History of Genii and Familiar Spirits
By John Beaumont

Copyright Topaz House Publications, 2017.

No part of this book may be reproduced except brief quotations and scholarly usage except by permission of the publisher. No guarantee is given to the efficacy or safety of the practices described.

ISBN: 978-0-9906682-7-5

Visit Topaz House Publications at www.topazbooks.pub

AN
Historical, Physiological and Theological

TREATISE
OF
SPIRITS,
Apparitions, Witchcrafts,
and other Magical Practices.

CONTAINING

An Account of the *Genii* or *Familiar Spirits*, both Good and Bad, that are said to attend Men in this Life; and what sensible Perceptions some Persons have had of them: (particularly the Author's own Experience for many Years.)

Also of Appearances of Spirits after Death; Divine Dreams, Divinations, Second Sighted Persons, &c.

Likewise the Power of Witches, and the reality of other Magical Operations, clearly asserted.

With a Refutation of Dr. *Bekker's World bewitch'd*; and other Authors that have opposed the Belief of them.

By *JOHN BEAUMONT*, Gent.

Edited by *John Madziarczyk*,
Printed for *Topaz House Publications, Seattle.* 2017.

THE CONTENTS OF THE CHAPTERS

INTRODUCTION
By John Madziarczyk
pg. 1

DEDICATION
pg. 13

TO THE READER
pg. 17

CHAP. I.
WHAT *the Ancients understood the Genii, that are said to attend Men, to be, as to their Nature and Offices.* *pg.* 21

CHAP. II.

Concerning the Genii, *that are ascribed to* Socrates, Aristotle, Plotinus, Porphyrius, Jamblicus, Chicus, Scaliger *and* Cardan.   *pg.* 37

CHAP. III.

What perception Men have had of Genii, *or* Spirits, *and their Operations by the Sight.*   *pg.* 67

CHAP. IV.

What perception some Persons have had of Genii, *or* Spirits, *and their Operations, by the Sense of Seeing, when others present at the same time have seen nothing.*
pg. 85

CHAP. V.

What perception Men have had of Genii, *or* Spirits, *and their Operations, by the Sense of Hearing.*
pg. 155

CHAP. VI.
What perception some Persons have had of Genii, *or* Spirits, *and their Operations by the Sense of Hearing, when others present have heard nothing.*
pg. 167

CHAP. VII.
What perception Men have had of Spirits, *and their Operations by all their Senses.*
pg. 179

CHAP. VIII.
What perception Men have had of Genii, *or* Spirits *and their Operations, by Dreams.*
pg. 191

CHAP. IX.
What Perception Men have had of Genii, *or* Spirits, *and their Operations, by Magical Practices.*
pg. 223

CHAP. X.

What may be suggested from Reason, concerning the Existence and Operations of Spirits.

pg. 269

CHAP. XI.

Considerations on Dr. Bekker's *Book, against* Spirits; *with a Conclusion to this Book.*

pg. 287

POSTSCRIPT

pg. 325

"GLEANINGS OF ANTIQUITIES"

Notes Concerning Genii or Familiar Spirits. (1724)

pg. 327

History of Genii

Introduction:

Genii and Familiar Spirits: Confounding Hierarchies.

By John Madziarczyk

John Beaumont, born c. 1650, died 1731, was a physician and antiquarian who lived in Somerset, in the southwest of England. He provided medical services to the miners in the area, and was a collector of the fossils that the mining brought up. Through his fossil collecting, as well as papers documenting new mining techniques, Beaumont became a fellow of the Royal Society. His first foray into writing was as a geologist, criticizing the efforts of Bishop Thomas Burnett to reconcile Biblical history with natural science. Burnett made a number of assertions on how the Flood could have transpired that Beaumont saw as unsound in light of current data. However, Beaumont also had a secret, one which he would first expose in his "History of Genii and Familiar Spirits" and later write about in "Gleanings of Antiquities"(1724).

For years, Beaumont had conversations with entities that he publicly labeled "Genii", but that in personal communications he labeled "Fairies". These beings gave him advice and told him about themselves, recommending, among other things, who he should marry. Their advice came to fruition as he did marry the recommended person. Beaumont's communication with these spirits, which he declares happened thousands of times over the course of some years, is what lead to the composition of the present work. "History of Genii and Familiar Spirits" was written to vindicate the idea of a personal Genius or Familiar Spirit, who advises and guides an individual in all the vicissitudes of life, as a valid phenomenon, one not caused by mental illness or other physical disorder, and also not the work of evil spirits.

By personal Genius, Beaumont was referring to a very long tradition that began in the west with the Daimon of Socrates. Socrates believed that he had a personal spirit that attended him, a Daemon, Daimon, or in Latin, "Genius". Socrates believed that his Daemon warned him when he was about to do something foolish. Plato documented Socrates' belief in his dialogues, and from there the story of the Daemon of Socrates proliferated through the classical world. It was the subject of commentaries by a number of authors in late antiquity.

In the classical world, though, the concept of a Daimon and Genii also had a much broader meaning than a personal spirit. Genii were also thought to attend particular cities and states.

Authors, such as Iamblichus, integrated the idea of the personal Daimon into these other realms, into practices such as theurgy, rituals to summon angelic beings in order to receive knowledge and enlightenment. Beaumont, though he mentions these other aspects of the Genius, confines himself to the personal aspect. Readers interested in these other aspects of Genii can consult volume one of "The Magitians Discovered" for a more thorough discussion.

As personal spirits, the Genii were variously thought to either attend the holy or to attend everyone, with the Renaissance writer Agrippa identifying three Genii as ruling different aspects of a person's life. These were given at birth and determined according to astrological configurations. Agrippa built on the notion that everyone was assigned a good and evil spirit at birth, an angel on one shoulder and a devil on the other. This, in turn, can be traced to the idea of the Good and Evil impulse in Judaism, also given at birth, between which an individual must choose. Beaumont examined all these traditions in his "History", and many more.

Beaumont identifies the Genius with Familiar Spirits, partially, but not exclusively, the domain of witches. Beaumont's characterization freely switches between referring to these lesser spirits as Genii and as Familiar Spirits. While as I'll argue, part of this convergence of terminology served a polemical purpose, I believe it's also indicative of popular usage at the time. The same interchangeability can be found forty years earlier in the anonymous additions to the 1665 "Discoverie of Witchcraft", documented in "The Magitians Discovered", where the concept of a personal Genius, as well as the Genius as a guardian figure of cities and towns, is discussed.

In addition to being a physician and a geologist, Beaumont was also part of the occult world of his day, although this aspect of his life has been little explored by scholars. He was a friend of Hans Sloane, the collector of the "Sloane Manuscripts", which contains many grimoires and other occult works. Sloane was the head of the Royal Society at the time. Beaumont was also friends with John Aubrey. Aubrey, an antiquarian and historian best known for his "Brief Lives", a collection of short biographies, showed his interest in the occult through his "Miscellanies", which is about supernatural phenomenon, and contains descriptions of the use of scrying crystals, trafficking with angels and entities, and the Second Sight, as well as documentation of ghosts and other supernatural activity. Beaumont quotes Aubrey's collection of questions and answers about the Second Sight extensively.

"History of Genii and Familiar Spirits" ranges over a great area. The work is divided up by the method by which the Genius or Familiar Spirit makes itself known, such as by sight, by hearing, by magic, or by dreams. This allows Beaumont to hold forth on topics that might otherwise be marginal to the subject, such as the nature of dreams and magic. In particular, it allows Beaumont to make a detailed study of the "Second Sight" as it existed in Scotland, the rationale being that the "Second Sight" allows individuals to perceive Genii and spirits, who advise them on matters. It should be noted that Beaumont's treatment of the "Second Sight" preceded the publication, but not the composition, of Robert Kirk's "Secret Commonwealth of Elves, Fauns, and Fairies". This is because, though the work was written in the late 17th century, it only circulated in manuscript form, as part of Kirk's papers, until it was published by Walter Scott in the early 1800s. Although religious, Beaumont's "History" is also notable for objecting to the activities of the witch finders. Beaumont devotes a substantial portion of chapter four to examining and debunking the story of witchcraft at Salem.

The question of personal communications with invisible spiritual entities naturally brings up the possibility of mental illness as its source. However, in the present volume Beaumont proves himself to be anything but unstable. He marshals sources from the Latin Renaissance, from Greece, and from the vernacular tradition, using them to great effect, and with great rationality. If Beaumont was mentally ill, it was a fertile mental illness that allowed him to make use of some of the most sophisticated sources of his day, and to synthesize them into a coherent whole, one which still holds up today. The diversity of sources that Beaumont employs, many of which are translated into English for the first time by the author, make the work especially valuable.

Beaumont's "History" challenges notions of high and low with regards to magic. While contemporary writers on high magic, a topic that includes practices such as the evocation of spirits, have linked high magic to the Greco-Roman world, the connection of low magic with the same has mostly been ignored. John Beaumont's "History" is unique in that his treatment of the low magical subject of Genii and Familiar Spirits includes extensive links to the Greco-Roman past. It's also unique in his assertion that Genii and Familiar Spirits are the same phenomenon. While there was a level of linguistic ambiguity in the 17th and 18th centuries about the terms "Genii" and "Familiar Spirits", Beaumont explicitly links the low magic concept of the Familiar Spirit to the late Neo-Platonic tradition of philosophy and theurgy. In doing so, he confounds the hierarchical positions of these phenomenon in the academy and in society, positions which they still, for the most part, occupy today.

The tradition of the personal Genius was, and is, connected with high magic, with Platonic and Neo-Platonic philosophy, the latter being among the most sophisticated manifestations of Greco-Roman thought. Socrates was thought to have a personal Genius. Familiar Spirits, on the other hand, are connected with low magic, and with disreputable magic. This difference in association carries over into the academic community, and into society. While Neo-Platonic theurgy has received sophisticated treatment, the world of the Familiar has largely been relegated to cross-cultural comparisons, with comparisons to the beliefs of 'primitive' societies. The notion that a Familiar spirit might be entitled to the dignity of the inspirer of Socrates is not often come across.

Partially, this is reflective of the picture of Greek and Roman religion that was painted in the 19th century Anglo-American world. The Greeks and Romans were cast as exemplars of contemporary Victorian society, as mostly atheistic except for a basic monotheism compatible with Anglican Christianity. The Greeks and Romans were associated with reason, and with civilization, not with magic. While this view has been challenged in recent decades, it still persists, and shapes Anglo-American culture, perhaps leading researchers into low magical phenomenon away from comparisons with the Greco-Roman world.

Indeed, there's an embedded bias to primitivism in the suggestion that the best parallels of Familiar Spirits are to be found in non-western cultures, particularly those with a low level of material culture. These are also often regarded as outside of history, which, in turn, feeds into a bias for a-historicism in analyses of pagan phenomenon that survive in the west. Popular, and low magic, is often as a whole viewed as existing in a historical vacuum, untouched from the beginning of time, or at the very least from the beginning of documentation. As such, the comparison of low magic practices in the west to cultures that are both non-Western and similarly outside of 'history', at least European history, such as the tribal peoples of the Americas, Africa, and Asia, also links one a-historical analyses with another.

This same primitivism, while sometimes praised because of the ennobling nature it occasionally attempts to give to its subjects, subtly denigrates the value of the subjects' experiences. The notion that Native American spirituality and religion could be as sophisticated as that of Greco-Roman philosophy is implicitly denied if Native American spirituality is associated with the 'noble savage', who lives in opposition to the world of civilization. Like the Familiar Spirit, the suggestion that the spiritual experience of a Native American religious specialist could be equivalent to that of Socrates is not often found.

Prehistory itself is sometimes also pressed into service, on its own, as when cave art in places such as Lascaux in France is used as evidence for one or another thesis about magical phenomenon. Conveniently, the creators of the art left no written records. We have no idea what they believed. As such, researchers are free to read into it whatever they want. Because there's no evidence to immediately contradict them, everything from radionics, to psychedelics, to musical intonations has been suggested as explanations for the art, along with more conventional suggestions of sympathetic magic. The latter, based on the paintings of animals in the caves, has no more implicit validity than the rest.

Searching for parallels in non-western cultures and in voiceless prehistory also distances the phenomenon from primary experience. While the notion of a Genius, or Daemon may be obscure, as Beaumont demonstrates there are many classical sources that present clues on how these phenomenon were actually experienced in antiquity. This, potentially, provides an insider view to the phenomenon that is not often come across in examinations of non-western parallels. The notion of the Daimon of Socrates, though obscure, is generally more immediately understandable for audiences in the west than the experiences of religious specialists in Siberia or Native America. These latter, while perhaps being rationally understandable, do not have the same sort of immediate significance to western individuals that they have for members of their own culture. A member of a Native American tribe would most likely have a vastly different understanding of the phenomena than a westerner, even if he or she was not a religious figure in the community. Beaumont uses evidence that is culturally familiar to him to piece together the significance of his own experiences in light of sources from outside his time, and outside of his immediate world of 18th century Britain.

Beaumont does include cross-cultural comparisons in his "History", but this is done only after the link has been made between his own experience, that of his contemporaries, and that of the Greco-Roman world. His "History" contains cross-cultural comparisons with the religious specialists of the Sami world, and with Native American figures in the West Indies and the northeastern United States. While it's up for debate whether the personal experience of Beaumont really was similar to the personal experience of Native Americans in New England, or the West Indies, or the Sami, nevertheless his account is valuable in that it tries to build connections between the experiences of the phenomenon through an inner, as opposed to outer, correspondence.

Beaumont, in making these comparisons, is also suggesting that the his experiences have the same value as both the Neo-Platonic Theurgists and the religious specialists of these non-Western cultures, and that these are equivalent in value with each other. He's also, rightly or wrongly, associating his personal prestige as a gentleman of 18th century Britain with practitioners in more humble, non-western, cultures. This, in turns, undermines distinctions between primitive and high culture, as well as between high and low magic, perhaps teaching us a lesson as relevant today as it was in its own time.

Within the greater series of books that Topaz has been releasing, Beaumont's "History" holds a special place. The subject matter of the personal Genius is integral to the anonymous material added to the 1665 edition of Reginald Scot's "Discoverie of Witchcraft". This material has been analyzed in volume one of "The Magitians Discovered". Volume two contains the actual texts of the 1665 "Discoverie". As such, Beaumont's "History" provides much documentation, and evidence for ideas talked about as theoretical possibilities in volume one of "The Magitians Discovered". This includes not only documentary evidence of beliefs about Genii in the late 17th and early 18th centuries, but also, unexpectedly, evidence of the influence of the Swedish Gothicist tradition of antiquarianism on the English occultism of the time .

Writing forty years after the publication of the 1665 "Discoverie", Beaumont shows himself familiar with the works of the Gothicists Olaus Rudbeck and Olaus Magnus, such the "Atlantica" and "History of the Goths". In looking at the beliefs of the Sami people, to provide a cross-cultural comparison of the personal Genius and of Familiar Spirits, Beaumont examines the work of Rudbeck, Olaus Magnus, of Rudbeck's great competitor Schefferus, and mentions other minor figures such as Cluverius, not strictly a Gothicist but working in a parallel tradition. The paraphrases that Beaumont takes from Rudbeck are very important in that they connect with the tradition identified in volume one of "Magitians" as informing the anonymous work of the 1665 "Discoverie".

Rudbeck was a later Gothicist who identified northern Scandinavia as being the home of Atlantis. However, a few things should be noted. First, Beaumont, though quoting Rudbeck extensively, does not reproduce Rudbeck's "Atlantis" doctrine itself. Secondly, Rudbeck's "Atlantic" speculations were based on a previous current of thought that made more modest assertions. What this tradition meant in practice, as opposed to fantasy, is indicated in volume one of "The Magitians Discovered", although the period of analysis in that volume ends just before the publication of Rudbeck's "Atlantica". Beaumont also gives extensive citations from Athanasius Kircher, the Catholic Hermeticist, and compares his work to that of Rudbeck.

Another connection between Beaumont and previous releases comes from his inclusion in the "History" of the story of Thomas Perks. Perks was an individual whose experiments with magic became a cautionary tale, one that was circulated throughout the 18th century. Beaumont provides one of the first examples of his tale, although he misidentifies Perks as "Jerps". Ebenezer Sibly, writing eighty years later, also provided a version of the story in his "A New and Complete Illustration of the Occult Sciences", which has been reproduced in "The Station of Man in the Universe: Ebenezer Sibly on the Spirit World and Magic", published by Topaz House Publications.

Finally, there are a few incidents that Beaumont repeatedly refers to which though familiar to contemporaries, are obscure today. These include references to supernatural phenomenon happening at "Tedworth" and "Mascon". By Tedworth, Beaumont is referring to what's been called "The Devil Drummer of Tedworth". This was a drumming sound that was supposedly manufactured by spiritual creatures as the result of a curse on a landowner for prosecuting a traveling musician.

By Mascon, Beaumont refers to the "Devil of Mascon", which was a spirit that tormented a Protestant minister in the town of Mâcon, in Burgundy, France, in the early 17th century. Claiming to be the Devil himself, the spirit supposedly carried on a mocking and argumentative dialogue with the minister, basically recreating a theme often found in Protestant literature, that of the Devil tempting a righteous individual. The difference between most Protestant literature and Mascon, for Beaumont at least, appears to have been that the phenomenon in Mascon was documented by a number of individuals around the minister, testifying to the reality of the phenomenon.

As a post-script, perhaps, there is the relation of Beaumont to Kenneth Grant. A "Mrs. Beaumont" and a "Beaumont Club" show up in Grant's novella "Against the Light", as well as in his non-fiction "The Ninth Arch". In these, he states that he got the name from the story "The Great God Pan" by Arthur Machen. Machen, a onetime Golden Dawn member, gives a "Mrs. Beaumont" as one of the identities assumed by the daughter of Pan. I believe, though I can't prove it, that Machen took the name "Beaumont" from this work, which is unique in that it doesn't condemn its subject.

Beaumont's history is a valuable resource for students of occult phenomenon, and I hope that readers toady find it as stimulating as it undoubtably was in its own time.

and Familiar Spirits

To the Right Honorouble

JOHN,

Earl of *CARBURY*,

Baron *Vaughan* of *Emblin* in *England*, and Baron *Vaughan* of *Molinger* in the Kingdom of *Ireland*, &c.

My Lord,

Y*OUR Lordship's great Genius to a Contemplative Life, which raises Humane Nature to an excellency above it self, and highly Influences the Oeconomy of this World, has naturally induc'd me to make an Humble Dedication to you* *of this Book. The Subject is abstruse, and treated of by few, and that sparingly. If I have enlarg'd my self upon it, it is, that some extraorinary Visitations having happen'd to me, in which I have had a Converse with those Genii I treat of, have made so strong an Impression on my Mind, that I could not well with-hold my self, from perusing the Best Authors I could Meet with, relating to it, in Order to draw an Abstract of what I found most Material in them, and to publish it together with my own Experience and Thoughts in that kind, as I have here done. I treat of this Subject Historically, Physiologically, and Theologically, tho' not in distinct Books, but promiscuously, as I found Occasion presented it self. As for my Performance herein, I could heartily wish it might prove to your Lordship's good liking, and humbly submit it to your Lordship's Great Judgment and Censure, being,*

My Lord,

Your Lordship's,

Most Humble and

Most Obedient Servant.

John Beaumont,

TO THE READER.

HAving long promis'd the World this Book, perhaps, the Jocose part of Mankind may now be apt to say,

Quid ferat hic tanto dignum promissor, hiatu?
Parturiunt montes, &c.

Be it as it may, I have here made good my Promise; and though I may not perswade my self, that all Men will acquiese in what I here deliver, I not pretending, in this Subject, to Mathematical Demonstration; yet I shall be free to say, That I fear no Man, who shall pretend to bring more Reason for an Opinion, contrary to that I assert; and I believe whoever shall peruse this Book, will find, that I am not Ignorant of what Opposers of all kinds may take upon them to offer against it. Indeed, while we relie meerly on Reason in Subjects of this Nature, I doubt we may have all too much cause to lament our selves with the Ingenious *Fracastorius*, in *Ep. ad Flaminium*.

Quid dicam diserum me agere, & quam ducere
  vitam,
Irrequietam animi, & quærentem indagine
  vanâ.
Naturam semper fugientem, quæ se ubi paulum
Ofendit mihi, mox facies in milla repenté,
Ceu Proteus conversa sequentem eludit & angit,
Maerenten. Seniíque horas, cassumque laborem.

Unhappy Man! What can I say, I do?
How lead my Life? thus restless to pursue,
Still flying Nature, which altho' by chance,
May now, and then present m' a little glance,
Strait, *Proteus* like, in thousand shapes she's
  rest,
So mocks my Toyle, and frets my pensive
  Breast.

We read of *Pentheus*, that upon his getting upon a Tree, and making himself a Spectator of the hidden Sacrifices of *Bacchus*, he was struck with such a kind of fury, that all things seem'd double to him; two Suns and two *Thebes* presented themselves to his sight; so that when he was hasting to *Thebes*, presently seeing another *Thebes*, he was drawn back: and thus he was continually carryed to and fro, in a restless Condition.

Eumenidum veluti demens videt agmina
    Pentheus,
Et solem geminum, & duplices se ostendere
    Thebas.

As *Pentheus* maz'd whole Troops of Furies Spyes,
Two Suns, two *Thebes* presented to his Eyes.

Now this Fable, as the Lord *Bacon* tells us, relates to *Divine Secrets*; for those who forgetting frail Mortality, rashly aspire to Divine Mysteries by high Flights in the Study of Nature and Philosophy, as tho' they were mounted on a Tree, have this for their Punishment, that they are perplext with a perpetual inconstancy and wavering in Judgment; for the Light of Nature being one thing, and the Divine Light another, it happens with them as though they saw two Suns; and since the Actions of Life, and the Decrees of the Will depend of the Understanding, it follows, That they hesitate no less in their Wills, than in Opinion, and are altogether at variance with themselves; and therefore they likewise see two *Thebes*; for by *Thebes*, which was the Habitation and retiring place of *Pentheus*, the ends of our Actions are represented:

hence it happens, that they know not which way to turn themselves, but being uncertain and wavering as to the main of things, they are Whirl'd about by sudden Impulse of Mind in every particular Matter; and I believe that those that will not acquiesce in what we have delivered us in the Scriptures, and by Christian Tradition, concerning Spirits, but will be medling in setting up other Hypotheses by their frail Reason, for solving Facts commonly ascribed to Spirits, will find their Judgment so perplext, and brought into such a Labyrinth, upon perusing what is here Written (and that even setting by what I affirm from my own Experience, as to an Existence of Spirirts, and their Operations, which I least rely on, or urge as Argumentative) that they will never be able to extricate themselves: And upon this issue I leave it; only adding this saying of the Learned Monsieur *le Clerc*; *Acerbos homines non moror, indignos quippe qui hæc studia tractent, aut quorum Judicii ulla ratio habeatur.*

In Pref. in Philos.

AN ACCOUNT OF GENII,

OR

FAMILIAR SPIRITS, that are said to attend Men in this Life, &c.

CHAP. I.

What the Ancients understood the Genii, *that are said to attend men, to be, as to their Nature and Offices.*

HAVING undertaken to write a Tract concerning the *Genii* that are said to attend Men during this Life, I think it proper for me, in the first place, to set forth what, according to the Ancients those *Genii* were understood to be, as to their Nature and Offices.

Censorinus tells us, that *Genius* is a God, under whose Tuition each Man is born and lives; and whether it be that he takes Care of our Generation, or is engender'd with us, or takes upon him our Guardianship after we are begotten, he says, he is called *Genius* from *Geno*, an ancient Latin Word, signifying to beget, in lieu of which the Word *Gigno* is now us'd. *Genius* is said to be Son of *Jupiter* and the *Earth*, as being held to be of a middle Nature betwixt Gods and Men, or for that he somewhat partakes of Body. Some have thought our *Genius* to be the Symmetry of the Elements, which

L. de Dies Nat c. 3.

preserves humane Bodies, and all living Creatures: Others, the secret Power of the Celestial Bodies, by which we are impell'd to do all things; and these were call'd *Geruli*, from *Gero* or *Ingero*; that is, from supporting us, or suggesting good or bad Thoughts into our Minds.

What the *Latins* call'd *Genius*, the *Greeks* call'd *Dæmon*; which Word, to pass by other Significations, according to its Etymology, signifies prudent, knowing, skilful in Affairs, and foreseeing things, they giving Answers to those that consulted them. In which Sense *Socrates* thought famous Men, after Death, for a Reward of their Vertue, were made *Dæmons*, of a middle Nature, mediating betwixt Gods and Men.

In Aug. de Civ. Dei l. 9. c. 9.

Ludovicus Vives says, it's a wonder to see how differing the Opinions of the *Gentiles* were, concerning the Gods and *Dæmons*: So that *Apuleius* thinks Otherwise than *Plato*; *Plotinus* than *Apuleius*; *Porphyrius* differs from them both; nor does *Proclus* agree in all things with *Jamblicus*, or any other. As for the *Genii*, some think them to be our own Souls, some our Inclinations, some a certain Light attending us, some the *Intellectus Agens*, *&c.* concerning which I shall set down what I find in several Authors.

L. de Deo, Socr.

Apuleius writes thus: In a certain Sense the Mind of Man, even while it is in the Body, is call'd a *Dæmon*.

> *Dii ne hunc ardorem Mentibus addunt*
> *Eurikle? An sua cuiq; Deus sit dira Cupido?*

And therefore, a good Desire of Mind, is a good God; whence some think those are call'd blest *Eudæmons*, whose *Dæmon* is good, that is, whose Mind is perfect with Vertue; which, I think, you may properly call a *Genius*, because that God which is each Man's Mind, tho' it be immortal, yet in some sort is engender'd within us; And there are some, who, as it seems to me, would have the Mind of Man freed from the Body, to be a second sort of *Dæmons*: This, I find, in the ancient *Latin* Tongue to be call'd *Lemur*. And he of these *Lemures*, who, taking Care of his Posterity, keeps the House as a calm and quiet Deity, is call'd a Family *Lar*: But he that, by reason of Demerits in life, is punished by a wandring in the World, having no quiet Seat, and becomes a vain Terror to good Men, and offensive to evil, is commonly called *Larva*. But when it's uncertain what Lot has happen'd to a Man, whether he be a *Lar*, or *Larva*, he is call'd the God *Manes*; the Word God being added for Honour's sake: They calling those Gods, who among them having justly and prudently govern'd the Course of their Lives, are afterwards Deify'd by Men, and admitted to Temples and Sacred Rites, as in *Bœotia, Amphiaraus*; in *Africa, Mopsus*; in *Egypt, Osiris*; others elsewhere; *Æsculapius* every where. And so far concerning those *Dæmons* that have had Bodies. But there is another kind of more august *Dæmons*, which being always free from the Fetters and Ties of Bodies, are drawn to us by certain Prayers. From this sort of sublime *Dæmons*, *Plato* thinks each Man has one given him, as a Witness and Guard in passing this Life; which tho' seen by no Man, are always present as Witnesses, not only of our Actions, but even of our Thoughts; and that upon our Return, at the End of our Lives, the said *Genii* presently carry us, as their Charge, to Judgment, and there stand as Witnesses at our Trial; where, if we falsifie in any thing, they reprove us; if we speak Truth, they vouch it, and Sentence is past according to their Testimony. So far *Apuleius*.

Porphyrius, L. de Abstinentia, says, That as evil *Dæmons* hurt Mankind, so good *Dæmons* never intermit their Offices, but foreshew us Dangers, as far as they may, hanging over our Heads from the evil *Dæmons*, while they make us Signs both by *Dreams*, and by the Soul divinely inspir'd, and many other things; and, that if any Man could distinguish these things which are signify'd, he would know and precaution himself against all Frauds; for they signifie to all Men, but all Persons do not perceive the things that are signified.

Agrippa says, that each Man has a threefold *Genius* to guard him, one Sacred, another of the *Geniture*, the third of the Profession a Man follows. The first is not deriv'd from the Stars or Planets, but given by God, it being universal, and above Nature. This directs the Soul, still suggesting good Thoughts, and enlightens us, tho' it be not always observ'd:

Occult. Phil. l. 3. c. 22.

But when we are purify'd, and live in a Calm, then it's perceiv'd by us; then it speaks, as it were, with us, and communicates its Voice, being present before in Silence, and labours continually to bring us to sacred Perfection. By the Assistance of this *Genius*, we may shun the Malignity of Fate: Whom if we religiously observe, by an Uprightness and Holiness of Life, (as we know *Socrates* did) the *Platonicks* think we are wonderfully aided by him, both by Dreams and Signs, for putting by Evils, and securing Good to us. The *Genius*, or *Dæmon* of the *Geniture*, descends to us from the Disposition of the World, and the Circuits of the Stars, that are concern'd in our Generation: This is the Sustainer and Guardian of life, it procures it to the Body, and takes care of it afterwards, and aids the Person for performing that Office for which the Heavens deputed him at his Birth. Those therefore who have received a fortunate *Genius*, are rendred strong, powerful, efficacious, and prosperous in their Works: Wherefore, by Philosophers, they are call'd *benê Fortunati*, and *benè Nati*, The *Dæmon* of the Profession is given from the Stars, to which such a Profession or Sect, as a Man professes, is subjected, and which the Soul, when it begins to use Election in this Body, and takes upon it Manners, secretly wishes; which *Dæmon* is chang'd for a more worthy or less, upon the Change of the Profession. When therefore the Profession agrees with our Nature, we get a *Dæmon* like us; and agreeing with our *Genius*, and our Life is made more calm, happy, and prosperous: But when we take on us a Profession unlike, or contrary to our *Genius*, our life is rendered more laborious and troublesome, by discording Patrons. Whence it happens, that a Man makes Proficiency in a little time, and with a little labour, in one Science, Art, or Ministry, who in others Toils, with much Sweat and Labour, to no purpose. And tho' no Science, Art, or Vertue is to be despised; yet, that you may live prosperously, and act fortunately, know, first of all your good *Genius* and your Nature, and what Good the Disposition of the Heavens, and God, the Disposer of all these, promises you, who distributes to each Man as he pleases: Follow these Beginnings, profess these, apply your self to that Vertue, to which the prime

Distributer raises and conducts you; and in what Virtue you find your self to profit most easily, endeavour to rise to the height of it, that you may excel in one, which you cannot do in all. However do not slight any perfection, as far as you are able to proceed in it; and if you have Guardians according to your Nature and Profession, you will find a double Proficiency of your Nature and Profession: But if they are unlike, follow the best; For sometimes you will find the Aid of an egregious Profession better than that of your Nativity. The same Author writes thus: As to each Man is given a good Spirit, so there is an evil one, both which seek an Union with our Spirit, and endeavour to draw it to them, and so mix themselves with it: The Good by good Works conformable to him, changes us into Angels by Union, as he that adheres to God, is made one Spirit with him: The Evil *Dæmon*, by bad Works, endeavours to make us conformable and united to him; and this is what *Hermes* says, when a *Dæmon* flows into an Humane Soul, he sprinkles in it of his own Notions; whence such a Soul, sprinkled with Seeds, raised in a Fury, brings forth wonderful things, and such as are the Performances of *Dæmons*. For a good *Dæmon*, when he passes into an holy Soul, he raises it to the Light of Wisdom; but an evil *Dæmon* transfus'd into a wicked Soul, incites it to Thefts, Murthers and Lusts, and whatsoever are the Performances of evil *Dæmons*. Good *Dæmons* (as *Jamblicus* says) most perfectly purge Souls, and others give us other things; being present, they give Health to the Body, Virtue to the Spirit, Security to the Mind, destroy what brings Death in us, foment the Heat, and render it more efficacious, for Life; and by an intelligible Harmony, always infuse Light into the Mind. I am of the Opinion of those, that think all Men are govern'd by the Ministery of many Spirits, and are led to all Degrees of Vertues, Merits, and Dignity, if they render themselves worthy of them: But those that render themselves unworthy, are cast down and detruded by the evil *Dæmons*, as well as by the good Spirits, to the lowest Degree of Misery, as their Demerits require. But those who are committed to the more sublime *Angels*, are preferr'd before other Men: For the *Angels* that have Care of them, raise them, and by a certain secret

Ib. c. 20.

power subject others to them, which tho' neither perceive, yet he that is subjected finds a certain weight of presidency, from which he cannot easily disingage himself: nay, he fears and reverences that force, which the superiour *Angels* influence the Inferiours with, and bring the Inferiours by a certain Terror into the fear of Presidency. So we read that *Mark Antony* formerly being join'd in a singular Friendship with *Octavian Augustus*, they were wont often to play together; but *Augustus* being always Conqueror, a certain *Magician* thus admonish'd *Mark Antony*: What do you do *Antony* with that young Man? Fly, and shun him; for tho' you are elder, and more experienc'd in Affairs, of a more Illustrious Family, and have been a great Commander in Wars, yet your *Genius* much dreads the *Genius* of this Youth, and your Fortune flatters his, and unless you fly far from him, it will wholly turn to him. Again, *Agrippa* tells us, the ancient Sages teach us to know the Nature of each Man's Genius from the Stars, and their Influences and Aspects at each Man's Birth, but by so differing and disagreeing Rules, that it's very hard to get these Mysteries out of their hands: For *Porphyrius* seeks the *Genius* from the Star that is Lady of the *Geniture*; *Maternus* either thence, or from the Planets that have been most dignified there; or from that whose House the Moon is to enter, after that it holds at the time of the Person's Nativity. But the *Chaldeans* seek the *Genius* only from the Sun, or Moon. Others again, and many of the *Hebrews*, from some cardinal Point of the Heavens, or from all of them. Others seek for the *good Genius* from the eleventh House, which therefore they call the *Dæmon*; and the evil *Genius* from the sixth, which they call the *evil Dæmon*. Since therefore the search of these is laborious and very abstruse, we may much more easily seek the nature of our *Genius* from our selves, attending to those things which our Mind suggests to us, the instinct of Nature dictates, and Heaven inclines us to from our first untainted Innocency; or when our Mind is purg'd of vain Cares, and sinister Effects and Impediments are removed from it. These doubtless are the kindly Suggestions of the *Genius* that is given to each Man at his Birth, leading and perswading us to that which our Constellation inclines.

Occult. Phil. Lib. 3. 2. 11.

So far *Agrippa*. He that would see more concerning the search after each Mans peculiar *Dæmon*, may read a little Tract on that Subject, printed at the end of a Book, entitled, *Trinum Magicum*, set forth by *Longinus*.

Natalis Comes says. The *Genii* or *Dæmons* present us with the Species or Images of those things they would perswade us to, as in a Glass; on which Images, when our Soul privately looks, those things come into our Mind; which, if consider'd with Reason, give us a right determination of Mind: But if a Man, setting Reason aside, be carried away with the guidance of evil Species, or Images, he will of necessity incur many Errors, especially if the Images are presented us by evil *Dæmons*. Whence many become wholly given over to Lusts, Cruelty, Covetousness, *&c.* all which are imputed to the *Genius*. *Myth. l. 4. c. 3.*

Maraviglia, in his *Pseudomantia*, writes thus, Tho' many have thought the *Genii* to be nothing but a certain Light plac'd by God in our Minds, at our Birth, whereby we understand all things; and being understood, if they are good, we love and pursue them; if bad, we decline and avoid them, yet the more common Opinion was, that the *Genii* were not only a light discovering and foreshewing future things to us, but certain pure Spirits standing by us always to guard and and admonish us; Tho' it be far more credible that those *Genii* in all Ages were the very Wills of Men, naturally predisposed with a desire and love, or an aversion and abhorrence of things Good or Evil, discus'd and propos'd to them by the Understanding. The same Author tells us, that *Pythagoras* thought the *Genii* were certain Lights naturally implanted in our Minds. *Apuleius* thought they were the Minds themselves, and Disposition of each Man. The ancient *Pagans*, that they were good and evil *Dæmons* appointed to each Man, from the beginning, for his Governance. Again, He writes as follows, The Prophecying Spirits, call'd in the Scriptures *Angels*, are call'd by the ancient Pagans, *Genii Fatidici*, as tho' generated from God, and sent from Heaven to us, to foretel future things; for they thought these fatidical Spirits, whom they variously worship'd, knew all things that were to come in the World, and could foretel them, because *Dissert.* 11. *Animadv.* 10. *Dissert.* 9.

themselves were a part, or a certain Particle of the Soul of the World, which is every where: For they were of Opinion, that this Soul was diffus'd through the whole World, but chiefly seated in the ætherial Region, and consequently in the Stars themselves; and more especially in the Sun, from which all inferior things are fomented, as it were, by Rays of a vivifying Soul transmitted to them; whence also they thought these kinds of Substances compos'd of a subtle Body, such as an ærial Body is; and that *Angels*, *Dæmons*, and *Souls* were from a particle of the mundane Soul. Which Substances *Apuleius* says, are plac'd in the ærial Region of the World, that they might profane a more easie Commerse betwixt Gods and Men, and more readily unfold the Secrets of the Gods, *&c.*

In Aug. de Civ. Dei. L. 9. c. 9.

Ludovicus Vives writes thus: *Plato* in his *Timæus* and *Cratylus*, calls the best part of our Mind a *Dæmon*: His words are these; You know what they are whom *Hesoid* calls *Dæmons, viz.*, that golden Race of Men, of whom he says thus:

> *But after Fate this Race has took away,*
> *They're pure terrestrial Dæmons call'd, and they*
> *Are Mens blest Guard, all Evils keep away.*

Tho I think that Race was call'd Golden, not that it consisted of Gold, but that it was good and excellent; and, I conceive, we are call'd an Iron-Age in companion of that; but if any one now living be good, *Hesiod* number'd him among his Golden Men. And what are the Good but the Prudent; and I conceive he call'd them *Dæmons* from their Prudence and Skill in Affairs, the Name it self, in our ancient Tongue, shewing it. Therefore it's well said of him, and most of the rest of the Poets, that when a good Man departs this Life, he is plac'd in some excellent Post of Honour, and made a *Dæmon* for his Wisdom. After this manner therefore I affirm, that a wise Man, so he be good, both living and dead, is a *Dæmon*, and justly so call'd. This we find in *Plato*, whence doubtless, *Origen* drew his Error, where he writes that human Souls are chang'd into *Dæmons*, and these again into those. *Porphyrius* also says, that each Mans peculiar *Dæmon* is a certain part of the Soul, *viz.* the Mind, and he is an happy Man, and one *Eudæmon*, that has got a wise Mind; and unhappy on the contrary: And that Souls Infested with Vices, pass into the nature of evil *Dæmons*, and are rendred like them in Lies and Impostures. *Proclus* explains all these things, laying down a threefold nature of a *Dæmon*: He writes thus: *Plato*, in his *Timæus*, says, our Animal Nature is a *Dæmon*: but this must be admitted but comparitively; for there is a *Dæmon* by Essence, another by Comparison, another by Reference or Respect; for every where that which next presides, being a certain order of *Dæmon*, in respect of the Inferior, is usually call'd a *Dæmon*. In which sense *Jupiter*, in *Orpheus*, calls his Father *Saturn* a *Dæmon*. And *Plato*, in his *Timæus*, call'd those Gods *Dæmons*, that immediately order Generation. Indeed, by comparison, such an one is a *Dæmon* which next provides for every one, whether it be God, or inferior to God. And in some respect, that Mind is said a *Dæmon*, which performs wonderful Actions, more like to those of a *Dæmon* than of a Man, and has his whole Life suspended from a *Dæmon*. After this way, I think, *Socrates* call'd those Minds *Dæmons* in a Republick, which had pas'd their Lives well, and were translated into a better State. Finally, a *Dæmon* by Essence is call'd a *Dæmon*, not by respect to Sequents, nor by reason of some Similitude to another thing, but has got his Property of himself, and has a certain distinct Existence, and his proper Powers, and his different ways of acting. Indeed the rational Soul in *Timæus* is always call'd an Animal *Dæmon*, but he does not mean it a *Dæmon* simply; for when we say a *Dæmon* simply, its a certain middle Nature betwixt Gods and Men. By *Plotinus* and others, its quæried, whether our Minds are mov'd of themselves to Desires and Determinations, or by the impulse of some Deity. And first, they said humane Minds were spontaneously mov'd but they found upon search, that we were impell'd to all honest Actions, by a certain Familiar *Genius* or *Numen*, given us at our Birth;

and that we desire or covet evil things by our Mind: For it cannot be that we covet evil things by the Will of a Deity, whom, its manifest, no Evil can please; tho' doubtless by many of the *Platonicks*, the Affections also with which we are carried away, are call'd *Dæmons*.

Hist. l. 21.   *Ammianus Marcellinus* writes thus: Divines tell us, that as all Men are born (saving the stedfastness of Fate) certain Divine Powers are associated to them, to be a sort of Governours of their Actions, tho' they are seen by few, whom manifold Vertues have dignified: And this Oracles and famous Authors have taught, among whom *Menander*:

> *Unicuique homini statim nascenti*
> *Adest Dæmon vitæ mystagogus.*

And so we are given to understand front *Homer's* Immortal Poems, that the Celestial Gods, have not spoke to Valiant Men, nor have been present to them, nor aided them in their Fights, but Familiar *Genii* attended them, by whose Aid *Pythagoras* and *Socrates* are said chiefly to have rais'd their Fame. *Numa Pompilius* also, and the Elder *Scipio* and, as some think, *Marius* and *Octavianus*, who had first the Title of *Augustus* given him, and *Hermes Trismegistus*, and *Apollonius Tyanæus*, and *Plotinus*, who has adventured at some Reasonings about this mystical Matter, and profoundly to shew from what beginnings these *Genii* become connected to the Minds of Men, which receiving, as it were in their Embraces, they defend as far as they may, and teach them great things, if they find them pure, and sever'd from the corruption of sinning, by an immaculate Society with the Body.

L. de Vit.
propr. c. 47.   *Hieronymus Cardanus* says, in general, there were manifold differences of *Dæmons* among the Ancients; forbidding, as that of *Socrates*; admonishing, as that of *Cicero* at his Death; teaching things to come by Dreams, Brutes, Casualties; advising us to go to a place, and deceiving us by

one Sense, or more, and by so much he is the nobler, likewise by natural, and also by non-natural things; and this we think the noblest; also a good and a bad.

Gilbertus Cognatus writes, that some think by the word *Manes*, Souls separated from the Body are signified; whence we see that ancient Monuments of Sepulchers are inscrib'd, *Diis Manibus*; and those that demolish Sepulchers are thought to violate the God *Manes*. In the Body, they are call'd *Genii*; separated from the Body, *Lemures*; when they infest Houses they are call'd *Larvæ*; on, the contrary, if they are good, *Familiar Lares*.

In not. in Lucian de Lucra.

That egregious Philologer *Kircher*, in his *Œdipus Ægyptiacus*, gives the following account of the *Genii*, according to the Doctrine of the *Ægyptians*. The *Ægyptians* had always in great veneration certain *Statues*, which they call'd *Serapes*; the *Latins*, *Penates* or *Lares*: Some say the *Penates* are nought but those *Genii* or Deasters, by which we Breathe, we Know, we See, we behold the Sun, *viz. Jupiter*, *Juno*, *Minerva*, and *Vesta*; for they call'd the middle Region of the Air, *Jupiter*, the lower, *Juno*; the top part of the Æther, *Minerva*, who is the power of divine Intelligence; the Earth, *Vesta*: These they call'd and believ'd to be the Gods of Provinces, and of our Births, and Presidents over Cities, and guards of private Houses. And *Dionysius Halicarnassæus* says, the *Romans* call these Gods *Penates*; and some translating them into *Greek*, call them *Genethlios*; or *Genitales*; others call them domestick and familiar Gods; some the Presidents of Possessions; others, secret Gods. They are call'd *Genethlii*, because they are thought to be appointed to the guard of Men, presently upon their being Born; or because by their vigilancy all things are generated; whence the *Genii* are also call'd the Presidents of things that are to be Generated. They are call'd *Patrii*, because they were thought to preside only over those things which are common to some Region, or Province; in which, with great diligence, they order'd things not only belonging to every City, but also to every House; to all Men, Plants, and Animals, according to the care committed to them. The *Serapes* of the *Egyptians*

Vol. 3. p. 474.

were nought but Images, without any eminency of their Limbs, roll'd, as it were, in Swadling-Cloaths, partly made of an appropriate Stone, partly of Metal, Wood, or Shell. Some of these, as tutelary Gods, were plac'd in publick Places, for a guard of them. Others of them were appointed for a guard of Persons, and were standing Tutelaries. Some others were portable, which whither soever Men went, they carried with them. Some also they, carried as *Amulets* about their Necks, at their Girdles, and about their Hand-wrists. Moreover, their Countenances were variously figured; for some had a Womanly Countenance, and their Heads veil'd; some were in the Form of Boys, with a *Vitta* about their Heads; others were represented other ways. They differed also in Instruments; some, which they call'd *Averrunei*, or *Apoptropæi* were figur'd with various Instruments, as Whips, Scourges, Nets hanging from their Shoulders; and these are the Images which the *Hebrews* call *Theraphim*, and which the Scriptures tell us, *Rachel* stole from her Father *Laban*, *Gen.* 31. which were brought from *Egypt* by the Servants of *Abraham* into *Palestina*, and propagated there. They call'd them *Theraphim*, because, as they could not pronounce *S*, changing *S* into *T*, according to the use of the Chaldaans; and changing the last *S* into *im*, they call'd those Images *Theraphim*, which the *Egyptians* call'd *Serapes*. Now the *Penates* of the *Egyptians* were the same with *Osiris, Isis, Nephte, Horus, Harpocrates, Arveris, Apopis,* and innumerable Deasters of this kind, which tho' they were accounted the universal *Genii* of all Nature, and the same as to Substance, only differing in effects, yet as they were deputed to the guard of private things, they had the Name of *Tutelaries*, and were worship'd as private Deities. So far *Kircher*.

From these *Genii* of the *Gentiles*, *Erasmus* in his *Adages*, thinks Christian Divines have ascrib'd to each Person two Angels, a good and a bad; tho' I think he says it with little reason, a Communion with Angels being so usual with the Patriarchs; from whom, in all probability, the *Gentiles* took their Doctrine of the *Genii*. The *Genii* were drawn under several Forms, as of a Serpent, a Boy, a Girl, a Youth, or an old Man, as *Cebes* in his *Table*. *Censorinus*, and many of the Ancients tell us, the *Lares* and the *Genii* were the same: Now the *Lares* were represented in the Form of Young-Men, cloath'd with Dog-Skins, and having a Dog to attend them, intimating, that they were friendly and fawning to Domesticks, and formidable to Strangers, as Dogs are wont to be. *Pierius* tells us, from *Chrysippus*, that the *Lares* were cloath'd with Dogs-Skins, because they represent the *Genii*, who are appointed for our Guard; and as Commissioners to inflict Punishments on us for all our evil Words and Deeds, and to avenge Crimes and all impiety, as often as Humanity laid by, we decline to a brutal Life; which the *Genii*, as sagacious Dogs, pursue and draw to condign Punishments. He adds, And as the *Genii* are given us for assiduous Attendants, never departing from us, it's with Justice he says, that the Dog, as a tutelary Animal, was hieroglyphically dedicated to the *Lares*, being the same with the *Genii* which we may more properly call *Angels*: And he says he cannot pass by what he has read among ancient Writers, *viz.* that there was a Temple of *Vulcan* at Mount *Ætna* in *Sicily*, in whose Grove there were Dogs, which fawn'd on those that came thither with Purity and Piety; but miserably rent the Impure and Polluted, as tho' divinely presaging the thing.

ierogl. l. 5. *c.* 5.

I could write more concerning the *Genii* of the Ancients, as, of the Sacrifices that were made to them, and other particulars, but it is beside my business here; and I shall only note, that beside the *Genii* attending each Person, the Ancients suppos'd others presiding over each Country, City &c. Those in the Figure prefixt to this Book being such, as I took them from *Cartarius* his Images of the Gods of the Ancients. The Explanation of which Figures is as follows.

The Figure on the left-hand represents the evil *Genius*, that Infested the Inhabitants of the Town *Temessa*, in *Italy*. The Story is thus: *Pausanias* writing of *Euthymus*, the Champion, tells us, that *Ulysses*, in his Wandrings, coming to the Town of *Temessa*, one of his Associates, for having ravish'd a Virgin, was ston'd to death by the Townsmen; whereupon his Ghost continually infested them; so that they

In Cliac. Poster.

were upon quitting the Town, till they were told by *Apollo*'s Oracle, that to appease him, they must build him a Temple, and sacrifice to him yearly the most beautiful Virgin they had among them; which, as they prepar'd to perform, it chanc'd, that one *Euthymu*, a Champion, came to the Town, and desir'd to be admitted into the Temple; who seeing the Virgin, and falling in Love with her, undertook to fight with the *Genius*, and overcame him, and forc'd him out of the Country, and married the Virgin. This *Genius* was of a very black Colour, and a formidable Appearance, having a Wolf's Skin fasten'd about him.

As to the little Figure in the middle, the Story is thus, as *Pausanias* relates it in the same Book: The *Eleans* Worship, as their Country God, *Sosipolis*, which signifies the Preserver of their City. His Sacrifices being wont to be yearly Celebrated in the Temple of *Lucina*. Concerning this God, what follows is recorded: When the *Arcadians* invaded the Country of the *Eleans*, and the *Eleans* presented an Army against them, a Woman, with a Child sucking at her Breast, came to the chief Commanders of the *Eleans*, and told them, that when she brought forth that Child, she was admonish'd in a Dream, to place him with the *Eleans* in the Battle: whereupon the chief Commanders of the *Eleans*, having thought fit to credit the Woman, plac'd the Child before their Standard. Upon the *Arcadians* Onset, the Boy, in their sight, turn'd into a Serpent; by which Prodigy being frighted, they presently fled, the *Eleans* smartly pursuing them: And upon getting this famous Victory, they gave him the Name of *Sosipolis*; and at a place where the Serpent was seen to go into a Cavern, a Temple was built after the Victory; and Honours were decreed to *Lucina*, because they thought the Boy was brought into the World by her. This God was drawn as a Boy, with a Garment of various Colours, sprinkled with Stars, holding in his Hand an Horn of Plenty; for in this Form he was seen by some Person in a Dream. I may here note, that the Form of Serpents under which the *Genii* were worship'd, denotes the wise and vigilant Care they have over us.

As for the Figure on the Right-hand: in some of *Adrian*'s Coin, this Inscription is found, *Gen. P. R.* where is seen the Image of a Military Man, compass'd about with a Garment, which reaches to the middle of his Legs, having in the Right-hand a Dish like a Sacrificing Vessel; and in the Left, an Horn of Plenty: This probably being the *Genius* of the People of *Rome*, under whose Guardianship their City was; the Horn and Dish shewing, that the *Roman* State, as all others are supported by outward Plenty, and Religious Devotion towards God.

In some of the Ancient Coins of *Trajan* and *Adrian*, is seen a Genius presenting with his Right-hand a Dish on an Altar, adorn'd with Garlands; and holding in his Left-hand a Whip, or somewhat like it, hanging down. This, by some, is thought to denote Rewards and Punishments. In the Coin of *Marcus Aurelius* is a *Genius*, having such a Dish in the Right-hand, and an Horn of Plenty in the other, with this Inscription, *Geniis Exerci: Et Genio Augusti*. So in the Coin of *Fl. Valerius Constantinus, Genio Populi Romani P. L. C.* where he holds in the Right-hand a Dish with a Star, in the Left, an Horn of Plenty. Again, in that of *Maximinus*, sometimes with this Inscription, *Genio Augusti sis*. Sometimes *Genio Populi Romani T. F.* sometimes *Genio Imperatoris*. These and the like Inscriptions are gather'd together in a particular Book, by the Learned Phycian *Adolphus Occo*. In the Antiquities also of *Appian* such Inscriptions of Monuments are found in the City of *Tarraco* in *Arragonia*. *And so much for a general Notion of the* Genii *of the Ancients*.

CHAP. II.

Concerning the Genii *that are ascribed to* Socrates, Aristotle, Plotinus, Porphyrius, Jamblicus, Chicus, Scaliger *and* Cardan.

THO' the *Genii* of these Men are reducible to the Chapters I shall go upon beneath, where I shall examine what perception Men have had of Spirits, or *Genii*, by their several Senses; yet, in regard the Learned *Naudæus*, in his *Apology for all the great Men that have been accused of Magick*, has Writ particularly concerning the *Genii* of these Men, and exploded them; and other Authors have writ against the *Genius* of *Socrates*. I shall here particularly consider what may be said concerning these *Genii*.

Part I. *c.* 13.

The most celebrated Instance of a *Genius* among the Ancients is that of *Socrates*. Testimonies for it are given by *Plato, Xenophon* and *Antisthenes*, his Contemporaries, confirm'd by *Lærtius, Plutarch, Maximus Tyrius, Dion Chrysostomus, Cicero, Apuleius, Ficinus*, and others, many of the Moderns, besides *Tertullian, Origen, Clemens Alexandrinus, Austin* and others. *Socrates* himself in *Plato's Theage* says, by some Divine Lot, I have a certain *Dæmon* which has followed me from my Childhood, as an Oracle; and this is a Voice, which, when it happens, always disswades the thing I am about to do, but never prompts, me to do any thing: and if any of my Friends communicate any thing with me, and the Voice is heard, it disswades, and is against the doing of it: And presently after he relates how a person lost his Life, for having despised the command of his *Dæmon*, warning him not to depart from him. Again, speaking to *Alcibiades*, he says, my Tutor, is Better, and Wiser than you: And speaking concerning the power of his *Dæmon*, e'en on other persons that used his Company and Conversation, he says, if it be grateful to my God, you will profit much, and in a little time; if on the contrary, not: And again, in his Apology, he says, going out of doors this Morning, the sign of God did not oppose me.

Many have been of opinion, that *Socrates* had not only a perception of his *Genius* by his sense of Hearing, but likewise by his Sight and Feeling. So *Apuleius* says, he judg'd *Socrates* perceived the sign of his *Dæmon*, not only by his Ears, but by his Eyes also; because he affirmed, that often not a Voice, but a divine Sign was presented to him; which he was the more induced to believe, for that it was so common a thing with the *Pythagoreans* to see *Dæmons*, that they wondred if any Man said he had seen none. Which Gift I impute to their great silence, and their deep recess of Mind; for as *Paracelsus* with others say, *Silence is the joy of all Spirits*. The Author of the small Tract, entitled, *De proprii cujusque nati | Dæmonis Investigatione*, Printed at the end of the *Trinum Magicum*, before mentioned, says the same, *viz.* that *Socrates* both heard his *Dæmon*, and saw him. And *Pictorius*, in his Dialogue *de Materia Dæmonum*, says, that *Socrates* affirms his *Dæmon* often to have spoke to him, who he sometimes saw and touch'd. So again, *Theocritus* in *Plutarch*, will have it, that a Vision attended him from his Childhood, guiding him in all the actions of his Life, which Vision going before him, was a light in Affairs, where humane prudence could not reach; and that the Spirit often spoke to him, divinely governing and inspiring his Intentions.

Lib. de Deo Socr.

L. de Daemo Socret.

Notwithstanding the opinion of these Men, and others, that *Socrates* had a perception of his *Genius* by more senses than one, I shall only here insist on the perception he had of him by his sense of Hearing; which in regard it's so well attested by *Plato* and *Xenophon*, his Disciples (who were envious Competitors for Learning, if it may be so said of *Philosophers*, so that they can no ways be suspected for having combined together to impose on the World) I wholly give credit to, tho' I well know there always have been, and still are some Men in the World, who have caveled at what is said of *Socrates's Genius*, as a thing feigned; whose reasons I shall now examine.

The learned *Naudæus*, in his laudable Work above-mentioned, and the 13*th*. Chapter of it, treating concerning the *Genii* ascrib'd to *Socrates*, and others, as above, writes thus, According to the Authority of all Authors, each of these Persons may boast of having been led into the Temple of Glory and Immortality, by the assistance of some *Genius*, or *Familiar Dæmon*, which was to them, as *Apuleius* says, a singular Guide, a domestick Inspector, an inseparable Judge and Witness, a disapprover of Evils, and an approver of Good; but since we cannot maintain this Opinion, without abating much of these Mens Merit, and the Obligation we owe to their labours; by the means of which, and not of those *Dæmons* and tutelary Gods, so many precious Relicks and Monuments of their learning are come to our Knowledge, I think it very proper to preserve the praise due to them, and to shew by the true Construction that ought to be given to this Conversation, how far those are out of the way in their imaginations, who perswade themselves it was such as that of *Angels* with Holy Persons, or of *Dæmons* with Magicians; for to come as near to the Truth as we may, we ought to observe, that the *Platonicks*, according to the Testimonies of *Jamblicus* and *Foxius*, suppos'd four sorts of rational Animals, under that they call'd the first Being, or the first Good, who is the Prime Author, and Mover of all things, *viz.* the Celestial Gods, or Angels, *Dæmons* that were Inferiors to them, *Heræs* and the Souls of Men in general, and that the chief Office and Duty of *Dæmons*, being no other (as *Proclus* says) but to concern themselves in the Affairs and Conduct of the last, and to serve them as Guides and Mediators towards the Gods. Men have taken an occasion from the resemblance of these Actions, to those that Souls exercise on their Bodies, to give these sometimes the Name of *Dæmons*, and especially when they come so to free themselves from the Slavery and Tyranny of the matter, where they are, as it were, interr'd, that they make themselves absolute Mistresses of all their Faculties, and no longer produce but Miracles, and Actions altogether like those of *Dæmons*, which is the true Sense according to which

L. de Deo Socr.

L. de myst. Ægypt. Jacomment in Phædon.

L. de Anim. & Dæm.

Apuleius said, that the Mind of Man, even while in the Body, is call'd a *Dæmon*; and *Heraclitus*, that the Spirit of Man serv'd him for a *Genius*; and the just desire, and good Operation of the Soul may be likewise qualified with the name of God, since ev'n *Porphyrius* said to this purpose, after *Plato*, in his *Timæus*, that God has given us the Superior faculty of our Spirit, as a *Dæmon* to guide us; and that he may rightly be call'd an *Eudæmon*, that takes Wisdom, as a watch Tower to guide him in all the Actions of his Life: which might serve us for a General solution to Answer all that is said of the Familiarity and Conversation of certain *Dæmons*, with Socrates, Aristotle, and others; if it were not rather requisite to satisfie particular Objections, that may be made against each of them, and to examine first what we ought to believe concerning the so famous and renown'd *Dæmon* of *Socrates*, no less celebrated by the Authority of those that have giv'n us the History of it, than by the great Diversities of Judgments that have been made of him; some saying, that there may be some likelihood of Truth for its being really so; others, that it was a meer Fiction of this Philosopher, or of his two Disciples, *Xenophon* and *Plato*, who as falsly publish'd the report of this Divine Assistance, as that of the Oracles declaring him the wisest of Men. And here *Naudæus* lays before us all the Dirt that envy or prejudice has thrown on *Socrates* and then goes on thus: But since I should but expose my self to the laughter of all Men, to follow the licentiousness of these dangerous Spirits, who so freely sham the Authority of these two great Philosophers, as also that of *Apuleius, Maximus Tyrius, Cicero, Plutarch*, and almost all the good Authors, to shew themselves more subtle and clear sighted than others, by crushing to pieces this old Image: I rather chuse to range my self of their side that respect it; since I cannot perswade my self, that so great a number of Writers would have loaded *Socrates* with so many Praises, or call'd him, as *Martial* did, the great Old-man; *Persius*, the reverend Master; *Valerius Maximus*, the Mind vetted with virile Strength; or finally, as *Apuleius*, the Old-man of Divine Wisdom, if he had not signalized himself

Marginalia:
L. de Deo Socr.

L. 7. Epigr. 68. Sat. 4. L. de Deo Socra.

by his Wisdom; so that we ought rather to excuse, than reprehend those, who do not judge without reason, that he had acquir'd it thro' the favour, and Assistance of some *Dæmon*. Tho' nevertheless there be no less uncertainty concerning, the Explication of his Nature, than of malice and calumny in the precedent Opinion; for *Apuleius* would have it to be a God, *Lactantius* and *Tertullian* a Devil; *Plato* thought he was invisible; *Apuleius*, that he might also be visible; *Plutarch*, that it was a sneezing on the right or left side, according to which *Socrates* foretold a good or evil Event of the thing undertaken; *Maximus Tyrius*, that it was a remorse of Conscience against the promptness and violence of his Natural Temper, which was neither heard, nor seen, by which *Socrates* was with-held, and hindred from doing some evil thing: *Pomponatius*, that it was the Stars that rul'd at his Nativity; and finally, *Montaigne* was of Opinion, it was a certain impulse of his Will that presented it self to him without Council of his Discourse. As for my self, I believe it may be said, conformably enough to truth, that this familiar *Dæmon* of *Socrates*, which, was to him a foreseer in uncertain things, a pre-admonisher in doubtful, a guide in dangerous, was nought but the good rule of his Life, the wise Conduct of his Actions, and the result of all his Virtues, that form'd in him this Prudence; which may with Justice be call'd the lustre and seasoning of all his Actions, the Eye that sees all, guides and orders all, and in a Word, the Art of Life, as Physick is the Art of Health. So that there is much more seeming ground to believe, that the Soul of this Philosopher, purifyed from its violent Passions, and enrich'd with all kinds of Vertues, was the true *Dæmon* of his Conduct; than to imagine, that he entangled himself with Illusions, and *Phantomes*, gave credit to them, or follow'd their Counsels; being a thing wholly absurd, which *Plutarch* seems to have a mind to root out of our Fancies, when he says in the Book he has compos'd concerning this *Dæmon*, that *Socrates* did not despise Celestial things, as the *Athenians* would perswade him at his Condemnation, though it be very true, that many Apparitions, Fables and Superstitious things being crept into the Philosophy of *Pythagoras*, and his Disciples, which rendered it wholly ridiculous and contemptible, he did what he could to manage it with prudence, and to clear it of all these Tales, and to believe of it but what he judged reasonable; and beneath, having solv'd some difficulties to be met with concerning the *Dæmon* of *Socratus*, he adds, but beside that this would be a too manifest interfering with the Precept of *Horace*.

De Art. Poet.

Nec Deus Intersit, nisi dignus vindice nodus. Inciderit ——

to refer the Predictions of *Socrates*, and the Counsel he gave his Friends, to some Divinity, we may more reasonably say, that as he was wholly carried to moral Actions, so he had particularly considered all the accidents that happen'd to Men, and that the least thing made him foresee and judge of the future. This is what *Naudæus* has writ concerning the *Dæmon* of *Socrates*.

Pseudom. vet. Disser. II.

Maraviglia writes, that *Socrates* being wholy taken up in giving Moral Precepts, ascribed all to a *Genius*, thinking thereby to give weight to his profitable Arguments, which he every where used for Instruction; well knowing what authority a Man carries, who is believed to give his Instructions, by the direction of a Divine *Afflatus*: Hence though *Plutarch* and *Apuleius* believed *Socrates*'s *Genius* was a true *Dæmon*, which by reason of his most pure and calm mind, convers'd with him from his Infancy, yet nothing evinces it to be ought but the natural Subtilty, Sagacity, Reason and Prudence of his Mind, cultivated by Meditation and Practice, which as a right *dictamen* admonisht and proposed to him things to be rightly done, and judged well of Futurities: for its reason, which continually whispers unto as what is to be hop'd for, or feared, and that is wont to be called our *Genius*, and Inward Voice always speaking to us, without having need of a separate *Genius*. And *Timarcus*, in *Plutarch*, who went into *Trophonius*'s Cave to enquire after the truth of *Socrates*'s

Genius, could receive nothing more probable, but those *Genii* were portions of the Mind, seated about the head of Man, as being naturally endow'd with a greater Wisdom.

The Learned *Anton. Van Dale, M. D.* in his last Edition of his Book of *Oracles*, rejects the *Dæmon* of *Socrates* thus: What have not the Ancient *Pagans* said concerning the *Dæmon* of *Socrates*? what not even the *Christians*? but from what Men of Authority does it appear that *Socrates* ever had such a *Familiar Dæmon*? since all of them ought to have had it from the mouth of *Socrates*, or of the *Socraticks*, *Cherephon*, and others, to whom *Socrates* had told it. And after having exploded what the Oracle is said to have deliver'd of *Socrates*, *viz.* that he was the Wisest of Men, he concludes the Chapter thus: But truly those things which were so rashly believed, and delivered by so many, both *Christians* and *Pagans*, concerning his *Dæmon*, which is testified only by himself (for so he boasts of himself in *Plato*'s *Dialogue* Entitled, *Theage*, and others of his Disciples forsooth) carry the same, or rather the like shew of Truth; for, who may not as well believe *Pythagoras*? who, as *Lærtius* testifies from others, said he was first *Æthalides*, then *Euphorbus*, then *Hermotimus*, then *Pyrrhus*, a Fisherman of *Delos*, before he was, in the last place, *Pythagoras*; for the Reasons and Arguments of *Socrates* concerning his *Dæmon*, in *Plato*, carry the same weight.

Dissert. I. *c.* I.

Monsieur Le Loyer delivers himself in a different way concerning the *Dæmon* of *Socrates*, writing thus: Do we not find that the Idolatrous *Egyptians* believed there were *Genii*, who admonished Men committed to their Care and Government, by a well form'd and articulate Voice: and from whom had they this, but from the *Hebrews*? Those that examine the Doctrine of the *Egyptians*, and their Priests, know that they are but the *Hebrews* Apes, tho' concealing as much as possible their Authors, and those whose Doctrine they follow; which they do with such an affected dissimulation, that he that does not look near to them, shall never be able to discover the traces and footsteps of these Thieves. They had learnt that, the *Hebrews*, by a secret Tradition, held their

Hist. des. Spectres. l. 9. *c.* 16.

Patriarchs had *Angels* which guarded them, and that the Patriarch *Jacob* had not concealed his having an *Angel*, which had preferred him in all places where he had been; they held also that these *Angels* Invisibly admonisht the said Patriarchs, and that their Voice was heard.

From this Hebrew Tradition and Doctrine, the *Egyptians* forged their *Genii*, confounding them with the *Angels*, tho' the *Genii* are but *Dæmons*, and gave them a Voice by which they advertized Men: and I certainly believe, that from the *Egyptians*, *Plato* drew and took the *Genius* or *Dæmon* of *Socrates*, which he makes Invisible, and to be heard Speaking, and forming some Voice. And tho *Plato*, imitating in this the *Egyptians*, seems to day, that the *Genius* which governed and guided *Socrates* was a good *Dæmon* and yet I take him but for a Devil, which led *Socrates* to an unhappy Death. The same *Le Loyer*, in his said Book, says he concludes with several Doctors of the Church, that *Socrates* was a Magician, because he used Divination.

Cap. 17.

Now, to consider what these Authors have said, concerning the *Genius* of *Socrates*, we find that even those that deal the most mildly with him, as *Naudæus* and *Maraviglia*, deny any Voice coming to him from without, which the words in *Plato* plainly and naturally import he had. And I believe it must be granted me, that the main ground these Men, and others of the same Opinion go upon, is, that not having had any experience of any such thing in themselves, and not being fully convinc'd, that any other Person has, notwithstanding the Testimonies of Men in all Ages, and the Instances I shall give, they are uneasie to yield the Point, even in the Case of *Socrates*. And I must here say, I have hundreds of times, seen, heard, and convers'd with those they call *Genii*, *Angels*, Spirits, or *Dæmons*, appearing to me in humane Shapes; of which I shall give some Relation beneath, beside the Experiences of many other Persons, known to me, and now living, in the same kind; whom opposers, (notwithstanding any reluctancy) must give me leave to believe to be Men of as sound Sense as themselves.

When such Persons of an over cautious belief, meet with any thing in History, or hear something related in this kind, we find they proceed two ways; either being somewhat tender of the Authority such things are deliver'd by, they excogitate various Explications of the Fact, as each Man's Fancy suggests to him; so that they will allow somewhat of Truth in it, after the way they explain it; as we find in the Case of *Socrates*, *Naudæus*, and *Maraviglia* have done; which is like the Complement young Philosophers have been taught to pay to *Aristotle* in distinguishing his Text, when it has seem'd to make against them; or they flatly deny it, and explode it as a Fable, with Dr. *Von Dale*, *Galleus*, and many others; as any Man may easily do of any Historical Fact, however attested (since it will not bear a demonstrative proof) and boldly cry out, *Affirmanti Incumbit probatio*.

It was a laudable Undertaking of *Naudæus*, to write an Apology for all the Great Men accused of Magick by some narrow Understandings; and which, I think, he has generally well perform'd: But as to his way of Apologizing for the Men above-mentioned, I cannot see how it should abate of their Merit, or of the Obligation we have to them, for the Works they have left us (as he seems to think it would) tho' they had receiv'd a good part of their Knowledge from the Suggestion of Intellectual Beings; for the World has been long under a Mistake, if prophetick Learning (which beside what has been immediately inspir'd from the prime Cause, Men may have sometimes had by a suggestion from Intelligences) be not of as great a Merit, and has not laid as great Obligations on Mankind, as any excogitated by Humane Wit; and we are as well owing to the prime Cause for what we deliver by our ordinary Faculties, as for what in this extraordinary way.

Again, Tho' the primary end of good *Angels*, in directing Mankind, be in things relating to their eternal Salvation; yet I know not why they may not sometimes, inspire or openly direct them in humane Studies, and in things relating to humane Life, so they are of a good tendency; as I find not but the knowledge of *Socrates*, and that of others, whom I shall mention beneath were; tho' that some have had

Knowledge inspir'd them by Evil Spirits: its what Divines generally teach: Neither shall I here take upon me to maintain, that the *Genii* which attended some of the Persons above mentioned by *Naudæus* (if they had any) were of the better sort.

There is one thing I shall note in *Naudæus*'s account of the *Dæmon* of *Socrates, viz.* Where he tells us, *Plutarch* said it was a Sneezing on the right or left side, according to which, *Socrates* foretold a good or evil event to the thing undertaken;. Now, tho' *Plutarch*, in his Academical way of Writing, in his Tract of *Socrates*'s *Dæmon*, introduces one *Polymnis*, who set forth this Opinion, *viz.* that *Socrates* was guided in his judgment by a Sneezing, happening to himself, or some stander by, yet I see no colour of reason, why this opinion should be fathered upon *Plutarch* himself, more than others there set forth. Mr. *Bogan*, tho' otherwise a learned Man, in his additions to Mr. *Rouss*'s *Archeologiæ Atticæ*, seems to me a little over-comical in sporting with *Socrates*, and his *Genius*, saying, *Socrates* (as *Emuncte naris* as he was) had so little Sense himself, as to fetch advice himself from another mans Nose, and to make a Sneeze serve instead of a *Genius*, or *Dæmonium* to tell him the Good and the Bad, *&c.* but all men are not admirers of Pedantick Railery.

L. 7. Sect. 2. c. 2.

To come to *Maraviglia* we find he will have it, according to his prejudice, that *Socrates*'s *Genius* was only his pretence to gain authority to the Doctrine he delivered; tho' still he allows somewhat extraordinary in him, that may be call'd his Genius, *viz.* the wonderful Sagacity of his Mind, cultivated by a long Meditation, which might in a particular manner have directed his Judgment, as to present and future things. But I think this suspition of *Socrates*'s design in his *Genius* is poorly grounded, since it no way appears that ever *Socrates* imputed the Doctrine he delivered to the Suggestion of his *Genius*, as *Numa* and others did, but only his being withheld by him, from doing some Actions which would have prov'd prejudicial to him.

As for Dr. *Van Dale*, he allows *Socrates* no more than other Men, and wholly rejects his *Genius*, as not being well attested, and charges Christians and Pagans for having over rashly believ'd, and deliver'd as a truth the Story concerning him.

Now as to this (with reverence to the Learning of so great a Man) I must take freedom to say, it seems to me he has overdone the matter in this case, by pressing things too far; as I conceive he has in several other parts of his Works: for as to his rejecting the testimonies of *Xenophon* and *Plato*, as not worth minding, I believe, by unprejudiced Readers they may be look'd upon as unexceptionable Testimonies in that matter, as any two Men now living on the face of the Earth; for what they shall deliver by hear-say, if we shall be led by suspicions, and remote possibilities of Fraud, and contrivance of such Men, all historical truth shall be eluded, when it consists not with a Mans private humour, or prejudice to admit it. As for what he further urges, that if we believe *Socrates*'s boast (as he calls it) of his *Dæmon*, we may as well believe *Pythagoras*, who said he was first *Æthalides*, then *Euphorbus*, &c. before he came to be *Pythagoras*; I think there is a great disparity in the case; for, as to Divine Voices being heard, its no more than what all the Ancient Prophets testified, besides what we find recorded of them in all Christian and Pagan Histories, nor are living Testimonies wanting: whereas, for the other, its well known how all the learned have expounded the *Pythagorean* Transmygration: concerning which the very learned *Joan. Reuchlin* writes thus. The *Pythagorean Metempsycosis* signify'd nothing among the truly learned, but a similitude of notions and studies, which were formerly in some Men, and afterwards sprung up again in others: and so it was formerly said, that *Euphorbus* was reborn in *Pythagoras*, because that warlike Valour which was celebrated in the *Trojan Euphorbus*, some way appear'd again in *Pythagoras*, by reason of the love he bore to the *Athletæ*, or those that gave themselves to manlike exercises. *Ficinus* also testifies the same, affirming, that the Transmigration also, as it respects brutes and Men, according

De Art. Cab. l. 2.

In Ep.

to the sense of all the learned *Platonicks* (except Plotinus) imported only that as affects of Brutes became habituated in Men, Man seem'd to have past into their Natures. But if Dr. *Van Dale* will have it that *Pythagoras* declared this as a truth, in a litteral sense: when he shall produce some others, who have declared the like experience of a Transmigration in themselves, as I have given instances backing what is said of *Socrates*, we may allow it a like motive of credibility. And if the opinion of *Origen* (whom the Dr. praises as more discreet in his opinion concerning the Pagan *Oracles*, than the other primitive Fathers) weighs any thing with him, he will find him pretty smart against those that reject the *Genius* of *Socrates*, where he says; Nor will there ever be wanting calumny to the uncandid, who have a malicious sense even of the best of Men, since they make a sport even of the *Genius* of *Socrates*, as a thing feign'd.

L. de Orac. Dissert. I. c. 2.

Contra. Els. l. 6.

Since I have intimated it above, I shall here give a farther instance, or two, of this learned Persons over-arguing himself, as I conceive, in the Third Chapter of his First *Dissertation*, treating of the Origen of *Oracles*, where he writes against the Imposture of the *Gentiles* in that kind, he charges them for having contrived generally the feats of their Oracles on Mountains, where were Caves and Subterraneous Vaults, partly made by Nature, partly by Art, for carrying on their Cheats; and that none but Kings, Princes, and Great Men, conscious of the Cheat, were admitted to consult them. Now, if any of the *Gentiles*, who had a belief in their *Oracles*, as I think it beyond dispute, that many, even of the most learned of them, had; nay, if they knew them to be Cheats, as some thought them to be, would they not presently reply, that a Mountain was made choice of for *Moses* to receive the Law of God, and that no Man under pain of Death, was to approach the Mountain but himself and *Aaron*? and likewise that the *Jews* kept their *Sanctum Sanctorum* altogether as private, and as liable to a suspicion of a Cheat, and admitted none but the Prince, the Senate, or some great Person to consult the *Oracle* of *Urim* and *Thummim*; and the High-Priest only saw the sign of God in the Brestplate, directing an Answer, as the learned *Joan. Leusden* has set forth in his *Philologus Hebro mixtus*. So that we find the force of this Argument wholly evacuated, it pressing equally on both sides. And I am sorry I must say if, I find too many Arguments made use of by some Writers, against the Religion of the *Gentiles*, which fall indirectly, I will not say designedly, on all Religion. *Disser.* 25.

Again, the said Author, in his Tract *De Divinatione Idololatricâ*, after having told us of the Superstitious Practice of the *Gentiles*, in driving away the *Lemures* with a noise of Brass, adds; Those that will believe these things, may as well believe what *Pliny* writes, *viz.* Above all things that have ever been heard of, is the prodigy happening in our Time, by a mine in the *Marrucine Territories*, where the Olive-field of *Vectius Marcellus*, a chief Person of the Equestral Order, past over the whole common Road, and on the contrary Plow'd Lands came thence into the Olive-field. Now, this seem'd very strange to *Pliny* (who, tho an admirer of great things, and a Man excellently qualified for recording historical Facts, was never lookt upon by the learned as a diligent enquirer into causes) and wholly incredible to the Author; tho' I think it no such extraordinary *Phænomenon* of Nature, there being several Instances to be given of the like kind, as well within our Nation as elsewhere. *Ch.* 8.

L. 17. *c.* 15.

Stow tell us, in his *Summary* that *An.* 1582. *Jan.* the 13*th* at *Hermitage* in *Dorcetshire*, a piece of Ground of three Acres, remov'd from its place, and was carryed over another Close, where Alders and Willows grew, the space of forty Rods, or Perches, and stopt up the Highway that leads to *Cirne*, a Market-Town, and yet the Hedges it was inclos'd with, inclose it still, and the Trees stand bolt upright, and the place where the Ground was before is left a Pit. So *An.* 1571. *Marcley-hill*, in the East part of *Herefordshire*, with a roaring noise removed it self from the place where it stood, and for three days together travell'd from its old Seat. It began first to remove *Febr.* the 17*th* being *Saturday*, at Six of the clock in the Evening, and by Seven of the clock the next Morning, it had gone forty Paces carrying with it Sheep in their Folds,

Hedge-rows and Trees, whereof some were overturn'd, and some that stood upon the Plain, are firmly growing upon the Hill, those that were East were turn'd West, and those in the West, were set in the East: In this remove it overthrew *Kinnaston-Chappel,* and turn'd two High-ways near an hundred Yards from their old Course. The Ground that thus removed was about 26 Acres; which opening it self with Rocks and all, bore the Earth before it 400 Yards space, without any stay, leaving Pasturage in the place of the Tillage, and the Tillage over-spread with Pasturage; at last overwhelming its lower parts it mounted to an Hill of twelve Fathoms high, and so rested after three Days travel. More instances may be giv'n of the same Nature, this being wrought by that kind of Earthquakes, we call *Brastæ* or *Brasmatics,* from βραζζω *ferveo, bullio, vi æstus ejicio,* which raise, and protrude the Earth, many Islands having been so cast up from the bottom of the Sea on a sudden. As for the Plough'd Lands coming in the place of the Olive-field, we may easily conceive this to have happen'd by a Gyrative motion of that piece of Land following upon the protrusion from the deep.

I intimate these things only to caution Men not to be over hasty in rejecting things that may seem Strange, and do not presently fall within their Comprehension; and that in opposing Adversaries they use due Circumspection in attending to the vast extent of the Power of Nature, and the various Manifestations of God in Men, many things being evident to some Persons, which to others seem wholly incredible.

In the last place; as for the Suggestions of *Monsieur le Loyer, viz.* that *Plato* had his Notion of *Socrates*'s *Genius* from the *Egyptians, &c.* I think them altogether groundless, since *Pythagoras,* who liv'd before *Socrates,* is averr'd to have made his great Proficiency in Learning from his Converse with Spirits, and since it was so usual a thing for the *Pythagoreans* to see Spirits, as *Apuleius* acquaints us. And why must it be an evil *Genius,* bringing *Socrates* to an unhappy end? If we believe *Plato,* we find *Socrates* did not think it so, but on the contrary was desirous to die; and I think no considering Man, who has liv'd an upright Life, would think it an unhappy thing to be freed from the grievances of decrepit Age; *Socrates*, according to the lowest Computation, being 70 Yeas of Age when he died; *Suidas* says 80, others 90. And as for his being a *Magician*, this need not to have been feign'd to procure him a *Genius*, since his *Dæmon* is said to have attended him from his Infancy. And so much concerning the *Genius* of *Socrates*.

I shall now proceed to give an Account from *Naudæus*, of the *Genii* ascrib'd to the other Men before-mentioned by him. As for the *Genius* of *Aristotle*, he thinks it a Jest in those Men that have ascrib'd one to him; it being manifest, according to all his Interpreters, that he never admitted other *Intelligences*, but those he assign'd as movers to each Sphere of the Heavens, rejecting all other kinds of *Dæmons*, so standing firm to his Principles, and not admitting any thing, that was not known to him, either by Motion or Operation: He likewise referring all that is wont to be ascrib'd to *Dæmons*, to Nature, that is, to the Properties of Natural things; to Humours, and Temperaments of Animals, to the Nature of Places, and to their Vapours and Exhalations, leaving nothing to do for these Substances. And after *Naudæus* has giv'n several Reasons against Aristotles admitting of *Dæmons*, he adds, I think, one probable Argument may be drawn from his Book concerning Divination by Dreams, where, to shew that there is nothing Supernatural in them; he says, but because some Animals likewise Dream, certainly Dreams are not sent from God, nor caus'd by him, but must be *Dæmoniacal*, since Nature is *Dæmonical*, not *Divine*. And though it be greatly controverted among Interpreters and Commentators, in what Sense we must explain this *Epithet* giv'n by *Aristotle* to Nature; it seems *Leonicus* has better hit on it than the others; and that the Learned *Charpentarius*, has found the whole Energy of this Phrase, when he says, *Aristotle* would shew by it, that that force may be found in Nature well order'd, depending on the Conversion of the Celestial Orbs, which may serve to explain all these things, for which others have

In comment. in hurclos. In c. 13. Alvin. Digress. 4.

recourse to *Dæmons*; by the means of which Explication he says, he may answer the sole Reason, giv'n by *Cæsalpinus*, for establishing *Dæmons* according to the Doctrine of *Aristotle*.

L. de Invest. Dæm. perip. c. 7.

In reference therefore to the *Genius* of *Aristotle*, ascrib'd to him by some Persons; I shall set down what *Piccolomini* and *Cæsalpinus* have writ concerning his Opinion, as to the Existence of *Dæmons*, the former contending against his Admission of them, the latter for it, and shall subjoyn my own Sense in the Matter.

Piccolomini states the case, whether *Aristotle* thought there were *Dæmons*, and concludes in the Negative, writing as follows: The word *Dæmon* may be taken, either metaphorically, or properly, if metaphorically, *Aristotle* may be allow'd to have granted *Dæmons*, he saying, that *Xenocrates* affirms him to be an *Eudæmon*, who has a studious Mind; for this is to each Man an *Eudæmon*; so we may also say with *Aristotle*, that the Mind coming from without, and governing a Man, is his *Eudæmon*; so in his Book of *Divination by Dreams*, he says, That Dreams are not sent by God, but are *Dæmonical*, because Nature is *Dæmonical*, not *Divine*; intimating that Nature, by a Metaphor, may be call'd a *Dæmon*; which name agrees to it, because it is God's Messenger, is powerful, and Works secretly and wonderfully; all which things are ascrib'd to *Dæmons*, so when the name of *Dæmon* is given to a part of the Mind leading us, we may say with *Aristotle*, that two *Dæmons* are born and live with us, *viz.* Reason, and the sensual Appetite: and he that is led by right Reason, is led by a good *Dæmon*, and he that is led by Anger, or Concupiscence is carryed away by an evil *Dæmon*; but the doubt is concerning a *Dæmon* properly taken, whether it be a *Dæmon* by its Nature, or a foregin *Dæmon*: the former of which may be aptly enough destin'd to be, *An Animal having a reason, and understanding Superior to Man, using a subtle body, and mediating betwixt God and Man*; the latter is the Soul of a Man, departed this Life, being freed from the gross Body, and using a subtle vehicle. And in this Sense *Aristotle* did not

L. de invest. Dæm. perip.

2 Top. loc. 19.

think there were *Dæmons*; not *Dæmons* by Nature, First, because as he profest to explain all particular degrees of things, to set forth a compleat Philosophy, he no where speaks of *Dæmons*. Secondly, in his third Book of the *Soul*, he plainly rejects them, setting forth, that no Animal can consist either of Air, or Fire, or any other simple Body; though he makes particular mention of Air and Fire, because the *Academicks* thought the Bodies of *Dæmons* to be aiery, and in some sort fiery. But to pass by many other Passages of *Aristotle* against *Dæmons*, he thinks this a most firm Reason, That there is nothing in the Universe in vain, speaking of the Degrees and Species of things; whereas if there were *Dæmons*, they would be of no use, according to *Aristotle*, which hence appears, because all those things which are commonly judg'd Works of *Dæmons*, are ascrib'd by him to other Causes, never any to *Dæmons*: For those things which excited the ancient Philosophers to excogitate *Dæmons*, were chiefly Divinations by Dreams, which *Aristotle* ascrib'd to Nature; the various kinds of Furies or Raptures, of which he attributes to a various temperament of Melancholy; the Answers of *Oracles*, which he refers to the property of certain Steams proceeding from the Cavities of the Earth; the saying of a Verse by an ignorant Person, by which *Aristotle* likewise refers to Melancholy: Since therefore Philosophers are rais'd by Works to the search of Causes, and *Aristotle* ascrib'd all those Works to other Causes, and not to *Dæmons*, we gather, he thought there were none. And so as to *Foreign Dæmons*, or the Souls of Men separated from the Body, *Aristotle* held there were none: For in his Second Book of the *Soul*, he says, there is no Soul without the Body: And in the Seventh of his *Metaphysicks*, he says, there is no Man without Flesh and Bones: And in his Second Book of the *Generation of Animals*, he says there is no Instrument without a Faculty, nor an organical Faculty without an Instrument: Now, the Soul of Man is organical, *&c.*

 Cæsalpinus, after having quoted *Plato*, introducing *Socrates*, concluding against his Calumniators, who charg'd him of admitting no Gods, that he that grants there are

Test. 66.

Test 26.

Cap. 13.

L. de Invest. Dæm. Perip. cap. 7.

Dæmonical Works, of necessity admits *Dæmons*, which are either Gods, or Sons of Gods, in his Seventh Chapter he writes thus: We may gather in *Aristotle*, that there are *Dæmons*, by that Argument, by which *Socrates* gather'd there were. He that asserts there are *Dæmonical Works*, is compel'd of necessity to confess, there are *Dæmons*. *Aristotle* asserts, there are *Dæmonical Works*, viz. Dreams and Nature; therefore of Necessity he must confess there are *Dæmons*, whence they are so denominated. And the Philosopher seems to have understood that middle Nature betwixt God and Mortal things, mention'd before by us, to be a *Dæmon*; for when he had deny'd Dreams to be sent by God, (as some thought they were) because they happen not only to the wisest of Men, but indifferently to Idiots, and some other Animals yet he says Dreams are *Dæmonical*, because Nature is *Dæmonical*, not Divine; tho' therefore somewhat Divine be contain'd in Nature, yet it does not merit the Name of Divine, but *Dæmonical*, because it follows the Wisdom of an Intelligence, whence it's rendred admirable, even in the least things, and Dreams are *Dæmonical*, by reason of the wonderful force of the Imagination.

Now, these two Authors consider'd, I think it may be agreed, that *Aristotle* did not admit a *Dæmon* properly taken, as *Piccolini* has set forth; but he admitted the Facts commonly ascrib'd to *Dæmons*, which he accounted for from other Causes; as we find by what is quoted from *Charpentarius*, by *Naudæus*, according to which (as *Naudæus* says) *Cæsalpinus*'s sole reason for establishing of *Dæmons*, according to *Aristotle*'s Doctrine, may be solv'd. Yet however, since *Aristotle* admits the Facts Commonly ascrib'd to *Dæmons*, I see not why he may not properly enough be said to have had a *Genius*, tho' it may be explain'd by an *Intllectus Agens*, coming from without, or by an orderly influx from the Intelligences that move the Heav'ns, he having a mind to set up for himself, by an hypothesis of his own, contrary to that of *Plato* receiv'd before, and which is more consonant to Christianity. Nor can I think *Aristotle*'s so plausible for solving *Phænomena*, tho' it may more gratify the Humour of some Persons. In reference to *Aristotle's Genius*, I may add what *Rhodiginus* writes, *viz.* That, among the Ancients, *Plato* had the Symbol of *Divine* given him, and *Aristotle* of *Dæmonical*; the reason why *Aristotle* was so stil'd, seems to be, that he chiefly treated of natural things, the consideration of which lies, in a manner, in the sublunary World, where they thought *Dæmons* had their abode: But *Plato* raising himself Higher, being addicted to the Contemplation of Intelligible Beings, got him a more eminent guide of Life, and despising those things which others admir'd, even to a Madness, he strove with all his force to bring that which is Divine in us, to that Divine Being which only is truly so, whence he got his name of *Divine*.

Lact. Antiq. l.2.c.2.

Naudæus, after he has rejected the *Genius* of *Aristotle*, proceeds to the others; but first tells us, That what all the *Platonicks* have set forth concerning *Dæmons* and *Magick*, can neither be prov'd by Reason nor Experience; and as for the Reason they draw from many Effects, which they say must necessarily be referr'd to these Causes, before he obliges himself to receive it, he first wishes they would well satisfy *Pomponatius*, *Cardan*, and *Bernardus Mirandulanus*, who shew, pertinently enough, that its better to have recourse to the Proofs of our Religion, to believe *Angels* and *Dæmons*, than to that heap of Experiences, of which a reason may be rendred by the Principles of Natural Philosophy. After which he says, We ought no longer to make doubt, but all that is said of the *Genii* of *Plotinus*, *Porphyrius*, and *Jamblicus*, ought to be referr'd a to what he has said before concerning the *Dæmon* of *Socrates*.

To this I reply, that even setting by the Proofs of our Religion for *Angels* and *Dæmons*, I see not but as for solving the Experiences he speaks of, by natural Principles, *Aristotle's Hypothesis of Intelligences* moving the Heavens, is altogether as precarious, and less satisfactory than the other, us'd by others of the *Gentiles*: And as for his referring what is said of the *Genii* of the three Philosophers before-mention'd, to what he has said of the *Genius* of *Socrates*, I think I have shewn above, that he has not validly refuted his *Dæmon*.

As to the *Genius* of *Plotinus*, *Porphyrius* his Scholar, who has writ his Life, which is prefix'd to *Plotinus*'s Works, set forth with Commentaries, by *Ficinus*, says thus in it:

"An *Egyptian* Priest coming to *Rome*, and being soon made known, by a Friend of his, to *Plotinus*, and having a desire to shew a Specimen of his Wisdom at *Rome*, perswaded *Plotinus* to go along with him, and he would presently shew him his *Dæmon*, or *Familiar Spirit*, whom *Plotinus* readily obey'd. The Invocation of the *Dæmon* was made in the Temple of *Isis*; for *Plotinus* said, this was the sole place in *Rome*, which the *Egyptian* found pure: But when the *Dæmon* was call'd to present himself to his view, instead of a *Dæmon*, a God appear'd, which was not of the Species of *Dæmons*; the *Egyptian* thereupon thus presently cry'd out, *You are happy*, O Plotinus! *who have a God for your* Dæmon, *and have not light on a Guide of an Inferior kind.*"

Plotinus therefore having a Familiar of the Order of Divine *Dæmons*, it was with reason that he always sublimely rais'd the Divine Eye of his Mind to that; and for this reason he afterwards compos'd a Book concerning each Man's particular *Dæmon*, where he endeavours diligently to assign the Causes of the difference of Familiar Spirits. *Porphyrius*, to shew the Divine Spirit of his Master, *Plotinus*, adds beneath:

"I had once thoughts of killing my self, which *Plotinus* wonderfully perceiv'd; and as I was walking in the House, he presently came to me, and said. *What you meditate*, O Porphyrius ! *is not like that of a sound Mind; but rather, of a Mind grown mad with Melancholy*; and therefore he commanded me to depart from *Rome*."

Those that would read *Plotinus*'s Tract concerning each Man's *Familiar Spirits*, may find it in his Works.

Naudæus proceeds next to the *Genii* of *Chicus, Scaliger,* and *Cardan*. As for *Chicus*, he looks upon him, by what he has writ, as a Superstitious Person, who affirm'd, he often made use of Revelations from a Spirit call'd *Florom*, which he said was of the Order of the *Cherubims*. But *Naudæus* rejects this, with other fabulous Relations of other Persons, saying with *Lucretius*:

Quis dubitat quin omne sithoc rationis ægestas.

a short way of refuting.

Concerning the *Genii* of *Scaliger* and *Cardan*, *Naudæus* writes as follows. If it were permitted me, and it became me to follow rather my will, than my duty, I should freely excuse my self from saying any thing against the *Genii*, which the two sole great Persons, whom we may oppose to the two most learned, and famous among the Ancients, have attributed to themselves, and who have been, as it were, the last effort, and miracle of Nature, *Scaliger* and *Cardan*: for I certainly believe, either they deceived themselves, in admitting these *Genii*, because, after having well examined themselves, they could not find in them the cause of such, and so extraordinary Perfection; or that they did it thro' modesty, not to discover by their Learning, how much all the rest of Mankind were inferior to them; or, finally, that they would cover from envy, under this particular assistance, and free from the jealousy of Men, that great renown they had acquir'd to themselves, by their studious diligence and labours. However, as truth is sooner found out when many Persons employ themselves in the search of it, the opinion of those is not to be rejected, who, say *Scaliger*, practised this stratagem, in imitation of all great Persons, and not to yield in Ambition to his Antagonist, attributing to himself for a *Genius*, in his *Art of Poetry*, a meer sally or emotion of Mind; by which the Soul is heated, as it were, in it self, to raise it to the knowledge of somewhat, during which, a Man may at any time say, and write many things, which he understands not after the heat of this enthusiasm is over. And as for *Cardan*, he speaks so

L. 3. *c.* 26.

variously of his *Genius*, that after having said absolutely in his *Dialogue* entitl'd *Telion*, that he had one, which was *Venereal*, mixt with *Saturn* and *Mercury*; and in his Book, *De libris propriis*, that he Communicated himself to him by his Dreams, he doubts at the same place whether he had really one, or whether it were the excellency of his Nature, *I perceived* (said he) *whether it were from the* Genius *set over me, or that my Nature is placed, in the extremity of an human State, and in the confines of the Immortals, &c*. And finally concludes in his Book, *De Rerum Varietate*, that he had none, frankly saying, *I truly know not that any* Dæmon, *or* Genius *attends me*. Whence we may surely judge, that he and *Scaliger* had no other *Genius*, but the great Learning they had acquired, by their diligence and labours, and the experience they had of things; on which coming to raise their judgments as on two Pyramids, they judg'd pertinently of all matters, and let nothing escape from being known, and manifest to them.

We here see what conjectures *Naudæus* has made concerning the *Genii* of these Men, which are as easily rejected as they are groundlesly suggested by him. And tho' *Cardan* says, in his Book *De Rerum Varietate*, he knew no *Genius* attended him; we know that Book was writ many Years before he writ his Life, which was but a little before his Death, and on which I think we have most reason to rely; where he plainly says, he had a *Genius* tho' not well discovered by him till his latter Years. And this Book writ by *Cardan*, of his own Life, was set forth by *Naudæus* himself, which makes it seem somewhat strange that he should deny he had any *Genius*. But, for the Readers satisfaction, I shall here set down what these two great Men say themselves of their *Genii*, and shall leave it to him to judge of it, as he shall think fit.

L. 15.

To pass by the *Genius* of *Facius Cardanus*, which his Son *Hierom Cardan* says, his Father own'd to have attended him for Thirty Years, and where he gives an account of Seven

L. De Dæ-mon.

Dæmons more, whom he saw and converst with; I here give you several particulars, tho' not all, which *Hierom Cardan* has left recorded concerning a *Genius* that attended himself.

In his Book of his own Life, set forth by *Naudæus*, where he writes of his good Spirit, he says, its received as a manifest truth, that familiar Spirits (which the *Greeks* call *Angels*,) have forewarned some Men, *Socrates, Plotinus, Synesius, Dion, Flavius Josephus*, and even my self: All lived happily besides *Socrates* and my self, who neverthelses am in a very good condition: but *G. Cæsar* the Dictator, *Cicero, Antony, Brutus* and *Cassius* had evil, tho' illustrious Spirits. Those of *Antony* and *Cicero*, were Glorious, but both Pernicious; that of *Josephus* was particularly famous, and of a rare excellency for Warlike Valour, favour with *Vespasian* and his Sons, Riches, Monuments of Histories, a threefold Offsping, and in his contest with the calamities of his Nation; also in a foresight of future things, wherewith he was illustrated in Captivity, being freed from the outrage of his Friends, and preserved from the Waves of the Sea. But these were manifestly *Dæmons*, tho' mine, as I believe, a good and merciful Spirit. I was long perswaded that I had one, but could not find how he should certify me of imminent events, till after the Seventy Fourth Year of my Age, when I set upon writing my life; but that so many imminent things should be foreknown to me, and truly foreseen, and that just before they happened, and precisely, seems to me a greater Miracle to be done without a Divine Aid, than with a Spirit; for Instance, When my Spirit saw what was ready to befall me, *viz.* that my Son was to Marry the next day, an Unfortunate Match, in the Night-time he raised such a beating of my Heart, by a way peculiarly known to him, that the Chamber seem'd to tremble; my Son perceiving the same, at the same time, so that both of us thought there was an Earthquake, which no body else perceived.

He adds beneath; There may be some doubts, why this care for me, and not for others; for I do not excel in Learning, as some think, but haply on the contrary? Is it an immence love of Truth, and Wisdom, with contempt of Riches, even

C. 47.

in this state of Poverty? or by reason of my desire of Justice? or that I ascribe all to God, nothing to my self? or haply for some end known to God alone?

Again, why does he not openly admonish me (as I could wish) of those things, of which he does admonish me? but teaches one thing for another, as by those disorderly Noises (*of which he gives several instances, happening before Deaths, in his* 43d. *Chapter of the same Book*) for me to assure my self that God beholds all things, tho' I see him not with my Eyes; for he could have admonish'd me openly by a *Dream*, or some clearer way of manifestation: but haply this shew'd more the Divine Care, and those greater things that hapned to me, Fears, Impediments, Anxieties, *&c*. there is need also of Obscurity, for us to understand that they are the Works of God, and ought not to be opposed; its folly therefore to be overhastily sollicitous for knowing these things.

At the end of the same Chapter, he writes, that having stuck to a splendor that attended him above Forty Years, he had all his art of Writing and publick Teaching, from his Spirit and Splendour, tho' this kind of Science had got him among Men, more Envy than Renown, and more Glory than Profit: but it gave him no small, nor vulgar Pleasure, and contributed to the prolonging of his life, being a comfort to him in many Calamities, an aid in Adversities, an help in Difficulties and Labours; upon the whole, he says, the fact was plainly so, he might err in the Causes, and refers himself to such as are Wiser, *viz*. Divines.

Chap. 38.

In the same Book he writes thus, Hitherto I have spoken of my self, as of a Man, and that is somewhat beneath other Men, in my Nature and Learning, but now I shall speak of some admirable Disposition of my self; and so much the more wonderful, that I find somewhat in my self, which I know not what to make off: And that that thing is my self, tho' I do not perceive such things to proceed from me: That it's present, when its meet, and not when I will have it. That which rises thence is greater than my Abilities; which was first discover'd to me, in the Year 1526. So that it's above

Forty four Years since. I perceive a thing from without enter into my Ear with a noise from that part directly, where People are talking of me: If it tends to Good in the right side, or if it comes from the left, it penetrates to the right, and an orderly noise is made: And if the Discourse be contentious, I hear a wonderful Contention; if it inclines to Evil in the left side, it comes exactly from the part where those tumultuous Voices are. Therefore it enters on both sides of my Head; and very often when the thing falls out ill, the Voice on the left side, when it should end, grows louder, and Voices are multiply'd, and very commonly, if the thing be in the same Town, it happens that the Voice being scarce over, a Messenger comes in to call me to them; and if it be from another City, and a Messenger comes, upon computing the time betwixt the Deliberation, and the beginning of the Journey, they come to the same, and I find Sentence past after the form it is concluded, and this continued with me to the Year 1568, and I wondred it ceas'd.

In the Year 1534. I began to see in Dreams what things would happen in a short time, and if the same Day, I saw them clearly, and after Sun rising; so that I saw a Sentence past in a Cause of the College, and that I should be Professor at *Bononia*; this ceas'd *An.* 1567.

The third thing was a Splendor, this I encreas'd by Degrees; it began about the Year 1575, 1573 or 74, but particularly this Year 1575, it seems to me I have it perfect, and it's a thing which does not leave me; but instead of the two foregoing which are ceas'd, it fortifies me against Emulators, and as necessity requires. Its compos'd of an Artifical Practice, and a Circumfluent Light, being very Pleasant, and alone performs much more, as to Efficacy, Exercitation, Advantage, and Solidity of Studies, than those two joyn'd together; and does not take a Man from his common Studies, and humane Conversation, but makes him ready at all things, and is most excellent for composing Books, and seems, as it were, the utmost reach of our Nature, for it represents all things together, that make for the matter under Consideration; and if it be not a Divine thing, certainly it's the most perfect of Mortal Works.

Chap. 37. In the same Book he writes as follows: While I liv'd at *Pavia*, and profest Physick there, looking casually on my Hand, I saw at the root of my ring Finger, of my right Hand, the form of a bloody Sword, I was presently struck with a great fear. In the Evening a Messenger came with a Letter from my Son in Law, acquainting me that my Son was taken into Custody, and that I should come to *Milan* the next Day, and for fifty three Days the Mark increas'd, and went upwards, and behold, the last Day reacht to the top of my Finger, and look'd red like a flaming Sword. I, suspecting no such thing, and being frighted, and not my self, knew not what to do, say, or think; at midnight my Son was beheaded; in the Morning the Sign was almost gone, in a Day or two it wholly vanish'd.

Chap. 4. In the same Book, having giv'n an account of some strange Noises, and Voices he had heard, and of a strange Smell he perceiv'd before Deaths, he concludes thus. But concerning these wonderful things, it's thus with Men, that when they are present, or a little before they have happ'ned, they draw the whole Man; after they are a while over, they are so little heeded, that unless they are brought fresh to the Mind by some force, they doubt, as it were, whether they have seen or heard them; which, I suppose, chiefly happens both by Reason of much more profound Causes, and for the distance of our Nature from the Causes that produce them. I know what Scoffs and Laughter, some, that would seem wise, raise at such things; the chief ring Leader of whom is *Polybius*, a Philosopher, without Philosophy, who understood not even the Duty of an Historian, but by extending it too far, became ridiculous, sometimes admirable, as where he speaks of the

L. 2. Hist. *Achæans*. In short, *Tartalia*, rightly said, that no Man knows all things, and those nothing, that do not know their Ignorance of many things. You see *Pliny*, who has deliver'd so clear an History, shews himself a Blockhead, where he treats of the Sun and Stars; what wonder therefore that

Polybius, (while he meddles of the more sublime and Divine things) has so clearly expos'd his Ignorance. I religiously Swear, that a Sense and Consciousness of only one of these things, is more dear to me, than a long lasting Reign over the whole Earth would be. And beneath, but let this suffice, for I have only here set down in short, when these things happen'd, and how, and such in which these could be no Suspiscion of Error or Imposture; and I only beg you, Reader, when you read such things, do not propose humane Pride for your Scope, but the greatness and amplitude of the World, and of the Heavens, and the vile Darkness in which we live, and you will easily Understand, I have related no incredible things. The same Author, in his Dialogue, intitl'd *Tetim*, or of *Humane Counsels*, where he makes *Tetim* and *Ram*, Interlocutors, makes *Ram* say, I believe *Cardan* has a *Genius* for his Companion, which discover'd himself late to him, being wont before to admonish him by Dreams and Noises; and beneath, so many and so wonderful things have happen'd to him, in his Life, that I am forc'd to believe, being intimate with him, he has a great, powerful, and rare *Genius*, so that he is not Master of his Actions; but those things he desires, he has not, the things he has he did not covet or hope for.

At the end of his fourth Book of *Wisdom*, he writes as follows, concerning the *Genii* of other Men. All great Men seem to be led by some Divine Spirit, or *Dæmon*; *Socrates*, before his Death, had warning of the Day in a Dream, *Dion* saw a Spectre in his House, what was it open'd *Gaius Cæsar*'s door the Night before he was slain? What was it said to *Brutus* as he was alone, I am thy Evil *Genius*, thou shalt see me again at *Philippi*? What was that august figure seen by *Cassius* in his Tent, that, was like to *Cæsar*? What foretold *Sylla* in his Dream, of his imminent Death? Or what was it he heard so Pleasant in a clear Sky? What from a *Mausolæum* call'd *Nero* before his Death? What admonish'd *Caligula* of his Death in a Dream? Why did *Antony* hear the departure of *Bacchus* from *Alexandria*, the Night before his Death? What mixt a sleeping Potion for *Adrian* in a Dream before his Death? Certainly, the *Dæmon* that was in them; for

Humane Nature, when highly exalted, rises to the force of a *Dæmon*. These foresaw their Deaths, but could not prevent the violence of it. Neither are these the only Persons, who having this Wisdom have had violent ends: For *Paul*, who, added by the Divine Spirit, could see the Secrets of God, and *Stephen* the Heavens open, and *Philip*, who was carry'd invisible through the Desart, died all by the Hands of others. But there is this great difference betwixt these Spirits, that the Divine is joyn'd with Justice and Piety, and the other Vertues, and has tranquility and rest always attending it; the *Dæmonical* is rais'd by Murthers, Robberies, and False-dealings; and is always accompanyed with suspiscious and manifold Disquiets. Who but a Person of troubled Senses, and a discompos'd Mind would chuse to embrace the *Dæmonical?* But as in sick Persons, the vitiated taste abhors Sweet and Fat things, and is more delighted with such as are sharp and insipid; so the Nature of Mortals being corrupted with Vice, abhors the best, and adheres to the worst; and this is done chiefly by the likeness of these two kinds, which, how great it is may easily be understood by this, that *Simon* and *Elimas*, the *Magicians*, were accounted Divine Men, and *Christ*, who was God, was thought by many to have a Devil. And so much for *Cardan*.

L. 3. c. 25.   *Scaliger*, speaking of the *Genius* ascrib'd by *Virgil* to Æneas, viz. *Achates*, so called from ἄχος ἄξης writes thus of the *Genii* that attend Men. We read in the Books of the *Pythagoreans*, enricht by the *Platonicks*, that we have two *Genii* attending us a Good and a Bad; by the guidance and counsels of the Good, Good and Elect Persons joyn themselves to God, from whom they have received him as a Mediator. To some *Heroes*, he shews himself, by others he is never seen but is heard, which *Socrates* professes of his, in more than one place in *Plato*, by some Divine Spirits he is neither seen, nor heard, but so introduces and presents himself, that by his light he discovers an intelligence of secret things, for Men to write: wherefore it often happens, that when that Celestial Heat is over in us, we our selves either admire those our Writings, or do not own them for ours, and do not understand some things after the way they were directed and dictated by him; nor do I think it hapned otherwise to *Plato*, to whose Writings a light is added by Interpreters, much greater than may proceed from vulgar judgments. As for my self, who think I am not to be compared even with the least, if any thing falls from me at any time unawares, I may not hope so much may be performed by me afterwards, which is the reason I never set upon meditating, or writing, unless invited by my *Genius*, who speaks inwardly with me, tho' not heard, shewing the spacious fields of the Divinity in our Minds, which being abstracted and suspended from the offices of the Body, it deputes to other Functions; so that he did not speak wholly at random, who thought, that *Aristotle's Intellectus Agens*, were the same with *Plato's Genius*; we have instances of both in History, for an Evil one appear'd to *Brutus*, and foretold him an unhappy end; A Good one to *Cæsar*, when he past *Rubicon*, shewing him the way to that, in which he plac'd his chief bliss, *&c*.

Heinsius says, in a manner, the same thing of himself with *Scaliger*, writing thus; Here are some things to which, being my self, I am not able to aspire, which after the heat has left my Mind, I consider as a Reader of another Man's Works. *Scaliger* also elsewhere calls his *Genius*, most Learned, whose desire is vast and immence: And *Heinsius* says, uninitiated Persons do not understand these things. *In Dedic. Hippon. sui.*

Excer. 344. *Ib.*

Scaliger also, on *Aristotle De Plantis*, writes thus; *Jamblicus*, in his *Mysteries*, says, he that being inspir'd, receives the Deity, has a sort of appearance of Fire before its ingress, and it's seen the God either coming, or departing; therefore those Spirits that apply themselves to our Mind with Darkness, bring us frivolous, wavering and doubtful things: And I know a Person to whose Eyes a Fire presents itself often, either meditating, or expecting Messengers. *P.* 9. 2. *in f.*

This is what *Scaliger* and *Cardan* have said concerning their own *Genii*, and those of others; from which the judicious Reader may easily discern their sense concerning them.

CHAP. III.

What perception Men have had of Genii, *or* Spirits, *and their operations by the Sight.*

AS I come now to give an account of the perception Men have had of *Genii*, or Spirits, and their operations, by their particular senses; I shall begin with the most spiritualized sense, *viz.* the Sight, and set forth what perception Men have had of them by that; and whereas in my account, according to the several senses, it may sometimes happen, that more than one sense may be concerned at one and the same time, in a perception of them, I shall entitle the Chapters, according to the predominant sense in that Action. And whereas it often happens that some particular Persons have a perception of Spirits, both by the Sight and Hearing, when other Persons present perceive nothing, I shall treat of these Persons in particular Chapters.

To begin therefore with instances of Persons perceiving Spirits by the Sight; *Campanella* tells us, there are *Angel Guardians* for each *Species*, and individual Person, as St. *Hierom* writes, and himself has found by experience, which he did not understand before. *De Sens Rer. l. 1. c. 7.*

In the same work, he tells us of a Friend of his, who was no ignorant, nor timerous Person, nor given to speak untruths, who assured him he had often seen and conversed with Evil *Dæmons*; and he says, he met with many others afterwards, who had been incredulous in this kind, but upon their seeing and conversing with Spirits, chang'd their Opinions, and their Lives, *L. 2. c. 25.*

Elsewhere he Writes thus, *Porphyrius* and *Plotinus* say there are *Angels* Good and Bad, as daily experience teaches; and my self also have found by manifest experience, not when I greatly endeavoured it, but when I was minding another thing; and therefore it's no wonder if they did not appear to curious *Nero*. *Ib. l. 4. c. 1*

C. 11.   In his *Atheismus Triumphatus*, he also tells us of a Friend of his that had a sensible experience of Spirits, whose Voice he used to hear betwixt sleeping and waking, and especially when any evil was to happen to him.

Father *Le Brun* Printed a Book two Years since at *Paris*, in *French*, which has for Title, *Historire Critique des pratiques Superstitieuses &c.*

In the Second part of this Book, *Chap* 7. he writes concerning *Trithemius*, as follows: The Abbot *Trithemius*, after an ardent desire of knowing Secrets unknown to all Mankind, learned such as were Astonishing by a Revelation, which has no way the character of being Divine. I examine not whether all he said he had learnt, be natural; I know some Persons pretend it; but it's plain it was without making a due reflexion. However it may be, I shall only speak of the manner after which *Trithemius* learnt these Secrets: He Writ it confidently to a *Carmelite* Father, a Friend of his, call'd *Borstius*, who died at *Ghent*, before the Letter came to him: It was open'd and communicated to many Persons, and *Trithemius* did not disown it. I have in hand, says he, in his Letter, a great Work which will amuse the whole World, if ever it sees the Light; it's divided into Four Books, and the First has for Title of it, *Steganography*; the Work throughout is full of great and astonishing things, which Man has never heard of, and will seem incredible. If you ask me, how I learnt these things? It's not by Man, but by the Revelation of I know not what Spirit; for thinking, on a day, this Year 1499. if I could not discover secrets unknown to Men; after having a long while ponder'd on those I have mentioned, and being at length perswaded that what I sought for was not possible, I went to Bed, being somewhat ashamed for having carried my Folly so far, as to attempt an Impossible thing. In the Night-time some one presented himself to me, and calling me by my name, *Trithemius*, said he, do not believe you have had all these thoughts in vain, tho' the things you search are not possible to you, nor to any other Man, they will become so. *Teach me then, I reply'd, what I must do to succeed.* Then he laid open the whole Mystery, and shew'd me that nothing was more easy. God is my Witness, that I speak the Truth, and that I have taught these Secrets but to a Prince, who by an evident proof has been convinced of the possibillity of it. It Imports that none but Princes should know these sorts of Secrets, least Traitors, Impostors, or other Ill Men make use of them for doing many Mischiefs.

Boissardus L. de Magia, Genius & Angelis, mentions this Letter of *Trithemius*, and says he there adds, that he could teach all the things he had of the Spirit, in all the Languages of the World; and that he clears himself of the Crime of Magick, and any commerce with Evil Spirits, by a Sacred Oath and Execration. *Naudæus* writes that *Trithemius* indeed lay under a suspicion of Magick, on the account of that Letter, and endeavours to clear him of it, but I leave it to the Readers, to consider what *Trithemius*'s Words import, as to a conversation with some Spirit, be he Good or Bad.

C. 5.

Apol. des Grands homines, &c. *p. 2. c. 17.*

The same *Boissardus* writes, that an Illustrious *German* Count, whom he knew, profest, he had a *Familiar Spirit*, whom he affirm'd to be of the Celestial Order, whose Counsel he used in all things he undertook, at home and abroad.

C. 6.

Philip Melancthon tells us, that he had seen *Spectres*, and that he knew many Men worthy of credit, who affirm'd they had not only seen *Spectres*, but had likewise discoursed with them. So *Maximus Tyrius* says, he saw *Æsculapius*, but it was in a Slumber, but *Hercules* he saw, as he was Waking.

L. de Anime.

Serm. 27.

There was a Pamphlet Printed in *London, Anno* 1645. in Quarto, Entitled, *A True and exact Relation of the several Informations, Examinations and Confessions of the late Witches Arraigned and Executed in the County of* Essex.

Who were Arraigned and Condemned at the late Sessions held at *Chelmsford*, before the Right Honourable *Robert Earl of Warwick*, and several of his Majesty's Justices of the Peace. *July* the 29*th*. 1645.

Before this Sessions several Informations concerning Witches, and their Practises, were taken before Sir *Harbottel Grimston*, and Sir *Thomas Bowes*, His Majesty's Justices of Peace for the said County. Some of which Informations are as follows.

I. *The Information of* Matthew Hopkins *of* Manningtree, Gent. *Taken upon Oath before us, the* 25th. *of* March, 1645.

This Informant saith, that the said *Elizabeth Clarke*, alias, *Beddingfield* (suspected for a Witch as aforesaid, and whose Mother and some others of her Kinsfolk, did suffer Death for Witchcraft and Murther) being by appointment of the said Justices, watcht several Nights, for the better discovery of her wicked Practises: This Informant came into the Room, where the said *Elizabeth* was watcht, as aforesaid, the last Night, being the 24*th*. of this Instant *March*, but intended not to have stay'd long there, but the said *Elizabeth* forthwith told this Informant, and one Mr. *Sterne*, there present, if they would stay, and do the said *Elizabeth* no hurt, she would call one of her white *Imps*, and play with it in her Lap; but this Informant told her they would not allow of it; but that staying there a while longer, within a quarter of an Hour after, there appeared an *Imp* like to a Dog, which was White with some Sandy Spots, and seem'd to be very Fat, and Plump, with very short Legs, and forthwith Vanisht away: and the said *Elizabeth* said the name of that *Imp*, was *Jarmara*; and immediately there appeared another *Imp*, which she called *Vinegar Tom*, in the shape of a Grey-hound, with long Legs; and the said *Elizabeth* then said, that the next *Imp* should be a black *Imp*, and should come for the said Mr. *Sterne*, which appeared, but presently Vanisht; and the last that appeared was in the shape of a Pole-cat, but the Head somewhat bigger; and the said *Elizabeth* then told this Informant, that she had five *Imps* of her own, and two of the Imps of the Old Bedlam *West*, (meaning one *Ann West*, Widow who is now also suspected to be guilty of Witchcraft) and said sometimes the *Imps* of the Old Bedlam Suck'd on the said *Elizabeth*, and sometimes her *Imps* Suck'd on the Old Beldam *West*; and the said *Elizabeth* farther told this Informant, that Satan would never let her be at rest, or quiet, till she did consent to the Killing of the Hogs of one Mr. *Edwards* of *Mannintree*, and the Horse of one *Robert Taylor*, of the same Town.

II. *The Information of* John Sterne, *Gent. Taken upon Oath before us, the* 25th. *Day of* March, 1645.

This Informant saith, that Watching with *Elizabeth Clarke* (suspected for Witchcraft, as aforesaid) she desired this Informant, and the rest that were in the Room with her, to sit down, and said she would shew this Informant and the rest some of her *Imps*; and within half an Hour, there appear'd a white thing in the likeness of a Cat, but not altogether so big, and being ask'd if she would not be afraid of her *Imps*? She answer'd, what do you think I am afraid of my Children? and that she call'd the name of that white *Imp Hoult*. And this Informant farther saith, that presently after there appear'd another white *Imp* with Red Spots, as big as a small Dog, which she then called *Jamara*; and that immediately after there appear'd at the Threshold of the Door another *Imp*, about the bigness of the first, but did presently Vanish away: and then the said *Elizabeth* being ask'd if any more *Imps* would come? she answer'd that *Vinegar Tom* would come by and by, and forthwith there appear'd another in the likeness of a Dumb Dog, somewhat bigger than any of the former; and the said *Elizabeth* also told this Informant, that she had three *Imps* from her Mother, which were of a Brown Colour, and two from the Old Beldam *West*; and that there had five *Imps* appear'd; but she had one more call'd *Sack and Sugar*, which had been hard at Work, and it would be long before it came, but it should Tear this Informant.

III. *The Information of* Frances Mills, Grace Norman, Mary Phillips, *and* Mary Parley: *Taken upon Oath, before the said Justices, the* 25th. *Day of* March, 1645.

These Informants say joyntly, that watching with the said *Elizabeth Clarke*, suspected as aforesaid, about Twelve of the Clock last Night, the said *Elizabeth* smack'd with her Mouth, and beckon'd with her Hand, and Instantly there appear'd a white thing, about the bigness of a Cat; and that these Informants saw five *Imps* more, which the said *Elizabeth* named, as abovesaid, *&c.*

IV. *The Information of* Edward Parsly *of* Mannintree; *Taken Upon Oath before the said Justices, the* 25th. *of* March, 1645.

This informant saith, that watching with the said *Elizabeth Clarke* the last Night, he ask'd her if he should continue still in the Room with her: and the said *Elizabeth* desired he should, if he would Fight for her with the Devils; for they would come this Night, and that which she call'd *Hoult* would come first, and then that which she call'd *Jarmara*; which did appear in the likeness of a white Dog, with red Spots; and presently after there appear'd that *Imp* which she call'd *Vinegar Tom*; and then that which she call'd *Sack and Sugar*: and the said *Elizabeth* then told this Informant, that the Devil had had possession of her Six or Seven Years, and that he had oftentimes knock'd at her Door in the Night-time, and that she did rise, open the Door, and let him in, and that he went to Bed to her three or four times a Week and had the Carnal knowledge of her, as a Man.

V. *The Information of* John Banks *of* Mannintree, *Taken upon Oath before the said Justices, the* 25th. *of* March, 1645.

This Informant saith, that watching with the said *Elizabeth Clarke*, he did Inform and Confirm all the particulars exprest, and set down in the Information of the said Mr. *Sterne*.

To the Five Informations before set down, I shall add the Examination of *Ann Leech* of *Misley*, in the County aforesaid, Widow, taken before the said Justices, *April* the 14*th.* 1645. as follows.

This Examinant saith. That she had a *Grey Imp* sent her, and that she, together with *Elizabeth Clarke*, and *Elizabeth Gooding*, did about a Year since, send their *Imps* to kill a Black Cow, and a White Cow belonging to Mr. *Edwards*, which was done accordingly; and says, That she sent her *Grey Imp*,

Elizabeth Clarke a *Black Imp*, and *Elizabeth Gooding* a *White Imp*; and that about 30 Years since she sent a *Grey Imp* to kill two Horses, of one Mr. *Bragg*, of *Misley*, which were kill'd accordingly. That she, and the said *Elizabeth Gooding*, sent either of them an *Imp*, to destroy the Child of the said Mr. *Edwards*; this Examinants *Imp* being a White one, and *Elizabeth Gooding*'s a Black *Imp*; and that about thirty Years since this Examinant had the said *White Imp*, and two others, a *Grey* and a *Black* Imp, of one *Anne*, the Wife of *Robert Pierce*, of *Stoake*, in *Suffolk*, being her Brother; and that these *Imps* went commonly from one to another, and did mischief where-ever they went. And that when this Examinant did not employ them abroad to do mischief, she had-not her Health; but when they were employ'd, she was healthful and well; and these *Imps* did usually suck those Teats, which were found about the privy Parts of her Body; and that those *Imps* did often speak to this Examinant, and that in an *Hollow Voice*, which she plainly understood, *&c.* she was executed at *Chelmsford*, as also *Clarke* before mention'd.

Now, as to the five Informations before set down (in which Eight Persons are concern'd) all given in upon Oath, that they saw such *Imps*, as they mention, I cannot well conceive what an opposer of any real Apparitions of Spirits can say: for here I do not tell you of afflicted Persons, who pretended to see *Spectres*, which were seen by none but themselves, nor of an Old distracted Woman, who fancies she has and sees Spirits, attending her, when there is no such thing: Nor do I give you the Testimonies of Crafty, Melancholy Wenches, or Old Women, as some such there may have been; but here are the Testimonies of Eight unexceptionable Persons, as I conceive, concurring in one thing: And if this be not a fair Proof, I know not what is so.

As to the Examination of *Anne Leech*, concerning her *Imps*, though the Fact stands but upon her Testimony, yet in regard it relates to somewhat that I shall write elsewhere in this Book, I thought fit to insert it. And I here forbear to insert the Spirits raised by Mrs. *Bodman*, who was executed at *Salisbury*, for which Fact there was also but one Testimony,

Sometime since, I drew the Account before set down from the foremention'd Pamphlet printed *Anno* 1645. I casually met with a Pamphlet publish'd in *London, Anno* 1648. by Mr. *Stearne* above mentioned; the Title of it is, *A Confirmation and Discovery of Witchcraft,* &c. *by* John Stearne, *now of* Laws-Hall, *near* Bury St. Edmonds, *in* Suffolk, *sometimes of* Manningtree *in* Essex.

In this *Pamphlet,* among other things, he gives an Account of the Facts abovemention'd, as follows.

Mr. *Hopkin*, and my self went together to *Elizabeth Clarke,* of *Manningtree* in *Essex*; who had been kept three Days, and three Nights under a guard, and when I had ask'd her, who she had accus'd as Witches, we were going away; but she said to us, if you will stay, I will shew you my *Imps*, for they are ready to come; then said Mr. *Hopkin, Besse* ! Will you do us no harm? No said she, What? Do you think I am afraid of my Children? You shall sit down; so we did, where fhe appointed us; then one of the Company, who was appointed to be with her that Night, said to her, *Besse*, I ask'd you a Question of late, but you answer'd not; then she said. What is it? He reply'd, tell the Truth, has not the Devil had the use of your Body? She said, Why should you ask me such a Question? He answer'd, I desire to know the Truth, and no otherwise, then she fetch'd a deep Sigh, and said, it is true; then said Mr. *Hopkin*, in what manner and likeness came he to you? She said, like a Tall, Proper, Black-hair'd Gentleman, a Properer Man than your self; and being ask'd, which she had rather lie withal, she said the Devil; and so particulariz'd every thing, and how he came in, and his Habit, and how he lay with her, and spake to her, and she then affirm'd this to be Truth, and so presently fell a smacking with her Lips, and call'd *Lought*, two or three times, which presently appeared to us eight, (for there were six which were appointed to be with her that Night before we went) in the likeness of a Cat (for she told us before in what shapes they would come, and so that presently vanish'd. Then she call'd again, as before, *Jarmara*! Then appear'd another like a Red, or Sandy spotted Dog, with Legs not so long as a Finger, to our perceivance, but his back as broad as two Dogs, or broader of that bigness, and vanish'd: After that she call'd more, as before by several Names, which came in several shapes, one like a Greyhound, with Legs as long as a Stags; another like a Ferrit; and one like a Rabbit, and so in several shapes they appear'd to us, till there were some seven or eight seen. Some by some of us, and others by other some of us; then I ask'd her if they were not all come, for there were more come than she spake of, she answer'd, that they came double, in several shapes, but said one was still to come. Which was to tear me in pieces: I ask'd her why? she said, because I would have had her try'd by Swimming, and told me, that now she would be even with me; and so told in what manner it should come, black and like a Toad, and so afterwards it did come, as the rest averr'd that saw it, &c.

This Account we find somewhat differs from the former, but whether enough to invalidate the Testimony, I must leave it to the Readers Consideration.

Mr. *Glanvil*, in his Collections of Relations, for proving Apparitions, Spirits, and Witches, tell us of an *Irishman*, that had like to have been carry'd away by Spirits; and of the Ghost of a Man who had been seven Years dead, that brought a Medicine to his Bedside. The Relation is thus.

A Gentleman in *Ireland*, near to the Earl of *Orrery*'s, sending his Butler one Afternoon to buy Cards; as he pass'd a Field, to his wonder, he espy'd a Company of People sitting round a Table, with a deal of good Cheer, before them in the midst of the Field: And he going up towards them, they all arose and saluted him, and desir'd him to sit down with them; but one of them Whisper'd these words in his Ear: *Do nothing this Company invites you to.* Hereupon he refus'd to sit down at the Table, and immediately Table and all that belong'd to it were gone; and the Company are now dancing and playing upon Musical Instruments. And the Butler being desir'd to joyn himself with them, but he refusing this also, they all fall to Work, and he not being to be prevail'd with, to Accompany them in working any more than in feasting, or dancing, they all disappear'd, and the Butler is now alone, but instead of going forwards, home he returns as fast as he could drive, in a great Consternation; and was no sooner entred his Master's Door, but falls down, and lay some-time Senseless, but coming again to himself, he related to his Master what had pass'd.

The Night following there comes one of this Company to his Bed-side, and tells him, *That if he offered to stir out of Doors the next Day, he would be carryed away*. Hereupon he kept within; but towards the Evening, having need to make Water, he adventur'd to put one Foot over the Threshold, several standing by, which he had no sooner done, but they espyed a Rope cast about his Middle; and the Poor Man was hurried away with great Swiftness, they following him as fast as they could, but could not overtake him, at length they espy'd an Horse-Man, coming towards him, and made signs to him to stop the Man, whom he saw coming near him, and both ends of the Rope, but no Body drawing; when they met, he laid hold on one end of the Rope, and immediately had a smart blow given him over his Arm with the other end; but by this means the Man was stop'd, and the Horse-Man brought him back with him.

The *Earl* of *Orrery* hearing of these strange Passages, sent to the Master to desire him to send this Man to his House, which he accordingly did; and the Morning following, or quickly after, he told the *Earl*, that his *Spectre* had been with him again, and assur'd him, that that Day he should most certainly be carry'd away, and that no endeavours should avail to the saving of him; upon this he was kept in a large Room, with a considerable number of Persons to guard him, among whom was the Famous Stroker, Mr. *Greatrix*, who was a Neighbour. There were beside other Persons of Quality, two Bishops in the House at the same time, who were consulted concerning the making use of a Medicine, the *Spectre*, or Ghost prescrib'd, of which mention will be made anon, but they determin'd on the Negative.

Till part of the Afternoon were spent all was quiet, but at length he was perceiv'd to rise from the Ground, whereupon Mr. *Greatrix*, and another lusty Man clapt their Arms over his Shoulders, one of them before him, and the other behind, and weigh'd him down with all their strength; but he was forcibly taken up from them, and they were too weak to keep their hold, and for a considerable time he was carried in the Air, to and fro over their Heads, several of the Company still running under him, to prevent his receiving hurt, if he should fall, at length he fell and was caught before he came to the Ground, and had by that means no hurt.

All being quiet till Bed time, my *Lord* order'd two of his Servants to lye with him, and the next Morning he told his *Lordship*, that his *Spectre* was again with him, and brought a Wooden Dish, with grey Liquor in it, and bid him Drink it off; at the first sight of the *Spectre* he said he endeavour'd to awake his Bed-fellows, but it told him, that that endeavour should be in vain; and that he had no cause to fear him; he being his Friend, and he that at first gave him the good advice in the Field, which had he not followed, he had been before now perfectly in the Power of the Company he saw there; he added, That he concluded it was impossible, but that he should have been carryed away the Day before, there being so strong a Combination against him; but now he could assure him, that there would be more Attempts of that Nature, but he being troubled with two sorts of sad Fits, he had brought that Liquor to Cure him of them, and bid him Drink it; he peremptorily refusing, the *Spectre* was angry, and upbraided him with great Disingenuity, but told him, however, he had a kindness for him, and that if he would take Plantane Juice, he should be well of one sort of Fits, but he should carry the other to his Grave; the Poor Man having by this time somewhat recover'd himself, ask'd the *Spectre*, whether by the Juice of Plantane he meant that of the Leaves, or Roots? It reply'd the Roots.

Then it ask'd him, whether he did not know him? he aswered no; it reply'd, I am such an one: the Man answered, he had been long Dead: I have been Dead, said the *Spectre*, or Ghost, Seven Years, and you know that I liv'd a loose Life, and ever since I have been hurried up and down in a restless condition, with the Company you saw, and shall be to the day of Judgment; then he proceeded to tell him, that had he acknowledged God in his ways, he had not suffer'd such severe things by their means; and further said, you never Pray'd to God that day before you met with this Company in the Fields.

This Relation was sent to Dr. *Henry More*, by Mr. E. *Fowler*, who said, Mr. *Greatrix* told it several Persons: The Lord *Orrery* also own'd the Truth of it; and Mr. *Greatrix* told it to Dr. *Henry More* himself, who particularly enquired of Mr. *Greatrix* about the Mans being carried up into the Air, above Mens Heads in the Room, and he did expressly affirm he was an Eye-Witness thereof.

De prestig. Dæm. l. 1. c. 12.

Wierus tells us, that a Young Woman, was miserably tormented with an Evil Spirit, in the Castle of *Caldenbroc*, in *Guelderland*, and had been carried away in the Air by him, if himself had not with-held her by Violence. He says also,

l. 2. c. 7.

that at *Magdeburg*, a certain Magical juggler, who was wont to lead about a little Horse for a Show, would let him walk about in a Circle in an open Theatre, and at the end of the Show, would tell the Company, that he could get but little Money among Men, and therefore he would go up to Heaven; whereupon he would throw a Cord up in the Air, and the little Horse would go up after it, himself taking hold of the Horses Tayl, would follow him, his Wife taking hold of him, would follow also, and a Maid Servant would follow her, and so mount up in the Air, as it were link'd together, the Specators standing in great admiration; till a certain Citizen coming by chance that way, and asking, what was done? It was answered that a Jugler with his little Horse was gone up into the Air: whereupon he assured them that he saw him just before going into an Inn in the Street; therefore finding themselves deluded, they went away. *Wierus* adds, no Man may deny but all this kind of allyance with *Dæmons*, by whatever means gotten, and all the way of these delusions is a pestiferous Fraud, introduc'd for the utter destruction of Men.

Mr. *Thomas Tilson*, Minister of *Aylesworth* in *Kent*, in a Letter dated *July* the 6*th*. 1691, which he sent to the late Mr. *Baxter* in *London*, gives an Account of an Apparition at *Rochester*; which Account Mr. *Baxter* has Printed in his *Historical Discourse of Apparitions and Witches*. It is as follows.

Mary the Wife of *John Goffe* of *Rochester*, being Afflicted with a long Illness, removed to her Fathers House at *West-Mulling*, which is about Nine Miles distant from her own, there she Died *June* the 4*th* this present Year 1641. The day before her departure, she grew very impatiently desirous, to see her two Children, whom she had left at home, to the care of a Nurse; she pray'd her Husband to hire an Horse, for she must go home, and Dye with the Children; when they perswaded her to the contrary, telling her she was not fit to be taken out of Bed, nor able to sit on Horse-back, she entreated them, however to try, if I cannot sit, said she, I will lie along upon the Horse, for I must go to see my Poor Babes.

A Minister, who lives in the Town, was with her at Ten of the Clock that Night, to whom she express'd good Hopes in the Mercies of God, and Willingness to die, but, said she, it is my Misery that I cannot see my Children.

Between One and Two of the Clock in the Morning she fell into a Trance; one Widow Turner, who watch'd with her that Night, says, That her Eyes were open, and fixt, and her Jaw fall'n; she put her Hand upon her Mouth and Nostrils, but could perceive no Breath; she thought her to be in a Fit, and doubted whether she were alive or dead.

The next Day, this dying Woman told her Mother that she had been at home with her Children. That is impossible, said the Mother, for you have been here in Bed all the while; yes, reply'd the other, but I was with them last Night, when I was a sleep.

The Nurse at *Rochester*, Widow *Alexander* by Name, affirms, and says, she will take her Oath on't before a Magistrate, and receive the Sacrament upon it, that a little before Two of the Clock that Morning, she saw the likeness of the said *Mary Goffe*, come out of the next Chamber, (where the Elder Child lay in a Bed by it self) the Door being left open, and stood by her Bed-side about a Quarter of an Hour; the Younger Child was there lying by her; her Eyes mov'd, and her Mouth went, but she said nothing. The Nurse moreover says, that she was perfectly awake, it was then Daylight, being one of the longest Days in the Year. She sate up in her Bed, and look'd stedfastly upon the Apparition; in that time she heard the Bridge Clock strike Two, and a while after said, *In the Name of the father, Son, and Holy Ghost, what art thou?* Thereupon the Appearance remov'd, and went away. She slipt on her Cloaths and followed, but what became on't she cannot tell; then, and not before, she began to be grievously affrighted, and went out of Doors, and walk'd upon the Wharf, (the House being just by the River side) for some Hours, only going in, now and then, to look to the Children; at Five of the Clock she went to a Neighbour's House, and knock'd at the Door, but they would not rise; at Six she went again, then they arose and let her in: She related to them all that had pass'd; they would perswade her she was mistaken, or Dreamt; but she confidently affirm'd, If ever I saw her in all my Life, I saw her this Night.

One of those to whom she made the Relation (*Mary* the Wife of *John Sweet*) had a Messenger came from *Mulling* that Forenoon, to let her know her Neighbour *Goffe*'s Wife was dying, and desir'd to speak with her; she went over the same Day and found her departing. The Mother, among other Discourse, related to her how much her Daughter had long'd to see the Children; and said, she had seen them. This brought to Mrs. *Sweet*'s Mind, what the Nurse had told her that Morning, for till then she had not thought to mention it, but disguis'd it rather, as the Woman's disturb'd Imagination.

The substance of this I had related to me, by *John Carpenter*, the Father of the Deceas'd, next Day after her Burial, *July* the 2*d*. I fully Discours'd the Matter with the Nurse, and two Neighbours, to whose House she went that Morning.

Two Days after, I had it from the Mother, the Minister that was with her in the Evening, and the Woman that sate up with her that last Night; they all agree in the same Story, and every one strength'ns the others Testimony.

They appear to be sober intelligent Persons, far enough from designing to impose a Cheat on the World, or to mannage a Lye, and what Temptation they lie under for so doing, I cannot conceive. So far the Letter to Mr. *Baxter*.

According to the foregoing instance, *Helmont* tell us of a Boy, who through an excussive desire of seeing his Mother, fell into an Extasy, and gave her a visit, she being many Miles distant from him, and that upon his coming to himself, remembring all things, he gave People many Marks of his having been with her. *Marcus Marci*, having set down this Relation from *Helmont*, adds, though we should grant the Boy's Mind or Imaginations had reach'd to that place, it would be ridiculous to think he could have perceiv'd those sensible things being present, unless we likewise admit the Organs of his Senses also, with which he could have receiv'd those Images, had pass'd thither: Therefore we must say, that as the Imaginative Faculty comes sometimes to the Knowledge of future things, so it does to the Knowledge of things absent; and as for the manner after which it is done, he has explain'd it elsewhere.

Phys. vet. rest. part 5

Captain *Henry Bell*, in his Narrative prefixt to *Luther's Table*, printed in English, *An.* 1652. having acquainted us how the *German* Copy printed of it, had been discover'd under Ground, where it had lain hid Fifty two Years, that Edition having been supprest by an Edict of the Emperor *Rudolphus* the Second, so that it was Death for any Person to keep a Copy thereof; and having told us, that *Casparus Van Sparr*, a *German* Gentleman, with whom he was familiarly acquainted while he negotiated Affairs in *Germany*, for King *James* the First, was the Person that discover'd it *An.* 1656. and transmitted it into *England* to him, and earnestly desir'd him to translate the said Book into *English*, says, he accordingly set upon the Translation of it many times, but was always hindred from proceeding in it by some intervening Business. About six Weeks after, he had receiv'd the Copy, being in Bed with his Wife, one Night between Twelve and One of the Clock, she being asleep, but himself awake, there appear'd to him an Ancient Man, standing at his Bed's-side, array'd all in White, having a long and broad White Beard, hanging down to his Girdle, who taking him by his right Ear, said thus to him. Sirrah! Will not you take time to translate that Book which is sent unto you out of *Germany?* I will shortly provide for you both place and time to do it; and then he vanish'd; hereupon being much affrighted, he fell into an extream Sweat, so that his Wife awaking, and finding him all over Wet, she ask'd him what he ail'd? He told her what he had seen and heard; but he never regarded Visions nor Dreams, and so the the same fell out of his Mind. But a Fortnight after, being on a Sunday at his Lodging in *Kingstreet, Westminster,* at Dinner with his Wife, two Messengers were sent from the whole Counsel Board, with a Warrant to carry him to the *Gatehouse, Westminster,* there to be kept till farther Order from the Lords of the Council. Upon which Warrant he was kept there ten whole Years close Prisoner; where he spent five Years of it in translating the said Book, having good cause to be mindful of the Old-Man's saying: I will shortly provide for you both place and time to translate it.

De Rer. variet. l. 16. c. 93.

    Cardan tells us, That *Jacobus Donatus*, a rich Senator of *Venice*, was wont to relate how himself being in Bed with his Wife one Night, and having a Wax Candle burning by him, and two Nurses at the same time lying there in a Truckle-Bed with a Child under a Year old; he saw the Chamber Door to be open'd by degrees, and I know not what Man to put his Head in; the Nurses saw him too, but neither knew his Face; the young Man being affrighted, arose, and snatch'd his Sword and Buckler, and the Nurses each of them great Wax Candles, he goes into the Hall adjoyning to the Chamber, there he found all things fast shut, he return'd with great Admiration. The Infant who was well in Health, dyed the next Day. This he never related without sighing.

We have also several instances in History of frightful *Spectres* appearing before Pestilences and other Afflictions. *Procopius*, where he writes of the great and wonderful Pestilence, that in time of *Cosræ* and *Justinian* dispeopl'd the Earth, says, there were then seen publickly, and in private Houses *Dæmons* in an Humane shape, which struck those they met, and those they struck were presently seiz'd with the Disease, and this happen'd to some waking, in open Day, to others in the Night time.

De bell. pers. l. 2.

CHAP. IV.

What Perception some Persons have had of Genii, *or* Spirits *by the Sense of seeing, when others present at the same time have seen nothing.*

Lucas Jacobson *Debes*, M. A. and Provost of the Churches in the Seventeen Islands of *Fœræ*, subject to the King of *Denmark*, in his Description of the said Islands, and Inhabitants, and his Account of several Observables there, in his eighth Chapter tells us, how Satan, even since the pure Light of the Gospel there, as well as before, has behav'd himself in deluding and seducing those Inhabitants: They having many Examples how he has taken away some, and carry'd away others, restoring them afterwards, but weaken'd in their Understandings; whereof he gives us some certain Relations, that are yet in the Memory of Man, and some others that happen'd while he himself was at *Fœræ*; he tell us, That Apparitions of Spirits is a thing so generally known in *Fœræ*, that almost every where in the Country, where they have read no Books thereof, nor heard any Relation from other Places, know it so perfectly by the Works and Apparitions of Satan, that they are in no doubt at all of it. And that they they may be seen by same Persons, and not by others, might be prov'd by many Examples in *Fœræ* that being a meer endowment of their Nature; and, he says, People grow much alter'd upon seeing such Apparitions, which Apparitions they call *Hollow Men*. An expression exactly agreeing with that of *Virgil* where he tells us what the *Sybil*, who undertook to carry *Æneus* as to the *Elysian Fields*, said *Æn*. 6. to him at the entrance of Hell, where the Ghosts, came against him.

> *Et ni docta comes tenues sine corpore vitas,*
> *Admoneat, volitare cavâ sub imagine formæ,*
> *Irruat & frustra ferro dinverberet umbras.*

and such they always appear'd to my self, not with solid Bodies of Flesh and Bones.

For particulars, I refer the Reader to Mr. *Debes*'s Book, and shall only set down one Relation from him of a thing which happen'd, *An.* 1667. It is as follows: A Person call'd *Jacob Olufson*, being then at *Giow*, in *Osteræ*, in the 24th Year of his Age, on the 17th of *Jan.* fell into a Sickness, lying a Bed during a Fortnight, and on the 14th Day of his Illness, as he lay asleep at Night, there came one into him with shining Cloaths on, whereat he awaken'd, and perceiv'd him in that Figure, in the Bed by him, the Room appearing full of Splendor, and it ask'd the Man where his Pain was? Whereunto he answer'd nothing; afterwards the Apparition stroak'd him with his Hand along his Breast, and round about, whereby he was presently heal'd.

Now, though *Dæmonologers* generally give instances of some Persons seeing Spirits, when others, in the same Room, at the same time, see them not, and some Men undertake by *Physiognomy*, to tell who shall have Visions of Spirits, or Angels, and who shall never see Apparitions of them, though they are in the Room with others that see them; yet the most convincing instance of this peculiar Sight, that I know of in the World, is, that of the *Second sighted Persons* in *Scotland*, who are call'd *Second sighted*, because they have the Gift of seeing more than others can that are with them.

My late Friend, Mr. *John Aubrey*, at the end of his Book of *Miscellanies*, Printed in *London*, *An.* 1695, gives an Account of these *Second sighted Persons*, which was sent him from a Learned Person in *Scotland* whose Letters he shew'd me before he Printed them: And I shall here set down a few Particulars, taken from that Account, relating to my purpose.

I. They generally term this Second sight, in Irish *Taishitaraugh*, and such as have it, *Taishatrim*, from *Taish*, which is properly a shadowy Substance, and such as can only be some way discern'd by the Eye, but not lay'd hold on by the Hands; for which they assign'd it to *Bugles* or *Ghosts*, so that *Taishtar* is as much as one that converses with Ghosts, or Spirits, or as they commonly call them the *Fairies*, or *Fairy-folks*; others call these Persons *Phissichin*, from *Phis*, which is properly foresight, or foreknowledge.

II. Those that have the *Second sight*, see a multitude of Men and Women, Night and Day, round about them, and a particular Relation is made of one of those Persons, a Man of an upright Conversation, who us'd ordinarily by looking to the Fire, to foretel what Strangers would come to his House the next Day, or shortly after, by their Habit, and Arms, and sometimes also by their Names; and if any of his Goods or Cattle were missing, he would direct his Servants to the very place where to find them, whether in a Mire, or upon dry Ground: he would also tell if the Beast were already dead, or if it should die e're they could come at it; and in the Winter, if himself with others with him sate thick about the Fire-side, he would desire them to make Room for some others that stood by, though they did not see them: He saw two Spirits continually, and sometimes many more, though others, say he continually saw more, and would often seem very angry, and something troubl'd, nothing visible to others moving him. The two particular Spirits that constantly attended him were call'd, one *Brownie*, in the shape of a *Boy*, the other *Meig Malloch*, or *Meg Mullack*, in the shape of a *Girl*, who were two Ghosts, which (as it's constantly reported) of Old haunted a Family in *Straths Pey*, of the Name of *Grant*; of which Name and Family this Person was.

Note, That King *James* in his *Dæmonology* mentions also a Spirit, call'd *Brownie*, that was wont formerly to haunt divers Houses, without doing any Evil, but doing, as it were, necessary turns up and down the House; he appear'd like a rough Man, nay, some believ'd their House was all the *Sonsier*, as they call'd it, that is, the more lucky, or fortunate, that such Spirits resorted there. *L. 3. C. 2.*

III. As to the extent of these Peoples knowledge this secret way, it reaches both present, pass'd, and future Events. They foresee Murthers, Drownings, Weddings, Burials, Combats, Manslaughters, &c. of all which there are many instances to be given; they commonly foresee sad Events a little while before they happen; for instance, if a Man's fatal end be hanging, they'll see a Gibbet, or a Rope about his Neck; if beheading, they'll see a Man without a Head; if drowning, they'll see Water up to his Throat; if stabbing, they'll see a Dagger in his Breast; if unexpected Death in his Bed, they'll see a Winding Sheet about his Head: They foretel not only Marriages, but of good Children, what kind of life Men shall lead, and in what Condition they shall die; also Riches, Honours, Preferments, Peace, Plenty, and good Weather. There is one instance of a *Second sighted Person*, who saw a young Man, attending a young Gentlewoman, as she went up and down the House, and this was about three Months before her Marriage with him; and sometimes they foretel things which fall out several Years after. It's likewise usual with Persons that lose any thing to go to some of these Men, by whom they are directed how; with what Persons, and in what place they shall find their Goods. It's also to be noted, that this Gift bears Latitude, so that some have it in a far more Eminent degree than others.

IV. As for the way of receiving this Gift, and communicating it to others, the Account tells us, that in the Isle of *Skye*, especially before the Gospel came thither, several Families had it by Succession, descending from Parents to Children, and as yet there are many that have it that way. So *Cardán* tell us, it runs in a Blood among the *Turks*, for Persons to cast themselves into an Extasy at Pleasure. Some say, they get this Gift by compact with the Devil, others, say, by converse with those *Dæmons*, we call *Fairies*. They say, they can communicate the Gift to others in a few Days, and have offer'd to do it for a small Matter; and, they say, that if at any time, when they see those strange sights, they set their foot on the foot of another who has not the second sight, that other will, for that time, see what they are seeing. And as I am told by a Person who has convers'd with those *Second sighted Persons*, the Gift will continue with the Man that has so receiv'd it, all his Life.

De Rer. varit. l. 8. c. 43.

V. This Gift is very troublesome to those that have it, and they would gladly be rid of it; for if the object be a thing that is terrible, they are seen to sweat and tremble, and screek at the Apparition; at other times they laugh and tell of the thing cheerfully; just according as the thing is Pleasant, or astonishing. A certain Person desir'd a *Second sighted Man* to teach him his Skill; who told him he could do it in three Days time, but said he would not advise him, or any Man to learn it; for upon learning it he would never be a minute in his Life, but he would see innumerable Men and Women, Night and Day, round about him, which he believ'd would be troublesome to him: Whereupon the Person would not learn it. And those that have it wish to be rid of it, judging it a Sin, and that it came from the Devil; and some of them have apply'd themselves to the Ministry, desiring their Prayers for their being freed of it, and they have been freed accordingly. In the Isle of *Skye*, if a Woman has it her self, and be marryed to a Man that has it also, unless a Child of theirs be baptiz'd just upon the delivery, he has it all his Life; if he be then baptiz'd, he is freed from it.

VI. The Persons that have this Gift, are observ'd, for the most part, to be vicious, tho some very honest Persons, of an upright life, have it.

Mr. *Aubrey*, in a small Addition, which he has annext to his *Account* of *Second sighted Persons*, gives us a Relation from *Diembroke*, of an old Woman with whom it was usual, where any Friend of hers dyed, to see their Apparitions without an Head, and this though the Persons were never so far off. And I have been credibly inform'd of a Gentleman in the *Low-Countries*, who, as he walk'd the Streets of a Town would often meet People without Heads, as it seem'd to him, and would ask the next Person he met with, who such Persons were, and would acquaint his Friends that those Persons would die within a Year, which always came to pass.

L. de Peste.

Relating to this we find it's a Custom with the *Jews*, on the 7*th* Day of their Feast of *Tabernacles, viz.* the 21st Day of the Month of *Sept.* to go forth in the Night time, in the Moonshine, because they think all things that will happen to them that Year, are reveal'd to them that Night in the Moonshine. *Leusden*, in his *Philologus Hebræo mixtus*, has giv'n us a cut of this Practice, which I have also here inserted: Where *Jews* are going forth in the Moonshine with Branches of Palms, Olives, and Willows in their Hands, to search out the Events of the whole Year; but the Head of one of them lies hid, and is not seen in the shadow, whence the Person concludes he shall die that Year. *Buxtorf*, in his *Synagoga Judaica*, thus sets forth all these things. They go forth in the Night time, in the Moonshine, some having only their Heads bare, some with a Shirt on only, or also naked, having a Sheet about them, which they let fall, and stretch forth their Arms and Hands; if any Man's Head be seen wanting in the shadow, he is in danger of Life, and it's a sign he will die that Year; if a Finger be wanting, the Death of a Friend is foreshown; if the right-hand, a Son; if the left, a Daughter will die; if he see no shade at all, he must prepare for Death, for there is no hope of avoiding it; and if he be upon undertaking a Journey, it's a sign he will never return home, *&c.* This the *Rabbins* make out from the Words, *Numb.* 14. 9. *Their shadow is departed from them*; but they write, it is not to be understood of the *simple shadow*, because it cannot be but a Man must see his shadow in the Moonshine; but of the *shadow of the shadow*; for if it be well minded, we shall find a twofold shadow, whereof the second is a Reflection of the first, which the *Rabbins* call the shadow of the shadow.

 I know not how far this may relate to the Doctrine of the *Cabalists*, for as *Boissardus* tells us, the *Arabian* Priests held with them, that there are Three parts of the Soul, the First is Called, *Neschama*, and is wholy Divine, abstracted and separated from the Body; this *Virgil* calls *Aurai simplicus Ignem*. The Second is called *Ruah*, and it is the Rational Soul which partakes of the Divinity and the Body, joyning both together with a wonderful Harmony, it gives Life to the Body, and causes that it has not an abhorrence for the Frail and Mortal Flesh, in which it lives. The Third part of the Soul is that which dissolves this Harmony, and it is as the Idol, Image, Shadow, and as the out-coat, drawn from the surface of the Body; the *Cabalists* call it *Nephes*, it wanders about Sepulchers, and is sometimes visible, but to the eyes of those whom God Illuminates; and this *Nephes* is that Fatal Hair in the Crown of Mens Heads, Sacred to *Pluto* and *Proserpine*, which before it be cut, and drawn away from the Crown of the Head, the Soul cannot be separate from the Body; so also unless this *Nephes* be drawn, as it were from the outmost surface of the Body, a Man cannot leave this life; and this part of the Soul (if we believe the Doctrine of the *Cabalists*) is that which is called out by *Magicians* and *Necromancers*, *Pluto* and *Proserpine* being first appeas'd, which if they put on their former Bodies, and such an Habit, as they wore alive, their Answers are called *Necromantical*, if they appear'd only in flitting and subtile Shadows, their answers were laid to be *Scyomantical*; So far *Boissardus*. Whence I only Note, that if there be such a shadowy and wandring part of the Soul, as is here mentioned, call'd *Nephes*; its probable the Woman mentioned by *Diembroke*, saw that at the death of Persons.

As to my own experience, relating to that of the *Second-Sighted Persons* abovemention'd, I shall here set it down, in reference to two of the particulars above Written, from Mr. *Aubrey's* Account, *viz.* the Second and Fifth. As, in the second particular, it's said, that those that have the *Second Sight*, see a multitude of Men and Women, Day and Night, about them: So it was with my self for some time, for I saw Hundreds, tho' I never saw any in the Night time, without a Fire, or Candle-light, or in the Moonshine, and as the Person mention'd in that Paragraph, had two particular Spirits there Named, which constantly attended him, besides others without Names; so it was with my self, two Spirits constantly attending me, Night and Day, for above Three Months together; who call'd each other by their Names, and several Spirits would often call at my Chamber Door, and ask, whether such Spirits lived there, calling them by their Names, and they would answer, they did. As for the other Spirits that attended me, I heard none of their Names mentioned, only I ask'd one Spirit which came for some Nights together, and rung a little Bell in my Ear, what his Name was, who answer'd

Ariel. We find that one of the Spirits which attended the *Second Sighted Person*, appeared as a Boy, the other as a Girl: but the two that constantly attended my self, appear'd both in Womens Habit, they being of a Brown Complexion, and about Three Foot in Stature; they had both black, loose Network Gowns, tyed with a black Sash about their Middles, and within the Network appear'd a Gown of a Golden Colour, with somewhat of a Light linking thro' it; their Heads were not drest with Topknots, but they had white Linnen Caps on, with Lace on them, about three Fingers breadth, and over it they had a Black loose Network Hood.

As the foresaid *Second Sighted Person*, sitting by the Fire with others in the Winter-time, would see Spirits standing by, and often seem angry and disturbed, tho' nothing visible to others mov'd him; so, as I have been sitting by the Fire with others, I have seen several Spirits, and pointed to the places where they were, telling the Company they were there. And one Spirit, whom I heard calling to me, as he stood behind me, on a sudden, clapt his Finger to my Side, which I sensibly perceived, and started at it; and as I saw one Spirit come in at the Door, which I did not like, I suddenly laid hold of a pair of Tonges, and struck at him with all my force, whereupon he Vanish'd.

As in the Fifth Particular above Written; He said that the Gift of the *Second Sight* is very troublesome to those that have it, and they would gladly be rid of it. So I must declare, that I would not for the whole World, undergo what I have undergone, upon Spirits coming twice to me; their first coming was most dreadful to me, the thing being then altogether new, and consequently more surprising, tho' at the first coming they did not appear to me, but only called to me at my Chamber Windows, Rung Bells, Sung to me, and play'd on Musick, *&c.* but the last coming also, carried terrour enough; for when, they came, being only Five in Number, the Two Women before mentioned, and Three Men (though afterwards, there came Hundreds) they told me they would kill me, if I told any Person in the House, of their being there, which put me in some Consternation, and I made a Servant sit up with me Four Nights in my Chamber, before a Fire, it being in the *Christmas* Holydays, telling no Person of their being there. One of these Spirits in Womans dress, lay down upon my Bed by me every Night: and told me, if I Slept, the Spirits would kill me, which kept me waking for three Nights: In the mean time a near Relation of Mine, went (tho' unknown to me) to a Physician of my acquaintance, desiring him to prescribe me somewhat for Sleeping; which he did, and a Sleeping Potion was brought me, but I set it by, being very desirous and inclined enough to Sleep without it. The Fourth Night I could hardly forbear Sleeping, but the Spirit lying on the Bed by me, told me again, I should be Kill'd if I Slept, whereupon I rose, and sat by the Fire side, and in a while return'd to my Bed; and so I did a Third time, but was still threatned as before: whereupon I grew impatient, and ask'd the Spirits what they would have? told them, I had done the part of a Christian, in humbling my self to God, and fear'd them not, and rose from my Bed, took a Cane, and knock'd at the Ceiling of my Chamber, a near Relation of mine lying then over me, who presently rose, and came down to me, about two of the Clock in the Morning; to whom I said, you have seen me disturbed these Four Days past, and that I have not Slept, the occasion of it was, that Five Spirits which are now in the Room with me have threatned to kill me if I told any Person of their being here, or if I Slept, but I am not able to forbear Sleeping longer, and acquaint you with it, and now stand in defiance of them; and thus I exerted my self about them, and notwithstanding their continual Threats, I Slept very Well the next Night, and continued so to do, tho they continued with me above Three Months, Day and Night.

A Gentleman having lately supply'd me with another Account, concerning the *Second Sighted Persons*, which was sent some Years since to a Lady, by a Person of whom she had desired it. I shall here set down the particulars of it, as follows.

I. He says the more general Account given of the *Second Sighted Persons*, is, that many *Highlanders*, but far more *Islanders* are qualified with this Sight. That Men, Women and

Children, are indifferently gifted with it, some Children have it, whose Parents have it not, and some Parents have it, whose Children have it not; some adult Persons have it, who had it not in their Youth, and cannot tell by what means or cause it was produc'd in them. It is a great trouble to those that have it, and they would be rid of it at any rate. The Sight is of no long duration, continuing for the most part, but as long as they can keep their Eyes steady, without twinkling; the most Assured therefore fix their look, that they see the longer, but the Timerous see only by glances, their Eyes always trembling at the first sight of the object.

II. That which is seen generally by them, is the species of Living Creatures, and of Inanimate things, as Ships, and the Habits upon Persons: They never see the Species of any Person already Dead; what they foresee fails not to exist in the mode and place where it appears to them; they cannot well know what space of time shall intervene betwixt the Apparition and the real Existence, but some of the boldest and longest experienced, have some Rules of Conjectures. As if they see a Man with a Shroud in the Apparition, they will conjecture at the nearness, or remoteness of his Death, by the more or less of his Body that is cover'd with it. They will ordinarily see their absent Friends, tho' at a great distance; sometimes no less than from *America* to *Scotland*, sitting, or standing, or walking in some certain place, and then they conclude with assurance, that they shall see them so, and there. If a Man be in Love with a Woman, they ordinarily see that Man standing by her, and so if a Woman be in Love. They conjecture of their enjoyments by the *Species* touching the Person, or appearing at a distance from her. If they see the *Species* of a Person, who is Sick in any other place, in an Healthful Pasture, or Action, they conclude a recovery; but if they are to Dye, they see them cover'd with a Winding-Sheet.

These generals were verified to Persons of Honour, by such of them as did See, and, were esteem'd Honest and Sober by all the Neighbourhood. And because there were more of these Seers, in the Illes of *Lewis*, *Harris* and *Vist*, than elsewere, some Persons of Quality intreated Sir *James Macdonel*, who is now dead, Sir *Norman Maclod*, and Mr. *Daniel Morison*, a very honest Minister who are still alive, to inquire into this *Sight*, and to acquaint them therewith, which they did, and all of them found an agreement in these generals, and Informed them of many particular and notorious Instances, confirming what they said.

He sets down some remarkable Instances, which he says were of very knowing and ingenious Persons, who had made it their business to be well informed concerning the *Second Sight*; which Instances being not Printed in any other Author, that I know of, I shall insert them here.

The First Instance, he says, is from a Person of great Learning, and eminent Quality, who gave the following Relation.

I was once Travelling in the *Highlands*, with many Servants, one of them going a little before me, and entring into a House, where I was to stay all Night, suddenly stept back with a screech and a noise, and fell by a Stone which hit is Foot: I askt what the matter was (for he look'd as one very much Frighted) he told me very seriously, I must not Lodge in that House; I ask'd why? he said, he wish'd so, because a Dead Corps would very shortly be carried out of it, and that several Persons carrying of it, met him at the Door, when I heard him cry; and therefore he would not have me Lodge in so unlucky a place; and seeing me Laugh and go in, he said to the other Servants, he was very sorry I did so, for he was sure what he saw would very shortly come to pass; this made me inquire if there were any sick Person in the House, but there was none; the Landlord was a strong Healthy *Highlander*, yet before I went from the House, the next Day, he Died of an Apoplectick Fit.

The Second Instance is from another Person, who writes thus.

In the Year 1653. *Alexander Monro*, who was afterwards Lieutenant Collonel to the Earl of *Dunbarton*'s Regiment, and my self were walking in a place called *Ulabill* in *Logh Broome*, in a little Plain at the foot of a rugged Hill; there was a Man working with a Spade, in the walk before us, and his Face to the Hill; he did not mind us as we past near him, which made me look at him, and perceiving him to stare a little strangely, I conjectured him to be a *Seer*, I called him, at which he stared and smiled: what are you doing said I? he andwered me, I have seen a very strange thing; an Army of *Englishmen*, leading their Horses down that Hill, and a number of them are come down to the Plain, and eating the Barley which is growing in the Field, near to the Hill. This was on the Fourth of *May*, for I noted the Day, and it was Four or Five Days before the Barly was Sown in the Field he spoke of. *Alexander Monro* ask'd him, how he knew they were *Englishmen*? he said because they had on Hatts and Boots, which he knew no *Scots* would have there; we as little set by what he said, as other foolish Visions, but in the beginning of *August* following, the Earl of *Middleton*, then Lieutenant for the King in the *Highlands*, having occasion to march a Party towards the South *Highlands*, sent his Foot thro' a place called *Innerlawel*, but was forced to send his Horse, with *Alexander Monro* to pass down the very forementioned Hill, as less rugged, tho bad enough, than that of *Innerlawel*; and the formost Party, which was first down the Hill, fell to eating the Barly, on the little Plain under it; and *Monro* call'd to mind what the *Seer* had told us, in *May* before; he writ of it, and sent an express to me with it.

The Relator of the Third Instance writes as follows.

I had once an occasion of being in Company with a Young Lady, and was told there was a notable *Seer* in the Company; I call'd him to speak with me (as I did ordinarily when I found any of them) and as he had answered me to several Questions, I ask'd him if he knew any Person to be in Love with that Lady, he said he certainly knew that there was a Man in Love with her (but he did not know the Man) for in the Two Days he had been in Company with her, he perceived one standing near her, and his Head leaning on her Shoulder; which he said, according to his Observations, foretold, that the Man would Marry her. This was in the Year 1655. I desired him to describe the Person, which he did, so that I could conjecture by the description, it was such an one of the Lady's Acquaintance, tho' there were no thought of their Marriage, till Two Years after; and happening, in the Year 1657. to find this *Seer*, who was an *Islander*, in Company with the other Person, whom I conjectured to have been described by him; I call'd him aside, and ask'd him, if that were the Person he saw by the Lady's side, Two Years ago? he said it was truly the same, and he had seen that Lady just then standing by him Hand in Hand. This was some few Months before their Marriage; and the Man is since Dead, and the Lady still alive.

The Fourth Instance is thus.

In *January* 1652. (says one of great Note) Lieutenant Collonel *Monro*, and my self hapned to be in the House of one *William Maclod* of *Ferrinlia* in *Rosse*, the said *Monro*, the Landlord and my self sitting in Three Chairs near the Fire, and in the corner of a great Chimney were two *Islanders*, who came that very Night to the House, and were related to the Landlord: while one of them was talking to *Munro*, I perceived the other to look odly towards me; from his Look, and being an *Islander*, I conjectured him a *Seer*, and ask'd him what he star'd at? he answered by desiring me to rise from that Chair, because it was an unlucky one. I ask'd him why? he said there was a Dead Man in the Chair next to me: well, said I, if he be in the Chair next me, I may keep my own, but what kind of Man is he? he said he was a tall Man, with a long grey Coat, having Boots on, and one of his Leggs hanging over the arm of the Chair, and his Head hanging down to the other side; and his Arm backward, as if it were broken. There were some Troops of *English-Men* then Quartered near that place, and there being at that time a great Frost after a Thaw, the Country was covered all over with Ice: Four or Five of the *English* Riding by this House, some Two Days after the Vision; while we were sitting by the Fire, we heard a great Noise, which proved to be these Troopers, who with the help of other Servants, were carrying one of their Number, who had got a very mischievous fall, and his Arm Broken, and falling frequently into Swooning Fits, they brought him into the Hall, and set him in the very Chair, and in the very Posture the *Seer* had described; but the Man did not Die, tho' he recovered with great difficulty.

The Fifth Instance is taken from the Account given in by Sir *Norman Maclod*.

There was a Gentleman in the *Isle* of *Harris*, who was always seen by the *Seers*, with an Arrow in his, Thigh: Those in the *Isle* who thought these Prognostications Infallible, did not doubt but he would be Shot in the Thigh, and Die of it. Sir *Norman* said, he always heard it the Subject of their Discourses for many Years, when that Gentleman was present, at last he Died without any such Accident; Sir *Norman* was at his Burial, at St. *Clement*'s Church in the *Isle* of *Harris*. At the same time another Gentleman was brought to be Buried in the same Church. The Friends on either side came to a debate who should first enter the Church, and from Words came to Blows; one who was Arm'd with a Bow and Arrows let fly amongst them (every Family in that *Isle*, have their Burying Places in the Church, in a Stone Chest, and their Bodies are carried in open Biers to the Burial Place.) Sir *Norman* having appeased the Tumult, One of the Arrows was found sticking in the Dead Man's Thigh. To this Sir *Norman* himself was Witness. Mr. *Aubrey*, in his Account of the *Second Sight*, has a Relation much of the same with this, tho' with some variation.

The Sixth Instance is taken from the Account which Mr. *Daniel Morison*, Minister in the *Isle* of *Lewis*, gave in.

This Relation, tho' somewhat of a different Nature from the others, may be worth Notice. He tells us of a Young Woman in his Parish, who was mightily Frighted by seeing her own Image still before her, when she went into the open Air, the Back of the Image being always towards her: So that it was not a Reflexion, as in a Mirror, but the Species of such a Body as her own, and in the very same Habit; the Minister kept her a long while with him, but she had no Remedy, till she was about Four or Five years Elder, and then it left her.

The Gentleman who writ the foregoing Relations, in a Letter to a Lady, adds in the close of it, that in order to solve the *Phænomenon* of the *Second Sight*, a hint may be taken from this Image, which appeared to the Woman abovementioned, and from such another mention'd by *Aristotle*, in the Fourth Book of his *Metaphysicks*; as also from that common Opinion that Young Infants see Apparitions, which are not seen by Elder Eyes; and like-wise from this, that several who have had the *Second Sight*, when in the *Highland*, or *Isles*, upon their being transported to Live in other Countries, especially in *America*, lose this quality, as it's reported by Gentlemen, who knew some of them in *Barbadœs*, that saw no Visions there, tho' they were known to have been *Seers*, when they lived in the *Isles* of, *Scotland*.

Laurentius Ananias, Printed a Book in *Latin* at *Venice*. *An.*1581. concerning the nature of *Dæmons*, where he writes somewhat which seems ally'd to this Gift of the *Second Sight*. It is thus.

L. 2. circa sinem.

Some *Dæmons* so miserably delude some Old Women, and Children, that they certainly perswaded themselves, that on set Nights, and at set Hours, their Souls being called, depart from their Bodies, and joyn themselves to the Souls of the Dead; which proceeds but from *Dæmons* corrupting the Imagination of those Creatures, thro' Infidelity after that manner; and as they relate this to credulous Old Women, they Predict the Deaths of certain Persons; and if the event sometimes answers, they confidently affirm, even upon their Oath, that they were Souls from whom they said it, when in truth they are nothing but Illusions of the Devil, perverting their Fancy; which error has possest the Minds of some Persons, above the Vulgar: though it hence appears they are all under a delusion; for it hapned some Years since, that in a Town where some Persons were found obnoxious to these affects and illusions of the Devil, one *Mark Antony*, who was look'd upon as an Honest Upright Person, no way given to speak Untruths, was seized with it, and often gave true Predictions concerning certain Persons, especially such as were near their Deaths: this Man being sent for by my

Brother, *John Antony Ananias*, who is a Priest, and he coming to him, my Brother ask'd him, whether what was reported of him were true, and he did not deny it, whereupon my Brother advised him to quit that erronious Opinion, telling him, that those could not possibly be the Souls of the Dead, but that they were deceitful *Dæmons*, and that he greatly offended God in giving Credit to them, wherefore he begg'd him, that for Gods sake, and the well-fare of his Soul, as he perceived that *Dæmonaical* seizure coming upon him, (as he always perceived it beforehand) or, when he began to be seized with it, he would seriously protest against obeying them any longer, and that he would earnestly Pray to God to Free him from that Diabolical Delusion and Madness of Mind. *Mark Antony* being somewhat astonished at what was said to him, believed my Brother, and promised him to follow his Advice, to the utmost of his Power, and so went Home, and when the usual Day came, that he was obnoxious to those Illusions, he was not seiz'd with them, and was very Joyful, and gave God thanks for it. But upon the next return of the Day, and Hour (for he was not wont to be Infested with those Illusions every Day of the Week, but only *Tuesdays* and *Thursdays*) finding his wonted seizure coming upon him, and that he was called by those unclean Spirits, and being greatly afflicted in Mind by their Signs, he cry'd out with great Vehemency, that he would no longer follow them. Upon which outcry, almost all the People in the House were Awaken'd, and went to him, to whom he related all that had past, and shew'd how he was severely Beaten by those Spirits, and from that time he was wholly freed from them; for which he gave God great Thanks.

> *Note, in Reference to this Relation, what is written by* Henry Boguet, *a Judge in Cases of Witchcraft, in the Country of St.* Claude, *in* Burgundy, *concerning the particular Nights on which Witches have their* Sabbaths, *or meetings. In his Discourse of Witches, printed in* French, *at* Lyons, 1605. *Chap.* 19. *he writes as follows.*

I formerly thought that the *Sabbath* was held only *Thursday* Nights, because all the Witches, I have seen, have so declar'd: but since that I have read that some of them have confess'd, they assembled, some the Night betwixt *Monday* and *Tuesday*, some the Night betwixt *Friday* and *Saturday*; others the Night preceeding *Thursday*, or *Sunday* thence I have concluded, that there is no Day prefixt for their *Sabbath*, but that the Witches go to it when the Devil requires them. I shall add here, that *Antide Coles*, a Witch, confess'd, she had been at the *Sabbath*, each good Day of the Year, as at *Christmas, Easter*, and the like Holidays. So far *Boguet*.

Conformably to the Relation of *Laurentius Ananias*, I have been well inform'd of a Woman in *Gloucestershire*, who, when any Person of the Neighbourhood was taken Ill, would generally predict their Death, or recovery, and was much resorted to on that Account; at length she was seized, and had to an *Assizes* at *Gloucester*, concerning this Fact; where being ask'd by the Judge, how she came by her knowledge, as to the Death or Recovery of Persons sick; she told him, she could give no other Account of it, but that when any Person was sick, and she had a Mind to know the Issue, a Jury of *Fairies* came to her in the Night time, who consider'd of the Matter; and if afterwards they look'd cheerful, the Party would recover; if they look'd sad, he would die. Nothing else being brought against the Woman, she was clear'd. The Person from whom I had this Information, was a Justice of Peace of that County, then on the Bench. And here I must say, that before I heard this Relation, or had read *Ananias*, I saw a Jury of *Fairies*, or *Ghosts*, or what you please to call them, summon'd, and pass a Verdict on a Person known to me.

Cardan tells us, That *Genii* sometimes appear before the Deaths of Persons, and gives an instance in *Julian* the Emperor, who being near *Clesiphon*, and studying Philosophy, saw his *Genius* looking sad (whom formerly he had seen in *France*, looking cheerfully, and I know not what Verses foretelling the Death of *Constantius*, and consequently his Happiness) and the Horn of *Amalthæa*, with which the

De Rer var.
l. 15. *c.* 78

Genius of the Republick was wont to be drawn, being shut, and his Chamberlane, or Steward of his House, going from him, and so the next Day the Emperor was kill'd.

Baptistia Fulgosus tells us, That sometimes the Spirits remain inclos'd in Humane Bodies, but their Motions are so occult, and the Senses so bound, that we cannot easily know whether those Bodies are alive, or not: Hence some are said to be rais'd from the dead, who were never really dead, experience having shewn they were still living; of these Persons some relate wonderful things, as that they had been where they never were; but their Spirit being collected in it self, comprehends, and sees those things, which being in its usual State, through various distracted Thoughts, by reason of the Corporeal Sight, it does not know. As St. *Austin* testifies, of one *Curina*, who liv'd in the Country of *Hippo*, in *Africa*, and falling into an ill Distemper, was look'd upon by all Men as in a manner dead, having lost his Senses, so that he took no Food; and having continued in this State for some Days, his Friends would have buried him, only they perceiv'd a little breathing at his Nostrils, but when afterwards all Persons thought him to be departed, on a sudden, opening his Eyes, he desir'd that some one should be presently sent to *Curina*, the Blacksmith, his Neighbour, to see how he did, and when it was found he was dead at that very hour, he affirm'd, that he was led before a certain Judge, who vehemently chid those Spirits by whom himself was brought before him, because he would have *Curina* the Blacksmith, and not him, and for that cause he was restor'd to Life. In this Extasy he said, he saw Paradise, and many other things; and among others, that he was baptiz'd by St. *Austin*, at *Hippo*, and he was admonish'd so to be, because what then seem'd to be done was a Vision; therefore being restor'd to his Health, he had fulfil'd what he was admonish'd.

So, as *Bonaysteau* tells us, The Spirit of *Hermotinus*, as it seem'd, leaving his Body as dead, wandred about various Places, and afterwards related those things which could be

L. 1. fact. & dict. Memorab. c. 6.

In Disc. de excel. & dig. hominis.

known only by those Persons, which were present to the things themselves. *Herodotus*, and *Maximus Tyrius* write the same of *Aristæus*.

Possidonius tells us, That a certain *Rhodian* dying, nominated six of his equals, and said, who should die first, who next, and so on, and the Event answer'd the Prediction.

A Vision which happen'd to the Ingenious and Learned Dr. *Donne*, may not improperly be here inserted. Mr. *Isaac Walton*, writing the Life of the said *Doctor*, tells us, That the *Doctor* and his Wife, living with Sir *Robert Drury*, who gave them a free Entertainment at his House in *Drury-lane*; It happen'd that the Lord *Hay*, was by *King James* sent in an Ambassy to the *French King, Henry the 'Fourth*; whom Sir *Robert* resolv'd to accompany, and ingag'd Dr. *Donne* to go with them, whose Wife was then with Child at Sir *Robert's* House. Two Days after their arrival at Paris, Dr. *Donne* was left alone, in that Room, in which Sir *Robert*, and he, and some other Friends had dined together. To this place Sir *Robert* return'd within half an hour; and as he left, so he found Dr. *Donne* alone; but in such an Extasy, and so alter'd in his Looks, as amaz'd Sir *Robert* to behold him, insomuch, that he earnestly desired Dr. *Donne* to declare what had befall'n him in the short time of his absence. To which Dr. *Donne* was not able to make a present answer; but after a long and perplext Pause, did at last say, I have seen a dreadful Vision since I saw you; I have seen my Dear Wife pass twice by me through this Room, with her Hair hanging about her Shoulders, and a dead Child in Her Arms: this I have seen since I saw you. To which Sir *Robert* reply'd, sure, Sir, you have slept since I saw you, and this is the result of some Melancholy Dream, which I desire you to forget, for you are now awake. To which Dr. *Donne's* reply was, I cannot be surer that I now live, than that I have not slept since I saw you, and am as sure at her second appearing she stopt, and look'd me in the Face and vanish'd. Rest and Sleep had not alter'd Dr. *Donne's* Opinion the next Day; for he then affirm'd this Vision with a more deliberate, and so confirm'd a Confidence, that he inclin'd Sir *Robert* to a faint belief that the Vision was true; who immediately sent a Servant to *Druy-House*, with a Charge to hast'n back, and bring him word whether Mrs. *Donne* were alive; and if alive, in what Condition she was as to her Health; the Twelfth Day the Messenger return'd with this Account: That he found and left Mrs. *Donne* very sad, and sick in Bed; and that after a long and dangerous Labour, she had been deliver'd of a dead Child; and upon Examination the Abortion prov'd to be the same Day, and about the very hour that Dr. *Donne* affirm'd he saw her pass by in his Chamber. Mr. *Walton* adds, This is a Relation which will beget some wonder, and well it may, for most of our World are at present possess'd with an Opinion, that Visions and Miracles are ceas'd; and though 'tis most certain, that two Lutes, being both strung and tun'd to an equal pitch, and then one play'd upon, the other, that is not touch'd, being lay'd upon a Table at a fit Distance, will (like an *Eccho* to a Trumpet) warble a faint audible Harmony, in Answer to the same tune, yet many will not believe that there is any such thing as a Sympathy with Souls, *&c.*

An Ancient, and Learned Gentleman, now living, and well known in *London*, has told me, that being at a Widow Gentlewoman's House, about seven Miles from *London*, one Day about three of the Clock in the Afternoon, he retir'd to his Chamber; where he had not long been, but a strange Light, such as he had never seen before, appear'd in the Room, in which Light, he saw a Child of the Gentlewoman of the House, which had been left sick in *London*, lye dead, as also a Friend of his own; he was much surpriz'd at this, and after the thing was over, he went down from his Chamber to the Gentlewoman of the House; and as he had been desir'd to come tho' next Day, to the House of a Lady, who liv'd in the same Parish, he desir'd the foresaid Gentlewoman to send word to the Lady, that he could not wait on her the next Day, as he had promis'd, for he knew that both the said Gentlewoman and himself should be sent for to *London*; and then he told the Gentlewoman what had pass'd; and in a while a Coach came for them from *London* accordingly. The same Gentleman told me, that upon his falling into a Trance at *Cambridge*, he saw also a Friend of his dead in *London*, who upon enquiry was found to have died just at the time he saw him.

Cardan gives a Relation somewhat of this Nature as follows: My Kinsman *Bapiſta Cardan*, studying at *Pavia*, on a certain Night, tryed to make a little Fire as he rose, and in the interim heard a Voice say, farewel my Son, I am going to *Rome*; and he saw a vast Splendor, as that of a bundle of Straw all on Fire; being affrighted, and throwing by the Fire-Shovel, he hid himself under his Bed-cloaths, till his School-fellows return'd from the Academy; upon their return, thinking him to be sick, they knock'd at his Door, he open'd it, and they asking him the cause of his stay there, he answer'd, he thought his Mother was dead, and told them what he had seen and heard, and wept withal: They turn'd the thing to a Jest, some laughing at him, some comforting him; the Day following, having heard nothing of his Mother's sickness, he was certifyed of her Death, and that she expir'd at that very hour that he perceiv'd those things. The Town *Cardan* is distant Two and Forty Miles from *Pavia*. That Man was not given to Lyes, vain or superstitious, and who said he had never seen, or heard any preternatural thing till then.

De Rer. var. l. 8. c. 84.

A Book newly coming to my Hands, which contains a more particular Account, in some respects, of the *Second sight* in *Scotland*, than any I have met with, I shall give here some Account of it.

Mr. *M. Martin*, Printed the last Year in *London*, a Book in 8*o*. intitl'd, *A Description of the Weſtern Isles of Scotland*, call'd by the ancient Geographers *Hebrides*. It contains many curious Particulars, relating to the Natural and Civil History of those *Islands*, with a Map of them, and in his Preface he tells us, that perhaps its peculiar to those *Isles*, that they have never been describ'd till now by any Man, that was a Native of the Country, or had travell'd them, as himself has done; and in the Conclusion of the said Preface, he tells us, he has giv'n here such an Account of the *Second sight*, as the Nature of the thing will bear, and which has always been reckon'd sufficient among the unbyass'd part of Mankind; but for those that will not be so satisfyed, they ought to oblige us with a new Scheme, by which we may judge of Matters of Fact. The chief particulars he has giv'n us concerning the *Second sight* are, in a Chapter by it self, as follows.

I. In the *Second sight* the Vision makes such a lively Impression on the *Seers*, that they neither see, nor think of any thing else, but the Vision, as long as it continues; and then they appear pensive, or jovial, according to the Object, which was presented to them.

II. At the sight of a Vision, the Eye-lids of the Person are erected, and the Eyes continue staring till the Object vanish, as has often been observ'd by the Author, and others present.

III. There is one in *Skye*, an Acquaintance of whom observ'd, that when he sees a Vision, the inner part of his Eye-lids turns so far upwards, that after the Object disappears, he must draw them down with his Fingers; and; sometimes employs others to draw them down, which he finds to be much the easier way.

IV. The faculty of the *Second sight* does not lineally descend in a Family, as some imagine, for he knows several Parents that are endow'd with it, but not their Children; and so on the contrary, neither is it acquir'd by any previous compact; and after a strict enquiry, he could never learn from any among them, that this faculty was communicable any way whatsoever.

Note, That this Account is differing from the Account giv'n before from Mr. *Aubrey*. And I think Mr. *Martin*'s reason here against the descent of this faculty from Parents to Children, is not generally conclusive, for tho' he may, know Parents endow'd with it, and not Children, and so on the contrary, yet there may be Parents who are endow'd with it, being qualifyed as Mr. *Aubrey* has said, (*viz.* both being *Second sighted*) whose Children may have it by descent. And as to this faculty's being any other ways communicable, (since the Accounts differ) I must leave it to a farther Examination.

V. The Seer knows neither the object, time, nor place of a Vision before it appears, and the same Object is often seen by different Persons, living at a considerable distance from one another. The true way of judging, as to the time, and circumstance of an Object, is by Observation; for several Persons of Judgment, without this faculty, are more capable to judge of the design of a Vision, than a Novice that is a *Seer*. As an Object appears in the Day or Night, it will come to pass sooner or later accordingly.

VI. If an Object be seen early in the Morning (which is not frequent) it will be accomplish'd in a few Hours afterwards: If at Noon, it will commonly be accomplish'd that very Day: If in the Evening, perhaps that Night: if after Candles be lighted, it will be accomplish'd that Night: it's later always in accomplishment by Weeks, Months, and sometimes Years, according to the time of the Night the Vision is seen.

VII. When a Shroud is perceiv'd about one, it's a sure Prognostick of Death; the time is judg'd according to the height of it, about the Person; for if it be not seen above the middle, Death is not to be expected for the space of a Year, and perhaps some Months longer; and as it is frequently seen to ascend higher; towards the Head, Death is concluded to be at Hand within a few Days, if not Hours, as daily Experience confirms. Examples of this kind were shown the Author, when the Persons of whom the Observations were made, enjoy'd perfect Health.

There was one instance lately of a Prediction in this kind by a *Seer*, that was a Novice, concerning the Death of one of the Author's Acquaintance; this was communicated to a few only, and with great Confidence; the Author, being one of the Number, did not in the least regard it, till the Death of the Person, about the time foretold, confirm'd to him, the certainty of the Prediction; the foresaid Novice is now a skilful *Seer*, as appears from many late instances: he lives in the Parish of St. *Mary*'s, the most Northern in *Skye*.

VIII. If a Woman be seen standing at a Man's left Hand, it's a presage that she will be his Wife, whether they are Marryed to others, or Unmarryed at the time of the Apparition. If two or three Women are seen at once standing near a Man's left Hand, she that is next him will undoubtedly be his Wife first, and so on, whether all three, or the Man be single, or Marryed at the time of the Vision, or not, of which there are several late instances of the Author's Acquaintance. It's an ordinary thing for them to see a Man that is to come to the House shortly after; and if he be not of the *Seer's* Acquaintance, yet he gives such a lively Description of his Stature, Complexion, Habit, *&c.* that upon his Arrival he Answers the Character giv'n of him, in all respects. If the Person so appearing be one of the *Seer's* Acquaintance, he can tell by his Countenance whether he comes in good or bad Humour. The Author has been seen thus by *Seers* of both Sexes, at some Hundreds of Miles distance: Some that saw him in this manner, had never seen him Personally, and it happen'd according to their Visions, without any previous Design of his to go to those places, his coming there being purely Accidental. And in the 19*th* Page of his Book, he tells us that Mr. *Daniel Morison*, a Minister, told him, that upon his Landing in the *Island Roma*, the Natives receiv'd him very affectionately, and Address'd themselves to him with this Salutation. God save you, Pilgrim! you are heartily welcome here, for we have had repeated Apparitions of your Person among us, *viz.* after the manner of the *Second Sight*.

IX. It's ordinary with them to see Houses, Gardens, and Trees, in places void of all three, and this in Process of time uses to be accomplish'd; of which he gives an instance in the *Island* of *Skye*.

X. To see a spark of Fire fall upon ones Arm, or Breast, is a fore-runner of a dead Child to be seen in the Arms of those Persons, of which there are several fresh Instances.

To see a Seat empty at the time of ones sitting in it, is a presage of that Persons Death quickly after.

When a Novice, or one that has lately obtain'd the *Second sight*, sees a Vision in the Night time without Doors, and comes near a Fire, he presently falls into a Swoon.

Some find themselves, as it were, in a crowd of People, having a *Corps* which they carry a long with them; and after such Visions the *Seers* come in sweating, and describe the

People that appear'd; if there are any of their Acquaintance among them, they give an Account of their Names, and also of the Bearers, but they know nothing concerning the Corps.

All those that have *Second sight*, do not always see these Visions at once, though they are together at the time; but if one who has this faculty designedly touch his Fellow *Seer*, at the instant of a Visions appearing, then the second sees it as well as the first.

XI. There is a way of foretelling Death, by a Cry, that they call *Taisk*, which some call a *Wrath*, in the Low-land. They hear a loud Cry without Doors, exactly resembling the Voice of some particular Person, whose Death is foretold by it; of which he gives a late instance which happen'd in the Village *Rigg*, in *Skye Isle*.

XII. Things are also foretold by *Smelling* sometimes, as follows: Fish, or Flesh is frequently smelt in the Fire, when at the same time neither of the two are in the House, or, in any probability like to be had in it, for some Weeks, or Months. This smell several Persons have, who are endued with the *Second sight*, and its always accomplish'd soon after.

XIII. *Children*, *Horses*, and *Cows*, have the *Second sight*, as well as Men and Women advanc'd in Years.

That *Children* see it is plain, from their crying aloud at the very instant, that a *Corps*, or any other Vision appears to an ordinary *Seer*: Of which he gives an instance in a Child, when himself was present.

That *Horses* see, it's likewise plain, from their violent and hidden starting, when the Rider, or *Seer*, in Company with them, sees a Vision of any kind, Night or Day; it's observable of an Horse that he will not go forward that way, till he be led about at some distance from the common Road, and then he is in a sweat; he gives an instance of this in an Horse, in the *Isle* of *Skye*.

That *Cows* have the *Second sight*, appears from this; that if a Woman Milking a Cow, happens to see a Vision by the *Second sight*, the Cow runs away in a great fright at the same time, and will not be pacifyed for some time after.

In reference to this, *Paracelsus, Tom. 9. l. de Arte presagâ*, writes thus, Horses also have their Auguries, who perceive by the sight and smell wandring Spirits, Witches and Spectres, and the like things; and Dogs, both see and hear the same things.

Here, in the next place, the Author answers Objections that have lately been made against the reality of the *Second sight*.

First, It's objected, that these *Seers* are Visionary, and Melancholy People, who fancy they see things that do not appear to them.

He Answers, The People of these *Isles*, and particularly the *Seers* are very Temperate, and their Diet is Simple and Moderate, in Quantity and Quality; so that their Brains are not, in all Probability disorder'd by Undigested fumes of Meat, or Drink. Both Sexes are free from Hysterick Fits, Convulsions, and several other Distempers of that sort. There are no Mad-men among them, nor any instance of self Murther. It's observ'd among them, that a Man drunk never has a Vision of the *Second sight*. And he that is a Visionary, would discover himself in other things, as well as in that; nor are such as have the *Second sight*, judg'd to be Visionaries by any of their Friends, or Acquaintance.

Secondly, It's objected, That there are none among the Learned, able to oblige the World, with a satisfactory Account of these Visions, therefore they are not to be believ'd.

He Answers, If every thing for which the Learned are not able to give a Satisfactory account, shall be condemn'd as False and Impossible, we shall find many other things, generally believ'd, which must be rejected as such.

Thirdly, It's objected, That the *Seers* are Impostors, and the People who believe them are Credulous, and easily impos'd upon.

He Answers, The *Seers* are generally Illiterate, and well meaning People, and altogether void of Design, nor could he ever learn that any of them made the least gain of it; neither is it reputable among them to have that faculty: beside, the People of the *Isles* are not so Credulous, as to believe an

Impossibility, before the thing foretold be accomplish'd; but when it actually comes to pass, afterwards it is not in their Power to deny it, without offering Violence to their Senses and Reason; beside, if the *Seers* were Deceivers, can it be reasonable to imagine, that all the *Islanders*, who have not the *Second sight*, should combine together, and offer Violence to their Understandings and Senses, to force themselvs to believe a Lye from Age to Age? There are several Persons among them, whose Birth and Education raise them above the suspicion of concurring with an Imposter, merely to gratify an illiterate and contemptible sort of Persons. Nor can a reasonable Man believe, that Children, Horses, and Cows could be engaged in a combination to perswade the World of the reality of the *Second Sight*.

Every Vision that is seen, comes exactly to pass, according to the Rules of Observation, tho' Novices and heedless Persons do not always judge by those Rules: concerning which he gives Instances.

There are Visions seen by several Persons, in whose days they are not accomplished; and this is one of the reasons, why some things have been seen, that are said never to have come to pass; and there are also several Visions seen, which are not understood till they are accomplish'd.

The *Second Sight* is not a late discovery, seen by one or two in a Corner, or a remote *Isle*, but its seen by many Persons, of both Sexes, in several *Isles*, separated about Forty or Fifty Leagues from one another; the Inhabitants of many of these *Isles*, never had the least Converse, by Word or Writing: and this faculty of Seeing Visions, having continued, as we are informed by Tradition, ever since the Plantation of these *Isles* without being disprov'd by the Nicest Sceptick, after the strictest Enquiry, seems to be a clear proof of its Reality.

It's observable, that it was much more common Twenty Years ago, than at present; for One in Ten does not see it now, that saw it then.

The *Second Sight* is not confin'd to the *Western Isles* alone, the Author having an Account, that its likewise in several parts of *Holland*, but particularly in *Bommel*, where a Woman has it, for which she is courted by some, and dreaded by others. She sees a Smoak about ones Face, which is a forerunner of the Death of a Person so seen, and she actually foretold the Deaths of several that lived there; she was living in that Town this last Winter.

The *Second Sight* is likewise in the *Isle of Man*, as appears by this Instance; Captain *Leaths*, the chief Commander of *Belfast*, in his Voyage 1690, lost Thirteen Men by a violent Storm, and upon his Landing in the Isle of Man, an Ancient Man, Clerk to a Parish there, told him immediately, that he had lost Thirteen Men; the Captain enquired how he came to the knowledge of that, he answered, that it was by *Thirteen Lights*, which he had seen come into the Church-yard; as Mr. *Sacheverel* tells us, in his late description of the *Isle of Man*. Note, That this is like the sight of the *Corps-Candles* in *Wales* which is also well attested.

Here the Author adds many other Instances concerning the *Second Sight*, of which I shall set down only a few.

A Man in *Knockow*, in the Parish of St. *Mary*'s the Northermost part of *Skye*, being in perfect Health, and sitting with his fellow Servants, at Night, was on a sudden taken ill, dropt from his Seat backward, and then fell a Vomiting, at which the Family was much concern'd, he having never been subject to the like before; but he came to himself soon after, and had no sort of Pain about him. One of the Family who was accustom'd to see the *Second Sight*, told them that the Man's Illness proceeded from a very strange cause, which was thus. An illnatured Woman (whom he named) who lives in the next adjacent Village of *Bornskittag*, came before him in a very furious and angry manner, her Countenance full of Passion, and her Mouth full of Reproaches, and threatned him with her Head and Hands, till he fell over, as you have seen him. This Woman had a Fancy for the Man, but was like to be disappointed as to her Marrying of him. This Instance was told the Author by the Master of the Family and others who were present when it happened.

Sir *Norman Mackleod*, and some others, Playing at Tables, at a Game call'd in *Irish*, *Falmermore*, wherein there are Three of a Side, and each of them throw the Dice by turns, there happened to be one difficult Point in the disposing of one of the Table-men; this obliged the Gamester to deliberate before he was to change his Man, since upon the disposing of it, the Winning or Losing of the Game depended; at length the Butler, who stood behind, advised the Player, where to place his Man, with which he comply'd, and won the Game. This being thought extraordinary, and Sir *Norman* hearing one Whisper him in the Ear, ask'd who advised him so skilfully? he answer'd it was the Butler; but this seem'd more strange, for he could not Play at Tables. Upon this Sir *Norman* ask'd him how long it was since he had learnt to Play? and the Fellow own'd that he had never Play'd in his Life, but that he saw the Spirit *Brownie* (a Spirit usually seen in that Country) reaching his Arm over the Players Head, and touching the part with his Finger, on the Point where the Table-man was to be plac'd. This was told the Author by Sir *Norman* and others, who happen'd to be present at the time.

Daniel Bow, alias *Black*, an Inhabitant of *Bornskittag*, who is one of the precisest *Seers* in the *Isles*, foretold the death of a young Woman, in *Minginis*, within less than 24 Hours before the time, and accordingly she Died suddenly in the Fields; tho' at the time of the Prediction she was in perfect Health; but the Shroud appearing close about her Head, was the ground of his Confidence, that her Death was at hand.

The same Person, foretold the Death of a Child in his Master's Arms, by seeing a spark of Fire fall on his Left Arm: and this was likewise accomplish'd soon after the Prediction.

Some of the Inhabitants of *Harries*, Sailing round the *Isle* of *Sky*, with a design to go to the opposite Main-land, were strangely, surprised with an Apparition of Two Men Hanging down by the Ropes that secured the Mast, but could not conjecture what it meant; they pursued their Voyage, but the Wind turning contrary, they were forced into *Broadford*, in the *Isle* of *Skye*, where they found Sir *Donald Mac Donald* keeping a Sheriffs Court, and Two Criminals receiving

Sentence of Death there; the Ropes and Mast of that very Boat were made use of to Hang those Criminals. This was told the Author by several who had this Instance related them by the Boat's Crew.

Several Persons, living in a certain Family, told the Author that they had frequently seen two Men standing at a Gentlewoman's Left Hand, who was their Master's Daughter; they told the Mens Names, and being her equals it was not doubted but she would be Marry'd to one of them; and perhaps to the other, after the Death of the First. Sometime after, a Third Man appeared, who seemed always to Hand nearest to her of the Three, but the *Seers* did not know him, tho' they could describe him exactly; and within some Months after, this Man who was seen last, actually came to the House, and fully answer'd the description given of him by those who never saw him, but in a Vision, and he Marry'd the Woman shortly after: they live in the *Isle* of *Skye*, and both themselves and others confirm'd the truth of this Instance, when the Author saw them.

Archibald Mac Donald, of the Parish of St. *Mary*'s in the *Isle* of *Skye*, being reputed famous for his Skill in foretelling things to come, by the *Second Sight*, hapning to be in the Village *Knockow* one Night, and before Supper, told the Family that he had just then seen the strangest thing he ever saw in his Life, *viz.* a Man, with an ugly long Cap, always shaking his Head; but that the strangest of all was a little kind of an Harp, which he had, with Four Strings only, and that it had Two Hart's Horns fixt in the front of it: all that heard this odd Vision fell a Laughing at *Archibald*, telling him that he was Dreaming, or had not his Wits about him, since he pretended to see a thing which had no being, and was not so much as heard of in any part of the World. All this could not alter *Archibald*'s Opinion, who told them, that they must excuse him, if he Laught at them after the accomplishment of the Vision. *Archibald* returned to his own House, and within Three or Four Days after, a Man with a Cap, Harp, *&c.* came to the House, and the Harp, Strings, Horns and Cap answer'd, the description of them at first view, and he shook his Head when he play'd; for he had Two Bells fixed to his Cap. This Harper was a Poor Man, who made himself a Buffoon for his Bread, and was never seen before in those parts, and at the time of the Prediction he was in the *Isle* of *Barray*, which is about Twenty Leagues distant from that part of *Skye*. This Relation is Vouch'd by Mr. *Daniel Martin*, and all his Family, and such as were then present, and live in the Village where this happened.

One *Daniel Nicholson*, Minister of St. *Mary's* in *Skye*, the Parish in which Mr. *Archibald Mac Donald* liv'd, told the Author, that one *Sunday*, after Sermon, at the Chappel *Uge*, he took an occasion to inquire of *Archibald*, if he still retained that unhappy Faculty of Seeing the *Second Sight*, and wish'd him to get rid of it, if possible, for said he, it's no true Character of a Good Man. *Archibald* was highly displeased, and answered that he hop'd he was no more unhappy than his Neighbours, for seeing what they could not perceive. I had, said he, as serious Thoughts as my Neighbours, in time of hearing a Sermon to Day, and even then I saw a Corps lay'd on the Ground close to the Pulpit; and I assure you it will be accomplish'd shortly, for it was in the Day time. There were none in the Parish then Sick, and few are buried at that little Chappel, nay sometimes not one in a Year. Yet when Mr. *Nicholson* return'd to Preach in the said Chappel, a Fortnight, or Three Weeks after, he found one buried in the very Spot, named by *Archibald*. This Story is Vouch'd by Mr. *Nicholson*, and several of the Parishioners still living.

Note, That it's an Argument of somewhat Evil, attending this faculty of the *Second Sight*, because there are Instances given of some Persons, who have been freed of it, upon using some Christian Practices.

Sir *Norman Mac Lead*, who has his Residence in the *Isle* of *Bernera*, which lies between, the *Isles* of *N. Vist* and *Harries*, went to the *Isle* of *Skye* about Business, without appointing any time for his return; his Servants in his absence, being all together in the large Hall at Night, one of them, who had the *Second Sight*, told the rest they must remove, for there would be abundance of other Company in the Hall that Night; one of his Fellow-Servants answered, that there was very little likelyhood of that, because of the Darkness of the Night, and the danger of coming thro' the Rocks, that lie round the *Isle*: but within an Hour after, one of Sir *Norman's* Men came to the House, bidding them provide Lights, &c. for his Master had newly landed.

Sir *Norman* being told of this, call'd for the *Seer*, and examined him about it; he answer'd, that he had seen the Spirit *Brownie*, in humane shape, come several times, and make a shew of carrying an Old Woman that sate by the Fire, to the Door, and at last, seem'd to carry her out by Neck and Heels, which made him Laugh heartily, and gave occasion to the rest to conclude him Mad, to Laugh so much without any reason. This Instance was told the Author by Sir *Norman* himself.

Four Men from the *Isle* of *Skye* and *Harries*, went to *Barbadœs*, and stay'd there some Years, who tho' they had wont to see the *Second Sight* in their Native Countrey, never saw it in *Barbadœs*; but upon their return to *England*, the First Night after their Landing, they saw the *Second Sight*; as the Author was told by several of their Acquaintance.

John Morison, who lives in *Bernera* of *Harries*, wears the Plant called *Fuga Dæmonum*, Sewed in the Neck of his Coat, to prevent his seeing of Visions, and says, he never saw any since he first carry'd that Plant about him.

A Spirit, by the Country People call'd *Brownie*, was frequently seen in all the most considerable Families in the *Isles*, and *North* of *Scotland*, in the shape of a tall Man, having very long brown Hair: but within these 20 Years past, he has been seen but rarely.

There were Spirits also that appeared in the shape of Women, Horses, Swine, Cats, and some like Fiery Balls, which should follow Men in the Fields; but there have been but few Instances of these for 40 Years past.

These Spirits us'd also to form sounds in the Air, resembling those of an Harp, Pipes, the crowing of a Cock, and of the grinding of Hand Mills: and sometimes Voices have been heard in the Air at Night, Singing *Irish* Songs; the words of which Songs some or the Author's Acquaintance still retain; one of them resembled the Voice of a Woman, who died some time before, and the Song related to her State in the other World. These Accounts the Author says, he had from Persons of as great Integrity, as any are in the World. So far Mr. *Martin*.

As for Sounds in the Air resembling that of Musical Instruments, crowings of a Cock, Singing, &c. I have often heard them my self.

In my reading, I have met with many well attested Instances, which may strongly induce a belief of what is said concerning the *Second sight*: Of which Instances I shall here give a few.

Sicillus, an *Herald* to *Alphonsus* King of *Aragon*, in his Book entitl'd, *Le Blason des Couleurs*, writes thus: There is a Town in *Italy*, call'd *Teridon*, where this Miracle is wont to happen, if any Citizen or Labourer be to die that Year, when he labours his Field, there clearly appears a great effusion of Blood, and the Blood signifies a near ensuing Death of the Possessor of that Field.

The Lord *Henry Howard*, in the Book he writ against *Suppos'd Prophecies*, writes thus. *Chap.* 17.

It chanc'd, after the Decease of a certain honest *Gent.* (whom I forbear to Name in some Respects) the Devil appearing (*so he Expresses it*) first to one of his Daughters, in his wonted shape, and with a Voice and Countenance answerable; and so again to another, he brought the Young Woman into so strange a Condition, that it would have griev'd any Man to have seen them; and this seem'd strange withal, that at the time his Appearance haunted them, they could as well tell who came into the House, what they said and did, &c. as any that were present in their Companies. The like Story, for all the World, is written of *Hieronymo* an *Italian*, and likewise of one of the *Greek* Emperors. So far the Lord *Howard*; who I think may be look'd upon as an unexceptionable Testimony, in the Story he relates of his own Knowledge, he having otherwise little Faith in things of this kind.

Hor. sub. cis. cent. I. *c.* 70

The Learned *Camerarius* writes thus: I could easily Name, and shew a Man living in my Neighbourhood, while I write this, who formerly having been Famous for his Mannagement of Serious Affairs, as well as other ways, has now for many Years been kept under a Guard, because now and then, for certain intervals of time, he is acted by a wonderful and troublesome Spirit; for he does not only (when in a sedate Mind) call many that come to him (though Strangers and such as he had never seen before) by their proper Names, and talk to them Pleasantly concerning their Parents, Relations, and the Coats of Arms of their Families, and this as Familiarly as tho' he had been a long time Conversant with them (and which he did to my self) and if he be in a troubl'd State, mixes False and Obscene things with what he says; but also sometimes he speaks and does other unusual and strange things; particularly it was observ'd, that some Years since, about that very time that *Cispar Castalion*, Admiral of *France*, with his Son in Law, and many Noblemen of his Religion, were by surprize kill'd in their Beds at *Paris*, he had wonderful Visions, from which it might have been gather'd, that some cruel Enterprize was somewhere contriv'd and executed. Among other things, the very Night of that cruel Butchery made at *Paris* he often cry'd out, all is in Blood; and a little after, see, see, what great Troops of Devils do I see wandring in the Air, on every side, coming from several remote Parts, Congratulating each other, and skipping for Joy, as tho' they had executed some strange and cruel Enterprize, long desir'd by them; but he added, crying out, that all those things were acted out of *Germany*.

I think this a great instance from a Learned Man; and if any Men can satisfie themselves with *Aristotle*, to solve Facts of this Nature, by saying, they are Operations of Melancholy, I leave them to their Fancies. If this Fact, and others set down before by me may be receiv'd as a Truth, I see not what difficulty there may be in admitting for a Truth, what is reported of *Apollonius Tyanæus*, viz. that as he was disputing in an open Auditory at *Ephesus* he cry'd out on a sudden, that he saw *Domitian* stab'd at *Rome*, at the very time that it was done.

To give one instance nearer home. There liv'd not many Years since, a very aged Gentlewoman, in *London*, in *Water-Lane*, by *Fleet-Street*, whose Name was *Pight*, who was endow'd with a Prophetick Spirit, she was very well known to many Persons, of my Acquaintance, now living in London. Among others, a Gentleman, whose Candor I can no way suspect, has told me, that he often referred to her, as to an Oracle; and that as soon as he came into her Presence, she would usually tell him, that she knew he was coming, for that she had seen his Spirit for some time before: And without his saying any thing to her, she would commonly tell him, what the Business was, which he came to consult her about, and what the Event of it would be: Which he always found to fall out, as she said; and many other Persons, now living can testifie the like Experience of her, as to themselves.

Joan. Marcus Marci, in his *Philos vet. Restituta*, tells us of a Boy seiz'd with the Plague at *Rome*, who being thought dead, on a sudden came to himself; and calling his Master, told him he had really been in Heaven, and there had understood how many, and who were to die out the House, and naming them; he affirm'd his Mastar should survive, and to create a belief of what he said, he shew'd that he had learn'd all Languages; and presently thereupon spake in *Greek* with his Master; he made a Tryal also in other Tongues, by conversing with those who were skill'd in them, whereas before he had only learn'd the *Roman* Language; and when he had liv'd thus three Days, falling into a Rage, he lay'd hold of his Hands with his Teeth, and really died; and the others whom he had nam'd died, his Master remaining alive.

Part 2. p. 274.

To the foregoing Account of the *Second Sighted Persons* in *Scotland*, I shall subjoin a thing no less strange, *viz.* An Account of the *Spectre-sighted Persons* in *New-England*; so call'd, because upon their being seiz'd with strange Fits, as of

Weeping, Laughing, Roaring, Convulsions, violent Agitations, &c. they were wont to see the *Spectres* of those Persons, who they said tormented them.

Mr. *Cotton Mather*, a Minister of *New-England*, in his Relation of the *Wonders of the invisible World*, inserted in his *Ecclesiastical History* of that Country, Printed in *London, An.* 1702. in *fol.* has giv'n us several instances of this kind, as also of many other Diabolical Operations. And Mr. *Robert Calef*, a Merchent of *Boston*, in *New-England*, has giv'n us a pretty full Account of the same, in his Book, intitl'd, *More wonders of the invisible World*, or, *The wonders of the invisible World display'd*, in five Parts, Printed in *London, An.* 1700 in 4o. And whereas these two Authors seem to differ in Opinion, the former thinking things to have been real, and proceeding from the Operations of Evil Spirits, and the later looking upon them generally to have been Illusion and Imposture, I shall give here an Abstract of both, for Men to see what they may Rationally judge in the Matter.

Chap. 7.

Mr. *Mather*, in the sixth Book of the said History, relates many of these Facts, and that with all sincerity, as he declares, and says, that no Rational Man of all that Country ever question'd them.

His First Instance is of one *Anne Cole*, a Person of serious Piety (as he writes) living in the House of her Godly Father at *Hartford* in *New-England*; who. *An.* 1662. was taken with strange Fits, so that she would express strange things, unknown to her self, her Tongue being guided by a *Dæmon*. The general purport of her Discourse was, that such and such Persons, whom she nam'd, were consulting how they might carry on Mischievous Designs against her, and several others, by afflicting their Bodies, or destroying their good Names. One of the Persons mention'd by her, was named *Greensmith*, who was then in Prison on suspicion of Witchcraft, and was brought before the Magistrates; to whom the Ministers, who had taken Notes of what *Cole* had said, reading what they had written, she with Astonishment confess'd, that the things were so, and that her self with other Persons, nam'd in the Paper, had Familiarity with the Devil, who told her, that at

Christmas they would have a Merry meeting, when the Agreement betwixt them should be subscrib'd: she declar'd, that her Devil appear'd to her first in the shape of a Deer, skipping about her, and at length, in that shape talk'd to her, and that the Devil had frequently Carnal Knowledge of her. On this Confession, with other concurring Evidences, the Woman was executed, and other Persons accus'd made their escape; whereupon *Anne Cole* was deliver'd of her extraordinary Vexations.

The Second Instance is *Elizabeth Knap*, who in *October*, 1671. was taken after a very strange manner, Weeping, Laughing, Roaring, with Violent Agitations, *&c.* and had a *Dæmon* speaking in her; among other things, she cry'd out in her Fits, that a certain Woman in the Neighbourhood appear'd unto her, and was the only cause of her Affliction; the Woman thus cry'd out on was a very Vertuous Person, who, by the Advice of her Friends, visited the afflicted, who though she were in her Fits, and had her Eyes wholly shut, yet when the innocent Woman was coming in, she shew'd her self wonderful sensible of it, and was in great Agonies at her approach; but the innocent Woman pray'd earnestly with, and for this possess'd Creature; whereupon, as she came to her self, she confess'd she had been deluded by Satan, who, in the shape of divers Persons, cruelly tormented her after divers Manners, and then told her it was not himself, but they were her Tormentors.

The Third Instance is of the House, of Mr. *William Morse* of *Newbury*, which, *An.* 1679. was infested with *Dæmons*, not unlike the *Dæmon of Tedworth*. Bricks, Sticks, Stones, Pieces of Wood, *&c.* were often thrown at the House, a long Staff danc'd up and down the Chimny, and afterward was hung on a Line, and swung to and fro; an Iron Crook was violently hurryed about by an invisible hand; and a Chair flew about the Room, till at last it light on the Table, where Meat stood ready to be Eaten, and was like to have spoil'd all. A Chest was by an invisible Hand carry'd from one place to another, and the Doors Barricado'd, and the Keys of the Family taken, some of them, from the Bunch, where they were tyed, and the rest flying about with aloud Noise of their Knocking against one another; and many other unaccountable things of this kind pass'd, too long for me here to set down; a little Boy belonging to the Family, was a Principal Sufferer in these Molestations, he was flung about at such a rate that they fear'd his Brains would have been beaten out; nor did they find it possible to hold him, his Bed Clothes were pull'd off from his Bed, his Bed shaken; a Man took him to keep him in a Chair, but the Chair fell a dancing, and both were very near being thrown into the Fire, he was prick'd on the Back, they found an Iron Spindle and Pins stuck in him, all the Knives in the House were one after anothers stuck in his Back, which the Spectators pull'd out: Sometimes he bark'd like a Dog, then clock'd like an Hen, he complain'd, that a Man call'd P—l appear'd to him, as the cause of all. Before the Devil put an end to these Tricks, the invisible Hand which did all these things, put on an astonishing visibility. They often thought they felt the Hand that scratch'd them, while yet they saw it not; but when they thought they had hold of it, it would give them the flip. Once the Fist beating the Man was discernable, but they could not catch hold of it: at length an Apparition of a Blackamoor Child shew'd it self plainly to them; another time a Drumming on the Board was heard, which was followed with a Voice that sang, *Revenge, Revenge, Sweet is Revenge*; at this the People being terrifyed call'd upon God; whereupon there follow'd a Mournful Voice uttering these Expressions. Alas! Alas! we knock no more, we knock no more, and there was an end of all.

The Fourth Instance is of the House of *Nicolas Desborough*, at *Hartford*, which, *An.* 1683. was troubl'd much after the same manner; it began upon a Controversie happening betwixt the Man of the House, and another Person, concerning a Chest of Cloaths, which the Man apprehended the other unjustly detain'd from him, and it lasted divers Months, till upon restoring the Cloaths the trouble ceas'd. He adds, at *Brighling* in *Sussex*, in *England*, there happened a Tragedy not unlike to this, *An.* 1659. It's Recorded by *Clarke*, in the Second Volume of his Examples.

His Fifth, and Sixth Instances are Relations of the same Nature.

His Seventh Instance is of one Mr. *Philip Smith*, aged about Fifty Years, a Deacon of the Church of *Hadley*, a Member of the general Court, a justice of the County Court, a Lieutenant of a Troop, and a Man very Exemplary for Devotion, Sanctity, and Gravity, who, *An.* 1689. was miserably Murther'd by Witchcraft, he was, by his Office, concern'd about relieving the Indigences of a wretched Woman in the Town, who being dissatisfy'd with him, express'd her self in a threatning manner, so that he apprehended receiving mischief at her Hands; he fell ill of a wearing Distemper, and at length became delirious, and cry'd out not only of Pains, but also of Pins tormenting him in several Parts of his Body. In his Affliction he exclaim'd much on the said Woman, and others, as being seen by him in the Room. Some young Men in the Town went and gave disturbance to the Woman so complain'd of, and all the while they were disturbing her, he was at ease and slept, as a weary Man. Gallipots of Medicines prepar'd for him, were unaccountably emptyed, audible screcchings were made about the Bed, when his Hands and Feet lay wholly still, and were held by others. Mr. *Smith*, at length dies; the Jury that view'd his Corps, found a swelling on one Breast, his Privities wounded, or burnt, his back full of Bruises, and several Holes that seem'd made with Awles; divers Noises were heard in the Room where the Corps lay, as the clattering of Chairs and Stools, whereof no account could be giv'n.

His Ninth Instance, to the Facts of which the Author was himself a Witness, is of Four Children of *John Goodwin* of *Boston*, all Religiously educated. These Children *An.* 1688. were wrought on by Witchcraft, by an Old Woman, whom the Eldest Daughter, who was about Thirteen Years of Age, had provok'd, so that she was immediately seiz'd with odd Fits: in a short time after, one of her Sisters, and two Brothers were horribly seiz'd with the same, all the Children were tormented still just in the same part of the Bodies, at the same time, tho' their Pains flew like Lightning from one part to another, and they were kept so far asunder, that they neither saw, nor heard one anothers Complaints; at Nine or Ten of the Clock at Night they still had a release from their Miseries, and Slept all Night pretty well; but when the Day came, they were again miserably handl'd; sometimes they were Deaf, sometimes Dumb, sometimes Blind, and often all Three at once, and many other unaccountable Symptoms attended them; they made most pitious out-cries, that they were cut with Knives, and struck with Blows, and the plain prints of the Wounds were seen upon them; the suspected Woman's House being search'd, several Images, or Puppets, or Babies, made of Rags, and, stuft with Goats Hair were there found, and the Woman confest that the way to Torment the Objects of her Malice, was by wetting of her Finger with her Spittle, and stroaking those little Images. The abused Children were then present in the Court, and one of the Images being brought to the Woman, she started up, and snach'd it into her Hand, when presently upon it one of the Children fell into sad Fits, before the whole Assembly. The Judges caused a repetition of the Experiment, and still found the same effect of it, tho' the Children saw not when the Hand of the Witch was laid upon the Images. To make all things clear, the Court appointed Five, or Six Physicians to Examine her very strictly, whether she were no way craz'd in her Understanding, who after spending several Hours with her, return'd her *Compos Mentis*, and Sentence of Death was pass'd on her. After her Condemnation, Mr. *Mather* says, he visited her several times, and she then told him, she us'd to be at Meetings where her Prince, and four more were present; she told him who the four were, and plainly said, that her Prince was the Devil; at her Execution she said, the afflicted Children should not be reliev'd by her Death, for others besides her self had a Hand in their Affliction: And accordingly, the Children continued afflicted far worse than before; one of the Children discern'd the *Spectres*, and told the Names of those that tormented them; a blow struck at the place where he saw the *Spectre*, was always felt by the Boy himself, in that part of his Body, which answer'd to that was struck at; and this, though his

Back were turn'd, and the thing so done, that there could be no Collusion in it, yet after the Agonies were over, to which a push, or a stab at the *Spectre* had put him to, as in a Minute, or two they would be, he would have a respite from his Ails, a considerable while, and the *Spectre* would be gone. The Affliction of the Children went on till they bark'd at each other like Dogs; and then pur'rd like Cats. They would complain they were in a Red hot Oven, and sweated, and panted, as if they had been really so. Then they would say, that cold Water was thrown on them, at which they would shiver very much. They would complain of being roasted on an invisible Spit, and lie, and roll, and groan as if it had been so; and by and by, screech out, that Knives were cutting them. They would complain that their Heads were nail'd to the Floor, and it was beyond an ordinary strength to pull them from thence. Mr. *Mather* says, the *Dæmons* did not know our Thoughts; for if himself, or others us'd a *Jargon*, and said, untie its Neckcloth, but the Party bidden understood their meaning to be, untie his Shooe, the Neckcloth, and not the Shooe has been, by wry then Postures, rendred strangely unaccessible; no good thing could then be endur'd near those Children, who while they were themselves, lov'd every good thing. The eldest Girl, being Mr. *Mather*'s House, a Chain invisible to any but her self, would be clap'd about her, and she, in much pain and fear, would cry out when they began to put it on; sometimes Persons present could with their Hands knock it off, as it began to be fastn'd; but ordinarily when it was on she would be pull'd out of her Seat, with much violence towards the Fire, that it was as much as one or to two could do, to keep her out; if Persons present stamp'd on the Hearth, just between her and the Fire, she scream'd out, that by jarring the Chain they hurt her. An unseen Rope with a cruel Noose was put about her Neck, whereby she was choak'd, till she was black in the Face; and though it were got off before it had kill'd her, yet there were the red Marks of it, and of a Finger and a Thumb near it, remaining to be seen for some while afterwards; these Children were often near burning and drowning, and strangling themselves with their

Neckcloths, but still seasonably succor'd; and, to omit many other Circumstances, they were at length deliver'd from this great Affliction.

Mr. *Mather*, at the end of Fourteen Instances of this kind, written by himself, lays before us an Account of Visitations of the same Nature, which happen'd in *New-England*, *An.* 1692. and written by Mr. *John Hales*, a Person, who, as Mr. *Mather* says, would not for a World be guilty of overdoing the Truth, in an History of such Importance. The Account is as follows.

At the latter end of the Year, 1691. Mr. *Paris*, Pastor of the Church in *Salem Village*, had a Daughter of about Nine Years of Age, and a Niece of about Eleven, sadly afflicted with unaccountable Distempers, as Physicians that were consulted thought, and one of them judg'd they were betwitch'd. Mr. *Paris* had an *Indian* Man Servant, and his Wife an *Indian* Woman, who confess'd that without the Knowledge of their Master and Mistress, they had taken some of the afflicted Persons Urine, and mixing it with Meal, had made a Cake, and baked it, to find out the Witch, as they said. After this the afflicted Persons cry'd out of the *Indian Woman*, nam'd *Tituba*, that she pinch'd, prick'd, and grievously tormented them, and they saw her here and there, where no Body else could, and could tell where she was, and what she did when she was absent from them, these Children were bitten and pinch'd by invisible Agents, their Limbs were rack'd and tormented, and miserably contorted, &c. *Tituba* was Examined, who confess'd the making of that Cake, and said, her *Mistress* in her own Country was a Witch, and had taught her some means to be us'd for the discovery of a Witch, and for preventing of being bewitch'd. In a short time other Persons, who were of Age to be Witnesses, were molested by Satan, and in their fits cry'd out upon *Tituba*, and *Goody Orburn*, and *Sarah Good*, that they, or *Spectres* in their shapes, did grievously torment them. The Justices at *Salem* examin'd the Afflicted and Accus'd together, and upon the Examination, *Tituba* confess'd, that she was a Witch, and that she, and the other two accus'd, did torment and bewitch the Complainers;

and that these, with two others, whose Names she knew not, had their Witch-Meetings together, relating the times when, and places where they met, with other Circumstances. Upon this *Tituba*, *Osburn*, and *Good* were committed to Prison, on suspicion of acting Witchcraft. Soon after these Afflicted Persons complain'd of others afflicting them in their Fits; and the Number of the Afflicted, and Accus'd began to increase; and upon Examination more confess'd themselves guilty of the Crimes they were suspected of; the Number of Confessors amounting at length to Fifty. The Justices, Judges, and others concerned, us'd all Conscientious endeavours to do what was right, according to former Presidents in *England*, in the like Cases. The Matter was carried on chiefly by the Complaints and Accusations of the Afflicted, and by the Confessions of the Accus'd, condemning themselves and others: Yet Experience shew'd that the more were apprehended, the more were still afflicted; and the Number of the Confessors enereasing, did but increase the Number of the Accus'd; and the executing of some made way for the apprehending of others: for still the afflicted complain'd of being tormented by new Objects, as the former were removed; so that those that were concerned were amaz'd at the Number and quality of the Persons accus'd, and fear'd Innocent Persons suffer'd: and henceforth, the Juries generally acquitted such as were try'd, fearing they had gone too far before, and all were let at Liberty, ev'n the Confessors. The Number of the Accus'd was increas'd to above an Hundred, and many of them were Persons of blameless and holy Lives. Nineteen were executed, and all deny'd the Crime dying; and some of them were knowing Persons, and had before this been accounted blameless Livers. The Persecution ceasing, the Afflicted grew presently well, the accus'd were quiet, and for Five Years past there has been no Molestation by them. So in *Suffolk*, in *England*. about the Year 1645. there was such a Prosecution, till they saw, that unless a stop were put to it, it would bring all into Blood and Confusion. The like has been in *France*, till 900 were put to Death; and in some other Places the like. So that *New-England* is not the only place circumvented by the Wiles of *Satan* in this kind. He relates from *Wierus*, p. 678, that an *Inquisitor* in the *Subalpine* Valleys, enquir'd after Women Witches, and burnt above an Hundred, and was prosecuting more, till the Country People rose, and by force of Arms hindred them, and refer'd the Matter to the Bishop. Their Husbands affirm'd, that at that very time it was said of them, that they play'd and danc'd under a Tree, they were in Bed with them.

At *Chelmsford* in *Essex*, *An.* 1645. there were 36 at once before Judge *Coniers*, and Fourteen of them Hang'd, and an Hundred more detained in several Prisons in *Suffolk* and *Essex*.

As for the Case at *Salem*, he conceives it proceeded from some mistaken Principles as that *Satan* cannot assume the shape or an Innocent Person, and in that shape do Mischief to the Bodies and Goods of Mankind; and that when the Devil does harm to Persons in their Bodies or Goods, its at least, for the most part by the help of our Neighbours, some which are in Covenant with him. This is the substance of what Mr. *Hales* delivers; and Mr. *Mather* tells us, that Mr. *Hales*, from whose Manuscript he Transcribed this, does there Confute these mistaken Principles: yet spends whole Chapters to prove that there is a Witch, whom he thus defines. Tis a Person that having the free use of his Reason, does knowingly and wittingly obtain of the Devil, or of any other Divine Power, but the True God, an ability to do or know strange things, or things which he cannot by his own humane abilities arrive unto.

Mr. *Mather*, in an *Appendix*, at the end of his Sixth Chapter of his Sixth Book, before-mentioned, gives a short Relation of some practices of Witchcraft, used by the *Indians* of *New England*, as follows.

The *Indians* of *Martha's Vineyard*, who are now *Christians*, abundance of them acknowledge the Witchcraft, wherein they had actual Conversations, and explicit Confederacies with Devils, while they were *Pagans*. They know that many Persons among them have been, by the zeal of their Parents, dedicated to their Infernal Gods, and educated for their especial Service: but that the *Dæmons* accept only of some here and there to make *Pawaws* or *Wizards* of. They know that these *Pawaws* often Imploy their *Dæmons* to smite their Neighbours with Blindness, and Lameness, and other Mischiefs, and sometimes to Kill them, and sometimes to Cure their Maladies. They know that their manner is to form a piece of Leather like an Arrow's Head, and then tye an Hair to it; or to take a Bone of some dead Creature: over these things they use Magical Ceremonies, whereupon the *Dæmon* presently snatches them away, and conveys them into the Bodies of Persons to be afflicted; or sometime the *Dæmon* pretends to them, that he brings a portion of the Spirit of the Person, closely Imprison'd in a Fly; and as they deal with the Fly, so it fares with the Body of the Person intended. Some of the *Pawaws* faculty chiefly consists in discovering and recovering Stoln Goods, by the help of their *Dæmons*. A *Pawaw*, turn'd *Christian*, said he had often employed his God, who appeared to him still in the form of a Snake, to Kill, Wound, and Lame, such as he design'd Mischief to. So far Mr. *Mather*.

I shall now give an Account of what Mr. *Calef*, above mentioned, has deliver'd in his Book, Entitled, *More Wonders of the Invisible World*, &c.

In his Preface he tells the Reader, he publishes these his Collections and Sentiments, in hopes, that having well consider'd and compared them with the Scriptures, he will see Reason, as well as himself to question a belief so prevalent, as that there treated of, as also the practice flowing from thence; he declares his disbelief of the operations and effects of the Devil, exprest by Mr. *Mather*, in his *Wonders of the Invisible World*; as that the Devil exhibited himself ordinarily as a Black Man, and Decoy'd Miserable Malicious Creatures to Lift themselves in his Service, by entring their Names in a Book; and that they have had their Meetings and Sacraments, having each of them their *Spectres*, or Devils commission'd by them, and representing of them, to be the Engines of their Malice: By these wicked *Spectres* afflicting poor People with various Torments, even Killing some, and causing some to destroy themselves, and carrying some over Trees, and Hills, Miles together, many of them being tempted to sign the Devil's Laws.

He takes this matter to be, as others understand it, *viz.* that the Devil has been too hard for many in *New England*, by his Temptations, Signs, and Lying Wonders, with the help of pernicious Notions, formerly imbibed and profest; together with the accusations of a parcel of Possest, Distracted or lying Wenches, accusing their Innocent Neighbours, pretending they see their *Spectres*, that is, the Devil in their likeness, afflicting of them: whereupon many Tragedies followed, which tho' begun in one Parish, spread over the whole Country; and he thinks a Zeal led by Blindness and Passion, and former Presidents had herein precipitated Persons into these wickednesses, or Witchcrafts, and says, much the same has been affected this present Year in *Scotland*.

His Book being divided into Five Parts, he begins his First Part with a Letter sent by Mr. *Cotton Mather* to a Friend of his, containing a Relation of an Apparition happening to one *Margaret Rule*, living in the North part of *Boston*. This young Woman, on a *Sunday*, *December* the 10*th*. 1693. after some Hours of previous disturbance in the Publick Assembly, fell into odd Fits, which caused her Friends to carry her home, where her Fits in a few Hours appeared to be preternatural: She was assaulted by eight cruel *Spectres*, of which she thought she knew three or four, but the rest came still with their Faces cover'd: she privately told Mr. *Mather* the Names of those she knew, Who says, they were miserable Wretches, that for many Years had been strongly suspected for Witches. Those *Spectres* brought her a red thick Book, not very broad, about a Cubit long, and demanded her to set her Hand to it, or at least to touch it with her Hand, as a sign of her becoming the Devil's Servant; which she peremptorily refusing to do, they fell a Tormenting her cruelly, so that she was forced to keep her Bed six Weeks together. Sometimes, tho' not always, together with the *Spectres*, there look'd in upon her, as she laid, a Short *Black Man*, whom they called their *Master*, being exactly of the same Dimensions, Complexion and Voice with the Devil, that has exhibited himself to other Infested People; not only in other parts of *New England*, but also in other Countries of *Europe*, as relations from thence inform us. She was cruelly Pinch'd with Invisible Hands, very often in a Day, and the Black and Blue Marks of the Pinches became immediately visible to the standers by, she would also be miserably hurt with Pins, that were found stuck in her Neck, Back and Arms; though those Wounds made by the Pins, would in a few Minutes ordinarily be cur'd; she would also be strangely distorted in her Joints by Exorbitant Convulsions. To pass by other strange Relations of her, in which Mr. *Mather* thinks there could be no Imposture, once in the middle of the Night she lamented sadly, that the *Spectres* threatn'd the drowning of a Young Man in the Neighbourhood, whom she nam'd to the Company; and it was found, that at that very time, this Young Man having been Press'd on Board a Man of War, then in the Harbour, was attempting to Swim on Shoar, and had been drown'd in the Attempt, if a Boat had not seasonably took him up. There were wonderful Noises every now and then, made about, the Room where she lay, which the Persons present could ascribe to no other Actors, but the *Spectres*. Once her Tormentors pull'd her up to the Ceiling of her Chamber, and held her there before a very Numerous Company of Spectators, who found it as much as they could all do to pull her down again. She had also a White Spirit which came to her, whose bright shining and glorious Garments she had a frequent view of. He stood by her Bed continually heart'ning and comforting of her, and Counseling her to maintain her Faith and Hope in God, and never to comply with the Temptations of her Adversaries. Mr. *Mather* says, he has seen it fulfil'd more than three times in the Deliverance of inchanted and possess'd Persons, whom God has cast in his way, that their Deliverance could not be obtain'd before the third Fast kept for them, and the third Day still obtain'd the Deliverance; and after *Margaret Rule*, had been more than Five Weeks in her Miseries, the White Spirit said to her; Well, this Day such a Man (whom he nam'd) has kept a third Day for your Deliverance, now be of

Good Chear, you shall speedily be deliver'd. Mr. *Mather* enquir'd, whether what had been said of that Man were true, and was certainly inform'd, that it was precisely so. On the last Day of the Week her Tormentors, as she said, approaching towards her, would be forc'd still to recoil and retire, as unaccountably unable to meddle with her; and they would retire to the Fire side with their Puppets, but going to stick Pins in those Puppets, they could not make the Pins to enter, and she saw their Black Master to strike them, and kick them, to make them do their Work, and renew the Marks of his Vengeance on them, when they fail'd of doing it: At last, being as it were stir'd with their ineffectual Attempts to mortifie her, they furiously said, *Well, thou shalt not be the last*; and after a pause, they added, *Go, and the Devil go with you, we can do no more*. Whereupon they flew out of the Room; and she returning perfectly to her self, gave thanks to God for her Deliverance: Her Tormentors left her extream Weak and Faint, and overwhelm'd with Vapours, which would not only cause her sometimes to fall in a Swoon, but likewise now and then, for a little while discompose her Reason, though her former troubles returned not.

To this Relation Mr. *Mather* adds, He has always been of this Opinion, that we are Ignorant of what Powers the Devils may have to do their Mischiefs, in the shapes of some that had never been explicitly engag'd in Diabolical Confederacies; and that therefore though many Witchcrafts had been fairly detected, on enquiries provok'd and begun by *Spectre Apparitions*, yet himself has been so far for abating the excessive Credit of *Spectres Accusations*, that he still charg'd the Afflicted, committed to his Care, that they should cry out on no Body for afflicting them; though if it might be of any Advantage to them, they might tell their Minds to some one Person, of Discretion enough to make no ill use of it. Nor had the Civil Authority prosecuted those things, had not a Conscientious regard to the Crys of Miserable Families, overcome the Reluctancies of the Judges to meddle with them.

The Second Part of this Book begins with a Narrative of what past at two Visits, given by Mr. *Cotton Mather*, and his *Father*, to *Margaret Rule*, written by Mr. *Calef*, as he says, from the Mouths of some Persons who were then present; of which Narrative Mr. *Cotton Mather* greatly complains, as very unfairly and falsly representing things, in reference to his Father and himself.

It contains also Letters from Mr. *Calef*, to Mr. *Cotton Mather*, offering a meeting with him, and desiring an Information in some Doctrinals relating to Witchcraft; which meeting Mr. *Mather* declin'd at the place nominated by Mr. *Calef*, though he offered to Discourse with him concerning it in his Study, or any other Convenient place. There are also Papers attested by several Hands of Persons present, that *Margaret Rule* was lifted up to the Ceiling of the Room, where she lay, by an invisible Hand, and that several of the Persons present had much ado, with all their strength to pull her down. This is followed by another Letter from Mr. *Calef* to Mr. *Mather*, in which, notwithstanding the Attestations of the Persons present, he declares his disbelief of *Margaret Rule*'s being so lifted up; his reason is, that then Miracles are not ceas'd, (this seeming to him as true a Miracle, as for Iron to Swim) and that the Devil can work such Miracles.

Next follows, several Letters from Mr. *Calef* to Mr. *Mather* and others, relating to the Doctrinals of Witchcraft, both desiring Mr. *Mather* to explain it, and setting forth what himself conceives of it, according to the Scriptures: and having Inserted a Letter, which he writ to the Ministers, whether *English*, *French*, or *Dutch*, in *New England*, he concludes it thus, That the only Decisive Circumstance to Convict a Witch, as far as he can find in the Scriptures, is a maligning and oppugning the Word, Work, or Worship of God, and by any extraordinary Sign seeking to seduce any from it; tho' not excluding any other Branch, when as well prov'd by that Infallible Rule; and that the going to the afflicted, or possest to Divine who are Witches by their *Spectre-Sight*, is a great wickedness, and that the searching for Tets, the experiment of their saying the Lords Prayer, the falling at the Sight, and rising at the Touch of the supposed Criminal, being all of them foreign from Scripture, as well as Reason, are Abominations to be Abhorr'd and Repented of. Lastly, That their *Salem* Witchcraft, either respecting the Judges and Juries, and their tenderness of Life, or the multitude and pertinency of Witnesses, both afflicted, and confessors, or the integrity of Historians, are as Authentick, and made as certain, as any ever of that kind in the World have been, and yet every one now sees through it; and that it was the abovementioned Sentiments that procured this saddest Affliction, and most lasting Infamy that ever befel that Country. Mr. *Calef*'s next Letter is to Mr. *Samuel Willard*, a Member of *Harvard College* in *New England*, where among other things he says that by the late Prosecution, under the notion of Witches, Twenty suffered as Evil Doers (besides those that Died in Prison) above Ten more Condemned, and an Hundred Imprison'd, and about 200 more Accused; and the Country generally in Fears, when it would come to their turn to be Accused; that those very Accusers, which had been Imprisoned as Witnesses against so many, Accused at length those in most High Esteem, both Magistrates and Ministers, as guilty of Witchcraft, which shew'd their Rulers, that necessity lay upon them to confound what had so long confounded the Country, as being unwilling to run the same risque.

Mr. *Mather* having sent Mr. *Calef* a Book Printed by Mr. *Baxter*, Entitled, *The certainty of the World of Spirits*, for his Instruction in that kind; Mr. *Calef* has here inserted a Letter which he sent to Mr. *Mather*, containing Animadversions on that Book. And in another Letter which he Writ to the Ministers in and near *Boston*, he speaks of the Doctrine of the *Manicheans*, and endavours to shew that the present Age is not free from that Infection; and ascribes the deluge of Blood-shed among Christians, to this, that Men having taken up a belief of a Covenanting, Afflicting and Killing Witch, and finding no footsteps of such a Witch in the Scriptures, have concluded, that though the Scriptures be full in it, that a Witch should not Live, yet that it has not at all described the Crime, nor means whereby the Culpable might be detected; and hence they account it necessary to make use of those Diabolical, and Bloody ways, always heretofore practised for their Discovery; finding that the Rules given to detect other Crimes, are wholly useless for the discovery of such.

Mr. *Calef's* last Letter of his Second Part, is to Mr. *Benjamin Wadsworth*, a Minister, whom he seems to charge with not well explaining the Scriptures, in reference to Witchcraft, and says, the late dangerous Notion, that the Devil appears to Persons, and that they and the Devil make mutual Ingagements, Confirm'd by Signing the Devil's Book, and are from hence Inabled not only to know Futurities, and things done at a Distance, but are also Impower'd thereby to do harm to Neighbours, to raise Storms, and do things above and against the Course of Nature, has been the occasion of shedding so much Blood in the World. He adds, It's manifest that the belief of the Witches Power to do the things abovementioned, was an ancient belief of the *Heathens*; and that from them it was received by the *Papists* who have since Improved upon it, and brought in the notion of a Covenant; and that *Protestants* seem to have lately Improved it farther, by saying, that Witches can Commissionate Devils to do those Mischiefs, thereby setting the Witch in the place of God. He has writ also in a precedent Letter, that two Parties in dispute, were not agreed which to put it upon, whether the Devil Impowers the Witch, or the Witch Commissions him on the Contract: but both Parties are agreed in this, that one way or other the Mischief is effected, and so the Criminal becomes Guilty of Death; in the search after which Criminals, many Countries have fallen into such Convulsions, that neither the Devaluation made by a Conquering Enemy, nor the Plague it self has been so formidable.

The Third Part of this Book gives an account of the Differences happening at *Salem Village*, on the account of Prosecutions for Witchcraft, which began there, where one Mr. *Paris* was Pastor; who, notwithstanding his acknowledging some Errors he might have fallen into in that respect, was at last dismist from that Cure. In his acknowledgment under his hand, he owns, that the horrid Calamity of afflicting that Country, broke out first in his House, and that in his Family there were some of both Parties, *viz.* Accusers, and Accused.

The Fourth Part contains an Ingenious Letter, Writ by a Gentleman without a Name, endeavouring to prove the commonly receiv'd Opinion about Witchcraft; to which Mr. *Calef* has Written a Reply. And a Second Letter is Written by the foresaid Gentleman, to which Mr. *Calef* has a Rejoynder.

The Fifth Part, contains an account of the most Memorable matters of Fact, touching the supposed Witchcraft in *New England*. Now tho' Mr. *Calef*'s Account of Facts, contains many more Particulars, than what I have set down before from Mr. *Hale*'s, yet since they would be too tedious for me to insert here, I shall only note some odd passages in them.

He tells us, that about the end of the Year 1692, a new Scene relating to Witchcraft was begun: One *Joseph Ballard* at *Andover*, whose Wife was Ill, and after Died of a Fever, sent to *Salem* for some of those Accusers, to tell him who Afflicted his Wife; others did the same, and Horse and Man were sent from several places to fetch these Accusers, who had the *Spectre Sight*, that they might thereby tell, who afflicted those that were any way Ill. When these came into any place where such were, usually they fell into a Fit; after which being ask'd who it was that afflicted the Person, they would for the most part name one whom they said sat on the Head, and another that sat on the lower parts of the afflicted. Soon after *Ballard*'s sending, more than Fifty of the People of *Andover* were complain'd of for afflicting their Neighbours: Here it was that many accused themselves of riding upon Poles through the Air, many Parents believing their Children to be Witches, and many Husbands their Wives, *&c.* when these Accusers came to the House of any Person upon such an Account, it was ordinary for other Young People to be taken with Fits, and to have the same *Spectre Sight*. Mr. *Dudley Bradstreet*, a Justice of Peace in *Andover*, having granted out Warrants and Committed Thirty or Forty Persons to Prisons, for the supposed Witchcrafts, at length saw cause to forbear granting out any more Warrants: soon after which, he and his Wife were cry'd out of, himself was by them said to have Kill'd Nine Persons by Witchcraft, and found it his fastest course to make his Escape.

 A Dog being afflicted at *Salem* Village, and those that had the *Spectre Sight* being sent for, they accused Mr. *John Bradstreet*, Brother to the Justice, that he afflicted the said Dog, and now Rid upon him, he made his Escape into *Petattequa* Government, and the Dog was put to Death, and was all of the afflicted that suffered Death.

 At *Andover* they complain'd of a Dog, as afflicting of them, and would fall into their Fits at the Dogs looking on them. The Dog was put to Death.

 Note, *In reference to this, that in my precedent Account of the* Second Sight, Children, Horses *and* Cows *had it as well as Men and Women.*

 A worthy Gentleman of *Boston* being about this time accused by those of *Andover*, he sent by some particular Friends a Writ to Arrest those Accusers in a 1000 *l*. Action, for Defamation, with Instructions to inform themselves of the certainty of the Proof; in doing which their business was perceived, and from thence forward the Accusation at *Andover* generally ceas'd.

 And now Nineteen Persons being Hang'd, and One Press'd to Death, and Eight more Condemned, in all Twenty Eight, about Fifty having confest themselves to be Witches, of which not One Executed; about One Hundred and Fifty in Prison, and above Two Hundred more Accused, the Special Commission of *Oyer* and *Terminer* came to a Period; after which Six Women, who had confessed themselves to be Witches, gave under their Hand that they did it only in complyance with their nearest Friends, who told them it was their only way to escape.

 As for the Tryals, and the Evidence taken for Conviction at *Salem*, they are set forth in Print by Mr. *Cotton Mather*, in his *Wonders of the Invisible World*, at the Command of Sir *William Phips*, then Governour of *New England*; but Mr.

Calef considering that his Book might fall into the hands of such as never saw those Wonders, has Transcribed here the whole Account he has given thereof, without any variation, but with one of the *Indictments* annext to the Tryal of each. After Mr. *Calef* has set down Mr. *Mather*'s said Account of the Proceedings at *Salem*, he writes some Animadversions on it, and then proceeds to give an Account of the proceedings in the like case at *Charles-Town*, *Boston*, and other places; and conclude with a Proclamation, at last, Issu'd out by the lieutenant Governour, Counsel and Assembly of the *Massachusetts Bay*, wherein they beg God Pardon for any Errors might have been committed in the late Prosecutions. And upon the Day of Fast, in the full Assembly at the South Meeting-House in *Boston*, one of the Judges, who had sat in Judicature at *Salem*, delivered in a Paper, desiring the Prayers of the People to the like effect. And some that had been of several Juries, gave forth a Paper sign'd with their own Hands, owning that they fear'd they had been sadly Deluded, and Mistaken, and beg'd Pardon of God and their Country Men, for what had past; and declaring that none of them would do such things again, on such Grounds for the whole World.

I thought good to give this Account at large of the two foregoing Books, because they give us a full Information of the last considerable Visitation by Witchcrafts, or so supposed, that, has happned to any Country in the World, and I hope it may be a farewel to them.

As to my own Opinion in these Matters, I am convinced by my own Experience (which to me is as a Thousand Witnesses) that there is such a thing, as a *Spectre-Sight*, so that one Person may see *Spectres*, when others present at the same time see nothing; wherefore I think it not Impossible that the afflicted Persons in *New England* should see; nay, I believe they saw the *Spectres* of Persons, who as they conceived, Tormented them; all Histories of Witches, both in *England*, and in all other Countries, testifying the same; tho' I no way think that such *Spectre-Sight* should be received a Judicial Proof against any Person, it being manifest by some foregoing Examples, that it's, at least sometimes, subject to Illusions, of which I shall here add a particular Instance from *Frommannus*, who in his Third Book of *Magical Incantation*, quotes the Author of Criminal Cautions, writing thus.

Part. 6. cap. 7. Dub. 48. p. 347.

A Prince of *Germany* Invited two Religious Fathers, of eminent Vertue and Learning to a Dinner. The Prince at the Table said to one of them, Father! Think you we do rightly in Hanging Persons, who are accused by Ten or Twelve Witches, to have appear'd at their Meetings or Sabbaths? I somewhat fear we are Imposed on by the Devil, and that it is not a safe way to Truth that we walk in by these Accusations; especially since many Grave and Learned Men every where begin to cry out against it, and to charge our Consciences with it; tell me therefore your Opinion. To whom the Father, being somewhat of an eager Spirit, said, what should make us doubtful in this Case? or what should touch our Confidences, being convinced by so many Testimonies? Can we make it a Scruple whether God will permit Innocent Persons should be so traduc'd? there is no cause for a Judge to stick at such a number of Accusations, but he may proceed with safety. To which when the Prince had reply'd, and much had been said *pro* and *con*, on both sides about it, and the Father seem'd wholly to carry the Point, the Prince, at length, concluded the Dispute, saying, I am sorry for you, Father, that in a Capital Case, you have Condemned your self, and you cannot complain if I commit you to Custody, for no less than Fifteen Witches have deposed, that they have seen you at their Meetings, and to shew you that I am not in Jest, I will presently cause the publick Acts to be brought, for you to Read them. The Father stood in a Maze, and with a Dejected Countenance, had nothing here to oppose but Confusion, and Silence, after all his Learned Eloquence. So far *Frommannus*.

It's observable, that when the *Spectre-Sighted* Accusers came to an House to discover who afflicted a Person taken Ill, it was ordinary for other Young People to be taken in Fits like the *Spectre-Sighted*-Persons, and to have the same *Spectre-*

Sight; as we know if a Person falls into Convulsion Fits in the presence of Young Persons, it's usual for these to fall into Convulsions also.

This strange Visitation in *New England*, in which Persons were seized with strange Fits, and came to have a *Spectre-Sight*, seems to be ally'd to what *Plutarch*, in his Book of the *Vertuous Acts of Women*, relates concerning the *Milesian Virgins*, as follows.

There was a time, that the *Milesian Virgins* fell into a strange Humour, and raving without any apparent Cause, only it was suspected, that there was some Venemous Constitution of the Air, which caus'd in them this *Delirium*, and alienation of Mind; for they all on a sudden were seiz'd with a desire to die, and a furious Inclination to hang themselves, and there were many that secretly did it; and no Remonstrance nor Tears of their Parents, nor Consolation of Friends avail'd any thing, but they would Destroy themselves, and they always found means to elude all the Subtleties and Inventions of those that Watch'd them: So that it was look'd upon as some Divine Punishment, which no Humane Provision could remedy; till at length, by the advice of a wise Citizen, an *Edict* was set forth, that if any Person should hang her self for the future, her Body should be carryed Naked through the open Streets in the sight of all Men; which put a full stop to this Tragedy. And if instead of an Indulgent *Non Compos*, found generally by our Juries of late, on all *Felo's da fe*, somewhat exemplary were order'd by the Government, possibly it might deter Persons from that Crime: *Plutarch* Notes it as a sign of a Good and Vertuous Disposition, that the fear of Infamy and Dishonour works more upon Humane Minds, than the fear of those horrible Accidents Death and Torments.

Ant. Lect. l. 30. c. 4.

Rhodiginus writes thus. Its said the *Abderites* while *Lysimachus* rul'd, began to be infested with a certain New and Wonderfull kind of Disease, the manner of it was thus. First there generally reign'd among them a fierce and burning Fever, when the Seventh Day was come, an abundance of Blood flow'd from their Nostrils, some fell into a plentiful

Sweat, and this ended the Fever; but a very Ridiculous affect seiz'd the Minds of them all, for they were stir'd up to Act Tragedies, and thunder'd out Iambicks with a very loud Voice, but chiefly the Tragedy of *Andromeda*, writ by *Euripides*, and the words of *Perseus*; the City was fill'd with these kinds of weekly Tragedies, the People bawling out these and the like kind of Words. *O King, thou Love of Gods and Men*! This unusual *Delirium* held a long while, till the Winter, and a fierce Cold coming, put an end to the Evil. It's thought the rise of this Disease proceeded from this, That at that time *Archelaus*, a Famous Tragedian, in the midst of the Summer, when the Heats were very great, Acted there *Andromeda*, whereupon the *Abderites* contracted the cause of their Disease in the Theater; and when (as its usual) the Appearances of what was Acted in that Tragedy, were presented to their Minds, they fell to the said Tragedy through a *Delirium*, upon their Recovery, *Andromeda* sticking in their Memories, and *Persus* with *Medusa*.

As to a Disposition of the Air in Reference to a *Spectre-Sight*, *Purchas*, in the Second part of his *Pilgrim*, writes, from a Relation of *Sandy's* Journey from *Venice* to *Constantinople*, as follows. We lay in a little Bay, and under a Clift, in the Gulf of *Calonus*, where not one of us but had his Sleep interrupted by fearful Dreams; he that watch'd affirming, that he had seen the Devil, so that in a great dismay we put from the shore about midnight; but whether it proceeded from the Nature of the Vaporous place, or that infested by some Spirit, I leave to decide. It's reported of a little Rocky Island hard by, nam'd Formerly *Æx*, Sacred to *Neptune*, that none could Sleep on it, for being troubl'd with Apparitions. The Gulf belongs to the Island *Mitylen*, or *Lesbos*. *L. 8. c. 8.*

Thus we find what Dispositions, of Mind Men may fall into sundry ways, and how far the Diabolical seisures, relating to practices of Witchcrafts, may be caus'd upon the Minds of Miserable People, being impregnated with Notions of *Dæmons*, and the like; and what Communication of Minds there may be betwixt such People, will deserve Consideration.

Hippocrates in his Tract of *Virgins Diseases*, (if it be his) enquires into the Nature and Causes of such Distempers, as Afflicted the *Milesian* Virgins, and considers the Disease call'd *Sacred*, which he says is attended with Frights, and Terrors, by which Persons are Vehemently scar'd, so that they grow Delirious and sometimes by Night, sometimes by Day, and sometimes both Night and Day, they think they see *Dæmons* infesting them, and that upon those Visions many have hang'd themselves, though more Women than Men, they being of a weaker Disposition of Mind; and Virgins that are almost ripe for Marriage, find this about the time of the first descent of their *Menses*, being free from those Evils before; but about that time the due Course of the Blood being stopt, it returns up to the Heart and Midriff, causing an acute Inflammation, and brings an alienation of Mind, with Crys and Terrors; and sometimes, he says, without *Spectres*, a certain Pleasure of Death seizes them, as seeming a good Thing; as they return to themselves, he says, the Women are wont to Consecrate their most precious Garments, with other things, to *Diana*, being deceiv'd by the Prophets, who Command them so to do.

Now though the Causes assign'd by *Hippocrates*, seems plausible enough for him, as a Physician, yet I doubt they will not reach all Cases, and we must have recourse to a Superiour Science for them. It's known to the Learned, that there has been a Science in the World, call'd *Scientia Umbrarum*, which, as to the publick teaching of it, has been suppressd upon good Politick grounds, though there are still some Societies of Men, in the World who allow the study of it, and teach it to Persons of whose Integrity they are satisfied; and as *Bœsatas* says, of Magick, of which this is apart, *Est tanquam res Sacra, que no nisiviris magnis, & peculiari beneficio de cælo instructis Communicatur, & nil ausi sunt aggredi quidam Principes in Politicis, in Sacris, in consibiis sine eorum arbitrio.*

Columella knew there was a science built on Higher Principles, than what are accountable for in *Physicks*, when he said, concerning the Cure of his Bees.

At sit nulla valet Medicina repellere pestem, *De cult.*
Dardaniæ veniant artes. — *Hort. l. 10.*

But if this Plague no Medicine can repel,
To Arts *Dardanian* let us fly. —

The *Scientia Umbrarum*, being a Branch of these Arts, the Ignorance of which possibly, may have been the occasion of many mistakes in Judicial proceedings relating to Witchcraft, the Dispositions of the *Astral Man*, being knowable only by that Science. And though many Severities have followed upon it, yet good Policy, perhaps, has rather chosen to suffer them, than to admit the Publick teaching of that Science, which might have been of more Pernicious consequence to the Publick. But I write these things only by the by, and as opening.

It seems to me, that Mr. *Calef* deals somewhat hardly with Mr. *Mather* in this, that when for his satisfaction, Mr. *Mather* had sent him a Paper, attested by several Subscribers, that *Margaret Rule*, with whom they were present, was lifted up to the Ceiling of the Room, and that several times, notwithstanding the Endeavours of strong Persons to keep her down, and there held her for a considerable time; and that they had much ado to pull her down; yet Mr. *Calef* declares his disbelief of it, for this reason, that then Miracles are not ceas'd; if as though a manifest Experience were to be so exploded. I have giv'n before two Experiences in the like kind, one from Mr. *Glanvil*, concerning a Person so lifted up in the Lord *Orery's* House in *Ireland*; another from *Wierus*, a Person well known to have been, of no Light belief, who declares that a Woman had been carried up in the Air by Spirits, if himself had not violently with-held her, and kept her down. As to his great Ground, of the Cessation of Miracles, I well know many Learned Divines, have been of that Opinion, though I think it no such Essential Point of Faith, that Christianity cannot well consist without it. Dr. *Brown*, in his *Religio Medici*, writes thus. That Miracles are *Sect. 27.*
ceas'd, I can neither prove, nor absolutely deny, much less

Sect. 28.

define the time and period of the Cessation. And again, Therefore that Miracles have been, I do believe, and that they may yet be wrought by the living, I do not deny, and Dr. *Stubbe*, in his Account of the *Miraculous Cures* wrought by Mr. *Greatrix* writes, according to the Impetuosity of his Spirit, That to say, Miracles are ceas'd, is a groundless Folly, if not a disingenious Impudence, in giving the Lye to various Religions: And if Mr. *Calef* admitted the point of *Margaret Rule*'s, being so lifted up, I cannot see why this must be concluded a Miracle, unless all things Providence permits the Devil to act, and which seem strange, shall be called Miracles.

And whereas Mr. *Calef,* so often urges Mr. *Mather,* with Mr. *Gaule*'s Fourth Head for Convicting a Witch, *viz.* That a Witch is one that maligns, and oppugns the Word, Work, or Worship of God, and by any Extraordinary signs seeks to seduce any from it; as appears, *Deut.* 13. 1, 2. *Matth.* 24. 24. *Act.* 13. 8. 10. 2 *Tim.* 3. 8. which Mr. *Calef* will have to be the only Head well prov'd in the Scripture for discovering a Witch, and often challenges Mr. *Mather,* to produce any other; and says, That his not bringing plain Scripture Proof, that there is a Covenanting Witch, is a sufficient Demonstration there is none; it's no consequence but there may be such a Witch, and that fairly reducable to the Head of Witchcraft mention'd in the Scriptures; for as there are New Diseases of the Body, which were unknown to the Ancients, so I know not why there may not be New Distempers of the Mind, all Crimes being such; and since Mr. *Calef* stands so much for plain Scripture Proof for what he Credits, he may do well to give us a plain convincing Scripture Proof (setting by his own Glosses) for the ceasing of Miracles; or of the time that Providence tyed up its Hands from doing any thing beside the ordinary course of Nature; or from commanding or permitting any Good or Evil Angels to do any such thing.

I think it worthy Consideration, that in the Account the abovemention'd Mr. *Greatrix* gave of himself and his Actions, in a Letter to the late Mr. *Boyle*, Printed in *London*, *An.* 1666. there seems a strange Agreement in some

Particulars, with what happen'd in the *New-England* Visitation; for as the Persons there Afflicted, assoon as they look'd on those that Afflicted them, would fall down in Fits, so Mr. *Greatrix* writes somewhat of the like Nature, relating to himself, addressing himself to Mr. *Boyle*, as follows.

"*Sir*, I hope you will Pardon me, when I relate to you my own Observations, and what my Experience inclines me to believe, in saying, that I have met with several Instances which seem'd to me to be Possession, by Dumb, Deaf, and talking Devils; and that to my Apprehension, and others present, several Evil Spirits, one after the other have been pursued out of a Woman, and every one of them has been like to Choak her, when it came up to her Throat, before it went forth; and when the last was gone, she was perfectly well, and so continued. There have been others, that have fall'n down immediately assoon as they have seen me, which the Mayor of *Worcester*, Colonel *Birch*, Major *Wilde*, and many Hundreds both at *Worcester*, and here in *London*, and other Places were Eye-Witnesses of: Many when they have heard my Voice, have been tormented in so strange a manner, that no one present could conceive it less than a Possession; as I will Instance in one at *York-house*, (where Sir *John Hinton*, Colonel *Talbot*, and many others were present) who had somewhat within her, which would swell her Body to that excessive Degree, on a sudden, as if it would burst her; and then assoon as I put my Hand on that part of her Body, where it did rise up, it would fly up to her Throat, or some other place, and cause her Neck to swell half so big again, and then almost Choak her, then Blind her, and make her Dumb, and Foam, and sometimes fly into her Hand, and so contract and fast'n it, that neither Sir *John Hinton*, or any else that did try (as there were many) could with all their strength open one Finger of her hand, nor would it fly his Hand in the least, nor any other Persons there, till I put my Hand on it, or my Glove; nay, I oftentimes brought it up into her Tongue, by running my Hand on her Body, on the outside of her Cloaths, up to her Throat, which was swoll'n in an Instant as big again, and has been seen plainly to fly from place to place, and at length with great violence of Belching, which did almost Choak her, and force her Eyes to start out of her Head, it went forth, and so the Woman went away well. Whether this were a Natural Distemper let any one Judge, that is either *Divine, Philosopher,* or *Physician.* I could Instance you on Forty as strange, or stranger; but I will go no farther then *London,* and Places adjoyning, for Instances of this Nature."

He adds beneath,

"That going to the Town of *Copoqueen* in *Ireland,* there were many Poor People that came out of *England,* for several Distempers they labour'd under; and among the rest, two that had the Falling-Sickness, who no sooner saw me, but they fell into their Fits immediately, and upon putting my Hands on them, they were restor'd to their Senses forthwith; and he pursued their Pains from place to place, till they went out of them." So far Mr. *Greatrix.*

Here we find, that as the Persons Afflicted in *New-England,* assoon as they look'd on the Afflictors, or so by them suppos'd, fell into their Fits, and were restor'd to themselves upon the Afflictors touching them, so the Distemper'd Persons, assoon as they look'd on Mr. *Greatrix* fell into their Fits, and upon his touching them were recover'd.

There was a Book Printed in *London, An.* 1656. intitl'd, *Enthusiasmus Triumphatus,* written by one who assum'd the Name of *Philosophilus Parresiastes*; near the end of which, we find a Relation of a Person, who had a Power of healing by stroaking, like that of Mr. *Greatrix.* The Relation is thus, *p.* 57. It's very credibly Reported, and I think cannot be deny'd, That one by the stroaking of a Mans Arm, that was dead and useless to him, recover'd it to life and strength. When I heard of it, and read some few Pages of that Miraculous Physicians writing, my Judgment was, that the

Cure was Natural, but that his Blood and Spirits were boil'd to that height, that it would hazard his Brain, which proved true; for he was stark mad not very long after.

Now, however, this Person might have valued his Skill in judging of an ensuing madness in such Cases, the effect having followed here according to his guess; yet we find it will not hold in all Cases, Mr. *Greatrix* having always liv'd free from any such Sequel.

To proceed to other Accounts of Persons, who have had a Perception of *Genii*, or Spirits not visible at the same time to others; The Famous *Torquatus Tasso*, Prince of the *Italian Pœts*, strongly asserted his own Experience in that kind. His Life was writ and publish'd in *French, An.* 1692. by *D. C. D. D. U.* who in his Preface tells us, that in what he has writ, he has followed chiefly the History given us in *Italian*, by *John Baptista*, a *Neapolitan*, Gent. who had been a very Intimate Friend to *Tasso*. In his Life, among other things, he acquaints us, that *Tasso* was Naturally of that Melancholick Temperament, which has always made the greatest Men, and that this Temperament being aggravated by many hardships he had undergone, it had made him sometimes beside himself; and that those Melancholick Vapours being dissipated, he came again to himself, like those that return from Fits of the Falling-Sickness, his Spirit being free as before. That near his later end he retired from the City of *Naples*, to his Friend *Manso*, at *Bisaccia*, a small Town in the Kingdom of *Naples*, where *Manso* had a considerable Estate; and pass'd an Autumn there, in the Divertisements of the Season, as Hunting, visiting Ladies, and frequenting other Companies, *&c.* And here the *French* Author gives us an Account of *Tasso's* Sensible Perception of a *Genius*, as follows. As after these Amusements he usually retir'd to his Chamber, to entertain himself there with his Friend *Manso*, the later had the Opportunity to enquire into one of the most singular effects of *Tasso's* Melancholy, of this Heroick Melancholy, as I may call it, which rais'd his Spirit, so far it was from rendring it obscure, and which, among the Ancients, would have caus'd them to have ascrib'd a *Familiar Damon* to him as to *Socrates*.

They were often in an hot depute concerning this Spirit, with which *Tasso* pretended to have a Communication. I am too much your Friend, said *Manso*, to him, one Day, not to let you know what the World thinks of you concerning this thing, and what I think of it my self. Is it possible that being enlightn'd as you are, you should be fall'n into so great a Weakness, as to think you have a *Familiar Spirit*; and will you give your Enemies, that Advantage, to be able to prove by your own acknowledgment, what they have publish'd to the World? You know they say you did not publish your *Dialogue of the Messenger*, as a Fiction, but you would have Men believe that the Spirit which you make to speak there, was a real and true Spirit; so that Men have thence drawn this Injurious Consequence, that your Studies have embroil'd your Imagination, so that there is made in it a confus'd Mixture of the Fictions of the Poets, the Inventions of the Philosophers, and the Doctrine of Religion. I am not Ignorant, answer'd *Tasso*, of all that is spread abroad in the World on the Account of my *Dialogue*: I have taken care divers times to disabuse my Friends, both by Letter, and word of Mouth. I prevented ev'n the Malignity of my Enemies, as you know, at the time I publish'd my *Dialogue*. Men could not be Ignorant that I compos'd it for the Young Prince of *Mantua*, to whom I would explain, after an agreeable Manner, the Principal Mysteries of the *Platonick* Philosophy. It was at *Mantua* it self, after my second flight from *Ferrara*, that I form'd the *Idea* of it, and I committed it to Paper a little while after my unfortunate return. I address'd it to this Prince, and all Men might have read in the *Epistle Dedicatory*, the Protestation I there make, that this *Dialogue* being writ according to the Doctrine of the *Platonicks*, which is not always conformable to reveal'd Truths, Men must not confound what I expose there as a *Philosopher* with what I believe as a *Christian*. This Distinction is by so much the more reasonable, that at that time nothing extraordinary had happen'd to me, and I spake not of any Apparition. This can be attested by all those with whom I lodged, or frequented in this Voyage; and therefore there is no reason for confounding the Fiction of my *Dialogue* with what has happen'd to me since. I am perswaded of all you say to me, reply'd *Manso*, but truly I cannot be of what you believe, at present, concerning your self. Will you Imagine to your self that you are in Commerce with a Spirit? And I ask you of what Order is that Spirit? Shall us place him in the Number of the Rebels, whom their Pride precipitated into the Abyss? Or of the Intelligences who continued firm in Faith, and Submission to their Creator? For there is no mean to take in the true Religion, and we must not fall into the Extravagances of the *Gnomes* and *Silphes*, of the *Cabalists*,

Now, the Spirit in question cannot be a *Dæmon*, you own, that instead of Inspiring you any thing contrary to Piety and Religion, he often fortifies in you the *Maxims* of Christianity; he strengthens your Faith by profound Reasonings, and has the same respect with you for Sacred Names and Things. Neither can you say that It's an *Angel*; for tho' you have always led a Regular life, and far from all Dissoluteness, tho' for some Years past you have apply'd your self after a particular manner to the Duties of a True Christian, you will agree with me that these sorts of Favours are not common; that a Man must have attained to an high degree of Sanctity, and not be far from the Pureness of Celestial Spirits to merit a familiar Converse, and bear an Harmony with them. Believe me, there is nothing in all these Discourses which you imagine you have with this Spirit. You know better than any Man those Symptoms, which the black Humours wherewith you are Tormented, causes in you. Your Vapours are the source of your Visions, and your self would not judge otherwise of another Person, to whom a like thing should happen; and you will come to this in your own respect also, if you will make a mature reflexion, and apply your self to blot out, by an effort of Reason, these Imaginations which the violence of your evil effect causes in you. You may have Reason, reply'd *Tasso*, to think so of the things that pass in me; but, as to my self, who have a sensible perception of them, I am forced to reason after another manner. If it were true that the Spirit did not shew himself to me but in the Violent Assault of my Vapours:

If he offer'd to my Imagination but wandring and confus'd *Species*, without Connexion or due Sequel, if he used to me frivolous Reasonings which ended in nothing; or if having begun some solid Reasoning, he left it off on a sudden, and left me in darkness, I should believe, with you, that all that passes, is but Dreams and Fantoms; but it's quite otherwise. This Spirit is a Spirit of Truth and Reason, and of a Truth so distinct, of a Reason so sublime, that he raises me often to Knowledges that are above all my Reasonings, tho' they appear to me no less clear; that he teaches me things which in my most Profound Meditations never came into my Spirit, and which I never heard of any Man, nor read in any Book. This Spirit therefore is somewhat of Real; of whatsoever order he be, I hear him and see him, nevertheless for its being impossible for me to comprehend and define him. *Manso* did not yield to these Facts, which *Tasso* would have pass'd for Proofs: he prest him with new *Questions*, which were not without *Answers*. Since you will not believe me on my Word, said *Tasso* to him, another Day, after having well Disputed, I must convince you by your own Eyes, that these things are not pure Imaginations: and the next Day conversing together, in the same Chamber, *Manso* perceived that, on a suden, he fixt his Eyes towards the Window, and that he stood, as it were Immovable; he call'd to him, and jogg'd him many times, but instead of Answering him; *See there the Spirit*, says *Tasso*, at last, *that has been pleased to come and visit me, and to entertain himself with me; look on him, and you will acknowledge the Truth of what I say.* Manso, somewhat surprised, cast his Eyes towards the place he shew'd him, and perceived nothing but the Rays of the Sun passing through the Glass: nor did he see any thing in all the Chamber, tho' he cast his Eyes round it with curiosity, and he desired him to shew him the Spirit, which he look'd for in vain, while he heard *Tasso* speak with much Vehemeney. He declares in a Letter, which he writ concerning this to the Admiral of *Naples*, that he really heard no other Voice but *Tasso*'s own; but they were sometimes *Questions* made by him to this pretended Spirit, sometimes *Answers* that he made to the pretended *Questions* of the Spirit, and which were conceived in such admirable Terms, so Efficacious, concerning Subjects so Elevated, and so Extraordinary, that he was Ravish'd with Admiration, and dared not to Interrupt him. He hearken'd therefore Attentively, and being quite beside himself at this mysterious Conversation, which ended at last by a recess of the Spirit; as he found by the last words of *Tasso*; after which *Tasso* turning himself to him, Well, said he, are your doubts at last dissipated; on the contrary, answer'd *Manso*, I am more Imbroyled than ever; I have truly heard wonderful things; but you have not shew'd me what you promised me. You have seen and heard, resum'd *Tasso*, perhaps, more than —— he stopt here; and *Manso*, who could not recover himself of his surprise, and had his Head fill'd with the *Ideas* of this extraordinary entertainment, found not himself in a condition to press him farther. Mean while he ingaged himself not to speak a word to any Man of these things he had heard, with a design to make them Publick, tho' he should have liberty granted him. They had many other conversations concerning this Matter: after which *Manso*, own'd he was brought to that pass, that he knew not what to think or say, only, that if it were a weakness in his Friend to believe these Visions, he much fear'd it would prove Contagious to him, and that he should become at last, as credulous as himself.

I was willing to set down this Relation at large, because I think it contains a sufficient Answer to what many Learned Friends have said to my self, on the like occasion.

Pernaps it may not be ungrateful to the Reader, if I subjoyn here the short *Eloge* writ on *Tasso*, by the Famous *Thuanus*, which is as follows.

Torquatus Tasso died about the Forty Fifth Year of his Age, a Man of a wonderful and prodigious Wit, who was seized with an incurable Fury in his Youth, when he lived at the Court of *Ferrara*; and nevertheless in lucid Intervals he writ many things both in Verse and Prose, with so much Judgment, Elegancy, and extream Correctness or Style, that he turn'd, at length, that Pity, which many Men had conceived for him, into an Amazement; while by that Fury, which in others makes their Minds outragious, or dulls them, after it was over, his Understanding became as it were purified, more ready in Inventing things, more accute in aptly disposing them after they were Invented, and more copious in adorning them with choice of Words, and weight of Sentences; and that which a Man of the soundest Sense would scarce excogitate at his Leisure, with the greatest labour and Care imaginable, he, after a violent agitation of the Mind, set beside it self, naturally perform'd with a wonderful Felicity, so that he did not seem struck with an alienation of Mind, but with a Divine Fury. He that knows not these things, which all Men know that have been in *Italy*, and concerning which himself sometimes complains, tho' modestly, in his Writings; let him Read his Divine Works, and he must necessarily conclude, either that I speak of another Man than *Tasso*, or that these things were written by another Man than *Tasso*.

What shall we say of *Horace*, as to a sensible perception of Spirits, who seems to desire Posterity to believe him, where he says,

Carm. l. 2.
Ode 19.

> *Bachum in remotis Carmina montibus*
> *Vidi docentem, credite posteri,*
> *Nymphasque discentes, & aures*
> *Capripedum satyrorum acutas*
> *Evoe recenti mens trepidat metu.*

> *Bacchus in distant Rocks I've seen*
> *Teach Charms, and Nymphs to learn of him.*
> *Believe it, and the prick'd up Ears*
> *Of Goat-feet Satyrs.* Oh ! *it Scares*
> *Me still to think on't with new Fears.*

And I know not why *Horace* (tho' an *Epicurean*) being Enthusiastically raised, might not have seen Apparitions, as well as other Men: as when with a Scalded Imagination, he cry's out,

> *Quô me Bacchæ raptis tui*
> *Plenum? quo nemora, aut quos agor in specus*
> *Velox mente novâ?*   *Cam. l. 3.*
> *Ode 25.*

Cruquius has writ a learned Comment on the former *Ode* of *Horace*, which I recommend to the Curious Readers perusal: he there reflects on *Lambinus*, who, in his Comment on the same *Ode*, says,

> ——————————*Credat Judæus Apella,*
> *Non Ego* ——————

he not having duly examined the Scope of that Divine Poet, in that *Ode*.

Having aver'd my own Experience in seeing *Genii*, or *Spirits*, I shall conclude this Chapter with what the most Ingenious Poet says of himself, in the like case,

> *Facta canam, sed erunt qui me finxisse loquantur,*
>   *Nulláq; mortali numina visa putuent.*
> *Est Deus in nobis agitante calessimus illo;*
>   *Impetus hic Sacræ semina mentis habet,*
> *Fas mihi præcipuè vultus vidisse Deorum*
>   *Vel quia sum vates, vel quia Sacra cano.*   *Fast. 6.*

> They're Facts I'll Sing, tho' some may say I feign,
> And think no Gods were ever seen by Man.
> God Reigns in us, by's Actings we take Fire
> Such Salleys, Seeds of Sacred Mind Inspire.
> Of all Men I may freely Gods behold,
> Or cause I'm Prophet, or Gods Truths Unfold.

CHAP. V.

What perception Men have had of Genii, *or* Spirits, *and their Operations by the Sense of Hearing.*

Thyræus tells us, That God proposed to Himself, in his way of acting with Men, First, to render Himself Familiar to them; afterwards, in succeeding Times, to remit somewhat of His Familiarity; at last to Govern Men, not by Himself, but by Men.

L. de Appar. Dei voc. c. 17.

The most familiar way that God has manifested Himself to Men, has been by presenting Himself in an outward appearance, and speaking to Men in an Humane Shape. He came somewhat short of this, when he was only heard and not seen. It's Inferior to both when he was neither seen nor heard, but insinuated Himself in a Dream, or the Fancy; the lowest degree was when he occupied only the understanding of Man.

If we run over, and examine all Gods manifestations of Himself, we shall find, for the most part, that to the first Men God oftenest presented himself in an outward humane Form: Afterwards, That with later Men he had Discourses, hiding his external Form. *Thirdly,* That he was neither seen in a personal Shape, nor his Voice perceiv'd, but he accomplish'd many things in Dreams. *Fourthly,* That he enlighten'd the Mind; yet it must no be thought that God so nicely observ'd this Rule, that he never pass'd it by; for when he has appear'd in an outward Form, he has often also been heard, often appear'd in Dreams, often enlighten'd the Understanding. Again, in later Times also, sometimes He has been seen, sometimes heard; but I relate what has happen'd for the most part.

The Minds of Men being at length practis'd, He afforded them his Presence, partly by *Oracles*, which he gave Viva Voce; partly the Understanding being enlighten'd by Himself, and the Ministry of Angels, He, in a manner, withdrew Himself, and govern'd Men by Men, as His Deputies; and left them, in a manner, to themselves, as He now Governs them. So far *Thyræus*.

I have premitted this from *Thyræus*, to give a general Notion of the Manifestations of God, and the Intellectual World to Man: This Doctrine being strongly back'd by the Scriptures, and deliver d down to us from all Ages; as likewise that *Genii*, *Spirits*, *Angels*, and *Dæmons*, have manifested themselves to Man after the like manners.

Appar. Dei. visib. c. 2.

Now *Thyræus* tells, us farther, That as these Manifestations differ in excellency according to the dignity of the Powers they are made to; and each Power has its Dignity, according as it is abstracted from Matter; so the Sight, in this regard, exceeding the Hearing; the Imagination, the Sight; the Understanding, the Imagination; the most excellent Manifestation will be the Intellectual, next the Imaginary, then the Visible, and, in the last place, the Vocal.

As I pretend to consider chiefly these two last ways, and have already giv'n Accounts in reference to the *Sense of Seeing*, I shall here give Instances of what perception Men have had of *Genii*, or Spirits by the *Sense of Hearing*, the manifestation of *Socrates*'s *Genius*, before-mention'd, being by a Voice, and many having heard strange Voices or Noises, who have never seen any thing. And as to these Voices or Noises heard, we must consider them in a two-fold respect: Either only the Person concern'd hears them, and not others present at the same time, (as it was the Case of *Socrates*;) or they are heard by all Persons present. I shall therefore first give a few Instances of the latter, and then of the others : only noting by the by, what *Wierus* says of these Voices or Noises, *viz.*

De Præs. Dæm. l. 7. c. 13.

"Spirits appear sometimes invisibly, so that only a Sound, or Voice, or Noise is perceiv'd by Men, *viz.* a Stroke, or Knocking, or Whistling, or Sneezing, or Groaning, or Lamenting, or clapping of the Hands, to make Men attent to Enquire, or Answer."

So far *Wierus*.

In *Luther's Colloquia Mensalia, &c.* set forth in *Latin* at *Francfort, An.* 1571, it being a different Collection from that of *Aurifaber*, which is translated from the *High-Dutch* into *English*, we have the following Relation.

Tom. I. c. *de Spectris.*

"It happen'd in *Prussia*, that as a certain Boy was Born, there presently came to him a *Genius*, or what you please to call it (for I leave it to Mens Judgments) who had so faithful a care of the Infant, that there was no need either of Mother or Servant; and as he grew up he had a like care of him: He went to School with him, but so that he could never be seen, either by himself, or any other, in all his Life. Afterwards, he travelled into *Italy*, he accompanyed him, and whensoever any Evil was like to happen to him, either on the Road, or in the Inn, he was perceived to foretel it by some touch or stroke; he drew off his Boots as a Servant; if he turn'd his Journey another way, he continued with him, having the same care of him in foretelling Evil; at length he was made a *Canon*, and as, on a time, he was sitting, and feasting with his Friends, in much Jolity, a vehement Stroke was struck on a sudden, on the Table, so that they were all terrified; presently the *Canon* said to his Friends, be not afraid, some great Evil hangs over my Head; the next Day he fell into a Fever, and the Fit continued on him for three whole Days, till he died Miserably."

The Second Instance, I shall give, is from *Bodin*, which though it has been Printed in *English* already, yet it relating to the Point I am treating of, and containing many pertinent Instances, I have thought fit to insert it here. He writes therefore as follows;

Dæmon. l. I. c. 2.

"I can assure you, a Person now living has told me, he had a Spirit Daily attending him, and that he began to have knowledge of him, about the 37th Year of his Age, though he believ'd he had accompanyed him all his life by preceding Dreams and Visions he had to keep him from Vices and Inconvenicies; but he never sensibly perceived him, as he had done since his 37th Year; which happen'd to him, he says, having for a Year before continually pray'd to God heartily, Morning and Evening, that he would please to send him a *Good Angel* to guide him in all his Actions. Since, as he told me, he begun to have very Instructive Dreams and Visions, sometimes for him to Correct one Vice, sometimes another, sometimes for keeping himself from Danger, sometimes for resolving him of one Difficulty, sometimes of another; and this not only concerning Divine, but likewise Humane things. Among others, he seem'd to hear a Voice of God, in his sleep, saying to him, *I will save thy Soul. It is I that appear'd to thee before*; since that every Morning, about Three or Four of the Clock, the Spirit knock'd at his Door, and he rose sometimes, and open'd his Door, but saw no Body; and every Morning the Spirit continued, and if he did not rise he knock'd again, and kept him waking till he rose, then he began to be afraid, thinking it some Evil Spirit, as he said; and therefore Continued to Pray to God, without failing a Day, that he would send him a *Good Angel*, and often sung the *Psalms*, which he could say in a manner all by heart, and then the Spirit made himself known to him, as he was awake, striking softly the first Day, so that he sensibly perceiv'd many strokes on a Glass Viol, which very much amaz'd him; and two Days after having a Friend of his, the King's Secretary, who is still living, dining with him, the Secretary heard the Spirit strike after that manner, on a little Stool standing by him; whereupon he begun to look Red, and to fear, but he said to him, be not afraid, it's nothing; however, to give him an assurance, he related to him the Truth of the Fact; now, he has assur'd me, that since the Spirit has always Accompanyed him, giving him a sensible sign, as touching him sometimes by the right Ear, if he did somewhat that was not Good; and by his left Ear if he did Well; and if any one came to deceive and surprise him, he presently perceiv'd the sign at his right Ear; and if it were some good Man, and came for his Good, he perceiv'd also the sign at his left Ear; and if he were about to Eat or Drink any thing that was Evil, he perceiv'd the sign; if he doubted of doing or undertaking something, the signal happen'd to him. If he thought of some Evil thing, and was at a stand, he presently perceiv'd the sign to put him off from it: Sometimes when he began to Praise God, with some *Psalm*, or to speak of his Wonders, he found himself seized with a certain Spiritual force, which gave him Courage. And for him to discern a Dream by Inspiration from those idle Fancies that happen, when a Person is indispos'd, or troubled in Mind, he was awak'd by the Spirit about Two, or Three of the Clock in the Morning, and falling asleep a little after, he had true Dreams of what he ought to do, or believe, or of doubts he had, or of what would happen to him; so that since that time, he says, there is scarce a thing that has happen'd to him, but he has had an Advertisement of it; nor a doubt of things that he ought to believe, but he has had it resolv'd, he duly Praying to God to teach him his Will, Law, and Truth; and as for his Comportment otherwise, he was of a Joyous Disposition enough, in all his Actions, and of a Gay Spirit, alledging to this purpose that Passage of the Scripture, which says, *I saw the Countenances of the Angels joyful.* If he chanc'd in Company to say some Evil word, or forbore some Days to Pray to God, he was presently advertiz'd in his Sleep. If he read in a Book that was not Good, the Spirit struck on the Book to make him leave off; and he was assoon directed, if he did any thing against his Health, and was carefully guarded in his Sickness. In short, he has told me so many Particulars, that it would be endless to relate them all; but above all, he was advertis'd to rise in the Morning, and commonly about Four of the Clock, and says, he heard a Voice in his sleep which said. *Who is it that will rise to serve God?* He says also, he was often advertis'd to give Alms, and the more Alms he gave, the more he found his Affairs to prosper; and as his Enemies had resolved to kill him, knowing that he was to go by Water, he had a Vision in his Dream, that his Father brought him two Horses, one Red, and the other White; which made him send to hire two Horses, and his Man brought him two Horses, one Red, and the other White, he having not told him of what Colour he would have them. I ask'd him, why he spoke not openly to the Spirit; he answer'd me, that he once pray'd him to speak to him, but presently the Spirit struck with violence against the Door, as though it had been with an Hammer; giving him to Understand, that he took no Pleasure in it, and often he put him by of reading and writing, that he might give rest to his Mind, and Meditate alone, he hearing often a very subtle and inarticulate Voice. I ask'd him if he had never seen the Spirit in a Form, he told me, he had never seen any thing waking, unless it were a sort of a light, in a round Form, and very clear. "

I omit some other Immaterial Particulars concerning this Person in *Bodin*, who concludes his Relation of him thus.

"I was willing to relate what I have known from such a Person to let Men understand that an Association with Evil Spirits ought not to be look'd upon as strange; if Angels, and Good Spirits have such a Society and Intelligence with Men. But as for what he says, that the Good Angel touch'd his Ear, this is well noted in the Book of *Job*, chap. 33. and in *Isaiah*, chap. 50. where he says, *Dominus vellicarit mihi aurem diluculo*; and *Job* says it better yet, discovering to understanding Men the Secret, by which God by little and little makes himself sensibly known; and as for what he says, he heard striking with an Hammer, we read it was the first Mark of the Prophets, for in the Book of *Judges*, it's said of *Manoa*, that the Angel of God began to knock before him, as *Rabbi David* says, where the *Hebrew* word, *Lepaghamo*, signifies to knock, and to sound, ring or ting, from the word *Pahamon*, which signifies a little Bell, or Tabrette, *&c*."
So far *Bodin*.

Mr. *Baxter*, in his, *Historical Discourse of Apparitions and Witches*, writes thus. There is now in *London* an Understanding, Sober, Pious Man, oft one of my Hearers, who has an Elder Brother, a Gentleman of considerable Rank, who having formerly seem'd Pious, of late Years does often fall into the Sin of Drunkenness; he often Lodges long together here in his Brother's House; and whensoever he is Drunk, and has slept himself Sober, something Knocks at his Bed's Head, as if one knock'd on a Wainscot; When they remove his Bed, it follows him: Beside other loud Noises on other Parts where he is, that all the House hears, they have often watch'd him, and kept his Hands, lest he should do it himself: his Brother has often told it me, and brought his Wife, a discreet Woman, to attest it; who averrs, moreover, that as she watch'd him, she has seen his Shooes under the Bed taken up, and nothing visible touch them. They brought the Man himself to me, and when we ask'd him, how he dare Sin again, after such a warning, he has no Excuse: but being Persons of Quality, for some special Reason of Worldly Interest, I must not Name him. Two things are Remarkable in this Instance. 1. What a Powerful thing Temptation and Fleshly Concupiscence is, and what an harden'd Heart Sin brings Men to; if one rose from the Dead to warn such Sinners, it would not of it self perswade them.

2. It Poses me to think what kind of Spirit this is, that has such a care of this Man's Soul, which makes me hope he will recover. Do good Spirits dwell so near us? or, Are they sent on such Messages? or, Is it his *Guardian Angel*? or, Is it the Soul of some Dead Friend? that suffers, and yet retaining Love to him, as *Dives* to his Brethren, would have him saved? God yet keeps such things from us in the Dark. The same Author, in his said Book has inserted a Relation sent him by a Gentleman in a Letter, concerning strange Noises, as follows.

"Mr. *Harlakenden*, who liv'd at *Coln Priory* in *Essex* (where I often was, his Son being my Pupil) formerly the House of the *Earls* of *Oxford*; off from the House was a Tomb-House, with a Chamber over it; his Butler, *Robert Crow*, and *William* his Coachman, us'd to lie in that Room; at two of the Clock in the Morning there was always the sound of a great Bell tolling; they affirming it so, Mr. *Harlakenden* slept in the Evening, so as to be awak'd at one of the Clock, and lay betwixt his two Servants to satisfie himself; at two of the

Clock comes the usual sound of a great Bell tolling, which put him into a fright and sweat, so as he jog'd his Servants; who awaking, said, Hark! *Tom* is at his Sport. It reviv'd him to hear them speak. Upon a particular occasion, Mr. *Thomas Shepherd* (who afterwards went to *New-England*) with some other Ministers, and good People, spent a Night in Prayer, and had some respect to the place, serving God, to call out the Devil; and from that time, never was any such Noise heard in the Chamber. This I had from Mr. *Harlakenden*'s own Mouth; and his Servants, ear Witnesses, when I was upon the place."

So far this Account.

Another Relation in this kind, I have sent me in a Letter by an Ingenious and Learned Clergy-Man of *Wiltshire*, who had given me the Relation before, by word of Mouth. It is as follows.

"Near Eighty Years since, in the Parish of *Wilcot* (which is by the *Devizes*) in the Vicar's-House there, was heard for a considerable time, the sound of a Bell constantly tolling every Night; the occasion was this; a Debauch'd Person who liv'd in the Parish, came one Night very late, and demanded the Keys of the Church of the Vicar, that he might ring a Peal, which the Vicar refus'd to let him have, alledging the unseasonableness of the time, and that he should by granting his desires, give a disturbance to Sir *George Wroughton*, and his Family, whose House adjoyn'd to the Church-Yard. Upon this refusal the Fellow went away in a Rage, threatning to be reveng'd of the Vicar, and going sometime after to the *Devizes*, met with one *Cantle*, or *Cantlow*, a Person noted in those Days for a Wizard; and he tells him how the Vicar had serv'd him, and begs his help to be even with him. The reply *Cantel* made him was this; Does he not Love Ringing? He shall have enough of it: And from that time, a Bell began to toll in his House, and continued so to do till *Cantel*'s Death, who confess'd, at *Filherton Gaol*, in *Sarum*, (where he was confin'd by King *James* during his Life) that he caus'd that sound, and that it should be heard in that place during his Life. The thing was so Notorious, that Persons came from all Parts to hear it: And *King James* sent a Gentleman from *London*, on purpose to give him satisfaction concerning the truth of the Report."

This Relation I had from *Francis Wroughton* Esq; Sir *George's* Son, who liv'd more than Ninety Years; he never heard the sound of the Bell, being abroad at School, but he has heard it averr'd to be true, by all the Neighbours of repute; and particularly often by his Father, who was at no small Expence in Entertaining Strangers, whose curiosity led them thither. I have only this Circumstance to add, That the sound was heard only by those who were in the House, nay, if any one put his Head out of the Window, he could not hear the sound, which yet they at the same time did, who were in the Room.

The Gentleman's Name who sent me this Relation, is *Wroughton*, and is of Sir *George's* Family.

Beda, treating of the *Seven Wonders of the World*, tells us, That in the *Capital* at *Rome*, there were Statues set up for all the Provinces Conquer'd by the *Romans*, or Images of their Gods; and that on the Breasts of the Statues the Names of the Nations were written, and little Bells were hung about their Necks, and Priests were appointed to attend there Successively Day and Night, to guard those Statues, and to observe them with great Attention, whether any of them mov'd, and caus'd the little Bell to ring, by which they knew what Nation was about to rebel against the *Romans*; of which the Priests gave the *Roman* Princes Notice, who presently provided for things accordingly.

Angelus Rocca, l. de Campan. c. 6. tells us of many Bells, that were wont to sound before Persons Deaths of their own accord. Accounts of the like Nature having been given us by other Writers: And Monsieur *de L'Ancre*, in his Book intitl'd, *Of the Inconstancy of Dæmons, and evil Spirits*, tells us, That in the Town of *Bourdeaux*, there was an honest *Canon* of a Church, who had his House for some time troubl'd with Spirits, and that among other things, there was heard almost every Night a kind of Musick, like that of an *Espinette*, set with certain *little Bells*, so Pleasant, that this partly took from him the fear and apprehension of the Spirits.

Kircher, in his *Obeliscus Pamphilius*, p. 544. tells us, The *Ægyptians* thought, that by the sound of the *Sistrum*, their Priests were variously inspir'd for performing Works of Divination, which *Jamblicus* well explains, saying,

"Various kinds of Motions in the World, answer to various Orders of the Gods, and certain kinds to certain of them; now from these various Melodies flow, which likewise agree, each by their Motions, to certain Gods in Order, the Principles of those Motions. These being every where, bellow their Gifts chiefly to those that belong to them, are chiefly present to Sounds and Melodies that chiefly agree to them, and insinuating themselves into our Spirits affected with them, they posses the Man, and presently wholly Work in him by their Essence and Power."

I shall conclude this Chapter, with a Relation somewhat in this kind from *Paracelsus*; tho' how far Spirits may be concern'd in the Matter, I shall not determine.

He begins the Sixth Book of his *Archidoxes*, thus.

"No Man can deny but Compositions of Metals, may Work wonderful things in Supernaturals, which may be made good by many Proofs, as I shall clearly shew beneath; for if you Compound all the Seven Metals in a due Order and fit time, and melt them together, as it were into one Mass, you will have such Metal, in which all the Virtues of the Seven Planets are joyn'd together; you will find all these Virtues in that one Metal, which we call *Electrum*. And beneath he writes; you must know that *our Electrum* (which is Compounded of the Seven Metals) drives away all evil Spirits; for in our *Electrum*, the Operation of the Heav'ns, and Influences of the Seven Planets are stor'd up. Therefore the Ancient *Persian Magi*, and the *Chaldeans* found out and perform'd many things by its means. I cannot here conceal a very great Miracle, which

I saw wrought by a *Spanish Necromancer*, who had a Bell not exceeding two Pounds Weight, which, as often as he rung, he could cause to appear about him many Spirits and *Spectres* of various Kinds; for when he pleas'd, he drew some Words and Characters on the inward surface of the Bell, and afterwards, if he rung it, a Spirit presently appear'd in any Form he would have him: By the sound also of the said Bell he could draw to him also, or drive from him many other Visions and Spirits, and even Men and Beasts; as I saw with my Eyes many of these things done by him: But as often as he would undertake some New thing, so often he renewed his Words and Characters; but he would not reveal to me the Secret of these Words and Characters; though deeply considering the thing my self, I, at length, casually found it; which I shall not here disclose: but I plainly enough observ'd, there was more Importance in the Bell than in the Words, for the Bell was certainly made of our *Electrum*."
So far *Paracelsus*.

I may here note, That some Persons have told my self, that they have seen a constellated Plate here in *London*, made of such *Electrum*, which, if put under a Man's Pillow at Night, will make him hear Heavenly Musick.

CHAP. VI.

What perception some Persons have had of Genii, *or* Spirits, *and their Operations by the Sense of Hearing, when others present have heard nothing.*

THO' as *Ludovicus Vives* says, Good and Evil Spirits have certain Actions unknown to us, as Men have among themselves, which Brutes understand not; for as Men move each others Fancies and Minds by Words, Nods, Gestures, Letters, or Signs which surpass the Knowledge of Brutes; so Spiritual Essences may agitate our Fancy by some Action, proper, and known only to themselves, the Imaginative faculty first mov'd; yet we do not ascribe all strange things wrought by the Fancy, to the Operation of Spirits; for as the same Author says, some by the meer Action of the Fancy, seem to have got themselves posted in a state of great Happiness, as we find of him in *Horace*.

L. de Anim. c. de Cogn. Inter.

>   ———*fuit haud Ignobilis Argis,*
> *Qui se credebat miros audire Tragædos,*
> *In vacuo Latus sessor plausorq; Theatro:*
> *Catera dum vitæ, servaret munia recto*
> *More: bonus sane vicinus, ambailis hospes,*
> *Comis in uxorem: posset qui Ignoscere Servis,*
> *Et signo læso non insanire Lagenæ:*
> *Posset qui rupem & puteum vitare patentem.*
> *Hic ubi cognatorum opibus, curisque refectus,*
> *Expulit helleboro morbum, bilemque meraco,*
> *Et redit ad sese, pol, me occidistis amici*
> *Non servastis, ait, cui sic extort a voluptas,*
> *Et demptus pervim mentis gratissimus error.*
> *Nimirum sapere est abjectis utile nugis,*
> *Et tempestivum pueris concedere ludum.*

Epist. l. 2. Ep. 2.

―――― *a Gentleman of Greece*
Thought he heard Acted wondrous Tragedies
And sate, and clapt them at an open Stage,
In all things else comporting his as sage:
Good Neighbour truly, hospitable Friend,
Kind to his Wife, if Servants did offend
Would easily Pardon, not o're stirr'd to Wrath,
Could shun a Rock and Precipice in his Path;
This Man by charge and care of Friends being cur'd,
His Sense with Hellebore and good Wine restor'd,
When come t' himself, cry'd, Friends, you've kill'd m' outright,
Not saved me, thus extorting my delight.
And robbing me of my minds delusive Joys;
It's good to please us thus with abject toys,
And in fit time to allow their sport to Boys.

This Instance we find relates to the Sense of Hearing (*Horace* saying he heard Actors) when only the Person concern'd Hears, though we may probably judge he saw the Actors, as well as heard them. So *Galen* tells us, of a certain Physician, nam'd *Theophilus*, who being ill of a Fever, heard Musical Instruments continually playing in his Chamber, and being recover'd persisted still to affirm the thing real. So *Bartholin* tells us, of a Student of a Melancholick Complexion, and distracted with Grief for the Death of a Sister, who said he heard a Celestial kind of Musick.

We know its said of *Pythagoras* and *Apollonius Tyanæus*, That they heard the Harmony of the Spheres, which tho' some interpret otherwise, I know not why it may not be thought, they heard some Celestial Harmony; this having hapned to several Persons beside themselves. An Ancient contemplative Gent. now living in *London*, has told me, That for Forty Years past he had never retired to Contemplation, as he daily did, but he heard an Heavenly Musick: And I know many others who have often heard the same, as I must declare I have often heard it my self, tho' other Persons present with us at the same time, hear it not, as we do.

L. de Symp. diff. c. 3.

Cent. 7. Hist. 83.

Delrio and *Torreblanca* write, That the Hearing being vitiated, is wont to deceive us, as it happens in Persons troubled with the *Morbus Imaginosus*; of which Distemper Learned Men make two kinds, one more commonly call'd a *Frensy*, when Phantasms are repsesented to the Mind in *viable Species*: Concerning which kind you may consult *Cornelius Celsus*, and *Clælius Aurelianus*, and this belongs to the depravation of the Fancy: the other kind is called *Corybantiasmus*, which takes Sleep from the Sight, and vitiates the Ears, whereby Men seem to hear Ringings and Sounds.

<small>*Disq. mag. l. 2. quest. 27. Sect.* I. *L. de Mag. operat. c.* 15.</small>

Concerning this Disease *Scaliger* writes thus. *Corybantiasmus* is a Disease of the Imagination, which superstitious Antiquity believ'd to be sent by the *Corybantes*. It seem'd to the Persons affected with it, that their Ears were always filled with a Noise of Musick and Singing: those who labour under this Disease are troubled with Watchings, or want of Sleep, or at least with a light Sleep, having their Eyes open; for they have always their Minds intent on Images; whence those that Sleep with their Eyes open were said to act like the *Corybantes*, such having no sound Sleep, by reason of Images and Sounds. So *Varro* in *Prometheo Satyr*,

<small>*In Catull.*</small>

> *Levisomna mens sonorinas Imagines*
> *Assatur, non umbræntur somno pupilla.*

To this relates that Passage of *Plautus*, in some Comedy of his, the name of which is still in question.

> *Mecum habet Patagus æs morbus.*

Which passage, in the Notes set forth by *Gronovius* on *Macrobius* is referr'd to the *Corybantes*, or Priests of *Cybele*. *Patagus* denoting the shaking of their Heads, *Æs* the confus'd sound of Brass. Whence is that of the Poet.

<small>*L.* 5. *c.* 19.</small>

> *Nec te progenitum Cybeleius ære sonoro*
> *Lustravit Corybas* ⎯⎯ ⎯⎯

The Disease it self is called *Corybantiasmus*. To this *Claudian* seems to have alluded.

L. 1. *in Ruff.*

Impatiensq; sui Morbus ——

And *Lucretius*,

Sollicitæ porro plenæque sonoribus aures.

The word *Patagus* comes from πατάσσω, *cum Strepitu palpito, Item Percutio, ferio*: For when the Corybantes were raised in a Fury, they shak'd their Heads, Danc'd, and run against each other; striking their Brass Bucklers, and causing a ringing of Brass, not without a Rhythmical Composition of the *Dactyle Foot*; from which Foot, and Mount *Ida*, they were called *Dactyli Idæi*.

Now tho' there be such a Disease, causing Musical Sounds in the Ear, this cannot rationally be imputed to *Pythagoras*, *Apollonius*, or the Gentleman I before mentioned, and others; they not being troubled with want of Sleep, or short disturbed Sleep, nor Sleeping with their Eyes open, which are set forth as Symptoms of it.

To proceed to give an account of a perception of other Sounds by the Hearing, which by some are imputed to Spirits, by others to other Causes, we find among the superstitious observations of the Gentiles, if any Person had a Ringing in his Ears, it was taken as an Omen; and as *Pliny* says, it was usual for Persons absent to perceive that others were talking of them, by a Ringing in the Ear: and to this purpose there is an Elegant *Latin Epigram*, writ by a very ancient *Poet*; and first made publick by *Joseph Scalliger*, as he says, in his Notes on *Ausonius*

L. 28. c. 2.

C. 16.

> *Garrula quid totis resonas mihi noctibus auris?*
> *Nescio quem dicunt nunc meminisse mei.*
> *Hic quis sit, quæris, resonant tibi noctibus aures,*
> *Et resonunt totis; Delia te loquitor.*

Non dubié loquitur me Delia: mollior aura
   Venit: & exili murmure dulcè fremit.
Delia non aliter secreta silentia noctis
   Summissa, ac tenui rumpere voce solet.

Why ring all night my pratling Ear? they say
I know not who is talking now of me.
Would you know who? your ear all night does sound,
All night: It's Delia's Voice there does rebound.
It's surely Delia talks of me, a noise
Comes soft and gently, with sweet murmuring voice,
Ev'n as my Delia with soft voice delights.
To break the secret Silence of the Nights.

And as *Ælian* tells us, *Pythagoras* thought somewhat Divine lay hid in these Ringings, he saying, the sound which very often happens in the Ears, is the Voice of the *Gods*, or *Dæmons*.

Var. hist. l. 4. c. 17.

As for the way that Men perceive these Sounds and Voices, *Rhodiginus* tells us, that Socrates perceived his Spirit by Sense, not by the Sense of his Body, but, as the *Platonicks* were fully perswaded, by the Sense of the Æthe-astreal Body lying hid within us; after which way also *Avicenna* thought Angels were wont to be seen and heard by the Prophets; for the words of *Dæmons* pass every where, as *Plutarch* says; but their sound is only heard by those that keep their Minds in a calm and composed State, undisturbed by Passions, whom we call Sacred and Demonial Men: unless we had rather explain *Socrates*'s perception of his *Dæmon*, according to *Proclus*, as follows. The Voice did not come to *Socrates* passively from without, but an Inspiration of his *Dæmon* from within, proceeding throughout the whole Soul, and passing to the Organs of the Senses, a Voice at length manifested it self, as coming to knowledge, not so much by Sense, as by Consent; for such illustrations are wont to happen from good *Dæmons*, and the *Gods*. Whence *Maximus Tyrius* says, You wonder *Socrates* came to a familiarity with a

Sect. Antiq l. 2. c. 10.

L. de Dæm. Socret.

In Alcib. Plat.

Dæmon, who was as a Friendly Prophet to him, and continually so attended him, that he seem'd, as it were, Interwoven with his Mind.

L. de Deo. Socr. L. de Rero vel c. Dæmon.

So *Piccolomeni* says, *Socrates* heard the voice of his *Dæmon*, not with the Ear of his Body, but of his Mind: wherefore others did not Hear it, for it was an internal representation of the Voice to the common Sense and Fancy.

James Gohory also, who took on him the Name of *Leo Suavius*, in his Comment on a Passage in *Paracelsus, l. 5. de vita longa c. 3.* tells us of a sound that is made by the Powder of Projection in the Transmutation of Metals, (which I think is to be taken in a Spiritual Sense) of which sound he says the mystical Books of the *Spagyrists* make mention, as *Augurellus*.

Indicio est etiam sonus hinc obtusus & aure
Deprehendi haud facilis ——

He adds, The Author of *The dangerous Fountain* says, There is made a certain Melody, which sometimes ceases as it were by the Magick Art. And elsewhere, the wonderful sound of a strange Bell strikes my Ear. And *Paracelsus* himself says, *Tympanaq; nobis Anonidica reddunt*: by the word *Anonididica*, meaning gentle Anodine Sounds, composing the Mind.

L. de vit. long. c. 5.

De Rer. var. l. 15. c. 87.

Cardan writes thus: Not only in all Sneezings, but in other kinds of Presagings, there are these things to be observed; First, that it be no natural thing, but something differing from the natural; as it was in that Ringing, wherewith I was admonish'd for many Years, of any Fame or Rumour concerning me; for this was not like to a Morbous affect, which now I have sometimes experience of; for this is inward, and as it were fix'd and troublesome, Light, and coming from without, and as it were separate; moreover it shakes my whole Head, as tho' it would compel me to take notice of it; a wonderful thing truly, and almost Incredible: and it's known chiefly from this, that it's Familiar, and in a manner always happens when I am upon some business of concern; nor does it happen in Diseases. So far *Cardan*. We know the causes of common Ringings in the Ear.

Motus, longa fames, vomitus, percussio, casus,
Ebrietas, Frigus, tinnitum causat in aure.

Schol.
Salern.

But these Ringings *Cardan* speaks of, are of another nature, of which I have had a wonderful experience my self; tho' I may not express it as *Luther* does, who in his *Table Talk* tells us, that *An.* 1530, he was at *Coburg*, where he was plagu'd in such sort with a sounding and ringing in his Ears, that it was as if a Wind went out of his Head, the Devil driving it.

C. 54.

Ricoldus, in his confutation of the Law given by *Mahomet* to the *Saracens*, writes thus.

C. 13.

Mahomet being troubled with the Falling Sickness (a Disease incident to Great Men, as *Aristotle* observes in *Socrates*, *Callimachus*, and *Hercules*, to whom we may add *Scotus* and many others) least others should think him really troubled with it, still as he fell down in his Trances, say'd that an *Angel* Convers'd with him, and gave him certain Answers, with the sound of a Bell in his Ear. *Instar Campanæ auriburscrcumsonantis.*

In Prob.

Now, as for hearing sounds of Bells, I never heard of any Person, who has had so much experience in that kind as my self; tho' I know one Person, and have been well inform'd of others, who have sometimes heard the Sounds of Bells after the same manner. But in two Spiritual Visitations that have happen'd to me, some Years distance the one from the other (of which I may give some account in this Book) I have heard Bells for several Weeks together, and that of all sorts, from the greatest Church Bells, to a little Hawk's Bell. Sometimes I have heard a Church Bell gently Tolling; sometimes Bells Ringing in Peal Solemnly, as at a Funeral; sometimes Merry round Ringing, as at Weddings: For some Weeks together, every Night, as soon as I was in Bed, a Spirit came with a little Bell Ringing in my Ear, and a Voice always Talking to me, and many other varieties I have had in that kind, and that both by Day and by Night; tho' no Person present with me at the same time, has heard any thing, as they told me, upon my enquiry of them. I have heard every Night, for some time, Hundreds of Spirits, coming, as it seem'd to me, first at a great distance, Singing, and Ringing hand Bells, who gradually approach'd my House, the Sound seeming nearer and nearer, till at length they came to my Chamber Windows, and some would come into my Chamber. The first Ringing Sound I heard, was of a Bell gently Tolling at one of my Chamber Windows, which looks to the *South*; and at, the same time, at the same Window, I heard a Spirit striking gentle strokes with a small Rod, as it seem'd to me, on a Brass Pan, or Bason, tuning his strokes to a call he us'd, *Come away to me, Come away to me*; and just upon it another Spirit, at another of my Chamber Windows, which look'd to the *East*, called to me in a louder and earnest Tone, *Come away to me, Come away to me*. I shall here forbear any farther particular Account in this kind, as to my own Experience, and shall set down somewhat relating to what is said before, as to Ringing of Bells and Brass, practised by the Ancient *Gentiles*.

L. de camp. c. 3. Fast. l. 5.

Angelas Rocca, tells us, It was believed by the *Gentiles*, that the *Manes*, or rather *Dæmons* were driven away by the ringing of Brass, or Bells, as it appears from *Ovid*, where he says of the *Ghosts* or *Manes*.

> *Rursus aquam tangit, Temesæáq; concrepat æra,*
> *Et rogat ut tectis exeat umbra suis;*
> *Cum dixit novies, manes exite paterni,*
> *Respicit, & purè, Sacra peracta putat.*

> *Again he washes, rings Tempsæan Brass,*
> *And prays the Manes from his House to pass;*
> *Then Nine times Cries, Paternal Ghosts be gone,*
> *So looks about, thinks Sacred Rites are done.*

Therefore the *Gentiles* thought that by the sound of Bells, Evil, or offensive *Genii* were driven away, or restrained from giving disturbance, because the *Manes* (as *Hieronymus Magius* says) were thought to love *Silence*. Whence by the *Pœts* they were called *Silentes*, as *Ovid* says in the same Book,

> *Mox etiam lemures animas dixere silentum,*

Wherefore as often as such Ghosts have spoken, they are said to have us'd rather a low and muttering Voice, than a clear one, as *Ovid* says, *Ib.*

> *Umbra cruenta Remi visa est assistere lecto*
> *Atq; hæc exiguo murmure visa loqui.*

> *Remus, his Bloody Ghost stood by the Bed,*
> *And with low murmur these words uttered.*

In reference to this *Remigius* writes concerning such as were accus'd of Witchcraft, and converse with evil Spirits, as follows. *Nicolæ Gramatiata, Eva Hesoletia, Jana nigra Armacuriana*, and many others, say, the Spirits have such a Voice, as one that puts his Head in an Empty Hogshead, or craz'd Vessel, and therefore always in speaking hold their Heads downwards, as Persons asham'd, or self conscious of some Crime are wont to do; or at least, they have a small and weak Voice. So *Hermolaus Barbarus*, said he heard a Voice of an hissing *Dæmon*, as he answer'd himself, and *Georgius Placentinus*, asking him concerning the meaning of *Aristotle's Entelechia*. The *Elm* also, mention'd in *Philostratus*, that is, as I conceive, the *Dæmon* of *Thespion*, speaking from the *Elm*, by his command, who was the Eldest of the *Gymnosophists*, saluted *Apollonius* coming to them, with a Slender Voice. The *Lecanomancy* also of the *Assyrians* and *Chaldæans*, was wont to effect this, that the *Dæmons* deliver'd their Words from the Bason with a stridulous and low hissing. So for *Remigius*. *Dæmona. latr. l.* I. *c.* 8.

To this I may add, what *Le Loyer* writes, in his History of Spectres, *viz. Damascius* a *Pagan* Philosopher, relates, that the *Familiar Spirits* lying hid in round consecrated Bowls, which he calls *Betyles*, answer'd those that consulted them, in a small and Inarticulate Voice, that it seem'd rather an hissing, than a Speech, and had need of Interpreters. The name *Betyles* is *Syriack*, and was taken from the *Hebrews*, who call'd those Places *Bethel*, where the Patriarch *Jacob* plac'd Stones, for a Mark that he had there ador'd God; the *L.* 4. *c.* 16. *In vitâ Isidori.*

Syrians turn'd this to their Superstition, and call'd *Betyles* their *animated Stones*, or Stones in which a *God* or *Dæmon* was hid. Our Learned *Selden*, writes of those *Betyles*. *L. de Diis Syris*.

But to pass by other Relations in this kind, and to speak of my own Experience; some Spirits that convers'd with me for some Months together, had a *Low-sunk Voice*, as many Persons have in Colds, but it was without any Hoarseness, being very clearly discernable; the Spirits I heard coming to me singing in the Evenings, had clear Voices; and that Spirit which came Nightly to me for some time, with a Bell in my Ear, had a very clear and resonant Voice.

Brass, and its ringing were also us'd by the *Gentiles*, on several other Accounts, and that for the same Reason, *viz.* It's purifying Nature; concerning which *Cæl. Rhodig.* writes thus: The Interpreter of *Theocritus*, in the poet's *Pharmaceutria* writes, that Brass was thought by the Ancients to be of great Virtue in *Sacred Rites*, and Excantations, and therefore was wont to be us'd in *Eclipses* of the Moon, and at Mens Deaths, because it was thought more pure than other things, and expiatory of Pollutions; therefore they us'd it in all Purifications, as *Apollodorus* has writ, *l. de Diis*. And *Sophocles*, in his Tragedy, which is call'd *Rhizotomi*, that is, *the Cutters of Roots*, writes of *Medea* cutting Herbs with a brass Knife, and putting the Juice into brass Vessels. And *Macrobius* writes, That brass Vessels were us'd chiefly in those *Sacred Rites*, with which they would compose the Minds of Persons, or consecrate them, or Cure Diseases. And the Priests of the *Sabines*, were wont to have their Hair Cut with a Brass Knife; and it's manifest, that the most Ancient *Greeks* us'd in many things the sound of Brass, as a most Powerful thing. As for the Reason of the Ancients in giving aid to the Moon, when in an *Eclipse*, by a confus'd noise of Brass, *Alexander* gives it us thus: Men rung Iron and Brass, because they thought *Dæmons* were driven away by it, at the time that the Planets cannot convey their Influence to the Earth, which is for the Benefit of Men.

L. 19. c. 1.

Some tell us, That by the ringing Noise of Brass, the force of Magick Charms was hindred from reaching to the Moon, the Charmers Voice being confounded by it, and that by this means relief was thought to be giv'n the Moon, when in a *Eclipse*; For Brass is the most sonorous of all the Metals, it having a shrill and penetrating sound; whence *Homer* gave *Juno* the Epithet χαλκεόφωνος, and *Spondanus*, on *Homer*, thinks a most resonant Voice was aptly giv'n her, because a Voice is nothing but the Air struck, and by *Juno* is meant the Air.

Magius, says the Searchers into Natural Causes, think by the sound of Bells the violent injury of Tempests, Winds and Hail-storms is driven away, because such ringing greatly agitates, cuts and breaks the Air, which appears from hence; that when Bees rise in a Swarm, and begin to fly away, they are forc'd by a gentle ringing of Brass, the Air being cut and sever'd, and scarce bearing their flight; though some think Bees then pitch upon the Air's being moved, because they are delighted with the ringing; which I leave to the judgment of others. *L. de Tintin. c. 11.*

Apollodorus says, the Priest of *Proserpina* was wont to ring a little Bell in her Sacred Ceremonies; and the Priest of the *Syrian Goddess*, also was wont to use a little Bell, as *Lucian* writes. The Priest, after he is come to the uppermost part of the Temple, Prays for the whole Congregation; and in praying he also rings a certain little Bell. *Robertellus*, also in *Octavian Augustus*, gives testimony of this Custom, when he speaks of the Gates and tops of Temples. The top is compass'd about with Bells; the Bells were wont to hang for the most part over the Gates of Temples. *L. de Diis.*

L. de Dea Syria.

L. 19.

Fungerus, in his *Etymologicum Trilinque*, tells us, the *Hebrew* word for *Æs*, is *Nechoscheth*, from the word *Nachosoh*, that is, he made an Auguration, he has Divin'd, he has Ominated, he has had certain Conjectures. Some think the reason of the Name to be, that haply from the sound of a ringing Bell, some Observation was made in *Auguries*, *Divinations*, and the like Conjectures; and *Gronovius*, in his learned Exercitations on *Stephan*'s *Byzantinus*'s *Fragment, de*

Dodina, tells us, That because Oracles, and Divinations are denoted by the word *Nechosoh*, which signifies also Brass and *Lebetes* hence in the *Dodonæan Oracle* Brass Bells, *Lebetes* and *Tripods*, were excogitated, when only Oracles and Divinations were to be understood. Mr. *Rosse* in his View of the Religions of *Asia* will have it, that the Bells hanging at the *Pallium* of the High Priest of the *Jews*, denoted Christ's Prophetick Office, though I know other Significations are ascrib'd to it by other Writers. And *Plutarch*, *In Symposi*, introduces *Metagenes*, an *Athenian*, who, as well for other Reasons there given, as for the *Jews* High Priests wearing the said Bells, which make a noise, as he walks, will have the God of the Jews to be the same with *Bacchus*, because in their Country, in the Nocturnal Sacrifices of *Bacchus*, call'd *Nyctelia*, they made a great noise, and the Nurses of *Bacchus*, were call'd *Chalcodristæ*, as much as to say, *Scrapers of Brass*. The strong Impression made on me by the noise of Bells in my Spiritual Visitations led me to draw these things together from the Ancients, which I leave to the Readers Consideration.

CHAP. VII.

What perception Men have had of Spirits, *and their Operations by all their Senses.*

THO' the Senses of Seeing and Hearing, are the chief Senses concern'd in a Perception of Spirits, and their Operations, yet the other Senses sometimes are some way affected by them. For, as St. *Austin* says, The Evil work of the Devil creeps through all the Passages of the Senses; he presents himself in Figures, applies himself to Colours, adheres to Sounds, introduces Odours, infuses himself in Savours, and fills all the Passages of Intelligence; sometimes cruelly tormenting with Grief and Fear, sometimes sportingly diverting Man, or taunting with Mocks.

According to this Passage of St. *Austin*, Mr. *John Pordage*, in his Book writ in vindication of himself from *Necromancy*, &c. publish'd in *London*, *An.* 1655. After having set forth, that his Maid-Servant, *Elizabeth Benwel*, had depos'd before the Commissioners, that she had heard Musick in his House, when she knew not that any Instruments or Musicians were in the House; and that she had heard it in the Kitchen, and in her Mistresses Closet, and thought the same to be near her, but saw none playing: Which Fact Mr. *Pordage* does not oppose. And he there confessing, that in *August* 1649, there appear'd in his Bed-Chamber, about the middle of the Night, a Spirit in the shape of one *Everard* (whom he suspected to be a Conjurer, and to be instrumental in raising up those Apparitions which himself and others saw) with his wearing Apparel, Bands, Cuffs, Hat, *&c.* who, after his sudden drawing of the Bed-Curtains, seem'd to walk once through the Chamber very easily, and so disappear'd: And that the same Night there appear'd to him a great Dragon, which seem'd to take up most of a large Room, having great Teeth and open Jaws; whence he often ejected Fire against him, which came with such a Magical Influence, that it almost struck the Breath out of his Body; and this Apparition continued 'till the Day began to dawn, and then disappear'd. I say, having set forth this, he proceeds to declare some extraordinary things, which few had been made acquainted with, and which at that time were seen and experimented by himself, and others with him. He writing as follows:

"Our inward spiritual Eyes being open'd in an extraordinary way, two invisible internal Principles were laid open and discover'd to us, which may be call'd *Mundi Ideales*, being two spiritual Worlds, which seem'd very much differing the one from the other, as having contrary Qualities and Operations, by which they work upon this visible Creation."

He says "One of those internal Worlds may be call'd *Mundus tenebrosus*, the dark World, whose Objects, by their correspondent inward Faculties or Senses were then discover'd and made known to them. The other World, he says, may be call'd, *Mundus luminosus*, or the light World, which, with its various Objects, was then likewise open'd to their inward Senses; for beside their internal Sight, they had their other internal spiritual Faculties of spiritual Sensation, open'd to discern their various Objects within these Worlds.

1. As to the Objects of the internal Sight, when the dark Principle or World was open'd, they beheld innumerable multitudes of evil *Sprits* or *Angels*, presenting themselves in appearing distinctions of Order and Dignity. The Princes of this dark World, and their Subjects, presented themselves, as passing before their Eyes, in Pomp and State; all the mighty ones appearing to be drawn in dark aiery Clouds, Chariots with Six, or at least Four Beasts to each one; beside, every figure or similitude of a Coach was attended with many inferior Spirits, as Servants to the Princes: The Animals that drew the cloudy Coaches, appear'd in the shapes of Lyons, Dragons, Elephants, Tygers, Bears, and such like terrible Beasts. Besides, the Princes and those that attended them, tho' all in the shapes of Men, yet represented themselves monstrously misshapen, and with Ears like those of Cats, cloven Feet, ugly Legs and Bodies, Eyes fiery, sharp, and piercing. Beside these appearances within, the Spirits made

some wonderful Impressions on Bodies without; as, Figures of Men and Beasts upon the Glass-Windows and the Ceilings of the House; some of which yet remain. But what was most remarkable was, the whole visible World represented by the Spirits upon the Bricks of the Chimney, in the form of two half Globes, as in Maps. After which, upon other Bricks of the same Chimney was figur'd a Coach and four Horses, with Persons in it, and a Footman attending, all seenming to be in motion; with many other such Images, which seem'd to be wonderful, exactly done. Now, fearing lest there might be any danger in these Images, through unknown Conjuration, and false Magick, we endeavour'd to wash them out with wet Cloaths, but could not, finding them engraven in the substance of the Bricks, which indeed might have continued 'till this Day, had not fear and suspicion of Witchcraft, and some evil design of the Devil against us in it, caus'd us to deface and obliterate them with Hammers."

He adds beneath. "But to shut up this relation of the Objects we saw in this dark World, I must add this, that were but the Eyes of Men open to see the Kingdom of the Dragon in this World, with the multitudes of evil Angels, which are every where tempting and ensnaring Men, they would be amaz'd, and not dare to be by themselves, without good Consciences, and a great assurance of the Love and Favour of God, in protecting them, by the Ministration of the Holy Angels.

2. As to the Objects of the inward and outward Smell, he says, That within three Weeks space, in which these Wonders appear'd, at several times, the evil Angels, or Spirits raised up such noisome poysonous Smells, that both the inward and outward parts of those that were exercised with them, became much disturbed and offended, for through the Sympathy betwixt the Body and the Soul, the sulphurous hellish Smells much exercised both by Magical Tincturation.

3. In reference to the Objects of the *Taste*, he says, That sometimes both Night and Day they were exercis'd with the loathsome Hellish Tastes of Sulphur, Brimstone, Soot and Salt mingled together; which were so loathsome to them, that

they were like to cause great Distempers, and Nauseousness in their Bodies, had they not been supported by God, beyond their own strength.

4. In Relation to their outward and inward *Touch*, they were much exercised both in Body and Soul; as to their Souls they sometimes felt such strange and Magical Wounds, and piercings by the fiery Darts of the Devil, that none can Express them, but those that have been exercis'd in some Measure, as *Job* was. As to their Bodies they felt Material Impressions from the Powers of Darkness, very noxious, in themselves, as to their Natural Spirits, and Life, but born by them, by quiet Submission to the Will of God."

As to the Internal *Light World*. "1. There appear'd then to their inward *Sight*, multitudes almost innumerable of pure Angelical Spirits, in Figurative Bodies, which were clear as the Morning Star, and transparent as Crystal, sparkling like Diamonds, and sending forth Beams like the Sun, powerfully refreshing their Souls, and enlivening their Bodies.

2. In Relation to the inward Sense of *Hearing*, there were many Musical Sounds and Voices, like those that St. *John* heard in *Mount Sion*, the Sweetness, Harmony and Pleasantness of which cannot be express'd; nor that Spiritual Joy and Delight which by them was infus'd into their Souls, be utter'd by the Tongue, it ravishing their Spirits, into the high Praises of *Jehovah*.

3. In Relation to the faculty of *Smelling*, the Tongue can hardly express those Heavenly Odours, and Perfumes which then were smelt, piercing into the very Spirit, beside the quickning Vertue, which by them was Communicated and Insinuated into the Spirits of their outward Bodies, which like a Cordial had been able to have renew'd the strength of their Languishing Nature.

4. Their Sense or Faculty of *Tasting* was very Pleasantly entertain'd with those invisible Dews, which were sweeter than Honey; with which, instead of Food, they were many times wonderfully refresh'd.

5. In Relation to the Sense of Spiritual *Contact*, that was also delighted with its Heavenly Objects: for he says, none can utter those pleasing Impressions, which the burning Tincture of the Light World afforded them, coming like an hot Cordial into the Center of their Spirits, being sensibly felt in the inner Parts, so as to cause much Joy and Heavenly Pleasures, which penetrated through their Souls, and gave them occasion to Praise and Magnify God.

Thus, he says, for the space of three Weeks, or a Month, they were exercised inwardly and outwardly, through that great Combat that was betwixt those two Worlds, and their Inhabitants; the Dark World sometimes Afflicting them with dreadful Shapes, abominable Smells, loathsome Tasts, with other Operations of the evil Angels; the light World, at other times opening, and relieving them with Odoriferous Perfumes, most sweet Dews, Glorious Visions, and Angelical Harmony. He adds, That now for the space of 4 Years, ever since the time of these great Manifestations, they have enjoy'd the exercise of their Spiritual Senses, which were never since shut, nor would be, unless through Transgression and Disobedience, they ran back into the earthly Nature."

I have set down this Relation, in short, from Mr. *Pordage*. And as for the Truth of it, it must rely upon him, and the other Persons then concerned with him; but for my self, I have no Reason to Question the Truth of it: it being usual with those that are train'd up to a contemplative Life; to have Visitations in that kind, both Internal and External.

The learned *Walter Hilton* (a great Master of a contemplative Life) in his *Scale of Perfection*, sets forth, that Appearances, or Representations to the Corporeal Senses may be both Good and Evil Writing as follows. *L.* 1. *Part* 1. *c.* 10.

By what I have said you may somewhat understand, that Visions, or Revelations, or any manner of Spirit in Bodily appearing, or in imagining, sleeping, or waking, or any other feeling in the Bodily Sense, made as it were Spiritually, either by sounding in the Ear, or savouring in the Mouth, or smelling at the Nose, or else any sensible Heat, as it were Fire glowing, and warming the Breast, or any other part of the

Body, or any other thing that may be felt by Bodily sense, though it be never so comfortable and liking, yet are they not contemplation it self, but simple and secondary (though they are good) in respect of the Spiritual Vertues, and of this Spiritual knowing and loving of God, accompanying true contemplation; but all such manner of feeling may be good, wrought by a good *Angel*, and they may be deceivable wrought by a wicked *Angel*, when he transfigures himself into an *Angel* of Light; for the Devil may Counterfeit in Bodily feeling the likeness of the same things, which a good *Angel* may Work; for as a good *Angel* comes with Light, so can the Devil; and as he can do this in Matters of Seeing, so can he do it in Matters of the ether Senses; he that has felt both, can well tell which were good, and which were evil; but he that has never felt either, or else but one of them, may easily be deceived.

These two are alike in the manner of feeling outwardly, but they are very differing within, and therefore they are not to be greatly desired, nor to be entertain'd lightly, unless a Soul can by the Spirit of Discretion, know the good from the evil; that it be not beguil'd, as St. *John* says, *Trust not every Spirit, but try first whether it be of God, or no.* And to know whether the Representation to the Bodily senses, be good or evil, *Hilton* gives the following Rule.

1 *Joh.* 14. 1.

Chap. 11.

"If you see any manner of Light, or brightness with your Bodily Eye, or in Imagination, other than every Man sees; or if you hear any wonderful pleasant sounding with your Ear, or have in your Mouth any sweet sudden Savour, other than what you know to be Natural, or any heat in your Breast like Fire, or any manner of Delight in any part of your Body, or if a Spirit appear Bodily to you, as it were an *Angel* to Comfort you, or teach you; or if any such feeling, which you know well comes not from your self, nor from any Bodily Creature, beware at that time, or presently upon it, and wisely consider the stirrings of your Heart; for if by Occasion of the pleasure and liking you take, in the said Feeling, or Vision, you see your Heart drawn from the minding and beholding of *Jesus Christ*, and from Spiritual Exercises; as from Prayer, and thinking of your self, and your defects, or from the inward desire of Vertues, and of Spiritual knowing and feeling of God, to set the sight of your Heart, and your Affection, your Delight and your rest Principally on the said Feelings or Visions, supposing that to be a part of Heavenly Joy, or *Angels* Bliss, and thereupon come to think that you should neither Pray, nor think of any thing else, but wholly attend thereto, for to keep it, and delight your self therein, then is this Feeling very suspiscious to come from the Enemy; and therefore though it be never so liking and wonderful, refuse it, and assent not thereto; for this is a flight of the Enemy to let, and beguile the Soul by such bodily Savours, or Sweetness in the Senses, to bring it into Spiritual Pride, and Into a False security of it self, flattering it self that it had thereby a Feeling of Heavenly Joy, and that it is half in *Paradise*, by reason of the Delight it feels about it, when indeed it's near to Hell Gates, and so by Pride and Presumption it might fall into Errors, or Heresies, of Phantasms, or other Bodily or Spiritual Mischiefs.

But if it be so, that this manner of Feeling lets not your Heart from Spiritual Exercises, but makes you more devout, and more fervent to Pray, more wise to think Spiritual Thoughts; and tho' it be so, that it astonishes you in the beginning, nevertheless, afterwards, it turns and quickens your Heart to more desire of Vertues, and encreases your Love more to God, and to your Neighbour; also it makes you more humble in your own Eyes. By these Tokens you may know it is of God, wrought by the presence and working of a good Angel, and comes from the goodness of God, either for the comfort of simple devout Souls, to increase their trust and desire towards God, to seek thereby the knowing and loving of God more perfectly, by means of such Comforts: or else if they be Perfect that feel such delight, it seems to them to be an earnest, and, as it were a shadow of the glorifying of the Body, which it shall have in the Bliss of Heaven; but I know not whether there be any such Men on the Earth."

He goes on. "Of this way of discerning the working of Spirits, speaks (St. *John* in his Epistle) thus, I *John* 4. 3. *Omnis spiritus qui solvit Jesum, hic non est ex Deo, Every Spirit that looses, or unknits Jesus, he is not of God.* This knitting and fastning of *Jesus* to a Man's Soul, is wrought by a good Will, and a great desire to him, only to have him, and see him in his Bliss spiritually. The greater this desire is, the faster is *Jesus* knit to the Soul; and the less this desire is, the looser is he knit. Whatsoever Spirit therefore, or feeling it is, which lessens this Desire, and would draw it down from the stedfast minding of *Jesus Christ*, and from the kindly breathing and aspiring up to him, this Spirit will unknit *Jesus* from the Soul; and therefore it is not of God, but is the working of the Enemy. But if a Spirit, or a Feeling, or a Revelation make this desire more, knitting the knots of Love and Devotion faster to *Jesus*, opening the Eyes of the Soul into spiritual knowing more clearly, and makes it more humble in it self, this Spirit is of God.

And hereby you may learn, that you are not to suffer your Heart willingly to rest, nor to delight wholly in any such bodily Feelings, of such manner of Comforts, or Sweetness, tho' they were good; but rather hold them in your sight nought, or little in comparison of Spiritual Desire, and stedfast thinking of *Jesus*: nor shall you fast'n the thought of your Heart overmuch on them."

He goes on. "But you shall seek with great diligence in Prayer, that you may come to a spiritual Feeling or Sight of God; that is, that you may know the Wisdom of God, the endless Might of him, his great Goodness in Himself, and in his Creatures; for this is Contemplation, and that other mentioned is none. Thus, says St. *Paul*, being rooted and grounded in Charity, we may be able to comprehend with all the Saints, what is the breadth, and length, and height, and depth. That you may know, he says, not by sound of the Ear, nor sweet savour in the Mouth, nor by any such bodily thing, but that you may know and feel with all Saints, what is the length of the endless Being of God; the breadth of the wonderful Charity and Goodness of God; the height of His

Ephes. 3. 18.

Almighty Majesty, and the bottomless depth of His Wisdom. In Knowing and spiritual Feeling of these, should be the exercise of a Contemplative Man; for in these may be understood the full knowing of all spiritual things, *&c.*

I have set down these things somewhat at large from this Author, because I conceive they may be useful to some Men, who lie under spiritual Visitations of this kind. We see he supposes it no uncommon thing, for Men to have their Spiritual and Corporal Senses wrought on in this extraordinary way, and teaches how they may discern Good from Bad in such cases. I know the Contempt many Men have for Studies of this nature; but its not to those I here write: Nor is it every Man's Talent to be Master of a Contemplative Life. This Person, by a deep Inspection into the disposition of Mens Minds, in all the gradations of a Contemplative Life, had a clear view of the *Figmentum* of Man in every posture of it, and that discretion of Spirits which the Scriptures mention.

Somewhat being occasionally said before concerning the inward Senses, I shall here give you a short account of the internal Senses, according to the *Platonick Philosophy*, by the benefit of which one Man perceives what another does not.

Cælius Rhodig. tells us, That the vivifying Act of the Soul on the Vehicle, that is, on the æthereal Body, is call'd the Idol of the Soul: But you must know this, that the Ancients thought there was in this Idol a confus'd energy of the Fancy without Reason; and such Senses, that the Sight is generally propagated throughout this whole Vehicle, as likewise the Hearing; but that many do not enjoy these Senses, nor is it often, but there is in them a power of an admirable nature; so that the harmony of the Spheres is perceiv'd by them, being otherwise silent; and there is heard also a Demonical Voice, and Bodies present themselves to the Sight, if the Soul withdraws it self in the ætherial corpuscle, being, after a manner sever'd from the Clog of the terrestrial and gross Body. So its said that *Tatius*, the Son of *Mercury*, being duly expiated by *Sacred Rites*, presently cry'd out, that he liv'd now in an Immortal Body, and being carry'd aloft, he saw and

Ant. Lect. l. 17. *c.* 16.

heard wonderful things; which *Mercurius* approving, said the same was usual with himself. There are some that write, and among others the *Platonick Olympiodorus*, that *Apollonius Tyanæus*, by the power of these Senses, when he was in the City, being rais'd, as it were, on a Watch-Tower, saw and told what things were done in *Egypt*. *Plotinus* thought that the first Intellect was the first Essence, from which, and in which other Intellects are; not only by *Idea*'s, but by their proper Intellectual Existences (as I may say) of the Soul, according to an Intellectual Faculty proper to themselves, even while they are in the Body, just as Lines drawn from a Center to a Circumference, do not depart from the Center while they touch the Circumference. Hence he will have it, that the Intellect of a Prophet and of an abstracted Man, tho' it seems to be only in the *East*, may have a prospect also of what things are done in the *West*, because all Intellects are every where, and in each other; since always they are all in the single Divine Mind, which is always wholly present every where. So far *Rhodig*.

Now, as the *Pythagoreans* and *Platonicks*, who, many of them had a sensible perception of what they call'd the Harmony of the Spheres, Divine Voices, &c, set up these *Hypotheses* for explaining things of this kind so it's no wonder, that the other Philosophers, who had not such abstracted Minds, and had no sense of such things, did not set up any *hypothesis* for explaining things they had no sense of, and rejected or ridicul'd any *hypothesis* of this nature.

I doubt what I have here deliver'd may be too speculative to please all Readers; and therefore I shall not dwell upon things of this nature, but only say in general, that in all Ages, and in all Religions there have been Contemplative Persons, or such as have much spiritualiz'd themselves in the study of Divine things, for detaching Souls from the Creatures, by bringing them to an opening of their Inward Senses, to fix them on the being infinitely Perect: As the *Esseens* among the *Jews*, and the *Platonicks* among the *Pagans*, who detach'd Minds, as much as possibly they could from Matter, to fix them on Metaphysical Meditations; and this is what is chiefly driven at by *Mystical Divines* among Christians: And it must be granted, that humane Reason stands much indebted to this Philosophy; for having driven the knowledge of GOD, and of a Being infinitely Perfect, and of the sole Creator of the World, much farther than other Philosophers have done; as Monsieur *Dureux*, asserts in the beginning of his Book, Intituled, *Traiteé historique sur la Theologie mystique.*

To add some farther explanation of the way that some Persons see Spirits, when others do not, *Cardan* tells us, that *Averrhœs*, in his *Collectanea*, seems fairly to have accounted for it, saying, When the Spirit which attends the Imagination, has, by Imagining, receiv'd forms of a Sound, or of any quality for discerning by the Smell or Taste, or of a dead Man, or of a *Dæmon*; and being imbued with it, is convey'd to the Sense which corresponds to that Action, as in Odours, to the proper Instrument of Smelling; in Hearing, to the Ears; in Spectres, to the Eyes, it will necessarily Smell, Hear, and See, without any Object; for if Seeing be nought but a Perception of a Species in the *Christalloides*, whether that Species comes from the Object or not, its manifest, as often as this happens it truly sees; and so it happens that Persons see *Dæmons*, or dead Persons, being awake; and also hear Voices of Persons they know, and smell Smells, and touch, as in the *Incubi* or *Succubi*: But these things are more seldom seen than they are heard or touch'd; because in the rest of the Senses it suffices to observe one difference, and one only Spirit, convey'd to the Sense with that Image may represent this: But as in the Eyes there are more differences necessary, Magnitude, Form, Colour, of necessity more Spirits must be convey'd; and for this reason Nature has made those Nerves hollow, which pass to the Eyes, and only those so, because those in their operations stand in need of far more Spirits, than any of the other Senses in discerning. Hence arises a solution of many Problems, which tho' carrying a certain truth, yet have brought many to such streights, that some have been fain to fly to Miracle, others to *Dæmons*, others have flatly denied the Facts. As in *Island* and *Norway*, &c. they think they see some of their Family who are dead, and think they embrace

L. de Mirab.

them; and say, they vanish in their Embraces: Now, *Island* is full of *Bitumen*, and the Inhabitants live on Fruits, Roots, Bread made of Fish and Water, and it lying in the frozen Sea, by reason of its great Cold, it cannot bear standing Corn, and much less Wine: Whence the Spirits, by reason of the Food; the Air, by reason of the Soil, are very gross; therefore, by reason of the thickness of the Air, and the Vapours concerted through Cold, Images wander about, as in the Clouds, which being conceiv'd, through Error, Fear, and Thought, the dense and earthy Spirit so long retains, till it be convey'd to the Instrument of Sense; therefore they perswade themselves they see and talk with them: They think they see Persons of their Acquaintance, and such as are dead, because they know they are not there living, and because they vanish in their Embraces; but no Man has feign'd to himself an unknown Figure in the Clouds, as of a *Chimæra*, or an *Hippocentaure*; for we are all carry'd to known things. So far *Cardan*.

But after all this Philosophizing, for shewing that all our Senses may be impos'd on by Phantoms, I do not find how this any way accounts for those Apparitions which have reveal'd future or hidden things, and the like, which were not possibly discoverable by any assistance of our Sense or Reason.

CHAP. VIII.

What perception Men have had of Genii, *or* Spirits, *and their Operations by* Dreams.

TO say absolutely, that all Dreams, without any distinction, are vain Visions, and sports of Nature, the Images of things at random coming into our Minds, and possessing them while we Sleep; and to banish all Divination from the Life of Man, as *Epicurus, Meterodorus,* and *Xenophanes* did, is contrary to Experience, and the common Consent and Agreement of Mankind. So that we may argue with *Averrhœs,* in his *Paraphrase,* there is no Man but has had Dreams, which have foretold him something, and therefore they are not only the Sports of Nature, and vain Appearances. *Pliny,* a Man little credulous in matters of Faith, writes, That the cures of many Diseases, unknown before, had been discover'd in Dreams. *Porphyrius,* to explain Divine Dreams, says, That God has given to each Man two Dæmons to attend him, a good and a bad; and that the good and propitious Dæmons, foreshew us, in our Dreams, Evils to come, prepar'd for us by evil Dæmons; adding, that if any Man could rightly discern those things that are intimated to us in our Sleep, he would be freed from all Evils, and become an egregious Prophet. *Psellus l. de Dæmon:* says, That Dæmons come to those that are worthy of their Society, and give them the knowledge of future things. And the *Platonicks* deride the *Peripateticks* for referring the Works of Dæmons, as Divinations, a manifestation of occult things, and the speaking of various Tongues to Humours, and the Steams of the Earth.

L. 25.

Dion Cassius, writes thus, The cause which moved me to write this History was this: When I had writ a Book of those Dreams and Prodigies, which had given *Severus* hopes of the Principality, and had sent it to *Severus,* and he had read it, and had writ me back many kind things; after receiving his

Rom. Hist. l. 72.

Letter in the Evening, I went to Bed, and in my Sleep it was Divinely Commanded me, to write an History; wherefore I writ the things I now treat of; which proving very pleasing to *Severus* and others, I presently resolved to go through writing the whole *Roman History*. And tho' I took upon me the Composing of this History with reluctancy, and, at first, wholly rejected it, my *Goddess* encouraged me in my Sleep, and gave me good hopes that this History should never Perish; which *Goddess* I take to be the Guardianess of my Life.

The same Author concludes the last Book of his History thus, At length being taken ill in my Feet, I was dismist of all Employs, to pass all the remainder of my Life in my Country, as my *Genius* had plainly signified to me in *Bythinia*: who also once seem'd to command me, in my Dream, to add these Verses to the end of my History.

Iliad. 3.
> *From Arms and cruel Slaughters, Dust and Pain Sustained in Wars,* Jove Hector *has withdrawn.*

Cardan, tho' he had writ ten Books of Dreams, yet in his Book *De Mirabilibus*, tells us how, he was often admonish'd in his Dreams to write his One and Twenty Books *De Subtilitate*; of which the foremention'd Book is one; and he says these did not seem Dreams to him, but somewhat greater, and that his Books *De Rerum varietate* were so likewise shewn him, and that it was a property belonging to his Family, which he had both by his Fathers and Mothers side, to Dream of what would happen to him; and this he has set forth, that Men may know there is some-what in us besides our selves. There is, he says, in all Men, but it incites some to Vertue, because they will have it so, others to Murther, Poisonings, &c. what, says he, do they think the Mind of a Wicked Man to be? is Man there alone? or are there Fears, Hatreds, Suspiscions, Angers and Torments of Mind, so that when a Man has given himself over to their power, he cannot be master of himself? In all of us there are buried Seeds and Sprouts of a contrary Faction; wherefore no Man can be excited to Vertue, nor have an experience of Truth in Dreams, who overwhelms and buries that which is in him beside himself; for there are three Factions within us, Evil *Dæmons*, a clear Light, and Pleasure; wherefore true Dreams, a foresight of Futurities, and wonderful things happen even to wicked Men. I know what may be objected against me, that, forsooth, I would seem a Divine Man: Do they think me of so little Sense, that I know not Men will rather impute this as a Vanity to me, than turn it to my Praise? but the things I have seen and know, I cannot conceal, tho' it be to my extream prejudice. It's no small comfort to me, that when the same things happened to *Galen*, the same Fear, the same Suspicion, which he confest he was not Ignorant of, yet he chose rather to obey his Impulse, and not to conceal the things he knew, to the hazard of his Fame, than to mind the Glory of Men. If any Man may haply suspect me for seeking from this, an opinion of Sanctity, let him know, that no Man among the Ancients more constantly asserted the Mortality of the Soul, than *Galen*, and that I am a Sinner. Wherefore the reason of these things must be deduct elsewhere; for they belong to the Books *De Arcanis Æternitatis & de Fato*, not to the present dispute, nor are they proper for it. So far *Cardan*. And I desire this may serve for an Answer to what some Men haply may be inclined to object to my self, in reference to what I have delivered in this Book, as to any experience of my own, in this, or the like kind; for I as freely own my self guilty of many Failings, as *Cardan* did, or any other Man may.

To come nearer to our Times, *Gessendus*, in the Life of *Peireskius*, writ by himself, relates so strange a Dream which happened to him, that *Peireskius* upon telling it him more than once, said that if another Man had related it, he should not have believed him.

In his return, *Anno* 1610, in the beginning of *May*, from *Montpelier* to *Nismes*, he had in his Company one *James Rainer*, a Citizen of *Aix*, who was wont to Lodge in the same Chamber with him, and now, did so in an Inn on the Road: as *Peireskius* Slept, *Rainer* observed he muttered somewhat to himself, after an unusual manner; whereupon *Rainer*

Awakened him, and ask'd him what was the matter? Oh! said he, from what a pleasant and grateful Dream have you roused me! *Rainer* asking him, what it was? I was Dreaming, said he, that I was at *Nismes*, and that a *Goldsmith* offered me a Golden Medal of *Julius Cæsar*, for four Crowns, and I was upon paying him his Mony for it; when upon your unseasonable Awaking me, both *Goldsmith* and Medal Vanished. They went on to *Nismes*, and being there, *Peireskius* took a turn in the City, till Dinner was ready, and, by a wonderful chance, he happened on a *Goldsmiths* Shop, and asked the *Goldsmith*, whether he had any Rarity to shew him? he told him he had a *Julius Cæsar* of Gold; he asked him the Price; and was answered four Crowns, which he presently paid him, and taking the Medal; by an admirable hit of Fortune he fulfilled his Dream. It may be said admirable, for he might easily have thought of *Nismes*, where he was to be the next Morning; he might have thought of that Coin of *Julius Cæsar*, which he had often wished for, being awake; he might have thought it found in that City, in which there were so many Footsteps of *Roman Antiquities*; he might have thought, at a *Goldsmiths*, to which sort of Persons, such things found, are commonly carried; he might have thought of a small Price, at which *Goldsmiths* rather value those things, than Antiquaries; he might have thought of four Crowns, with which moderate Price a *Goldsmith* might be content. In short, a *Goldsmith*, and that at *Nismes* might have a Medal of that Price; but its altogether wonderful, that all those things should have concurr'd, and the Event answer the Dream. And nevertheless, *Perieskius* was not the Man, who, for all this, thought the cause of this Dream preternatural, as haply he might have done, if the like Dream had often happen'd; but as he knew the sports of Chance, he only accounted this among those which by their rareness are wont to create a stupor in the vulgar. So far *Gassendus*.

Amyraldus writ a Discourse in *French*, concerning *Divine Dreams*, which Discourse was Translated and Printed in English, *An.* 1678. In it this Dream of *Peireskius* is inferred, and plac'd among Angelical Dreams. I shall here give you some account of that Discourse, as follows.

The First Chapter treats of *Natural Dreams*, which he concludes thus: It's true, sometimes it happens, that some of these Dreams come to pass, which makes us think, there is some resemblance or agreement betwixt the Dream and the Event; and by consequence that some *Angel* or *Spirit* is concerned therein; but, as *Aristotle* has observ'd, This happens by meer chance, as he that without any aim should shoot a thousand Arrows, may at last by chance, hit the Mark. So in our Dreams, such an infinite number of Visions pass in our Imagination, that it's not only no Wonder, if one should sometimes chance to be true, but it would be much more strange, if once or twice, in our Life, it did not so happen; but if any of our Dreams do not only come to pass, but there also is a remarkable Agreement betwixt it and the Event, and such as we ought necessarily to suppose the Operation of an Intelligent Agent to Intervene, we ought not then to reckon this among Natural Dreams, but to refer it either to God, or to some Action of Angels.

His Second Chapter treats of *Angelical Dreams* in general, with some Reflections on particular Dreams; he says, There are two sorts of Dreams, which we may impute to *created Intelligences*; one where the things signify'd are contain'd in symbolical and mysterious Representations, the other where they are propos'd naked, without any such resemblances. The common Rule of interpreting the former, he says, is to observe the Agreements which are betwixt the Dreams, and their Events; and some of these Dreams regard present, others future things; of both which he gives Instances. Those other Dreams which propose things nakedly, as they are in themselves, have no need of an Interpreter to understand them, but when the Event confirms them they are not the less wonderful, as the Dreams of *Peireskius*, and others which he mentions.

The Third Chapter treats of *Divine Dreams*, which are also of two sorts, one contains Future things, under enigmatical and mysterious Representations, the other are much more plain and naked; of both which he gives Instances. Concerning *Divine Dreams*, in general, he makes three Enquiries. 1. Why God has sometimes reveal'd himself in Dreams to his Servants. 2. How they could certainly know that those Dreams had God for their Author. 3. Whether this way of Revelation by Dreams be yet praised, and whether God does still make use of it, under the Dispensation of the Gospel. The first of these Questions is treated of in this Third Chapter, where he says, That as God made use of various means to reveal himself to the Prophets, and by them to others, so there is no reason why he should have excluded that of Dreams; and there is yet this farther reason, in particular, for them above the others, that though there be a great deal of Vanity in ordinary Dreams, and that those which proceed from Angels have very often much uncertainty, and ambiguity, and that some Philosophers, as *Aristotle* and others, suppos'd no regard to be had to that way of Divination, yet it has always been almost the universal Opinion of all Nations, that the Divine Being did principally communicate it self to Men by Dreams; and generally this Opinion in the Eastern Nations had a very great Reputation; so that it was Principally in those Nations, that they have reduc'd the Interpretation of Dreams into an Art, and have laid down Rules concerning it: and because the People of *Israel* were also of the same Opinion, God chose to send them such Dreams, as were truly Divine, thus to fix them to these; and so divert them from that Vanity, to which other Nations suffer'd themselves to be carryed by those others. Beside, the Church being then in her Infant State, the People were more easily instructed by Dreams, than by other ways, in which there was need of more clearness and strength of Understanding.

The Second Question, concerning the Characters by which we may know Dreams truly Divine, from vain Delusion, is treated of in his Fourth Chapter, where he would have first note, That among these Dreams that proceed from the

Operations of Angels, there may also be found Divine ones, inasmuch as God does not only permit, but may command the Impression of them; but those he properly calls Angelical Dreams, are meerly such as neither the Formation of the Images exceeds their Power, nor is the knowledge of the things which these Images represent above their Intelligence, nor above the quickness of their Conjectures and Divination. He calls some Dreams, *Divine*, because whether it were that God employ'd Angels to convey them, or whether they are immediately caus'd by himself, the things signifyed by them far exceed the Natural capacity of an Angels understanding; so that it was absolutely impossible they should ever attain to the Knowledge of them, but by a particular Revelation; therefore those Dreams may be reputed to come from God, which by what Messenger soever they are conveyed, yet contain such things as God only is able to know and reveal. As for the Marks of *Divine Dreams*, he says, it's certain that *Moses*, and others had some certain Marks which absolutely determin'd them to set upon such Actions as they did, though others might not know wherein those Marks did consist; he observes that God Rules in the Understanding of Wise and Vertuous Men; and powerfully inclines it to a Belief and Resolution, though it does not see in the object reasons, altogether proportionate to the effect it feels in the Soul; so that the extraordinarily determination of the Understanding is an evident Proof of the Divinity of the Dream.

The Third Question, *viz.* Whether God makes use of this kind of Dreams, now under the Dispensation of the Gospel, is treated of in his Fifth Chapter, where he says, That as for those *Divine Dreams*, which are designed to foretel things to come, under the Emblem of an Allegorical Representation, or to convey some new commands to Men in order to some great and extraordinary Design, for which there is need of Divine Authority for the undertaking and executing of it, he conceives that time is wholly expir'd, and those who pretend to, and boast of any such, are either Impostors, who would abuse the World by their feign'd Visions, to serve their own private Interest, or Fools, who have their Brains disturb'd by

Hypochondriacal Vapours; and here he delivers his Thoughts concerning a certain kind of People of both Sexes, who both in *Poland* and *Germany* have pretended to Divine Visions in these latter Days; he does not accuse them of Imposture, they having given a sufficient Experience of their Piety, but affirms, That in their Actions they had some transport of Understanding, which proceeded from some other Cause, than what was truly Divine. They were Persons that gave themselves extraordinarily to the reading of the *Apocalypse*, and the other Prophesies; and their Spirits were so possess'd with the Ideas of those things they there saw, where future Events were represented to them, that they perswaded themselves, their very Dreams, and the things they imagin'd they saw in those Extasies they sometimes fell into, were Real and Divine Visions; and what contributed to this belief, was, that they suffer'd themselves to be carryed away by the hopes of those, who expect in due time, a Prosperity of the Church of God on Earth, and a terrible Subversion of all those States and Powers which now oppose the Establishment of Christ's Kingdom: And as they zealously desired this, they easily imagin'd it to be certain and indubitable; divers Texts of Scripture also having some seeming appearance of some such Promises made to the Church of Christ: Beside the Melancholick Humour which was naturally predominant in them, the Afflictions, Hardships, and Anxieties they underwent, as well from the publick Affairs, as their own private Concerns made them very ready to receive all Impressions of Fancy, which might shew them any hope of Deliverance, or any mitigation of their Troubles; be it then that either they Dreamt, or that waking, they were surpriz'd with some transport of Fancy, in which their Soul was perfectly abstracted from the Body, and from all Commerce with their Senses (as this sometimes happens in Hypochondriacal Distempers) these Apocalyptical Images were thus put into a violent motion, and fram'd in their Imaginations those pretended Visions, which they have since related to us; though we have seen, in great part, by Experience, that those Images which they saw in their pretended Enthusiasms, either signified nothing at all, or if they did, yet their vanity and falseness have been confuted by the Events.

He subjoyns here a Reflexion on those are called *Quakers*, for boasting of Visions, Revelations, Divine Inspirations, extraordinary Gifts of the Spirit, of Extasies and strange Transportations; who by their tremblings and quakings would represent the Motions of Enthusiasts and Prophets; and he tells us, the Spirit of Christ is a Spirit of Understanding and Prudence, and of a sober and well settled Sense, and not a Spirit which fills empty Brains with Dark and Phantastical Imaginations, nor exposes the true Religion to the Laughter of its Enemies, and to the scandal of Sober and Intelligent Men, by its indecent, and unnatural Motions.

As for those Dreams which may proceed meerly from the Impression and Operation of *Angels*, both good and bad, he says, he will not deny but there may be yet some Examples of that kind to be seen; and though the Dispensation of the Law, under which good Angels were more especially Employed in things relating to Religion, be now pass'd, yet they continue still to be Ministers and Instruments of Divine Providence in what relates to civil Life and humane Society, and especially the Protection of the Faithful, and the Defence of the Church of Christ. And as it is not impossible, but they may sometimes appear to Men waking, so it is not incredible but God may make use of them, from time to time, to convey to Men the notices of some things by Dreams; he says, there are many Examples of both kinds in the Books of those who have made Collections of them, to which Books he refers the Reader; but gives us one Instance of Monsieur *Calignan*, Chancellor of *Navarre*, a Man of singular Vertue; who being at *Bearne*, one Night, as he lay asleep, heard a Voice which call'd him by his Name, *Calignan*; Hereupon awaking, and hearing no more of it, he imagin'd he Dreamt, and fell asleep again; a little after he heard the same Voice, calling him in the same manner, which made a greater impression on him than before, so that being awaken'd, he call'd his Wife, who was with him, and told her what had happen'd; so that they both lay waking for some time, expediting whether they might hear the Voice again, at last the Voice awaken'd him a third time, calling him by his Name, and advised him to retire presently out of the Town, and to remove his Family, for that the Plague would rage horribly in that place within a few Days; he followed the direction, and within a few Days after the Plague began in the Town, and destroyed a great number of People. Now, the Author says, whether the Plague came by the Infection of the Air, or by some Infectious Persons, or whether some Sorcerers and Witches, (as they say they sometimes do) diffus'd their Infectious Poysons in that place, neither exceeded the knowledge of the Angels that spake to him. He next relates a Dream as strange which happen'd to *Lewis de Bourbon*, Prince of *Conde*, and, in his Conclusion, he says, there is need of great Circumspection to Judge of these Nocturnal Visions; if any such Dream induce us to a good Action, and from whence there can follow no bad Event, such a Dream ought not to be suspected by us; but if it prompts us to evil, we ought absolutely to condemn, and reject it, as a Delusion of the Devil. So far *Amyraldus*.

Melancthon, l. de Anima, writes concerning the Nature of Dreams, as follows. I shall not follow the Ambages of Natural Philosophers, who striving to refer Dreams of all kinds to Natural Causes, ad foolishly; but I find four kinds of Dreams.

The First is of vulgar Dreams, which may be call'd Natural, because, the Natural and immediate Causes of them are in view, as when Images are presented of those things, which we think on being awake; or when Dreams answer to certain Humours; a redundancy or agitation of which moves the Imagation, or Spirits.

The Second kind I call presaging, which nevertheless is not *Divine*, but as by a Natural temperament, or peculiar property, or by a Natural Gift, one Person is more Musical than another, or has a greater Activity of Body, *&c.* so by a Natural Gift or property, many have presaging Dreams, painting forth future Events, as it were by certain Allegories. So *Pontanus* tells us, That a certain Soldier at *Genoa*, Dreamt he was devoured by a Serpent, wherefore on a Day, when the other Soldiers were put on board Ships to Fight with the Enemy, he kept himself at home; but a tumult casually arising in the City, he was kill'd by the Ball of a sort of Canon, which we call a Serpent. This kind of Dreams has not an apparent cause in the Motion, or Plenty of the Humours, or the first Qualities, as we said of the first kind, but there are certain presaging Natures, call'd by *Aristotle*, *Loquaces Naturæ*, that have frequent signifying Dreams; nor shall I be against it, if any Men shall contend, that the cause of this property is the excellency of the temperament, as Astrologers will have it; but those are idle who deliver ways of explaining them, and seek Causes in the Motion of Humors.

The Third kind is *Divine*, which God sends into Minds, either by himself, or by *Angels*; such as the Scriptures tell us were divinely sent, and these only are to be rely'd on, as certain, the others being all fallacious.

The Fourth kind is *Diabolical*, as when Witches (as it seems to them) are present at Feasts and Sports, when it has been often known by experience, that they never went to them, but as they lay Sleeping, signified by their Gestures and Cries, that they Dream'd of Feasting and Dancing. Of this kind have been many Superstitious Dreamers of Former Ages, and in these our Times we have heard of many Fanatical Dreams of *Anabaptists*, Commanding Crimes, and Confirming Errors; which are easily judged of by Pious and Prudent Persons.

Sennertus, in *Epit. Phys. l. 7. c. 9.* writes thus. To *Supernatural Dreams* we refer all those which are sent us from Superiour Causes, and External to us, be they from God, Angels or Devils. Those that are sent from God and Good Angels, are especially called Divine, whereof there are some instances in the Scriptures: for God is wont either to present new Species to Men in Dreams, or, so to order and conjoyn those that are in Men before, that they are signs of future things; and Angels are wont to stir up and aptly dispose those Species, Spirits and Humours that are in the Body, that they admonish Men of good and necessary things. And Diabolical Dreams are caused the same Way, as by Angels, but for a different end, *viz.* the Destruction of Men.

From these things it appears, how even absent and future things may be presented to us by our Dreams. The *Platonicks* think many Dreams may be referr'd to their *Genii* and *Dæmons*, which they think attend all particular Persons, and conclude, that they admonish them of many things; but our Divines much more rightly refer them to Angels, which attend each Man. To which we may add what *Tertull.* writes, *viz.* The gift of Divine Dreams descends ev'n on Prophane Persons, God equally affording Rain and Sunshine on the Just and Unjust: Since ev'n *Nebuchadnezzar* had a Dream sent him by God. And as the favour of God reaches even the *Pagans*, so the temptation of the Devil does the Saints, from whom he is never absent, that he may steal upon them unawares, when a Sleep, if he cannot prevail with them when awake.

L. de Anim.

He there further Philosophizes concerning Dreams, as follows.

Because in Dreaming Persons the Fancy is employed, and some Fantasm is presented to it, and we do not Dream only of those things which we have done in the Day, or of those things which lye hid in the Body, but also of those things which are at a vast distance from us, and which we have neither seen, heard, nor perceived by any Sense; nay, of those things which are not yet in being, but to come afterwards, its queried how the Images of things absent, and never perceived by the Senses, and which are not yet in being, can be presented to the Fancy? The *Epicureans* suppose that Images, which fly to and fro, and wander in the Air, are the causes of this thing. *Rhodig. Lect. Antiq. l. 27. c.* 11. denies those Images, but contends there are certain Motions, which exercise us instead of Images; and that those Motions proceed from certain beginings of those things, which are shortly after to be said, or done by us, the Air first chang'd, and then being conveyd through the passages of the Ears and Nostrils to the Heart, cause, that we seem to foreknow the events of future things; and these motions cannot at any time, bring a more ample sense of themselves, than in the Night. But how can there be motions of things that are not yet in being? or how can things absent Fifty, or an Hundred Miles presently affect the Air? or why do not those Motions affect all Persons indifferenly asleep in their way, but only those whom it concerns to know that thing? We refer all those Dreams which we have concerning things, that we never perceived before by Sense, or from causes that do not lye hid in our Body, to a Divine operation.

Quercitan Philosophizes of Supernatual Dreams thus: *L. de Diæt.* Supernatural Dreams are in the middle betwixt Divine and Natural; in regard their causes are neither referr'd Immediately to God, nor to the malignity of evil Humours, on which the rise of Natural Dreams depends; but to our Soul, which is awake, the Body sleeping; and which being stirr'd up by a certain Supernatural Rapt, especially the good *Genius* Inspiring, represents to us by Dreams and Visions, many Fantasms, which, for the most part, Presage somewhat certain, the certitude of which is commonly known by the event of things; many Instances of those Dreams occur, where it has oftem seemed to Persons in Dreams, that they fall into some Disease, or recover of it, to which Visions the Event afterwards answer'd to all things, that they had seen before in their sleep; though they were not desir'd nor sought for, as Diabolical Dreams are wont to be sought for. *Arnoldus de Villa Nova* Dreamt, That he was bit in the Foot by a Black Cat, the next Day there broke out in that part of his Foot a Cancerous and Malignant Ulcer. So far *Quercitan.*

So *Simlerus* tells us, in the Life of *Gesner,* That *Gesner* on a Night Dreamt, that he was bit by a Serpent, and the next Morning said, that he should be seiz'd with a Pestilential Carbuncle: a few Days after a Carbuncle appear'd in his left Pap, five Days before he dyed.

To procceed now to give some farther Instances of Dreams from other Authors. *Fracastorius* tells us, That *Marcus Antonius Flaminius,* being at *Genoa,* and somewhat indisposed in his Health, borrow'd a Book of a Friend, to divert him; which having read some Days, he chanc'd to leave it on a Couch, with some other Books, and that when the Person that lent it, came for it, it could by no means be found. In the Night time he saw, in his Dream, a Maid Servant of the House, take the Book from the Couch, and as she was laying it on a Table, the Book chanc'd to fall on the Ground, and one side of the Cover was broken, and the Maid hid it, for fear, in a secret place. *Flaminius* rising in the Morning, and remembring his Dream, sought for the Book and found it in that place, and charging the Maid Servant with what was done, she confess'd that all pass'd as he had said.

Celsus Mancinius of *Ravenna*, has writ an Ingenious Tract, intitl'd, *De Somniis, & Synesi per Somnia*, viz. of Dreams, and a sagacious perception of things by Dreams, in which he has inserted the Dream before set down. In his Work he has set forth the Opinions of the most Famous Philosophers concerning the Causes of Dreams; and though he allows the Divine and Angelical Dreams recorded in the Scriptures, yet for all other wonderful Dreams, he thinks a reason may be rendred of them according to the Doctrine of *Aristotle*, viz. as casually hapning. He gives Instances of many strange Dreams, and among others of that of *Flaminius*, and explains them all according to Aristotles Doctrine. In his 19th Chapter, he says, Its known that those who apply themselves to Philosophy, and other Arts and Sciences, in their sleep, by the help of a Powerful Imagination, a recent exercise, and a strong Attention of Mind, Discourse, find out and do many things which they had not done, nor were able to find out, waking; and he says, *Flaminius* saw those things in his Dream, because being troubl'd about the Book he had borrowed, and much concern'd, that he could not restore it, he began to think where the Book might be found; he did not Judge it stol'n, but seeing other Books remov'd from one place to another, *viz.* from the Couch to the Table, he began to consider who had done it; as he thought of this, no one could occurr to him more readily, nor more suspected than the Maid Servant, that constantly attended him. That Servant was doubtless free from any Suspicion of Theft; for the Book was not likely to yield her much Money, or to be of any use to her; therefore he must conclude within himself, that in carrying the Books from the Couch to the Table, that Book casually fell and broke its cover; and because People are wont to hide their Faults, or at least to lessen them by some excuse, that simple Maid fearing chiding, or beating, or lest some ill might follow, wisely to avoid all, hid the Book in the most secret place she could, as behind a Chest, or some like place. Having discourss'd these things by Night, in his sleep, and found upon waking in the Morning, remembring his Dream, he try'd whether it were true, and found all things exactly to answer his Dream. He explains other strange Dreams after the same manner, according to *Aristotle*'s Opinion, as casually hapning, by a lucky hit of the Mind, in its improv'd way of reasoning in our Sleep.

But I doubt this way of explaining will not do in all Cases, but we must often have recourse to the Direction of some Superior Intelligences.

Mr. *Cotton Mather*, in his *Ecclesiastical History of New England*, writes thus, Within a Fortnight of my writing this, a Physician, who sojourned within a Furlong of my House, for three Nights together, was miserably disturbed with Dreams of his being Drown'd; on the third of these Nights his Dreams were so troublesome, that he was cast into extream Sweats, by strugling under the imaginary Waters: With the Sweats yet upon him, he came down from his Chamber, telling the People of the Family what it was that had so discomposed him. Immediately there came in two Friends, that asked him to go a little way with them, in a Boat, upon the Water: he was, at first, afraid of gratifying them in it, but being very calm Weather, he recollected himself, why should I mind my Dreams, or distrust Divine Providence? he went with them, and before Night, by a Thunder Storm suddenly coming up, they were all three Drown'd. Mr. *Mather* says, he enquir'd into the truth of this Relation, just as he writ it, and could assert it.

L. 6. c. 9. Example 12.

So again, *Camerarius* tells us in the Life of *Melancthon*, that *Gulielmus Nessenus*, on a Day after Dinner, in a gentle Sleep he had Dreamt that he was passing a River in a Fisher Boat, (as he usually did for his Diversion) and that the Boat striking on the Trunk of a Tree, was overturned, and he was Drowned. This Dream he told to *Philip Melancthon*, who then casually came to see him, deriding withal the Vanity of Dreams; but that same Evening what he had Dreamt came to pass.

Mr. *William Smythies*, Curate of St. *Giles's Criplegate. An.* 1698, published an account of the Robbery and Murther of *John Stockden, Victualler*, in *Grub-street*, within the said Parish, and of the Discovery of the Murtherers, by several Dreams of *Elizabeth*, the Wife of *Thomas Greenwood*, a Neighbour to the said *Stockden*: An Abstract of which Account, I give you as follows.

Mr. *Smithies*, first telling us, that none can doubt but great Discoveries have been made by Dreams, who read the Life of Sir *Henry Wotton*; and our *English* Chronicles (particularly the Murther of *Waters*, and the Discovery of it by a Dream, recorded by Sir *Richard Baker*, in his Chapter of Casualties, in the Reign of *James* the First) and other Histories; he says, Mr. *Stockden* was Robb'd and Murthered by three Men, in his own House, on the 23^d day of *December*, 1695. about Midnight. A little after the Murther, there came a Woman into the Street, and said, she believed one *Maynard* to be one of the Murtherers, because she was informed he was full of Mony, both Silver and Gold; upon which there was a Warrant against him; but he could not be found. Soon after this *Stockden* appear'd to *Elizabeth Greenwood*, in a Dream, and shew'd her an House in *Thames-street*, near the *George*, and told her, that one of the Murtherers was there; she went the next Morning, and took one *Mary Buggas*, an Honest Woman, who lived near her, to go with her to the Place to which her Dream directed, and asking for *Maynard*, was inform'd that he Lodg'd there, but was gone abroad. After that *Stockden* soon appeared, again to Mrs. *Greenwood*, and then representing *Maynard's* Face, with a flat Mole on the side of his Nose (whom she had never seen) signified to her, that a *Wire-drawer* must take him, and that he should be carried to *Newgate* in a Coach. Upon enquiry they found out one of that Trade, who was his great Intimate, and who, for a reward of Ten Pounds, promised him on his Taking, undertook it, and effected it. He sent to *Maynard* to meet him, upon extraordinary Business, at a Publick House, near *Hockley in the Hole*, where he Played with him till a Constable came, who apprehended him, and carried him before a Magistrate, who Committed him to *Newgate*, and he was carried thither in a Coach.

Maynard being in Prison, confest the horrid Fact, and discover'd his Accomplices; who were one *Marsh*, *'Bevel* and *Mercer*, and said, that *Marsh* was the setter on, being a near Neighbour to *Stockden*, who knew he was well furnished with Mony and Plate; and though *Marsh* were not present at the Robbery, yet he met to have a share of the Booty. *Marsh* knowing or suspecting that *Maynard* had discoverd him, left his Habitation. *Stockden* appear'd soon after to Mrs. *Greenwood*, and seem'd by his Countenance to be displeas'd: he carried her to an House in *Old-street*, where she had never been, and shew'd her a pair of Stairs, and told her that one of the Men lodg'd there; the next Morning she took *Mary Buggas* with her to the House, according to the direction of the Dream, where she asked a Woman, if one *Marsh* did not Lodge there? to which the Woman replyed that he often came thither. This *Marsh* was taken soon after in another place.

After this Mr. *Greenwood* Dreamt that *Stockden* carried her over the *Bridge*, up the Burrough, and into a Yard, where she saw *Bevil*, the third Criminal (whom she had never seen before) and his Wife: upon her telling this Dream, it was believed that it was one of the Prison Yards; and thereupon she went with Mrs. *Footman* (who was *Stockden*'s Kinswoman and Housekeeper, and was Gagg'd in his House when he was Murthered) to the *Malshalsea*, where they enquired for *Bevil* and were inform'd, that he was lately brought thither for Coining, and that he was taken near the *Bankside*, according to a Dream which Mrs. *Greenwood* had before of his being there; they desired to see him, and when he came, he said to Mrs. *Footman, Do you know me?* she replyed, I do not; whereupon he went from them: Mrs. *Greenwood* then told Mrs. *Footman*, that she was sure of his being the Man, whom she saw in her Sleep. They then went into the Cellar, where Mrs. *Greenwood* saw a lusty Woman, and privately said to Mrs. *Footman*, that's *Bevil's* Wife whom I saw in my Sleep: they desired that *Bevil* might come to them, and first put on his Periwig, which was not on the time before; the lusty Woman said, why should you speak with my Husband again, since you said you did not know him? he came the second time, and said, Do you know me now? Mrs. Footman replyed, No; but it proceeded from a sudden Fear, that some Mischief might be done to her, who had very narrowly escaped Death from him when she was Gagg'd; and as soon as she was out of the Cellar, she told Mrs. *Greenwood*, that she then remembred him to be the Man. They went soon after to the Clerk of the Peace, and procured his removal to *Newgate*, where he confest the Fact, and said, *To the Grief of my Heart, I Killed him.*

Mrs. *Greenwood* did not Dream any thing concerning *Mercer*, who was a Party concern'd, but would not consent to the Murther of *Stockden*, and preserved Mrs. *Footman's* Life; nor has there been any discovery of him since, but he is Escaped, and the three others were Hang'd.

After the Murtherers were taken Mrs. *Greenwood* Dreamt that *Stockden* came to her in the Street, and said, *Elizabeth, I Thank thee, the God of Heaven Reward thee for what thou hast done.* Since which she has been at quiet from those Frights, which had much Tormented her, and caused an alteration considerable in her Countenance.

This Relation is Certified by the *Lord Bishop of Gloucester*, who, with the then *Dean of York*, the *Master of the Charterhouse*, and Dr. *Alix*, had the Particulars of the foregoing Narrative, from Mrs. *Greenwood* and Mrs. *Buggas*.

When Dr. *Harvey* (who was afterwards *Fellow* of the *College of Physicians in London*) being a Young Man, went to Travel towards *Padua*, he went to *Dover*, with several others, and shew'd his Pass, as the rest did, to the Governour there. The Governour told him, that he must not go, but he must keep him Prisoner; the Doctor desired to know for what reason, how he had Transgress'd; he said, it was his will to have it so; the Pacquet Boat hoisted Sail in the Evening (which was very Clear) and the Doctor's Companions in it. There ensued a terrible Storm, and the Pacquet Boat, and all the Passengers were Cast away. The next day the sad News was brought to *Dover*, the Doctor was unknown to the Governour, but by Name and Face; but the Night before the Governour had a perfect Vision, in a Dream, of Dr. *Harvey*, who came to pass over to *Calais*; and that he had a warning to stop him. This the Governour told the Doctor the next day, and the Doctor told this Story to several of his Acquaintance here in *London*. This Relation I took from Mr. *Aubrey*'s Miscellanies: and I think it hard (I may say impossible) to account for this Dream, and that of Monsieur *Calignon*, before set down, by any occult way of improv'd Reasoning in our Sleep.

Claude de Tisserant, a *Parisian*, Printed an *History of Prodigies, An.* 1575. where he writes, That the Wife of one of the Chief of the Parliament of *Provence*, Dreamt that her Husband was Executed, as he really was, in the City of *Paris*, and at her Awaking, found her Hand so stiff, that she could not ply it, and in it was the Image of her Husband represented, with his Head Cut off, the said Image being all Bloody; this Image having been seen by many Persons yet alive, it not being above 20 Years since the thing happen'd.

Alex. ab Alexand. tells us, That an Ingenious Young Man, who lived with him, he having the care of his Education, saw, in his Dream, his Mother carried in a Funeral, to be Interr'd; whereupon he fell into great Sighs and Lamentations, whom *Alexander* caused to be awaken'd, and then ask'd him why he so Lamented? he answered, his Mother was Dead, and in his Sleep, he saw her carrying to be Buried. *Alexander* observed the day and time that this Vision happen'd; a little while after, a Messenger came to him with the News of his Mother's Death; of whom asking the day, it happened he found she

Gen. Dier. l. 1. *c.* 11.

died the same day that the Vision was seen. By which Example, he says, with others of the like kind, we are prompted to believe that God has given us Divinatory Spirit, and Prophetick Foresight of future things, in our Dreams.

<small>Synes. Somn. l. 4. c. 20.</small>

Cardan writes thus, *Joannes Maria Maurosenus*, a Senator of *Venice*, my particular Friend, while he was *Prætor* in *Dalmatia*, saw in his Dream, one of his Brothers, whom he much lov'd, Embrace him, and bid him farewel, because he was going to the other World. *Joan. Maria* having followed him a little way Weeping, awak'd all in Tears, and was in a great fear for his Brother at *Venice*. On the third day Letters were brought him from home, signifying that his Brother (for that was his Name) died on that night and hour, after he had lain three days Sick of a Pestilential Fever. This he related to me more than once, with Tears in his Eyes.

The same Author writes in the next Paragraph, That *Ludovicus Modius*, his Countryman, had a Soldier Sleeping in a Chamber, who on a certain Night cry'd out in his Sleep, his Master ask'd him. What ayl'd him? he answered, That he Dreamt he had received a great Wound in the Head, and that he was upon Dying, and therefore he awak'd in a Fright; his Master, who Loved him, commanded him not to stir out of Doors: mean while, his Companions, the next day, had a mind to visit the Enemy; he forgetting his Dream, goes forth with them; the Enemy appearing, his Companions Fled, and he was Slain, his Head being Cloven asunder.

He there tells us also, That *M. Anton. Taurelus* was admonished by a Dream, wherein he saw himself a Drowning, whereupon he resolved not to go a Swimming that day, but forgeting his Dream, and returning to his Swimming, he was Drown'd.

S. Austin tells us. That one *Præstantius* desired a Solution of a Doubt of a Philosopher, which he refused to give him; the night following *Præstantius* being awake, saw this Philosopher stand by, and solve the Doubt, and presently to go away. *Præstantius* meeting him the next day, ask'd him, why having refused to solve the Question the day before, he came to him at midnight, of his own accord, and Solv'd it: to which the Philosopher reply'd, *I came not truly, but in my Dream I seem'd to do this to you.*

Magnenus, in his *Exercitations on Tobacco*, says, such Dreams as these happen, for that the Person that Dreams representing to himself such a Man, endeavours to produce a sense of things not beneath the authority of that Man, or the Idea he has of him; hence, sometimes, they have such Conceptions, which are owing, not to themselves, but to the reputation of so great a Man. Wise *Epictetus* very well knew this, who commands that our Mind be raised by some Man of great Repute, which we may propose to our selves to be Imitated, and may hear and behold him as present: *Propose to your self,* says he, *what* Socrates, *or* Zeno *would do in such a Case. Enchri. c.* 5.

^{Exer. c. 6.}

He adds beneath; That Sagacious Vertue which exerts it self in Man, freely discovers it self by an Instinctual Impetus, and I have often perceived in my Sleep, what exactly fell out the next day: So when I have gone to Sleep with a fixed thought on a Person Sick, a meet Remedy has been represented to me in my Dream, which nicely weighing in my Judgment the next morning, I have thought it Excellent, and given it with great Success. I had read the same had happen'd to *Hippocrates* and *Galen*, but doubted of its Truth; but I have found by my own experience that a Nature prone to a Business, finds most compendious ways for it, which others scarce ever, attain, *Invita Minerva*; as *Ptolomy* says *Cent.* 4.

Galen tells us, That Women, while they are with Child, often see their Childrens Fortunes in their Sleep, and that *Cypsalis*, and *Pericles* began to be formidable to *Greece*, from the Womb. Here *Cardan* adds, The Soul seems then to be most pure, as it newly comes from Heaven, and to foresee and shew future things to Parents.

In the Life of the late Sir *Henry Wotton*, we find an account of a Dream of his Father *Thomas Wotton*, Esq; as follows. A little before his Death, he Dreamt, that the University of *Oxford* was Robb'd by Townsmen, and poor Scholars, and that the Number was Five; and being that day to write to his

Son *Henry* at *Oxford*; he thought it worth so much pains, as by a Postscript to his Letter, to make a slight enquiry of it. The Letter was writ out of *Kent*, and came to his Sons hands the very morning after the night, in which the Robbery was committed; for the Dream was true, and the Circumstances, tho' not in the exact time; and when the City and University were both in a perplext Inquest of the Thieves; then did Sir *Henry Wotton* shew his Fathers Letter; and by it, such light was given to this work of darkness, that the Five Guilty Persons were presently Discovered and apprehended, without putting the University to so much trouble, as the Casting of a Figuer.

We are also told in the next Paragraph, That the said *Thomas Wotton*, Esq; and his Uncle *Nicholas Wotton*, who was Dean of *Canterbury*, both foresaw and foretold the days of their Deaths.

Selneccerus tells us in his *Calendar*, concerning *Christian* King of *Denmark*, That he foretold his Death; both to his Chaplain M. *Paulas Noviomagus*, and to *D. Cornelius* his Physician. *Jacobus Scutellarius*, a Famous Astronomer of *Prague*, Physician to the Emperour *Rodolphus* the Second; had a foreknowledge of his Death eight days before it happen'd, and affirm'd for certain, he should Die on the 10th of December, *An.* 1589. That Famous Astronomer *Leonardus Thurnisser* certainly foreknew the day of his death, made his Will, and commanded his Landlord that he should Bury him by the side of *Albertus Magnus*, which was done. He Died the 9th of *July, An.* 1596. There is at *Rome* this Monument.

> *To* Seraphinus Oductius Strancionicus, *Famous Physician, a most Ingenious Prophet, and a Man skilled in all manner of Learning; who being seized with a vehement Fever, foreknew, and most constantly foretold the day and Hour of his Death.* Theophilus *his Son erected this Monument: he Died the* 9*th of the* Calends *of Sept.* An. 1538. *having Lived* 54 *Years,* 9 *Months and* 22 *Days.*

This I take from *Kormannus, L. de Mirac. Part* 9. *c.* 102. who in the said Book, and the same *part. c.* 164. writes as follows, concerning *Presaging Dreams*. That Dreams sometimes presage Death, many examples testify. That of King *Pharaoh's* Baker, *Gen. c.* 4. The Dream of *Lucius Scylla* the *Roman*. The Dream of *Calphurnia*, the Wife of *Julius Cæsar*. The Dream of *Cicero*, in *Valerius*. The Dream of *Alexander the Great*, in the same. The Dream of *Simonides*. The Dream of *Cressus*, King of *Lydia*. The Dream of the *Arcadian* in *Megara*, in the same. The Dream of *Flav. Valerius*, of *Marcian* the Emperor. The Dream of *Elizabeth de l'Arche*, the Mother of the *Pucelle of Orleance*. The Dream of *Polycarpe*. The Dream of the Scholar of *Pavia*. All which M. *Ancermus Julianus*, has learnedly compiled in his *Book of Dreams and nocturnal Visions*.

An ancient Gentleman, now living in *London*, has told me, That many Years since he had occasion to make a Journey into the North, and that being a Bed in his Inn, the first Night of his Journey, a Friend of his, Dead not long before, appeared to him in his Dream, and told him, he had lodg'd 1000 *l*. in the hands of a Person, whom he named (and who was well known to the Gentleman I write of) for the use of his Daughter; and he desired him, That upon his return to *London*, he would put the Person in mind of it, and desire him to take care to pay the Mony. The Gentleman, after his return, took an oportunity to wait on the said Person, and after common-discourses were over, told him, That such a Friend of theirs (whom he nam'd) lately Dead, had communicated a Secret to him, *viz.* that he had lodg'd 1000 *l*. in his hands, for the use of his Daughter, and that, as she would grow Marriagable in a short time, he might do well to pay it: The Person freely own'd the thing, and pay'd the Mony accordingly; the Gentleman, from whom I had the Relation, having known nothing of it but in his Dream. And this is remarkable, that the Gentleman who paid the Mony, chanced to fail in about three Months after.

To give some Account of what experience I have had my self in Dreams. As *Cardan* tells us, that beside the Oracle and Prophecy, there are four kinds of Dreams, *viz. Monitory, Persuasive, Deterring* and *Impelling*; So I have had some of all these four kinds, and have been guided by them in many material circumstances of my Life; many times the *Genii* which have attended me, as I have lain in my Bed, have bid me go to Sleep, saying, That they would suggest something to me in my Dream which they have performed; and when the Dream was over, they having suggested what they pleased, they have sensibly push'd my Shoulder, or taken me by the Arm-rist, or toucht some other parts of my Body, to awake me, and have bid me consider of what I had seen in my Sleep. And though I have then generally found the things enigmatically represented, yet the meaning was obvious enough, and I have guided my self by it.

Synesi. Som. l. I. c. I.

Dr. *Bekker*, who takes upon him to solve all Appearances in *Dreams*, or others, by Natural Reason, without any Agency or Spirits; in the Third Volume of his Work, entitled, *Le Monde Enchanté*, *c.* 22. writes thus. There is a certain way of Presage, or of Prognostick Signs, which relates to certain particular Persons and their Concerns, when a Man by some extraordinary Vision, by the hearing or some sensible Perception of something, is advertis'd before hand of something which will happen to him, or of what is presently to happen. This is what I agree in, and I shall give the Reason of it in my Fourth Part; and here I shall only explain the thing after the way I conceive it: for Instance, some one Dreams, that himself, or one of his will die, or that he sees his own Figure, or that of another Person before him, or in a Coffin, or that he hears some one knocking on it to Nail him in, that he preceives some one to take him by the Hand, or to strike him on the Shoulder, and all other things of this Nature; but in the same degree, as those beforemention'd, without going farther: that is to say, in things that concern our selves, and those that belong to us, and in respect of what is Natural, not with Persons that have no Communication with us, or concerning things that are wholly contingent and casual, and that depend on the Choice of Mens Wills. If beyond this somewhat often happens, it is not against Nature, nor above it, nor out of its Power; for before such a Dream happens, a Man has thought, perhaps, more than once, with great Affliction of his Death; since a Dream comes from much thinking on a thing, and that the Affliction partly causes the Distemper, or having increas'd it, Death Naturally follows; but it's more difficult to comprehend how this may also happen in respect of other Persons; for a Man has not so strong a tye with another. Mean while, as I observe, that Naturalists assigns two Causes, that give Birth to *Sympathy*, or a mutual Inclination, which manifestly appears in Men, Beasts, Plants, Trees, and in many other Bodies, by which they naturally Unite themselves together, or keep far asunder from each other; and in their Operations, they find not Reason to reject as incredible ev'n these Apparitions, in a Dream, but we ought also to conclude from thence, that the Natural cause being thus known, the Devil has nothing to do in it.

We explain more particularly *Sympathy*, after the way following: We say then, first, That each Body, ev'n though so little it can scarce be perceiv'd, is compos'd of an Infinity of little Parts; and that these little Parts are interwoven the one with the other, after a very unequal manner; that it's for this that two Bodies whereof the least Parts or Atoms are woven after an equal manner, have also a tye one with the other; for they are invested with an object, which is the same, or at least of the same Nature, and of an equal manner; wherefore those which are of an equal Composition of Parts, will receive the one as well as the other, after such or such a manner, a like desire, or like food in eating and drinking, and as this texture has place particularly in the Naturnal mixture of Man's Body, we call this *Equality of Humors*, and according then as these Particles agree, and are woven and dispos'd well, or ill together, this is call'd *Good* or *Ill Humor* of a Man, but this is not yet all, the Particles thus Interlact for the Composition of a Body, are withal little volatile Parts, which pass away in Vapours continually both outwardly, and inwardly, whereof we may see, as far as the Eye can discover, some what a Proof in the Smoak, or Vapour of hot Blood, for this Vapour is nought but a quantity of those little Parts, mixt the one with the other, in a volatile and continual Motion; these Particles exhale from one Body into another: Now in all things this holds, that every where, like seeks its like, and joyns with its like; when in the commerce of Humane Life this does not happen so exteriorly, it's because this coupling or joyning is not made by a necessity of Nature, but by Deliberation: and nevertheless there will be still a secret cause in the Sympathy of these Natures, which does not appear so outwardly.

We must add to what we have said before, the force of the Imagination, whereof Experience teaches us amazing thinks; It is (to speak thus as openly, as we may) as out of the Operation of the Exteriour Senses, that Spirits, (that is to say) the said Exhalation, and Evaporation of the most subtle Parts mounting from the Heart to the Brain, where they expose a like Representation, as that of the common Sense of Man, by the means of the Senses, but otherwise brought from without; according then as the Brain is tender or hard, moist, or dry; or that a Person is old or young; a Man, or a Woman; that the one or the other finds himself Sick or in Health: According to all this, I say, something is imprinted, more easily or more difficultly in the Brain; the Spirits having more or less Communication with those of another Body, equal, to this, by the means of the Exhalation, and Evaporation of the least Parts, outwardly and inwardly; this happens most commonly in a Sickness; and above all in a Mortality; thence comes the contagion of the Air, and of the Blood. This being so, Men may also, in case of a Sickness, or Mortality, or of some Iminent danger, while the Blood and Spirits are particularly mov'd, have a lively fore-perceiving; that is to say, the Woman in respect of her Husband, the Child in regard of his Mother, and the Mother in regard of her Child; Brothers and Sisters in regard the one of the other; and even a Friend, and a Comrade in respect of those with whom they have contracted a Friendship and Society; and though they are far distant, they cease not to have this fore-perceiving, since the volatile Particles disperse themselves to many Leagues distance, and tend the one towards the other.

Experience wholly proves what I say, the most subtle Parts, and their Exteriour and Interriour attraction of one Body in another, causes that the Loadstone draws the Iron; for what draws reciprocally touches; This touch fortifies the texture of the Particles the one with the others; and so that what does not touch reciprocally does not draw. That these little Parts disperse themselves very far is what is taught us by the trace of a Dog; this Beast in following it, will find by the sole means of the smell, in which consists the Motion of these subtle Parts, the Tract of any one that has travell'd, to Fifty, nay, even to an Hundred Leagues of way, by Land and Water, in fair Weather, and Tempestuous. As for the Imagination, its a thing manifest, by the wonderful Experience and Operation it has while Women are with Child, on the Fruit; without speaking at present of other Examples which may find their place in the Sequel.

I conclude therefore, at present, that this Communication, and this Motion of the volatile Parts of the Bodies of Persons, that have love the one for the others, or that are of a very equal Nature, be it far, or near, produces such a thing. This admirable Participation makes an equal Impression on the Brain, as we find ill Weather causes it self to be fore-perceiv'd in a Man's Limbs, or chiefly in those of a Beast. I say, such an Impression is made, when there is a Person sick, or that a sickness Foments it self in his Limbs, or that he dies, or is on the point of Death: its to this Person as a Dream, he understands, he sees, he perceives something, and this also troubles him. When there has happen'd to him after an extraordinary manner, such a Perception or Dream Waking, it's the same thing as the Imaginations that never happen'd to him after the same manner, or near it, or that he has been used all the times he has made this experience, to see somewhat like this to follow, he may take it for a sign not of a Devil, or of a Spirit, but as being wholly Natural. We may also freely believe, that by reason of the unequal constitution of the Brain, Blood and Spirits in some Men, one also ought to be subject more to these kinds of rencounters than another; this causes that we may say in some manner with Reason, that one Man may see more Fantoms than another.

I shall forbear to incert more here from Dr. *Bekker*, referring the Reader to his Works; and I shall conclude this Chapter with a Relation, or two, for Men to consider how Dr. *Bekker*'s Philosophy before laid down, may serve to explain them, tho' in truth these Relations might have been somewhat more properly inferred in some precedent Chapter, than this of Dreams.

The first is concerning that Duke of *Buckingham*, who was Stabbed by *Felton*, *Aug.* 23. 1628.

Mr. *Lilly* the *Astrologer*, in his Book, Entituled, *Monarchy, or no Monarchy in England*, Printed in 4o. 1651. Having mentioned the Death of the Duke of *Buckingham*, writes as follows. Since I am upon the Death of *Buckingham*, I shall relate a true Story of his being admonished often of the Death he should Die, in this manner.

An Aged Gentleman, one *Parker*, as I now remember, having formerly belonged unto the Duke, or of great acquaintance with the Duke's Father, and now retired, had a *Dæmon* appeared several times to him, in the shape of Sir *George Villier*'s, the Dukes Father; this *Dæmon* walk'd many times in *Parker*'s Bed-Chamber, without any action of terrour, noise, hurt, or speech; but at last one Night broke out in these Words; *Mr.* Parker, *I know you loved me formerly, and my Son* George *at this time very well; I would have you go from me (you know me very well to be his Father, Old Sir* George Villiers *of* Leicestershire) *and to acquaint him with these, and these particulars,* &c. *and that he above all refrain the Council and Company of such and such, whom he then nominated, or else he will come to destruction, and that suddenly.* *Parker* though a very discreet Man, partly imagined himself in a Dream all this time, and being unwilling to proceed upon no better grounds, forbore addressing himself to the Duke, for he conceived if he should acquaint the Duke with the words of his Father, and the manner of his appearance to him (such Apparitions being not usual) he should be Laugh'd at, and thought to dote, in regard he was Aged. Some few Nights past, without farther Trouble to the Old Man, but not very many nights after, Old Sir *George Villiers* appeard again, walk'd quick and furiously in the Room, seem'd Angry with *Parker*, and at last said, Mr. Parker, *I thought you had been my Friend so much, and loved my Son* George *so well, that you would have acquainted him with what I desired, but I know you have not done it; by all the Friendship that ever was betwixt you and me, and the great respect you bear my Son, I desire you to deliver what I formerly commanded you, to my Son.* The Old Man seeing himself thus sollicited, promised the *Dæmon* he would, but first argued it thus, that the Duke was not easy to be spoken withal, and that he would account him a Vain Man to come with such a Message from the Dead; nor did he conceive the Duke would give any credit to him: to which the *Dæmon* thus answered; *If he will not believe you have this Discourse from me, tell him of such a Secret* (and named it) *which he knows none in the World ever knew but my self and him.* Mr. *Parker* being now well satisfied that he was not asleep, and that the Apparition was not a vain Delusion, took a fit oportunity, and seriously acquainted the Duke with his Father's words, and the manner of his Apparition. The Duke heartily Laught at the Relation, which put old *Parker* to a stand, but at last he assumed Courage, and told the Duke, that he acquainted his Fathers Ghost, with what he found now to be true, *viz.* Scorn and Derision; but my Lord, says he, your Father bid me acquaint you by this token, and he said it was such as none in the World but your two selves did yet know; hereat the Duke was amazed, and much astonished, but took no warning, or notice thereof, keeping the same Company still, advising with such Councilors, and performing such Actions, as his Father by *Parker* countermanded. Shortly after, Old Sir *George Villiers*, in a very quiet, but sorrowful Posture, appears again to *Parker*, and said, Mr. *Parker, I know you deliver'd my words to* George *my Son, I thank you for so doing, but he slighted them, and now I only request this more at your hands, that once again you repair* to my Son, and tell him, that if he will not amend, and follow the Counsel I have given him, this *Knife or Dagger* (*and with that he pull'd a Knife or Dagger from under his Gown*) *shall end him*; *and do you Mr.* Parker *set your House in order, for you shall die at such a time.* Mr. Parker once more engaged, though very unwillingly, to acquaint the Duke with this last Message, and so did, but the Duke desir'd him to trouble him no farther with such Messages and Dreams, and told him he perceived he was now an Old Man and Doted; and within a Month after meeting Mr. *Parker* on *Lambeth-Bridge*; said, *Now Mr.* Parker *what say you of your Dream?* who only return'd, *Sir I wish it may never have success,* &c. but within six Weeks after, he was Stab'd with a Knife, according to his Fathers Admonition beforehand, and Mr. *Parker* Died soon after he had seen the Dream or Vision perform'd.

This Relation is Inserted also in the Lord *Clarendon*'s *History*, and in Sir *Richard Baker*'s *Chronicle*. The Lord *Clarendon*, in his *History*, Vol. I. *L.* 1. having given some Relations, says, that amongst others there was one (meaning this of *Parker*) which was upon a better foundation of Credit, than usually such Discourses are founded upon. And he tells us, that *Parker* was an Officer in the Kings *Wardrobe* in *Windsor Castle*, of a good reputation for honesty and discretion, and then about the Age of Fifty Years, or more. This Man had in his Youth been bred in a School, in the Parish where Sir *George Villiers*, the Father of the Duke liv'd; and had been much cherished and obliged in that Season of his Age, by the said Sir *George*, whom afterwards he never saw. About Six Months before the miserable end of the Duke of *Buckingham*, the Apparition was seen; after the third appearance he made a Journey to *London*, where the Court then was; he was very well known to Sir *Ralph Freeman*, one of the *Masters of Requests*, who had Married a Lady, that was near allied to the Duke, and was himself well received by him. He Informed the Duke with the Reputation and Honesty of the Man, and Sir *Ralph Freeman* carry'd the Man, the next Morning, by Five a Clock to *Lambeth*, according to the Duke's appointment, and there presented him to the Duke, who received him Courteously at his Landing, and walked in conference near an Hour with him and Sir *Ralph*'s, and the Duke's Servants at such a distance, that they heard not a word; but Sir *Ralph* always fixt his Eyes on the Duke, who sometimes spoke with great commotion and disorder; and that the Man told Sir *Ralph* in their return over the Water, that when he mentioned those particulars that were to gain him credit, the Duke's colour changed, and he Swore he could come to that Knowledge only by the Devil; for that those particulars were known only to himself, and to one Person more, who he was sure would never speak of them. So far the Lord *Clarendon*. And I think Dr. *Bekker*'s Hypothesis will hardly clear this matter.

I shall only add here a small relation of a thing that happened to my self; About Six Years since, a Gentleman, whom I had never seen, nor heard of before, came to my Lodging (which was then in *Fetter-lane*) about Six of the Clock in the Morning, it being Summer time, he found a Servant of the House, and asked him whether I were stirring, and finding not, he desired the Servant to go to me, and acquaint me of his being there, and that he desired, if it might not be troublesome, he might be admitted to my Bed-side; I admitted it; and upon his coming to me, he told me he was directed to me by a Lady, a Relation of mine, whom he had met at *Hamstead*, he having a desire to discourse with me concerning an Affair in which he understood I had some knowledge: After some discourse was over I asked him his Name, which he told me; then I asked him where he Lived, he replyed, in *Cane-Wood* whereupon I was somewhat surprized; for that very Morning, at Three of the Clock, I was awaked out of my Sleep by aloud Voice, saying, *Cane, Cane, Cane*; now whether the intentness of the Gentlemans Thought of coming to me, wrought this upon my Mind, or how else it came to pass, may require consideration.

CHAP. IX.

What perception Men have had of Genii, *or* Spirits, *and their Operations by Magical Practices.*

THE Learned *Ludovicus Capellus* writ a Book, Entituled, *The Hinge of Faith and Religion*, which was Published in *English, An.* 1660. In the Tenth Chapter of that Book, he draws a reason to prove a Deity from *Wizards, Magicians, Inchanters,* and from all the *Heathen* Idolatry, and Superstition; where he writes thus:

It's a certain thing, which the experience of our days, and that of all Ages does averr, which the monuments of Histories, both Ancient and Modern confirm, and which the Writings, as well of Heathens, as of Christians certifie; that there are and have been at all times in the World, *Witches, Magicians, Diviners, Inchanters,* and such like notorious wicked People, that have a familiar Communication, and a frequent Commerce with Devils; by whose help and power they do many strange and prodigious things, above and beyond all humane Wisdom; all which consequently infers, that these things proceed from a supernatural and immaterial cause, such as *Dæmons* are.

The Laws made and promulgated in all well governed States and Commonwealths, as well that of the *Jews* by *Moses,* as that of the *Christians,* and of the *Heathens* themselves, do evidence this to us. The Executions and Supplices which Justice frequently inflicts on such Persons; the Processes, the Relations and Informations that are made about them, do assure us of this, and leave no doubt of it. The damnable curiosity of many Persons, which every day have recourse to such as they, to know, see, and do all those things that cannot be done by any other means, does also confirm this. The Writings of the *Heathens,* as well *Greeks* as *Romans,* are full of Instances of such Persons, and of their effects, which are stupendious and wonderful: so that a Man must wholly renounce his Reason, and believe nothing of those things that are done, if he will not also believe that there are such Persons; which is true and manifest by all those kinds of Testimonies, and Monuments, which may induce us to believe any thing.

Now, if there are any *Witches, Inchanters*, &c. it necessarily follows that there are *Dæmons*, by whose help and power, they cause these prodigious effects to come to pass, which Men wonder at, and look upon with horrour and amazement; it being not possible that those things should be done by any humane Power. The Histories therefore and Writings of all Nations, and even of the Heathens themselves, are full of examples of the *Devils* Apparitions, and of their strange effects. Now, he says, if there ware any *Dæmons* (as it cannot be denied) it follows that there is a Deity above them, which so restrains them, that they shall not overthrow all things by their might; for they have strength and malice enough to do it.

He adds beneath. The publick profession of *Magical Arts*, which has been sometime tolerated in some of the most famous Universities of Christendom; the common distinction of black and white Magick, which has been invented by some excellent Philosophers of the Sects of *Plato* and *Pythagoras*, who would have found a way by which they might have subjected the good *Dæmons* to them, and reconcile them to themselves, and which has from them past to the *Jewish Cabalists*, and from them to the *Christians*, are an invincible Argument, that there are *Magicians* and *Dæmons*: The certain and averred Relations of the *Northern Countries*, and of both the *Indies*, do testify, that all those do swarm with them, and that there is scarce one which has not his *Dæmon*, and *Familiar Spirit*. So far *Capellus*.

To give some account now of the Magick and communion with Spirits, practised in the *Northern Countries, Shefferus*, Professor of Law at *Upsal* in *Sweden*, has writ an History of *Lapland*, which was Printed in *English* at *Oxford, An.* 1674. and in his Eleventh Chapter, which is concerning the Magical Ceremonies of the *Laplanders*, he writes as follows.

It has been the received Opinion among all that have known the Name of the *Laplanders*, that they are a People addicted to *Magick*. This Judgment of Historians concerning the *Laplanders*, is no less verified of the *Biarmi*, their Predecessors, so that we may justly suppose both of them to have descended from the same original; for the *Biarmi* were so expert in these Arts, that they could either by their Looks, Words, or some other wicked Artifice, so ensnare and bewitch Men, as to deprive them of the use of Limbs and Reason, and very often to bring them into extream danger of their Lives: but though in these latter times they do not so frequently practice this, and dare not profess it so publickly as before, yet there are still many that give themselves wholly to this Study: for every one thinks it the surest way to defend himself from the injuries and malicious designs of others. And they commonly profess that their knowledge of these things is absolutely necessary for their own Security; upon which account they have Teachers and Professors in this Science; and Parents in their last Wills bequeath to their Children, as the greatest part of their Estate, those Spirits and Devils, that have been any way serviceable to them, in their life time. And *Sturlsonius* gives an account of the most Famous *Laplanders* of that Profession: and though some arrive at a greater knowledge in this Profession, and are more able Masters to teach it than others, yet it's very seldom but the Parents themselves are so learned, as to perform the duty, and save the expences of a Tutor. According to an aptness of disposition in Learning, some arrive at a greater perfection in this Art, than others, who may be excellently qualified for other Imployments.

As to their bequeathing their *Familiars* to their Children, they suppose it the only means to raise their Family: So that they excel one another in this Art, according to the largeness of the Legacies they receive. Thus each House has its peculiar Spirits, and of different and quite contrary natures from those of others. And not only each distinct Family, but single Persons in them also have their peculiar Spirits, sometimes one, two, or more, according as they intend to stand on the defensive part, or are maliciously inclined, and design to be upon the offensive: but there is a set number of obsequious Spirits, beyond which no one has; and some of these will not engage themselves, without great sollicitation and earnest entreaties, when others readily proffer themselves to little Children, when they find them fit for their turn; So that divers of the Inhabitants are almost naturally *Magicians*: for when the Devil takes a liking to any Person in his Infancy, as a fit Instrument for his designs, he presently seizes on him with a Disease, in which he haunts him with several Apparitions; from whence, according to the capacity of his Years and Understanding, he learns what belongs to the Art. Those which are taken thus a second time, see more Visions, and gain greater knowledge. If they are seized a third time, which is seldom without great torment, or utmost danger of their Life, the Devil appears to them in all his shapes, by which they arrive to the very perfection of this Art; and become so knowing, that without the *Drum*, they can see things at great distances, and are so possest by the Devil, that they see them even against their will: For instance, not long since a certain *Lap*, who is yet alive, upon my complaining against him for his *Drum*, brought it to me, and confest with Tears, that though he should part with it, and not make him another, he should have the same Visions he had formerly: and he instanced in my self, giving me a true and particular relation of whatever had happened to me in my Journey to *Lapland*; and he farther complained, that he knew not how to make use of his Eyes, since things altogether distant were present to him.

As for their *Magick Art*, it's according to the diversity of Instruments they make use of in it, divided into two Parts; one comprehends all that to which their *Drum* belongs, the other those things to which *Knots*, *Darts*, *Spells*, *Conjurations*, and the like, refer. Concerning their *Drum*, it's made of an hollow Piece of Wood, and must be either of *Pine*, *Firre*, or *Birch-tree*, which grows in such a particular place, and turns directly according to the Suns Course; which is, when the grain of the Wood, turning from the bottom to the top of the Tree, winds it self from the right hand to the left; from this perhaps they believe the Tree very acceptable to the Sun, which under the Image of *Thor* they Worship, with all imaginable Adoration. The Piece of Wood they make it of is the Root cleft asunder, and made hollow on one side, upon which they stretch a Skin; the other side being convex, is the lower Part, in which they make two Holes, where they put their Fingers to hold it. The shape of the upper side is Oval, and in Diameter about half an Ell. It's like a *Kettle-drum* but not altogether so round, nor so hollow, and the Skin is fasten'd with Wooden Pegs; some are sewed with the Sinews of *Rain Dear*. They Paint upon the Skin several Pictures in red, stain'd with the Bark of an Alder-tree. As for the particular Pictures of these Drums, I refer you to the Author. They put a Bunch of *Brass Rings* on the Drum, when they beat them. Several of the Drums have not the same Pictures upon them. They have the Pictures of several Animals on their Drums, to signifie when, and in what place they may find them. If a *Rain Dear* be lost, how they may get him again? whether the *Rain Dears* Young ones will live? whether their Fishing will be successful? if Sick Men will recover, or not? whether Women great with Child, shall have a safe delivery? or such, or such a Man shall die of such a Distemper, or of what other? and other things of the like Nature, which they are desirous to know. He says he can give no Account of the Reason for the Difference in their *Drums*, unless it be that some of them, are made for more malicious Designs; others again for each Man's private Purpose; On this Account he believes, according to the Nature of the Business they intend, they add, and blot out, and sometimes wholly change the Figures.

There are two things requir'd to fit a *Drum* for use, *an Index*, and *an Hammer*. The first shews, among the Pictures that thing they enquire after, with the *Hammer* they beat the *Drum*. The *Index* is the *bunch of Brass Rings* before mention'd. They first place one great Ring upon the *Drum*, then they hang several small ones upon that; the shape of the *Index*, is very different, he had one of *Copper*, of the bigness of a *Dollar*, with a squarehole in the middle, and several small

Chains hanging about it instead of *Rings*. Another has an *Alchimy-ring*, on which a small round plate of *Copper* is hung by little Chains; he had seen another of Bone, in shape of the *Greek* Δ, with rings above it, and others of a quite different make. As he has giv'n here Cutts of several *Drums*, so he has of the *Indexes*, and *Rings*; some Writers call those *Rings Serpents*, or *Brazen Frogs* and *Toads*, not that they resemble them, but because by them they signifie these Creatures, whose Pictures they often make use of in their Conjuring, as supposing them very grateful and acceptable to the Devil. They make the *Index* indifferently of any sort of Metal. The Hammer they use in raising their *Familiars*, as for the Head of it, it's made of *Rain-Dears Horn*; the other part serves for the Handle: and he has given us two Cuts of the *Hammers*; with this *Hammer* they beat the *Drum*, not so much to make a noise, as by drumming to move the ring, lying on the Skin, so as to pass over the Pictures, and shew what they seek after. This is the Description of the *Drum* with all its Necessaries, as it's us'd by the *Laplanders*, that are Subject to *Sweden*. The *Finlaps* also, that are under the Crown of *Denmark*, make use of *Drums*, though somewhat different in their make from the former; however, he conceives them not of a different kind, but made for some particular uses. The *Laplanders* use their *Drums* for divers Designs, and are of Opinion, that what ever they do, is done by the help of it; and therefore they keep it very choicly with the *Index* and *Hammer*.

There are three very strange things which they believe they can effect by their *Drum*, and these belonging either to their Hunting, their Sacred Affairs, or lastly, their enquiring into things far distant; he finds four things chiefly mention'd by another Writer; the first is the knowing the State of Affairs in Foreign Countries; the second what success their Designs in Hand will meet with; the third, how to Cure Diseases; the fourth, what Sacrifices their Gods will be pleas'd to accept, and what Beast each God desires, or dislikes most. The Artists that beat the *Drums*, beat not altogether in the same place, but round about the *Index*; they beat softly at first, presently quicker, and continue this till they have effected their intent.

The *Drummer* first lifts up the *Drum* by degrees, then beats softly about the *Index* till it begins to stir, and when it's remov'd some distance from its first place to either side, he strikes harder till the *Index* Point at something from whence he may Collect what he look'd for, both the *Drummer*, and those present are upon their Knees. Those who desire to know the Condition of their Friends, or Affairs abroad, whether 500 or 1000 Miles distant, go to some *Laplander*, or *Finlander* Skilful in this Art, and present him with a Linnen Garment, or Piece of Silver, as his reward. An example of this Nature is to be seen upon Record at *Bergen*, in *Norway*, where the effects of the *German Masters* are registred.

In this place one *John Delling*, a Factor to a *German*, enquired of a *Finlapper* of *Norway*, about his Master in *Germany*: the *Finlapper* readily assented to tell him; like a Drunken Man, he presently made a bawling, then reeling and dancing about several times in a Circle, fell at last upon the Ground, lying there for some time, as if he were Dead, then starting up on a sudden, related to him all things concerning his Master; which were afterwards found to agree to what he reported. A *Laplander* also, as *Schefferus* writes, gave *Tornæus* an Account of the Journey he first made to *Lapland*, though he never had seen him before that time; which though it were true, *Tornæus* dissembled to him, lest he might glory too much in his devilish Practices. *Schefferus* says, the Authority of this Man is so considerable, that it may give Credit enough to the Story.

As to the Method taken in making these Discoveries, its very different, *Olaus Magnus* describes it thus; the Drummer goes into some private Room, accompanyed by one single Person, beside his Wife, and beating the Drum, moves the *Index* about, muttering at the same time several Charms; then presently he falls into an Extasy, and lies, for a short time, as Dead; mean while his Company takes great Care that no Gnat, Fly, or other Animal touch him; for his Soul is carryed by some evil *Genius* into a Foreign Country, from which it is brought back with some sign, as a Knife, or Ring, as a token of his Knowledge of what is done in those Parts; after this,

Hist. Goth.
l. 3. c. 26.

rising up, he relates all the Circumstances belonging to the Business that was enquired after. *Petras Claudius* makes no mention either of the Drum, Charms, Company, or those things he brings with him; but he says, he casts himself on the Ground, grows Black in his Face, lying as if Dead for an Hour, or two, according as the Distance of the place is, of which he makes enquiry; when he awakes, he gives a full Account of all Affairs there. *Samuel Rheen*, in his History, says, The Drummer sings a Song, call'd by them *Joiike*, and the Men and Women that are present, sing like wise, some in higher, some in lower Notes, this they call *Duura*. As for their casting themselves on the Ground in a Trance; and what is said by some of their Souls parting from their Bodies, *Schefferus* believes, the Devil only then stifles the Faculties of the Soul for a time, and hinders their Operations. As the *Drummer* falls down, he lays the *Drum*, as near as possible on his Head. Those in the mean time, that are present leave not off singing all the while he lies sweating in his Agony; which they do not only to put him in Mind, when he awakes of the Business he was to know; but also that he might recover out of his Trance, which he would never do, as they imagine, if they either ceas'd singing, or any one stirr'd with their Hand or Foot: And this perhaps, is the reason, why they suffer no Fly, nor any living Creature to touch him, and watch him so diligently. It's uncertain how long they may lie in their Trance, but it's commonly according as the place where they make their discovery is nearer, or farther of; but the time never exceeds 24 Hours, let the place be at never so far a Distance. As for their farther Practice with the *Drum*, I refer you to the Book it self.

    Concerning their other Parts of *Magick*, the first is a *Cord* tyed with *Knots* for raising of Wind. *Schefferus* says, he thinks it not at all probable, that the *Laplanders* should be concerned in this Practice, since they live in an *Inland Country*, Bordering no where upon the Sea, wherefore this properly belongs to the *Finlappers* of *Norway*; and those that are skilled in this Art have command chiefly over the *Winds that blew at their*

Birth; now, he says, as this belongs chiefly to the *Finlappers*, and *Finlanders* of *Norway*, so does the stopping of the Course of Ships, which is altogether of the same Nature.

Somewhat relating to this I find in *Nicolaus Hemmingius*, who in his *Tract de Superstitionibus Magicis*, printed at *Copenhagen, An.* 1575. tells us, That *Petrus Palladius*, sometime Bishop of *Seelandt*, and Professor of Divinity at *Copenhaguen*, could from a Part of his Body affected, foretel from what Part of the Heavens Tempests would come, and was seldom deceiv'd.

Next, he comes to their *Magical Darts*, which they make of Lead, in length about a Finger; by these they Execute their Revenge on their Enemies, and Wound them with Cancerous Swellings, either in the Arms or Legs, which by the extremity of its Pain, kills them in three Days time; they shoot these Darts to what distance they please, and seldom miss their Aim. *Schefferus* thinks, that both *Olaus Magnus*, who writes this, and *Zeigler* from whom he transcrib'd it, as he has many other things, are mistaken, in setting down *Leaden Darts*, since he finds no Person now that knows any such thing, nor is there any mention made of such in any other Writers: he thinks the mistake may be, by misunderstanding the word *Skot*, which is commonly us'd for explaining those Darts; for when Man, or Beast is suddenly taken with a Disease, People call this that takes them so, *Skot*, that is a *Dart*. *Petrus Claudius* calls it a *Gan*, which they send abroad; he likens it to a *Flye*, but says its some little Devil, of which the *Finlanders* in *Norway*, that excel most in this Art, keep great Numbers in a *Leather Bag*, and dispatch daily some of them abroad; but he seems to intimate no more by this word *Gan*, than that very thing which endangers Mens Health and Lives; for he says, That these *Finlanders* cannot live peaceably, except they let out of their *Ganeska*, or *Gan-kiid*, which is the *Satchel*, every Day one of the *Gans*, that is a *Fly* or *Devil*; but if the *Gan* can find no Man to Destroy, after they have sent him out, which they seldom do upon no Account at all, then he Roves about at a venture, and destroys the first thing he meets with. Therefore this word *Gan* signifies no more than what *Zeigler* meant by his Dart, for the term by which they express going out, is, *de Skiuda devis Gan*, that is, he, as it were, shoots out his *Gan*, like an Arrow, for *Skiuda* is only proper to the shooting out of an Arrow.

This Magical Practice, they use as well against one another, as Strangers; nay, sometimes against those that they know are Equals in the Art. Some of the Conjurers are contented only with the power to expel the *Gan* out of Men, or Beasts, which others send; this is remarkable among them, that they can hurt no Man with their *Gan*, except they first know his Parents Name.

Now, all that the *Finlanders*, and *Finlappers* of *Norway* effect by their *Gan*, the *Laplanders* do by a thing they call *Tyre*. This *Tyre* is a round Ball, about the bigness of a Wall-Nut, or small Apple, made of the finest Hair of a Beast, or else of Moss, very smooth, and so light, that it seems hollow; its Colour is a mixture of Yellow, Green, and Ash, but so that the Yellow appears most. This *Tyre* they say is quicken'd, and moved by a particular Art. Its sold by the *Laplanders*, so that he that buys it may hurt whom he pleases with it, they perswade themselves and others, that by the *Tyre* they can send either Serpents, Toads, Mice, or what they please into any Man, to make his Torment the greater. It goes like a Whirl-wind, and as swift as an Arrow, and destroys the first Man, or Beast, that it lights on, but so that it often mistakes; of these we have two many Instances at this time, which are too long to insert here. So far *Schefferus*.

There are two things I shall note in reference to this Account of *Schefferus*. 1. As for Parents bequeathing to their Children their Spirits at their Deaths, we find in the *Tryals of Witches in England*, that the same has been practis'd here and that some have had Spirits given them by their Parents, others by other Relations, and other Friends, beside those which Originally came to themselves.

2. As for *Schefferus*'s particular Opinion, That the *Laplanders* did not really send Darts to those they had a Mind to destroy, I cannot easily agree in Opinion with him; for you find before in Mr. *Mather*'s Account of the *Indians* in *Martha's*

Vineyard, in *New-England*, that the *Indian Pawaws* were wont to form a piece of Leather like an Arrow's Head, and then to tye an Hair to it, and over these to use some Magical Ceremonies, whereupon the *Dæmon* presently snatch'd them away, and convey'd them into the Bodies of Persons to be afflicted; and as the *Laplanders* send their *Gans*, or *Flies* to destroy Persons, so Mr. *Mather* says, sometimes the *Dæmon* pretends to the *Pawaws* that he brings a Portion of the Spirit of a Person closely imprison'd in a Fly, and as they deal with the Fly, so it fares with the Body of the Person they intend to Afflict. The *Drums* also us'd by the *Laplanders*, are us'd by the *West-Indians*, so that there is a strange Agreement in their *Magical Practices* as I shall set forth beneath.

The Learned *Olaus Rudbeck*, in the *Second Volume* of his *Atlantica*, treats concerning the *Lapland Drums*, the Heads of which he says, are divided into three Parts, the uppermost Region contains the Heavens, and all Celestial things, and all Volatiles; the middle Region contains the Earth, with Men and all Animals; the lowermost Region contains all Infernals and Subteraneous Places: and then he gives a particular Explication of all the Figures, or Marks on the *Tympana*; and says, if the *Laplanders* would know whether, when they go a hunting, they shall have success, they beat their *Drum* with *Thors Hammer*, and diligently observe a certain Ring leaping on the *Drum*, which if they see to rest on the Image of a *Ranger*, they no way doubt but they shall kill a Ranger that Day, if it rests on the Figure of a Wolf, they conclude they shall have a Wolf for their Prey. He refers us for other things, relating to the use of the *Lapland Drums*, to *Schefferus*'s *Lapponia*, *Olaus Magnus*, and others; however, I shall give you here what seems to be *Olaus Rudbeck*'s Sense, concerning what may be expected from the Superstitious use of the *Lapland Drums*, inserted by him in the Fifth Chapter of the said Book, *p.* 283. it is as follows. Since the Doctrine of Christ came to *Lapland*, Men could not but forget many things relating to Superstition, and cast off others, or at least, be at an uncertainty in them; whether therefore the *Laplanders* themselves are now Ignorant of the true make of the most

Chap. 10.

Ancient *Drums*, or whether the very differing fitting of the *Drums* deprives them of the Knowledge of a thing so extreamly vain, they now suffer themselves with extream difficulty to be drawn to make known their Superstition to others; perhaps also shame, or fear deters some. To pass by that, the chief *Arcanum* of Superstition will not be Revealed; be it as it may, you shall now hardly find any Man, who knows rightly how to manage this *Drum*, or to explain it to others; and those who think they know somewhat of this kind, either so obstinately conceal it, or so dissemble their skill, that those Labour in a manner in vain, who with any Gifts, how great soever, or high drinking (which is wont to go a great way with them otherwise) endeavour to break or Conquer that silence; but among Gifts (if any Man will purchase this Art of them) the *Laplanders* are earnest Lovers of *Imperial Rix-Dollars*.

In the Sixth Chapter of his said *Second Volume*, he tells us of wonderful Performances, said to have been wrought by the means of their *Scipio Runicus*, or *Runestaffe* (by us call'd the *Runick Almanack*, of which there are many in *England*) being anointed with a certain Magical Ointment, *viz.* of Mens flying in the Air on it, and the like; and says a more constant Fame of nothing has remain'd in their Country, from the remotest times of *Paganism*, than of such flights in the Air; and that nothing is more readily believed, than that the present *Laplanders*, who continue still in *Paganism*, use the same kind of flights now and that beside *Runstaffe*'s *Sticks, Pales, Calves, Horses, Dogs,* and other living Creates anointed with the same kind of Ointment, were thought to be able to carry their Riders to Places design'd; and these things were wont to be ascrib'd to *Diana*, or *Disa* as the first Inventress of them.

He here tells us also, That the *Tympanum* of the Mother of the Gods, so much celebrated by the Greeks and Latine Writers, though explain'd by none of them, as it ought, was nothing but a Copy of the *Lapland Tympanum*, convey'd to Foreign Parts by *Disa, Isis, Idæa,* or *Diana*, whose *Ring* and *Hammer* were sometime found in the left Hand of the Figure of *Isis* at *Rome*, the *Tympanum* it self being over the Head of the Goddess, and there being Marks under her Feet like to those that are seen in the *Lapland Drums*. The *Egyptian Isis* also, according to a Cut giv'n of her by *Pignorius*, holds this *Ring* and *Hammer* in her left Hand. And the Mother of the Gods (as *Du Choul* has set forth) handles a *Tympanum*; and he says, he will make out in his *Chronology*, that *Isis* the Daughter of *Inachus*, going into *Egypt*, a little before the times of *Moses*, taught the *Egyptians* Incantations, and withal shew'd them that Infamous use of the Hieroglyphical Marks, with which Art the *Egyptian Magi* afterwards contended with *Moses* before *Pharoah*. But he does not think that all the *Goths* were giv'n to those Arts, because the Testimonies of the *Scalds*, and of *Snorro* himself free the most Valiant of the *Goths* from that Infamy, those Arts being beneath their Valour and Dignity, and seem'd much to prejudice the Fame and Renown due to Valiant Men; and therefore great Punishments was never inflicted on Men giv'n to such Arts, by Magnanimous Kings.

I must here note, That notwithstanding all this Discourse, concerning *Thor's Hammer*, and its being convey'd from *Sweden* to foreign Parts, given us by the Learned *Rudbeck*, I must wholly yield to what the Learned *Kircher* in his *Obeliscus Pamphilius*, has delivered us concerning it; he has there writ a Paragraph, with this Title to it; *Concerning the Tautick Character, or the Cross with an Handle to it*, (that is, a Ring annext to the top of it) *chief of all the Hierogliphicks*, (this being the same with what *Rudbeck* calls *Thor's Hammer*.)

Kircher there, among other curious things, tells us, that the *Egyptians*, in the Character *T. Tau*, as in a Looking-Glass, plac'd the Idea of the whole Pantomorphous Nature, by the Circle or Ring, which they commonly place on the top of it, they denoted the Celestial Orbs, in which the Spirit of the World mixes it self; first communicating its Virtue to them by the Cross, the virtue of the four Elements on the Sublunary World, through the mediation of the Celestial Bodies, from which the generation of all things arises; for they observed there were two motions chiefly appearing in Nature, *viz.* a

Strait, and a Circular one; they represented this by a Circle, the other by Strait Lines; for the Elements being moved out of their natural places, they found by experience, they return'd to them but by Strait Lines, *and beneath*, he quotes the following Passage from *Ficinus*'s Third Book *De vitâ Cælestus Comparendâ*.

The *Ægyptians* preferr'd the Figure of the Cross before all others, because Bodies act by the vertue diffused to the Superficies; now the first Superficies is described by the Cross, for so it has chiefly Longitude and Latitude; and this is the first Figure, and the straitest of all, and contains four Strait Angles; now the effects of the Celestial Bodies chiefly result from the Rectitude of the Rays and Angles; for then Stars are most powerful, when they hold the four Angles of Heaven, *viz.* the Points of the East and West, and of the mid Heaven, on either side; and being so disposed, they so cast their Rays against each other that they thence make a Cross, the Ancients therefore said the Cross was a Figure made of the fortitude of the Stars, and the Suscepticle of their fortitude, and therefore it had a mighty power in *Images*, and received the Powers of the Spirits and Planets.

Tom. 2. part 2. *p.* 399.

The same Author in his *Œdipus Ægypt.* says, The *Crux Ansata*, or *Isiaca* is seen carried almost in every *Images* Hand of the *Ægyptians*; which Character they had in so great Veneration, that they thought nothing could be rightly done without it, and it was the most powerful *Amulet*, and a Character made by a wonderful Subtlety of Wit, according to the pattern of Nature, the only guide and light to show the way to Happiness.

Ib. Tom. 3. *p.* 277.

Again, he tells us elsewhere, That by the *Crux Ansata*, which consisted of a Circle and a Cross, they denoted the motion of *Phtha*, *viz.* the Soul of the World artificially disposing all things that are in the World; and by the Circle, the circular motion of the Celestial Bodies, whereby it in some sort animates them, and renders them apt for influencing Inferiours: and by the Cross, or the lines cutting each other, they signify the motion which it performs in the Inferior World, for the Generation and Production of things, according to the nature of Elementary Bodies; for the motion of Sublunary things is according to strait Lines, as it appears in the motion of Light and Heavy things, and of such as are of a middle Nature; whereof those being carried, some upwards some downwards, according to Strait Lines, these participating equally of Gravity and Levity, having got a middle Nature, and diffus'd, as it were, on the sides, appositely express the cut Lines of a Cross, and therefore, by this only Character, for the said reasons, they do not unmeetly denote the whole process of Nature; wherefore also they reputed this Character, as the most Mysterious of all Hierogliphicks, and thought the same had the greatest force of all, both to allure *Good Genii*, and facinate the Evil ones; hence calling it the Symbol of Health, the greatest Spell, the Monogram *Phtha*; and by other Names, they had it put in all *Obelisks, Statues, Tables,* &c.

Here we find a pretty satisfactory Account of the Original Institution of this Character, which I cannot find in the the Works of the Learned *Rudbeck*; and therefore as far as it appears to me hitherto, I must conclude it of an *Ægyptian* Original.

To proceed now to some further account from *Olaus Rudbeck*, in reference to Magical Practices, in his 3 *d.* Vol. c. 11. he tells us, when we find any strange Relation in that kind, we ought duly to weigh what is really perform'd by the *Magick Art*, and what contains some abstruse sense, and is proposed translatitiously, and by way of *Ænigma*: he says it's a firm Argument with him for the practice of *Witchcraft* and *Horrible Magick* in the North, that Men came thither at the same time from *Greece, Ægypt,* and *Phœnicia,* as to a famous Academy, and gave themselves over wholly to the study of those Arts: and that *Pythagoras* was not the only Man that learnt to Fly of the *Hyperborean Abaris*, but others of the same Age, as we find from *Diogenes,* in *Photius,* viz. *Carmanus, Cylla, Dercyllis,* &c. who thinking themselves in *Thule,* on a sudden awaking, as it were from a Dream, found themselves in the *Temple of Hercules* at *Tyre*. And the Author setting down some of their chief Customs, agreeing with what the

Greeks and *Latins* write, tells us, that the *Golden Apples*, raising the Gods themselves from Death to Life, that is, which set forth the Acts of their Ancestors, encouragements to Vertue, and determents from Vice, are interpreted by him Letters which were cut on Stones, or Wood, or writ on Parchment; and those Stones, Tables, Parchments and *Lapland Tympana*, from their Oblong Figure, got the name of *Pine-apples*, *Apples* and *Eggs*: and those Letters which were writ on Parchment or *Magical Tampana* were done over with a Gold Colour, drawn from the Bark of an Alder; which Alder was much esteemed by their Ancestors, and is now by the *Laplanders*, because from its inward Bark chew'd with the Teeth, they get that Gold Colour wherewith they Paint all kinds of Letters and Figures on their *Tympana*. And as for its being said that some descended into Hell, being carried on *Alder Sticks*, it's on this account, that in their Divinations they used such Sticks, in the Barks of which, Letters and Circles were Cut, compassing about the Stick, like the various spires of Serpents. As for the God they call upon in their Divinations, he says its *Saturn*, and his Worshippers using the *Drums*, are called *Saturnines*. Therefore he that by the help of the *Drum*, would seek Counsel of the Gods, takes in one Hand a *Golden Apple*, in the other an *Hammer*, made like a *Cross*, of Alder or Horn, and has also a *Serpent* made of Copper, and not much differing from Gold in Colour, which upon the beat of the *Hammer*, on the Head of the *Drum*, leaps in and out, till it settles on some Letter or Figure, shewing that to be it, from whence the Answer is given; moreover, the *Saturnine*, upon beating the *Drum* a while, fell into a Trance, as tho' he were Dead, and the *Laplanders*, by mistake, then thought the Soul went out of the Body, and after having learnt many things, return'd again; whereas their Ancestors, with *Plutarch*, thought the Soul did not go out of the Body, but yielded for some time, and gave a loose to the *Genius*, which having rov'd about, told it inwardly many things, which it had seen and heard without. Now, the things they desire to see are of various kinds, either the Soul of the Dead, or the Actions of Men at a great distance, or past, or future things; and he gives instances of some eminent Persons, who came from other Countries to theirs, to see the Ghosts of their Ancestors, raised after this manner, and *Plato* owns that all the Tradition concerning the *Elisian Fields* and *Hell*, owes its rise to their North, which being cut on a *Table of Brass* was carried by *Ops* from the *Hyperboreans* to *Delos*, belonging to the *Greeks*.

In his Tenth Chapter of his said Third Vol. speaking of their *Cumæ* which lies beyond the *Baltick*, over-against *Phlægria*, he says, it was known formerly for *Horrible Magic*, and the Imposture of *Witches*; where *Ulysses* and *Æneas* were seduced, consulting the old Fate-telling *Cumæan Sibyl*, call'd the *Prophetess of Hell*, because she lived in the remotest part North, as it were in a Subteraneous place this *Sibyl* being different from the *Cumane Sibyl* in *Italy*; nay, and he here tells us, it is to be noted, that whatsoever of the *Magick Art* and Natural Science, is ascribed to the *Antediluvian Giants* by *Syncellus* and others, all this, both the *Greek Histories*, and those of their Country, unanimously ascribe to the North.

In his Twelfth Chapter of the same Volume, he tells us, that *Thor*, amongst other Names given him, was called *Fluge-Guden*, the God of *Flies*, driving away Magical Flies with his *Hammer*, he being the same with *Belzebub*, mentioned in the Scripture.

As for the *Magical Flies*, they were *Dæmons* in the shape of *Blue Flies*, which the *Finlanders* kept in a *Magical Pouch* or *Satchel*, they being called by them *Gan*, that is, *Spirits*, which they daily sent forth for their *Magical* purposes, viz. to bring them News from all parts of the Universe, and to do things destructive to Men, &c. and these *Flies* were driven away by Sacrifices to *Thor*, tho' the Victims offer'd by the *Jews* at the Temple of *Hierusalem* were freed from *Flies*, by reason of the *Jews* Faith in God.

I thought fit to subjoyn this account from *Olaus Rudbeck*, to that of *Schefferus*, they both relating to *Magical Practices*, and giving some light to each other.

I may here acquaint the Reader, that *Olaus Rudbeck*, Son to the Famous *Olaus*, before quoted, was deputed, *Anno* 1695. by the late King of *Sweden*, *Charles* XI. to Travel through the Northern Provinces of *Sweden*, viz. *Lapland*, *Finland*, &c. to Write a Natural History of them, giving an Account of things peculiar to those Countries, *viz.* the *Plants* and *Flowers*, *Stones*, *Metals*, *Quadrupes*, *Birds*, *Fish*, &c. and *Anno* 1701. he Printed a First Part of this intended Account, at *Upsal*, in *Quarto*, the General Title of the Work being, *Lapponia Illustrata*; and the particular Title of this First Part being *Iter per Uplandiam*. In his General Title Page, he says, he shall set forth in his Work, the Scituation of each of the Countries he there Names, and the *Genius* of the Inhabitants, but chiefly both the Habit of Body, and Disposition of Mind of the *Laplanders*, their Religion, Manners, Language, way of Converse, and their first Origin, beside the account of their Annimals, Minerals, Mountains, Woods, Lakes, Rivers, Cataracts, &c. so that, as he designs to divide this Work into several Parts, we may hope, in one of them, to have as accurate an Account, as may be of their *Magical Practices* and Superstitions.

Having intimated before the Magical use of *Drums*, with other Superstitious Practises in the *West-Indies*, I shall give you here what Mr. *Wafer*, in his Description of the *Isthmus* of *Darien*, Printed *Anno* 1699, writes of it, which is thus: We enquir'd of the *Indians* when they expected any Ships, who said, they knew not, but would enquire concerning it; and thereupon sent for some of their *Pawaws*, or Conjurers, who came, and went into an Apartment by themselves, stay'd for some time at their Exercise, and he and his Companions could hear them make most hideous Yellings, and Shrieks, imitating the Voices of all their Birds and Beasts: With their own Noise they join'd that of several Stones struck together, and of *Conch-Shells*, and of a sort of *Drums*, made of hollow *Bambœs*, which they beat upon, making also a jarring Noise with Strings fasten'd to the larger Bones of Beasts; and every now and then they would make a dreadful exclamation and clattering, all of a sudden, and as suddenly make a pause, with a profound silence: But finding, that after a considerable time, no Answer was made them, they concluded that't was because we were in the House, and so turn'd us out, and went to work again; but still finding no return, after an Hour or two more, they made a search in our Apartment, and finding some of our Cloaths hanging up in a Basket against the Wall, they threw them out of Doors in a great disdain; then they fell once more to their *Pawawing*, and after a little time they came out with their Answer, but all in a muck Sweat; so they first went down to the River, and wash'd themselves, and then came and deliver'd the Oracle to us; which was to this effect: That from the tenth Day, from that time, there would arrive two Ships; and that in the Morning of the tenth Day, we should hear, first one Gun, and some time after another; that one of us should die soon after; at that going aboard we should lose one of our Guns; all which things fell out exactly, according to the Prediction.

A Person who has spent many Years in Voyages, has also told me, that he has seen *Drums* us'd in *America*, particularly at *Dominico*, where the *Indians* use them to *Pawaw* with, for causing Rain or fair Weather; but those *Drums* have no Characters on them; they beat them with Sticks, and have some little piece of Iron or Stone on the Head loose, which plays while they are beating; they utter also many words all the while they are beating, and speak very loud. The same Person acquainted me, that he saw in *Norway*, near *Yarpin*, an Artist beat a *Drum*, like a *Lapland Drum*, with two Sticks, and he observ'd his *Lips* to move all the while; he beat thereon above a quarter of an Hour, till he was all in a Sweat, and then he fell into a Trance, in which he lay above half an Hour, or near three quarters; and upon his coming to himself, he answer'd the Question had been propos'd to him.

Concerning these Diabolical Extasies, Mr. *Pereaud*, in the seventh Chapter of his *Demonology*, prefixt to his *Antidæmon of Mascon*, printed in *French* at *Geneva*, An. 1656, writes thus: The Devil causes Witches sometimes to fall into Extasies in the Day-time, causing in their Bodies a destruction of their Spirits and Sense for some time; so that a Man would say their Soul were out of their Body, and then he puts lively Impressions of things into them; while they are in this Preternatural sleep, their Souls being, as it were retreated into themselves, and so fixt, by the Devil, to the Fancies and Illusions, wherewith he amuses them, that they firmly believe, by this Imagination thus lively impress'd, that they have done themselves, what the Devil represented to them by such Imaginations. There are many Histories of these Diabolical Extasies, but I shall content my self in alledging one, and so much the rather because it happen'd in my time, in the Country of *Vaux*; about the Year 1594, as I have been assur'd by very Credible Persons. There was at that time, and in that place, a Bailiff of Berne, who having, one Day, invited the Minister of the said place to Dinner, and being at Table, they came to a Discourse of Witches, occasion'd by the then Confinement of one, as a Prisoner, in the Castle of *Echalens* where they were, and which Prisoner was already Condemn'd to Die, for the Crime of Witchcraft, and was in a short time to be Executed, as he really was. This Bailiff spake his Mind freely to the Minister, his Pastor, concerning many things, which this Witch confess'd to have done, and which he had a difficulty to believe it possible for him to do, and hereupon being risen from Table, the Bailiff went to the Prison, and brought the Prisoner, and having spoken to him, among other things, concerning the Confessions he had made, and of his Condemnation following, thereupon he Courteously told him, that he should consider well whether he had not done himself injury, in having confess'd things that he had not done, minding him of some of those things in particular; hereupon the Prisoner, who was already dispos'd to die, seriously told him, that what he had said and confess'd, was really true, and that for Proof of this, if he pleas'd to permit him, he would kill the Cattle of a Neighbour, whom he nam'd, so he had his Box, and his Stick, which were at his House, in a place which he nam'd; hereupon the Bailiff, willing to satisfie his Curiosity, resolv'd to send for this Stick and Box, resolving also to pay for the Cattle to whom they belong'd. The Stick and Box being brought, were put into the Witch's Hands; who in the Presence of the Bailiff, the Minister, and some others perform'd all the Ceremonies that other Witches are wont to use with those Instruments of Satan, till he fell as Dead, at their Feet, without any Motion or Sense, till about an Hour, or three Quarters after, he came to himself, as from Death to Life, or as from a most profound Sleep; and then being ask'd by the Bailiff whence he came? He said, he came from killing the Cattle which he had mention'd to him, and according to the leave he had giv'n him; presently the Bailiff sent to know whether this were true, and the Cattle were found really Dead, as he had said.

Mr. *Pereaud* adds; The Question is, who then kill'd the Cattle, it could not be the Witch, his Body continued always in the Presence of the Bailiff and others; to say that he went in his Soul, separated from the Body, this cannot be, for Reasons which he gives. It follows then, it was the Devil himself that did it, having wrought, in the mean time, so powerfully on the Imagination of the Witch, that he believ'd it was done by himself.

Paracelsus has another way of explaining these things; which I shall leave to the Readers Consideration; it is as follows, The Constellation of a Man may be so great in its thought, that in a Man's sleep, it may send his Sydereal Spirit to another place, without the aid of the Elementary Body; that Astral Body has a Power of infecting with Poison, weakning, distorting, blinding, beating, killing, and inspiring, and that in a Moment, and afterward of returning to its Elementary Body. And its a thing very well known, that the Ancients, through a strong Imagination, by the force of the Astral Body, attempted and perform'd many things of this kind against their Enemies; so that some on a sudden, have been rendred Paralitical, no Natural Cause concurring; some depriv'd of their Sight, some made Leprous, some Strangl'd. These and the like Evils have been inflicted, which could scarce be cur'd again in a very long time. Therefore, let those Physicians, who meet with such Diseases know, that neither the Elements, nor Nature it self breeds them, but that they were the Works of the sole Sydereal Body of others; and these

Tom. II. *c.* 2. *prob. in Scien. Divi paragr.* 2.

things are caus'd in Dreams, when this or that Man Dreams such a thing; therefore according to this Dream, judge of the Disease of others.

He adds beneath, Though the Body, Soul, and Spirit are not together at the same time, yet the thought and Speculation, or Imagination remains still in the Spirit, wherefore they are often seen with such kinds of Thoughts. Since therefore the thought of a Man is of such a Nature, therefore by the Sydereal Spirit that thing is so express'd, and signified by a Dream, according as one Spirit is dispos'd to another before he be consumed; nor is this only so, but also in Mountains and Woody Places, and in the Alps, a great Number of these Sydereal Spirits have been sometimes seen, which have hurt Cattle and other Creatures, because the Sydereal Spirits of some maintain'd an hatred, and executed a Revenge after Death, against these Neighbours whose Cattle they were.

The following Relation, concerning an admirable Performance of Persons, who cast themselves into a Trance, is no less stranger.

Frommannas, in his Tract *de Fascinatione Magica part. 6. c. 3.* quotes *Maiolus* writing thus. No less admirable is that Judgment of seven Magicians, which I learnt at *Nantes, An.* 1549. when therefore they had took upon them to tell, within a little space, what was done ten Miles round, they presently fell all down as Dead, and lay so for three Hours; and then arising, they told whatsoever they had seen done in the whole Town of *Nantes*, and in the Country round about it to a good Distance; the Places, Facts and Men being observ'd, all which things upon enquiry were found true; therefore all of them being accus'd and found Guilty of many Malefices, were condemn'd to the Fire.

P. 3. l. 5. c. 3.

Purchas, in his Extracts from *Gonzalo Ferdinando Ovido*, his Summary and General History of the *Indies*, writes thus. Before the Inhabitants of *Hispaniola* had receiv'd the Christian Faith, there was among them a Sect of Men, who liv'd, solitarily in the Desarts, and led their Life in Silence and Abstinence, more strictly than the *Pythagoreans*, abstaining in like manner from all things that liv'd of Blood, contented only with Fruits, Herbs, and Roots, which the Desarts afforded them; the Professors of this Sect being call'd *Piaces*; they apply'd themselves to the Knowledge of Natural things, and us'd certain Secret Magical Operations and Superstitions, whereby they had a Familiarity with Spirits, which they allur'd into their Bodies at such time as they would take upon them to tell of things to come, which they did as follows. When any of the Kings sent for any of them out of the Desarts for this purpose, the *Piaces* comes with two of his Disciples waiting on him, of whom one brings with him a Vessel of a Secret Water, and the other a little Silver Bell; when he comes to the place, he sits down on a round Stool, made for him on purpose, one of his Disciples standing on one Hand of him, and the other, on the other, in the Presence of the King, and certain of his chief Retinue (for the common People are not admitted to these Mysteries) and turning his Face toward the Desart, he begins his Incantations, and calls the Spirit, with a loud Voice, by certain Names which no Man understands but himself and his Disciples. After he has done this a while, if the Spirit deferrs his coming, he drinks of the said Water, and therewith grows Hot and Furious, and inverts, and turns his Inchantment, and lets himself Blood with a Thorn, strangely turmoiling himself, as we read of the furious *Sibyls*, not ceasing till the Spirit comes, who presently overturns him, as a Greyhound overturns a Squiril; then, for a while, he seems to lie as though he were in great Pain, or in a Rapture, wonderfully tormenting himself; during which Agony, one of his Disciples shakes the Silver Bell continually; when the Agony is over, and he lies quiet (though without any Sense or Feeling) the King, or some other in his stead, asks of him, what he desires to know, and the Spirit Answers him by the Mouth, of the rapt *Piaces*, with a direct and perfect Answer to all Points. On a time a certain *Spaniard* being present at those Mysteries with one of the Kings, and in the Spanish Tongue, asking the *Piaces* concerning certain Ships, which they look'd for out of *Spain*, the Spirit answer'd in the *Indian* Tongue, and told them what Day and Hour the

Ship departed from *Spain*, how many they were, and what they brought, without failing in any Point. If he be ask'd concerning the Eclipse of the Sun or Moon (which they greatly fear and abhor) he gives a perfect answer, and the like of Tempests, Famine, Plenty, War, or Peace, and such other things. When all Questions are over, his Disciples call him aloud, ringing the Silver Bell at his Ear, and blowing a certain Powder into his Nostrils, whereby he is raised as it were from a Dead sleep, being yet somewhat heavy headed, and faint for a good while after. Since the Christian Faith has been dispersed through this *Island*, those Diabolical Practices have ceas'd.

Part. 3. l. 5. c. 5.

The same Author from the Fifth Book of *Josephus Acasta*, speaking of the *West-Indians* of *Mexico*, writes as follows.

When the Priests went to Sacrifice, and give Incense in the Mountains, or on the tops thereof, or in any dark and obscure Caves, where their Idols were, they us'd a certain Ointment, doing certain Ceremonies, to take away fear, and to give them Courage. This Unction was made with divers little Venemous Beasts, as *Spiders, Scorpions, Palmers, Salamanders* and *Vipers*. To make an Ointment of these Beasts, they took them altogether, and burnt them on the Hearth of the Temple, which was before the Altar, till they were consum'd to Ashes; then they put them in Mortars with much Tobacco (which Herb they much us'd to Benumb the Flesh, that they might not feel their Travail) with which they mingle the Ashes, making them to lose their force; they likewise mingl'd with these Ashes, *Scorpions, Spiders,* and *Palmers*, alive, then they put to it a certain Seed being ground, which they call'd, *Ololuchqui*, whereof the *Indians* make a Drink to see Visions; the Vertue of this Herb being to deprive a Man of Sense. They likewise ground, with these Ashes, *Black*, and *Hairy Worms*, whose Hair only is Venomous; all which they mingled together with the Black, or the fume of Rosin, and put it in small Pots, which they set before their God, saying it was his Meat; and therefore they called it a Divine Meat, by means of this Ointment they became Witches, and saw, and spake with' the Devil. The Priests being slubber'd with this

Ointment lost all fear, putting on a Spirit of Cruelty; by reason whereof they very boldly kill'd Men in their Sacrifices, going all alone in the Night to the Mountains, and into obscure Caves, contemning all Wild Beasts, and holding it for certain, and approv'd that *Lions, Tigers, Serpents*, and other Furious Beasts, which bred in the Mountains and Forests, fled from them by the Vertue of this Tobacco of their God.

The same Author tells us, There is a kind of *Sorcerers* among the *Indians* allow'd by the Kings, or *Ingua*'s, who take upon them what form and figure they please, flying far through the Air in a short time, beholding all that is done; they talk with the Devil, who answers them in certain Stones, or other things which they Reverence much; they tell what has pass'd in the farthest Parts before any News can come; as it has chanc'd since the *Spaniards* arrived there, that in the Distance of two or three Hundred Leagues, they have known the Mutinies, Battles, Rebellions and Deaths, both of Tyrants, and of those of the Kings Party, and of private Men, which have been known the same Day they happen'd or the Day after, a thing impossible by the Course of Nature. To work this Divination they shut themselves into a House, and became drunk till they lost their Senses, a Day after they answer'd to what was demanded, some affirm they use certain Unctions. The *Indians* say, their Old Women commonly use this Office of Witchcraft, and especially those of one Province, which they call *Coaillo*, and of another Town they call'd *Manchey*, and of the Province of *Gutirochivi*. They likewise shew what is become of things stoln and lost; there are of these kinds of Sorcerers in all Parts, they tell of the Success of things pass'd, or to come, whether Voyages shall be Prosperous, whether a Man shall be Sick, or shall Die, or return safe, or shall obtain that he pretends to; they give their Answers, yea, or no, having first spoke with the Devil, in an obscure place; so as the Enquirers hear the sound of the Voice, but see not to whom these Conjurers speak, neither do they understand what they say, they make a thousand of Ceremonies and Sacrifices to this effect, and grow exceeding

Ibid.

Drunk, for doing whereof they particularly, use an Herb call'd *Villea*, the Juice whereof they mingle with their *Chica*, or take it in some other sort.

P. 3. l. 1. c. 1. The same Author, from the *Journal* of *William de Rubruquis* a *French Minorite Friar*, concerning his Travels into the Eastern parts of the World, *An.* 1255. tells us, That when the *Cham* of *East-Tartary* purposed to do any thing, he caused Three *Shoulder Bones of Ramms* to be brought him; and holding them in his Hands, he thought of the thing whereof he would Consult, whether he might do it, or not, and then delivered the Bones to be Burnt; when they were burnt Black, they brought them to him; then he lookt upon them, whether the Bones, by the Heat of the Fire, were Cleft right length ways, if so he might do it; but if the Bones were Crackt athwart, or round pieces were flown out of them, then he did not proceed; for that Bone is always Cleft in the Fire, or the thin Skin which overspreads it, and if one of the three were Cleft forth right, yet he did it. In Mr. *Jenkinson*'s Voyage among the *Tartars*, we may read of such Divinations. So far *Purchas*.

Now in reference to this way of Divination, a Lady now in *London*, has told my self, that she knew a Person in Ireland who by looking on the Plate Bone of a Shoulder of Mutton, it being of a Sheep that belong'd to the Master of a Family, would predict the whole Fate of that Family, and that usually with success, as to who should first Die, and many other Accidents relating to them.

Mr. *Bedford*, Minister of *Temple* Parish in *Bristol*, writ a Friend of his the last Year, a strange Relation of an Acquaintance of his, who often conversed with Spirits, and the unhappy consequences of it. It is as follows.

About Thirteen Years since, I was acquainted with one *Thomas Jerps*, a Man about 20 years of Age, who lived with his Father, at *Mangerfield*, in the County *Gloucester*, by Trade a *Black-Smith*, he was a very good Temper'd Man, extreamly well Skilled in the Mathematical Studies, which were his constant Delight, *viz. Arithmetick, Geometry, Gauging, Surveying* and *Algebra*, and much addicted himself to

Astronomy; at length he applied himself to *Astrology*, and would sometimes Calculate Nativities, and resolve Horary Questions, *&c.* which he told me prov'd oftentimes very true; but he was not satisfied with it, because there was nothing in it, which tended to a Mathematical Demonstration.

Having not seen him for some time, he came to me one Day, and we being in Private, ask'd me very seriously concerning the Lawfulness of conversing with Spirits; and after I had given my Thoughts in the Negative, and confirm'd them with the best Reasons I could, he told me he had considered all those Arguments, and believed they all related only to Conjuration; but there was an Innocent Society with them, which a Man might use, if he made no contract with them, did no harm by their means, and was not curious to pry into hidden things; and that he himself had Discoursed with them, and heard them Sing, *&c.* to his great Satisfaction, and once made an offer to my self, and another time to Mr. *Bayly*, now Minister of St. *James's* in *Bristol*, that if we would go with him one Night to *Kingswood Forest*, we should see them, and hear them both Speak and Sing, and talk with them on whatsoever Subject we had a mind to, and we should return very safe; but neither of us had the Courage to venture. I told him of the Subtlety of the Devil to delude Mankind, and transform himself into an Angel of light; but he could not believe that it was the Devil. I had several conferences with him on this Subject, but could never convince him: In all which I never observ'd the least disorder of Mind, his Discourse being very rational.

I ask'd him several particulars concerning the method he used, and the discourse he had had with the Spirits; He told me he had a Book whose directions he followed, and accordingly, in the dead time of the Night, he went to a cross way, with a Lanthorn and Candle, which were Consecrated for this purpose, with several Incantations: He had also a Consecrated Chalk, having a mixture of several things within it; and with this he used to make a Circle at what distance he thought fit, within which no Spirit had power to enter; after this he Invoked the Spirits, by using several forms of

Words; some of which he told me were taken out of the Scriptures, and therefore he thought them lawful. The Spirits appeared accordingly to him, in the shapes of little Girls about a Foot and an half high, and play'd without the Circle: at first he was somewhat affrighted, but after some small Acquaintance, he became pleased with their company: He told me they spake with a very Shrill voice like an Ancient Woman; he asked them if there were a God, an Heaven, and an Hell? they Answered there were; he asked them what oeconomy they had among themselves? they told him they were divided into Three Orders: that they had a Chief, whose Residence was in the Air, that he had several Counsellors, which were placed in the form of a Globe, and he in the Center, which was the chiefest Order: another Order was imployed in going to and fro, from thence to the Earth, to carry Intelligence from the Lower Spirits, according to the Directions they received from those in the Air.

This Description being contrary to the account we have in Scripture, of the Hierarchy of Angels, made me conclude them Devils, but I could never convince him: He told me he bid them Sing, and they went to some distance, behind a Bush, from whence he could hear a pleasant Consort, but of such Musick, of which he never heard the like; and in the upper part he could hear something very harsh and shrill like a Reed, but as it was managed, gave a particular Grace to all the rest.

About a Quarter of a Year after this, he came to me again, and told me he wished now he had taken my Advice, for he thought he had done that, which would cost him his Life, and his Eyes and Countenance shew'd a great alteration. I asked him what he had done? he told me that being Bewitch'd by his Acquaintance, he resolved to proceed farther in this Art, and to have some Familiar Spirits at his Command, according to the directions of his Book, which were to get a Book made of Virgin Parchment, and Consecrated with several Incantations, as also particular Ink, Inkhorn, Pens, &c. for this purpose; with these he was to go out as usual to a Cross-way, call upon a Spirit, and ask him his Name, which he was to enter in the First Page of his Book, and this was to be his Chief Familiar. Thus he was to do by as many as he pleased. Writing their Names in distinct Pages, only one in a Leaf, and then, whenever he took the Book and opened it, the first whose Name presented, should appear: his Chief Familiar he said was called *Malchi*, after he had done this, they appear'd to him faster than he desired, and in most Dismal Shapes, as of Serpents, Lions, Bears, *&c.* and hist at him, and attempted to throw Spears, and Balls of Fire; he was very much Affrighted, and the more because, he found it not in his power to Lay them, insomuch that his Hair stood an end, and he expected every moment to be Torn in Pieces. This was in *December* about Midnight, when he continued there in a Sweat till break of Day, at which time they left him, and from that time he was never well as long as he liv'd. He always said he never made any Compacts with any of these Spirits, nor ever did any Harm by their means, nor pry'd into Future Concerns, relating to himself, or others, and exprest an hearty Repentance for his Sin.

A farther account of this Matter may, perhaps, be had from his Relations, of Neighbours in *Mangerfield* in *Gloucester-shire*, not above a Mile out of the Road, betwixt *Bristol* and *Bath*.

I formerly gave an Account of this Affair, to the late Bishop of *Hereford*, in which probably there are some things contain'd, which I do not now remember, and which, perhaps, may be procured from his Lady, now living near *Gloucester*, which Account would be more Authentick. So far Mr. *Bedford*.

Janus Mattheus, an *Italian* Physician, Printed a Book of *Problems*, at *Venice*, Anno 1567. The First *Problem* there treated, is this; Whether there are *Dæmons*, and whether they are the causes of Diseases, according to the Opinions of Divines, Philosophers and Physicians. In the Third Book of this *Problem*, he gives us a Relation much like the foregoing Relation of Mr. *Bedford*, and says, he had it from many Persons worthy of Credit, and from the Author of the thing himself. It is as follows.

After the Death of *Julius Albertus*, a Lawyer, a certain Friend of mine, a Lawyer also, seized on a certain *Necromantick* Book, which had been kept in a Box of the said *Albert*; having got it into his possession, he presently return'd into a Mountain, where his Wife was Born, before the discovery of the Theft; there he Lived a long time, and Died, never having tried the Power of the Book, he being wholly Ignorant of the Magick Art; but on a day unwarily whisper'd out something, concerning its Magical Power, to his only Son, named *Arrivabenus*, my familiar Acquaintance, his Father being Dead, and he having Married a Rich Wife, was drawn by some false Companions, into the Fallacious Practice of Chymistry, and when, after a while, he had spent much of his Wives Fortune, and almost all of his Paternal Estate in Chymical Practices to no purpose, he lights, on a day, on a certain *German* Traveller, who was Skilful in the Art of Chymistry, whom he carried to his House, and they there try'd Chymical Experiments together a long time, but still in vain; whereupon at length he discover'd to the *German*, that he had a Magical Book, and shew'd it him, but with engagement of Secresy; the *German* considering the Book, said to him, pray let us try whether this Book contains Truth or Dreams, and on an appointed Day; *Arrivabenus* took with him the Book, and a Sword (the *German* going with him unarm'd, (for so it was agreed betwixt them;) and before Sun Rising they went into a Valley, thro' which a Torrent ran, and so went into a thick Wood, on the left side of the Torrent, in the midst of which having cut some Bushes with the Sword, and made an *Area*, as it was necessary; presently some Ceremonies being premitted by the *German*, wont to be used for such end, and a large Circle being made with a Rod, with certain Geometrical Figures, they both enter into it. Then *Arrivabenus* himself, who would not deliver the Book to the *German*, (they having so agreed) held it firmly in his Left Hand, and the Sword in his Right, and at the *Germans* Command open'd it; which being done, the *German* in the *German* Tongue, called only two *Dæmons* to appear in Soldiers Habits; and presently with a great Wind and Noise, two *Dæmons* came, one a Horseman with an Head-piece and a Coat of Mail, and all other meet Arms, and Riding on a Black Horse; the other a Foot Soldier, going before him, girt with a Sword, and having a Snapsack on his Shoulder, whose Eyes shined with certain movable Flames, that you would have judg'd them Colliers, and would scarce have been able to look on them: presently as these *Dæmons* appear'd to the Men, they said, what do you Ask? to these the *German* made an Answer, and asked them many things in the *German* Tongue, and received their Answers to all things in particular. At length as he had Commanded them to return to Hell, as they were going away, *Arrivabenus* said, What think you will become of our *Alchimy?* to which as the *Dæmon* was going to Answer, begone says the *German*, in the *German* Tongue, Speak no more; whereupon, they return'd to Hell, with the same Wind and Noise as they came. After they were Vanished *Arrivabenus* began to upbraid the *German* for having done Ill, in hindring the Devil from giving them an Answer, as to their *Alchimy*, and the next day dismist him. And by reason that for two Years afterwards *Arrivabenus's* Wives Uncles would not Pay him what remaind in their Hands of her Fortune, as he desired, because he had managed, his Affairs Ill; being struck with a Rage, he takes his Dæmonical Book, and goes to the same Wood and *Area*; and having performed all things but one, which the *German* had done there before; behold, presently, with the same Wind and Noise of the Trees, innumerable *Dæmons*, with Frightful Countenances, and carrying rugged Staves in their crooked Hands, appear (for through Rage *Arrivabenus* had forgot to command, both how many, and in what appearance they should come to him, as the *German* had done before) and stood about the Circle he had made, within which the Miserable Man stood; and they fear'd him with threats, and endeavoured to pull him out of the Circle, all of them earnestly Asking, what will you have? what will you have? whereupon being Frighted and beside himself, and running to and fro within the Circle, in an horrid Fear, he fell at length out of the Circle unawares; the *Dæmons* then fell a Beating him, pulling him here and there, and strove to take the Book from him, but could not do it, he having hid it in his Bosom. Mean while *Arrivabenus* sometimes Running, sometimes Creeping, came at length to the Bridge, which is over the River, for he was not so far beside himself, that he had quite forgot his right way, but the *Dæmons* threw him from the Bridge into, the River, so that he was nigh Suffocated in the Mud and Water; now, a Country Man casually driving an Ass to fetch Wood, past over the Bridge, where his Ass being frighted, and flying back, he saw *Arrivabenus* tumbling in the Mud, half Dead, he called to him, and laying hold, of his Hair, drew him out of the Mud, and by the help of his Ass, carried him, with much ado, to his Wife in the Town; who finding the Book in his Bosom, which she had heard him speak of before, she took it privately from him, and had it burnt. *Arrivabenus* lookt Pale and Ill ever after it, tho' he Lived a long time: And *Anno* 1591. upon my request, freely gave me this Relation, word for word, I having heard of it long before from some others. *Janus Mattheus* adds for a close; Now what possibly may our great Philosophers, the *Perepateticks* here Answer? Truly they will either deny Instances of this kind, for that they consist of Particulars, which are neither known by Discipline, nor by the Understanding: or such things being granted, they would say that these are not Histories, but meer Dreams of some Melancholly Relators, for certain Melancholly Persons so fixtly Dream in the Night (as it sometimes happens to Lovers and Jealous Persons) of these things which with a most vehement affect they Desire, Hope, abhor or fear in the Day, that they seem most truly to see the same waking in the Day time; according to that of *Averrhœs*. Its no strange thing that some Man may see when awake, what sleeping he did in his Dream. Nay, perhaps he will see the very form of the thing, and not its likeness, as its said of *Gaumar*. So far *Janus Matthæus*.

<small>L. de Som. & Vig.</small>

Kircher, in his *Œdip. Ægyp. Tom.* 3. *p.* 82. tells us, That in the midst of the Subterraneous *Adyta* of the *Egyptians*, there was an Altar or Table plac'd, and in it the whole Concatenated Series of the *Genii*, were represented by such hidden Symbols, that they did not only notifie the hidden Recesses of the greatest Mysteries, but they had also an infallible efficacy, to make one of them which the Priests had a Mind, personally to appear, by horrible and execrable Adjurations, and Analogous Rites and Ceremonies.

There are many Relations of Houses infested with *Dæmons* by Magical Practices, causing Noises in them, throwing Stones, &c. of which I shall give only this Instance, *Joan. Cluverius* tells us, that *An.* 856, an evil Spirit infested the City of *Mentz*, and the Neighbouring Places: first throwing Stones, and making Noises against the Walls of the Houses, and then growing troublesome to Men, he began, in a while to speak, and to tell what things were stoln, and so to sow discord among Neighbours; at length he stirr'd up the Minds of all against one Man, as though they suffer'd all those things for his Sins; and into whatsoever House he went, it presently took on Fire: nor was he free in the Fields, for Fruits being there heap'd together, they were consum'd with Fire, and when the Neighbours for this fell upon him, and were about to kill him, he prov'd his Innocency by carrying a burning hot Iron in his Hands. He continued acting thus for three Years, till he had consum'd all the Houses with Fire.

In Epit. Histor.

There was an Instance of this kind, the last Year in *Somersetshire*, at *Butley*, near *Glastenbury*, where lives one Mr. *Pope*, whose Son being about 13 or 14 Years of Age, fell often into Fits, and in his Fits said, his Father's House would be Burnt by Spirits, whom he sometimes saw; and the House was Burnt down accordingly, and a Stall with three Oxen in it, and some Wheat Mows in his backside; and Stones were seen to come in at the Windows in the Day time, no Man perceiving from what Hand they came; as a Person of *Glastenbury* told my self, the last Summer, at *Wells*, in the said County; he, upon his being in the House, having seen many Stones so come in at the Windows. This Vexation continued a long time, though now I hear it's ceas'd, and the House is rebuilding; There are many more particulars to be brought concerning this Fact, and, if any Man can make out, that all these things were done by Trick, and Contrivance (as some say they were) they may do well to satisfie the World of it.

I know the late Dr. *Bekker*, in his Book entituled, *Le monde Enchanté*, laughs at all things of this Nature, as done by Humane Contrivance, and Mr. *Scot*, in his *Discovery of Witchcraft*, writes thus: I could recite a great Number of Tales, how Men have ev'n forsaken their Houses, because of such Apparitions and Noises; and all has been by meer and rank Knavery; and wheresoever you shall hear that there is in the Night Season such rumbling, and fearful Noises, be you well assur'd, that it is flat Knavery, performed by some that seem most to complain, and are least suspected; and hereof there is a *very* Art, which for some respects I will not discover. The Devil seeks daily, as well as nightly whom he may Devour, and can do his Feats as well by Day as by Night, or else he is a Young Devil, or a very Bungler.

I know not what may be offer'd to Men of such obstinate Prepossessions, who will have all things done by Imposture, which seem strange to them, and interfere with their Belief; I may indulge their Humour so far, that if only one Person tells a very strange Story, a Man may be more apt to think it possible for that Person to lye, than that so strange a Relation should be true; but if a considerable number of Persons, of several Countries, several Religions, several Professions, several Ages, and those Persons look'd upon to be of as if great Sagacity, as any the Countries afford, agree in Relations of the same kind, though very strange, and are ready to vouch the Truth of them upon Oath, after having well consider'd Circumstances, I think it a violation of the Law of Nature, to reject all these Relations as fabulous, meerly upon a self presuming Conceit, unless a Man can fairly shew the things to be Impossible, or wherein those Persons were impos'd on. Dr. *Bekker* rejects all the Facts alledg'd for proving the Operations of *Dæmons*, and among others the Facts of the *Dæmons* of *Mascon* and *Tedworth*, as being done by Combinations of Servants, or others; and would have the World acquiese in his Arbitrary say so, without any manner

L. 15. c. 49.

of Proof, only alledging this frivolous Pretence, that there have been Impostures in that kind, and therefore those must be so; a notable consequence which should a School-Boy infer, he would deserve lashing, but I shall say somewhat concerning Dr. *Bekker*'s Work beneath (it being *Instar Omnium* in its kind) and therefore shall say no more of it here; leaving the Facts at *Mascon* and *Tedworth* to Men of unbyass'd Thoughts to judge of them as they see cause: These Relations seeming to me well attested, and as well examin'd as if the Critical Dr. *Bekker* had been a Party concern'd on that Account. Indeed it may not be easy sometimes to discover how a thing is done by Trick, tho' it be really so; as the Lord *Howard*, in his *Defensative against suppos'd Prophecies*, c. 17. where he treats of Mens Conference with damn'd Spirits and Familiars, tells us, That himself was present with divers Gentlemen and Noblemen, who undertook to descry the finest Sights that *Schotto*, the *Italian*, was able to Play, by *Leger du Main*, before Queen *Elizabeth*, who notwithstanding were no less beguil'd than the rest, that presum'd less on their Dexterity and Skill in those Matters. And nevertheless I think it may not be difficult to discern that some Facts, and among others, those that pass'd at *Mascon* and *Tedworth*, were above all Humane Performance. Mr. *Scot*, indeed tell us, *There is a peculiar Art for doing these things, which for some respects he will not discover.* I suppose by this Art he does not mean a common Combination of Servants (as Dr. *Bekker* seems to be of Opinion it is, though he presently subjoins, that the Devil can shew Tricks as well by Day, as by Night, intimating as though those Noises, *&c.* only happen in Houses by Night (a time favouring Impostures) which is a great mistake; for in the Relations of the *Dæmons* of *Mascon* and *Tedworth*, and that I have given before, and in many other Relations of the like kind, we find that many Facts pass'd in the Day time, as well as by Night, and that Stones have been thrown at Persons in open Fields, in the Day time, by an invisible Hand, when many have been present. And notwithstanding this pretence of an Art, unless Men have an Art to make themselves invisible, (as *History* tells us, I know not with what truth, some have done) I shall never believe that any Man shall be able fairly to solve the Facts we have recorded of Houses and other Places infested, by any Performance of Man; allowing still that there have been many Impostures in this kind, and that many strange things may be performed, as to the Conveyance of Voices and Sounds by a deep insight in *Acousticks* and *Phonicks*.

I shall not conceal here, that, in reference to what pass'd at *Tedworth*, a Person lately told me, Mr. *Mompesson* own'd privately to the late King *Charles* the Second, that all that pass'd at his House at *Tedworth* was done by Contrivance: And another Person has told me, it was done by two Young Women in the House, with a design to scare thence Mr. *Monpsesson*'s Mother; this was told them by others, and I found them inclin'd to a Belief of it, but whoever related this, unless they were obstinate Opposers of the Truth, either had not seen, or duly Consider'd the Letter writ by Mr. *Monpesson* to Mr. *Glanvil, Nov.* the 8*th*. 1672, nor that writ by him to Mr. *Collins*, one of the Booksellers that undertook the Impression of his Book, it being dated *Aug.* the 8*th*. 1674. in the first mention'd of those Letters he writes thus: I have been very often of late ask'd, whether I have not confess'd to his Majesty, or any other, a Cheat discover'd about that Affair. To which I gave, and shall to my dying Day, give the same Answer, that I must belye my self, and perjure my self also, to acknowledge a Cheat in a thing, where I am sure neither was, nor could be any, as my self, the Minister of the Place, and two other honest Gentlemen, depos'd at the *Assizes*, upon my impleading the *Drummer*; and tho' I am sure this damnable Lye does pass for current among one sort of Persons in the World, yet I Question not but the thing obtains Credit among those, whom I principally desire should retain a more Charitable Opinion of me, than to be any way a Deviser of it, only to be talk'd of in the World, to my own Disadvantage and Reproach.

In his Letter to Mr. *Collins*, he informs him of what was depos'd upon Oath, and by whom at the *Assizes* at *Sarum*, concerning this Affair, where he writes thus; The Evidence upon Oath were *my self*, one Mr. *William Maton*, and one Mr. *Walter Dowse*, all yet living, and I think of as good Repute, as any this Country has in it; and one Mr. *John Cragg*, then Minister of the Place, but since dead: We all depos'd several things, that we conceiv'd impossible to be done by any Natural Agents, as the Motion of Chairs, Stools, and Bedstaves, no Body being near them, the beating of Drums in the Air, over the House, in clear Nights, with several other things of the like Nature. These Witnesses were Neighbours, and depos'd that they heard, and saw these things almost every Day or Night, for many Months together.

The proceeding Letters are Printed at the end of the Preface, to the Second Part of Mr. *Glanvil's Saducismus Triumphatus*, Printed together with the First Part, *Ann.* 1681.

After the foregoing Declaration of Mr. *Mompesson*, I must freely tell all Men, that shall pretend a Cheat in the Translation at *Tedworth*, that till they fairly make appear to the World, by whom the Cheat was play'd, and how the Facts Sworn to were perform'd, the Imposture must lie at their Door.

If we may believe *Luther*, he tells us, in his *Table Talk*, Chap. 35. That he departed from *Worms*, and not far from *Eisenach*, was taken Prisoner, and was lodged in the Castle of *Wartburg* in *Pathmo*, in a Chamber far from People, where none could have access to him, but only two Boys that twice a Day brought him Meat and Drink, among other things they brought him Hazle Nuts, which he put into a Box, and sometimes us'd to eat of them. In the Night times the Devil came, and got the Nuts out of the Box, and crack'd them against one of the Beds Posts, making a very great Noise, and a rumbling about his Bed, but he regarded him not; when afterward he began to slumber, he kept such a racket and rumbling upon the Chamber Stairs, as if many empty Hogsheads and Barrels had been tumbled down; and tho' he knew the Stairs were strongly guarded with Iron Bars, so that no Passage was either up or down, yet he arose and went towards the Stairs to see what the matter was, but finding the

Door fast shut, he said, *Art thou there? So be there still*; and so he committed himself to *Christ*, and laid him down to rest again. So far *Luther*.

I went my self once to see a Gentleman near *Bath*, and came to his House about Eleven of the Clock in the Morning, his Lady said to me, she wish'd I had come sooner, for about an Hour before, as she was coming in at the fore-door of the House, she saw the Minister of the Parish come into the Entry, at the backdoor, and to go into the Hall, whom she presently followed, but found him not there, whereupon she went up to her Chamber, where a Midwife was to attend her, she being near her time of being brought to Bed, and finding the Minister not there, as she expected, she was much surprised, and sent to his House to enquire for him, and it was found, he had not stirred out of his House that Day; but withal the Gentleman, I was to see, told me, they had every Night Noises in their House, as though a Man should strike Hundreds of strokes with a Mallet on an empty Hogshead, which kept himself, and his whole Family waking; and said, if I would stay a Night with him I should hear the same; but my occasions would not then permit me to stay.

There are a World of well attested Relations in this kind, but all must be Cheat and Imposture with some Men, because, forsooth, they will have it so.

To deliver somewhat of my own Opinion concerning the Power of Magick; I must own my self to have been long guided by the Caution giv'n us by *Corn Agrippa*, to prevent being impos'd on by Pretenders to Magick, and other curious and abstruse Arts, in an Epistle he sent to his Friend, the Abbot *de Aqua Pendente*, where he writes as follows: Have a care you are not deceived by those who have been deceived, for no reading of Books whatsoever can direct you in this, they being fill'd with meer *Ænigma*'s. O! How great things are written concerning the Power of the *Magick Art?* Concerning the prodigious *Images* of *Astrologers?* of the powerful Metamorphosis of the *Alchimists?* and concerning that Blessed Stone, with which baser Metals being touch'd, they are presently turned into Siver or Gold? all which things

Ep. l. 5.
Ep. 14.

are found vain, when they are practis'd according to the Letter. And nevertheless those things are delivered and written by great, and most grave Philosophers and holy Men, whose Traditions, who shall dare to Charge with Falshood? Nay, it would be impious to believe, that they purposely writ Lyes. Therefore there is another Sense in what they write, than is delivered by the Letter, and that covered with various Mysteries, but hitherto openly explained by none of the Masters; and which I know not whether any Man can attain, by the sole reading of Books, without a skillful and faithful Master, unless he be divinely inlightned, which is granted to very few. Therefore many labour in vain, who pursue these most Secret *Arcana* of Nature, applying their Minds to the bare words as they lie; for by an unhappy *Genius*, being fall'n from a right understanding, and intangl'd in false Imaginations, by the craft of exteriour Spirits, they become dangerous Servants to those, over whom they might Rule, and not knowing themselves, they go forth after the Footsteps of their Herds, seeking without themselves, what they possess within them. And this is what I would now have you know, that the Worker of all wonderful things is in our selves, who knows how to effect, and that without all Crime, Offence of God, or Injury of Religion, whatsoever the portentous *Astrologers*, the prodigious *Magicians*, the envious Persecutors of Nature, the *Alchimists*, and the wicked *Necromancers*, worse than Devils, dare promise. I say, that Worker of wonderful things is in us,

> *Nos habitat, non tartara sed nec sidera coeli.*
> *Spiritus in nobis qui viget, illa facit.*
>
> *He lives in us, not in the Stars, nor Hell,*
> *That Spirit does it, which in us does dwell.*

But these things are not to be committed to Paper, but to be delivered by Word of Mouth, which I may do when I see you. As to the Philosophy you require, I let you know, that to know God, the Maker of all things, and to pass into him by a whole Image of likeness, as by a certain Essential contact, or tye, whereby you may be transformed and made a God, this is the true and solid Philosophy, as the Lord speaks of *Moses*, saying, *Behold I have made thee a God of Pharoah*, this is the highest, and most occult Philosophy of wonderful Works. Its *Clavis* is the understanding, for the higher things we understand, the more sublime Vertues we put on, and the more wonderful things we Work with more ease and efficacy, but our understanding being inclosed in corruptible Flesh, unless it rises above the ways of the Flesh, and comes to its proper Nature, cannot be united to those Divine Powers (for they do not join but with their like) and is wholly impotent for perceiving those most hidden Secrets of God and Nature; shall a Man see God and Live? What Fruit will a Grain of Corn bring forth, unless it first dies? He must die, die to the World and the Flesh, and to all his Senses, and the whole Animal Man, who would enter the recesses of Secrets; not that the Body is separated from the Soul, but that the Soul leaves the Body; concerning which Death, *Paul* says to the *Colossians, You are dead, and your Life is hid with Christ*; and elsewhere he says, more clearly of himself, I know a Man, whether in the Body or out of the Body I know not, God knows, rapt to the third Heav'n, *&c.* I say we must die this Death, which is precious in the light of the Lord, which happens to very few, and haply not always; for,

> ——— *pauci quos æquus amavit,*
> *Jupiter, & ardens evexit ad æthera virtus,*
> *Diis geniti hoc potuere* ———

first those who are born, not of Flesh and Blood, but of God; next those who by a Privilege of Nature, or a Genethiliacal Gift of the Heav'ns are Dignified for it; the rest build on Merits and Art, concerning which I shall certifie you by Word of Mouth. So far *Agrippa*, who has much more to the same purpose.

Dr. *Flood*, as well elsewhere in his Works, as in his *Clavis to his Philosophy and Alchimy*, towards the end of it, writes conformably to what is delivered us by *Agrippa*, as follows. That the true *Cabalists*, and true *Alchimists* are employed about one and the same thing, and so the Magi, wise Men, and Philosophers, its what no Man of a sound Mind can be Ignorant of, since there is but one *summum bonum*, and one true Stone, at which Mark all that are truly Wise, most attentively Aim; some of whom are employed about the *Cabala*, others about *Alchimy*, others about the *Theo-Philosophy*, others about *Natural Magick*.

As to *Agrippa*, I have heard some Learned Men say, that in his Youth, when he writ his Books of *Occult Philosophy*, he had some esteem of *Magick*, but as he grew Elder, and when he writ his *Vanity of Sciences*, he shew'd his contempt of it; but I wonder Learned Men should talk thus; for in his *Vanity of Sciences*, he explodes *Magick*, no more than he does all other Arts and Sciences, and indeed he writes little there against it: And he says elsewhere, that he writ that Book sportingly, only to try what Young Students could say for the Arts and Sciences they were so fond of, and so valued themselves by. And in his Epistle to *Erasmus*, he says He writ that Book in a Declamatory way, in which all Liberty of Speech is used and allowed; this being as Scholars, that take a *Theme*, and declaim *Pro*, or *Con*, at Pleasure. If I look for *Agrippa*'s true Sense of a matter, I seek for it in the *Epistles* he writ to his Learned Friends and Correspondents, and there he sufficiently expresses the esteem he had of the true Magick. *Epist. l. 6. Ep. 35.*

As to the Death of the Animal Man, mentioned by *Agrippa*, as requir'd for initiating us towards the Performance of great things, Dr. *Willis*, as a skillful Phisiologer, in his Book *Of the Soul of Brutes*, excellently sets forth the Contest which happens betwixt the Corporeal Soul, and the Rational, in the Purgative Life, before the latter can settle the former in a due Subjection, and keep it self to its due Purity. He writes thus: The Corporeal Soul does not so readily obey the Rational in Desirables, as in Knowables, for that being nigher the Body, and so having a more intimate Affinity towards the Flesh, its *Exerc. 1. c. 7.*

wholly bound to take care of the good and Perservation of that; for the careful Performance of which Office, its very much drawn by the various Allurements continually presented by the Objects of each Sense; hence being employed about the care of the Body, and under that pretext being apt to indulge Feasting and Pleasures, she very often gives a Deaf Ear to Reason, perswading the contrary; moreover, the Inferiour Soul being weary of the others Yoak, on occasion being given, clears it self of its Fetters, affecting Liberty, or Rule; and then you may clearly observe Twins striving in the same Belly, or rather a Man wholly divided by two Armies fighting against each other within him.

Infestis obvia signis.
Signa, pares Aquilas, & vota minantia votis.

This Intestine contest does not wholly cease, till one of the Combatants being become Superior, leads the other wholly Captive, though, in the mean time, to establish the Empire of the Rational Soul, and to vindicate its Right and Empire from the Usurpation of the sensitive Soul, the Precepts of Philosophers, and Moral Institutions are put in use, and when these will not do, Sacred Religion furnishes a far more powerful Aid, whose Laws and Precepts being duly observ'd, they are able to raise a Man not only above a Brute, but ev'n himself, that is, above his Natural State; in as much as they subject the Sensitive Soul to the Rational, and both to God. Nevertheless this Divine Policy is not, ev'n so erected in Man, without a great Contention; for while Reason using its own strength, joyn'd with Moral and Sacred Precepts endeavours to draw the Faculties of the Corporeal Soul to its side, this rising on the contrary, obstinately adheres to the Flesh, and is hardly drawn from its Flatteries, nay, and which is to be lamented, she too often seduces the chief Soul in us, and carries it away with it, to wallow in the Dirt of sensual Pleasures; so that a Man becomes either like to, or worse than a Brute, insomuch that Reason being become Brutal, leads to every excess; and notwithstanding the Minds Empire is not always, and wholly overthrown, but sometime or other, either returning to her self, of her own accord, or being awaken'd by some occasion given, and conscious of her Lapse, she riles up against the sensitive Soul, as an Enemy and Traitor, and throwning her from her Throne, commands her Obedience. Nay, sometimes she compels her, by reason of Crimes committed, to torture her self, and her beloved Flesh, and so by inflicting Punishments on her self, to Expiate, as she may her own Faults; which kind of Act and Affect of Conscience of a Man's torturing himself, being proper to Man, plainly shews him either to have two subordinate Souls within him, or, at least that the Parts of his Soul are very differing; whereof, as the one opposes the other, and contends for the Mastery, it happens that Man is carryed away to contrary purposes, and is Exagitated little less than a Dæmoniack, obsess'd by a Legion.

The same Author, in the same Book, writes more of the said Contest as follows. Superstition, and Despair of Eternal Salvation are wont to imprint on the sensitive Soul, the Blood and Body, in a manner the like affects of Melancholy, as Love and Jealousie, tho' some way after a different manner of affecting; for in the former, the Object whose getting or loss is in danger, is wholly Immateral, and its design being first conceiv'd by the Rational Soul, is Imprinted on the Corporeal; in the prosecution of which, if this readily obeys, then no Perturbation of a Man's Mind arises; but if the Corporeal Soul withstanding, as it often happens, the Rational still insists with Admonitions and Threats, presently the other growing hot, moves the Blood and Spirits after a disorderly manner, opposes Corporeal Goods and Pleasures, to the Spiritual presented by the Understanding, and endeavours to draw the Man to her side; and as thus there is a continual struggle betwixt the two Souls, and sometimes the Will is Superior, sometimes the sensitive Appetite prevails; at length a Court of Conscience is erected by the Mind, where all particular Acts are scrupulously examined, by reason of these frequent Variances of the Souls, the Animal Spirits, as being too much, and in a manner perpetually exercised, and being

Dissert. 2. c. d' Melanc.

commanded here and there contrary ways, and almost distracted, fall somewhat at length from their Vigour, and Natural Disposition, and at last being rendred fixt and melancholick, as they are detained from their wonted Expansion, they frame out of Course, and unusal traces in the Brain, and so cause a *Delirium*, with an excess of Fear and Sadness. In those kinds of affects, the Corporeal Soul being carryed away, as it were by Violence, both Divorces it self from the Body, and being modified according to the Character of the *Idea* imprinted, is wont to take a New *Species*, either *Angelical*, or *Diabolical*; mean while the Understanding, inasmuch as the Imagination suggests to it only discorderly and monstrous Notions, is wholly perverted from the use of the right Reason.

After the like way of affecting, it happens that some melancholy Persons fall into Imaginary *Metamorphoses*, either as to their Fortunes, or their Bodies, one imagining himself and Acting as a Prince, another as a Beggar, one thinks his Body to be made of Glass, another thinks himself a Dog, a Wolf, or some other Monster; for after the Corporeal Soul, being affected with a lasting Melancholy, and blinded in Mind, has wholly departed from her self and the Body, she affects a New *Species*, or Nature, and, as much as in her lies, really assumes it. So far Dr. *Willis*.

I hope this may not seem an overlong Digression, in regard it seems to me to contain a more clear Explication, than may easily be found in other Authors, of the contest which happens betwixt our two Souls within us, in order to the Spiritual Death of the Animal Man, and our assuming a Divine Nature, capable of wonderful Works, as mentioned by *Agrippa*.

But after all the reasoning of *Agrippa*, in which he has excellently set forth what relates to Internal Operations of the Mind, and the way of bringing it to its highest Perfection and Purity, I do not see how he Accounts for the External Operations perform'd by Magicians of which there are a World of Instances, unless he will have it with the *Arabian* Philosophers, that the Soul by the Power of the Imagination can perform what it pleases; as penetrate the Heav'ns, force the Elements, demolish Mountains, raise Vallies to Mountains, and do with all Material Forms as it pleases.

Mr. *Blunden*, having sent a Letter from *London* to *Paulus Felgenbalder*, at *Amsterdam*, to desire his Opinion concerning *Magical Performances*, he returned him an Answer, in *Latin*, *An.* 1655, which Answer a Gentleman having favour'd me with a sight and perusal of, I give you here the Substance of it.

He divides Magick, and Magicians into three kinds, *viz.* Divine, Natural, and Diabolical. Now all Magick, he says, consists in the Spirit by Faith, for Faith is that *Magnet* of the Magicians, by which they draw Spirits to them, and by which Spirits they do great things; *viz.* either by the Spirit of God, or by Natural Spirits, or by the Spirits of *Dæmons*: Therefore all Magick consists in a Spirit, and every Magician Acts by a Spirit. Magicians that are of God Work by the Holy Ghost, and the Holy Ghost by Magicians, 1 *Cor.* 12. Natural Magicians Work all things by the Natural Spirits of the Elements, but Witches and Dæmoniacal Magicians, as *Jannes* and *Jambres* in *Ægypt*, Work their Magical Performances by the Spirit of *Dæmons*; he concludes therefore, that all Operations and Works of efficacy are wrought by a Spirit. Now, he says, it must be well observ'd, that the Magicians which are of God, and the Natural Magicians very much differ. Natural Magicians are shewn us, *Matth.* 7. 22. and by Natural Magick *Dæmons* are also cast forth, but not all kinds of *Dæmons*, and so many Works of efficacy are wrought by Natural Magick, also Natural Divinations and Prophecies, *Act.* 16. 16. such the *Pythonissa* was that raised *Samuel*, *Sam.* 28. who appeared in a Body of Wind and Air, as all the Bodies of the Dead, till the Resurrrection, which produces a Spiritual Body, consisting of a Spirit, Light, and the Heavens, Spiritual Elements. The Spirits of the Elements attend this Natural Magick, and obey the Magician: but we must know, that in some Persons the Natural Magick and Demoniacal are mixt and promiscuous, as the Magick which is from God, and the Natural Magick; and also in some part the

Dæmoniacal were mixt in *Balaam*, who also sought *Auguries*, *Numb.* 24. being willing to make himself gracious to God, and also to Man, and so to please both; and therefore the Angel of God resisted him, *c.* 23. and for this Hypocrisie, he died by the Sword, *c.* 30.8.

Though therefore, he says, Natural Magicians, do many Works of efficacy by Spirits, yet they do not do these in the Name of God and Christ, though they talk much of the Name *Adonai*, and call upon it, yet this Name may be taken in vain; and by the Permission of God Natural Spirits bring to pass *Auguries*. So also Natural Magick, and the Dæmoniacal are promiscuous in some Persons; but if a Person by Natural Magick should call out *Dæmons*, it does not follow, that this was also from Divine Magick; and if *Dæmons* are cast out by Natural Magick, by one that is in the fear of God, it does not follow, that he is a true Magician of God; for Natural Magick truly casts forth Spirits and *Dæmons*, if it be true Natural Magick, but if it exorbitates to Dæmoniacal, then it is condemn'd, and when Natural Magick keeps within its bounds, it is not condemn'd by Christ; read *Luke* the 9. 49. 50. wherefore the Name *Adonai*, and of *Christ* may be us'd both rightly, and in a sinister way; rightly, as in the place before quoted; in a Sinister way. *Act. c.* 7. 13. 14. and so the Magicians of Dæmons, resisted the Magicians of God, *c.* 13. 8. and 2 *Tim.* 3. 8.

He subjoins, that ev'n Natural Magick is not to be practis'd by any Christian, because all Magick is wrought by a Spirit, and we ought not to seek a Conversation with Spirits, and for that *Satan* mixes himself with the Natural Spirits. And whereas some allow the practise of Magick with the Angels of God, he says, That no Man ought to have to do with Angels without God's Command. And with this Abstract of that Letter, I conclude this Chapter of Magick.

CHAP. X.

What may be suggested from Reason, concerning the Existence of Spirits, and their Operations.

Kircher, in *Epist. Parænet.* prefixt to his *Obeliscus Pamphilius*, writes thus: We know a threefold Demonstration has been always us'd by the unanimous Consent of Philosophers in the Acquisition of Science; Mathematical, Physical, and Moral. Mathematical Demonstration, as it inquires into the affects and Properties of Quantity, by Principles known by the Light of Nature, of Eternal Truth, and void of all deceit, so it begets a certain, and properly called Science, all scruple of doubt being remov'd. Physical Demonstration, as it comes by Experiments of things, to the Secret knowledge of Causes, it begets indeed Science, but by reason of the Experiment, which for the most part is exposed to the false Representations of the Senses, it is not void of Deception, nor does arrive at the certitude of the former; yet according to *Aristotle*, it Triumphs with the Title of true Science. Moral Demonstration, as it depends on the Experience of Humane Actions, begets indeed Science, but such as the Nature of Moral things admits, and which is call'd Humane Faith, and for the most part, relies on the Authority of the Relater. For the like cause the Authority of the Revealer begets Divine Faith, more certain than all Science. Humane Authority is a certain imitation of this, on which we must relie, unless we will make void, and annihilate the Histories of all pass'd things; I speak not here of the Authority, and Histories of suspected Credit, but of those which have the clear Prescription of many Ages for their Authority. So far *Kircher*.

Now laying this before us, it is to be noted, That Christian Divines do not pretend to a Mathematical, or Physical Demonstration of the Existence of Spirits; for their Existence cannot be demonstrated from their Essence, or the effects ascrib'd to them, not from the first, because it's not from the Nature of Spirits, nor from that of any other Creature that they Exist; for God so freely created all Beings, that he might have left them uncreated; nor from their effects, because the concourse of God alone, or other Causes might be conceived to suffice for such effects; but Christian Divines build chiefly on Divine Revelation, which is superior to all Science, and on the constant Tradition of all Christian Divines, from the first Ages of Christianity; and all they pretend to, as Physiologers, in what they say concerning Spirits, is, that there is nothing in it, which implies a Contradiction, or is inconsistent with Reason; and as there have been, and are many *Phænomena* in the World, which it has concern'd Philosophers to Account for, the Doctrine of the Existence of Spirits has been Hypothetically introduc'd into the World, and back'd by as great Men among the *Gentiles*, as the World has had; and tho' other Philosophers have set up other Hypothesis for explaining those *Phænomena*; yet I think it would be a strange rashness in any Person owning the Law of *Moses* or *Christ*, to throw by an Hypothesis back'd by Divine Revelation, or rather introduc'd by the most Learned of the *Gentiles*, Consonant to it; and to adhere to any other Hypothesis, excogitated meerly by the Wit of Man; and which, in truth, does not so fairly account for *Phænomena* as the other does; or shamefully to deny Facts, which are to be accounted for; as I know not with what unbounded Confidence, some ev'n among Christians have done; whereas *Vanini*, who died a Martyr to Atheism, and *Pomponatius*, who has been look'd upon by some to have been of the same Opinion, and many others, freely own'd the Facts, which they found uncontestably manifested to them by Experience and Testimonies, though they did not think fit to explain them by the Agency of Spirits, but as free Naturalists, set up other Hypothesis as they thought good for explaining them. So *Alchindus*, in his Works, referred to Nature, all things that are ascribed to *Angels* and *Devils*, as since him *Petrus Aponus*, and *Pomponatius* have done, imagining that all Sublunary things were wholly subject to, and depending on Celestials;

and that they received all Vertues and Properties the one from the other, and each particular from the wholes together, by the means of certain Corporeal Rays, which pass from the least even to the greatest, and which they supposed the cause of all that is done in Nature. As *Marcus Marci*, of late referred all to *Ideas*; so *Avicenna* to *Intelligences*, *Galen* to the Temperament; and these, with many other Philosophers, have exerted all their force to take off the Admiration of many extraordinary Effects, by setting forth the most likely Causes of them they could imagine; but how far a Man may have Reason to acquiesce in any of those Hypothesis, will still be the Question.

For the Rationality of the Hypothesis of Spirits, *Plutarch* introduces *Cleombrotus*, thus delivering himself: As those say very well, who hold that *Plato* having invented this Element, whence Qualities spring and are ingendred, which is sometimes called the first Matter, and sometimes Nature, has freed the Philosophers from many Difficulties; so it seems to me, that those who have introduc'd the Nature of *Dæmons*, betwixt that of the Gods and Men, have resolv'd more Doubts and Difficulties, and greater; having found the tye, which conjoins and holds together as it were, our Society and Communication with them; be it that this Opinion came from the Ancient *Magi* and *Zoroaster*, or from *Thracia* and *Orpheus*, or from *Ægypt*, or from *Phyrigia* as we Conjecture, considering the Sacrifices that are made in those Countries.

L. de defect, Orac.

Father *le Brun*, in his Book quoted before by me, *c.* 3. after having set forth many odd Discoveries of hidden things, made by the *Virgula divinatoria*, in his second Part, *c.* 6. examines the Causes of its turning in order to Discoveries, and having (as I conceive) validly refuted all Natural Causes which others have pretended to assign for it, he concludes it is done by the Agency of evil Spirits; the Existence of which he proves as follows.

If there are Effects that cannot be produc'd by Bodies, there must necessarily be in the World other Beings than Bodies; and if among these prodigious Effects, there are some that do not carry Men to God, and make them fall into Error and Illusion, it's a farther invincible Argument that we must acknowlegde other Beings than the Being absolutely perfect and Bodies. So those extraordinary Effects which can neither be called in doubt, nor be Attributed to God, or to Bodies, are an Incontestable proof that we must admit created Spirits capable of amusing Men, and seducing them by Deceits. Though therefore the Scriptures had not clearly taught us the Existence of Spirits seperated from Bodies, I dare say, that extraordinary Effects, such as the discovery of many hidden things by the turning of the *Virgula Divinatoria*, would give a strong proof that there are wicked Spirits. But their Existence is clear enough in the Scriptures; and certainly its the best establish'd of all the Articles of our Faith, the least contested, and the most universally disperss'd through the World. *Maimonides*, in his *More Nevochan* proves with much Learning and Judgment, that before *Moses*, the *Sabeans*, *Æpytians* and *Chaldeans*, knew the good and evil *Genii*; all the Ancient Poets and Philosophers own'd this Dogma, and we find in the History of the Conversion of People, that it has been always found establish'd among the most remote Nations, nor can it be said (as some may pretend) that this is a proof of the stupidness of some Nations; for the most Polite People differ not in this, from those they call *Barbarians*; and we may see, in the Works of *Porphyrius*, *Jamblichus*, and *Clemens Alexandrinus*, how much the Doctrine of the *Greeks*, was like to that of the *Ægyptians*, concerning the Existence of good and evil Spirits.

Part 3. c. 46.

The new converted Christians of the Primitive Times, who, being disabus'd of the Follies of Paganism, were watchful on the practice of the *Gentiles* to discover their Impostures, own'd that sometimes Prodigies were wrought by the *Dæmons*. *Minutius Fœlix*, who liv'd in the second Century, has very well set forth what the Sense of the Christians of those Times was, concerning the Nature, and Operations of those *Dæmons*, whom the *Gentiles* Worship'd. *Tertullian*, and *Origen*, and almost all the Writers of the Three first Centuries have delivered the same, with all the Assurance that Truth may give: And what these great Men have said, is a very good

Answer to what is sometimes Objected, that Christ destroyed the Kingdom of *Satan*, and that the Prince of this World is now judg'd. *Joh.* 16. 11. St. *Peter*, St. *Paul*, and St. *John*, Men well instructed in the Words of Christ, and in the Sense that ought to be giv'n them, tell us, that the Devil, as a roaring Lyon, goes about to deceive us, that we ought to have recourse to Prayer, and keep us firm in Faith, to preserve us from his Artifices, and the snares he lays for us. The Devil therefore is not out of the World, so that he Acts no longer, but is driven from a great many Places where he had Rule. It's a Truth of our Faith, that God has left some Power to Devils, and he permits them, on many occasions, to put it in Execution. The frequent Possessions in the first Ages of the Church are authentick Testimonies of it, and the best averred Histories since Christ: And a thousand Superstitious Practices, producing extraordinary Effects, furnish us with incontestable Proofs of the Operation of *Dæmons*; and is there any Ecclesiastical Writer, who has not either proved or suppos'd this Truth? The Learned *Gerson* tells us, what we ought to believe in this Case, and whence it is that this Truth makes so little Impression on the Spirits of many Persons, saying, Certainly its an Impiety and an Error, directly contrary to the Scriptures, to deny, that *Dæmons* are Authors of many surprizing Facts; and those that look upon all that is said of it, as a Fable, and make a Mock of Divines, for ascribing Effects to *Dæmons*, deserve a severe Correction. Sometimes even the Learned fall into this Error, because they let their Faith be weaken'd, and their Natural Light be darken'd. Their Souls being all posses'd with sensible things, refer all to Bodies, and cannot raise themselves to Spirits detached from Matter. It's what *Plato* has said, that nothing so much hinders the finding of Truth, as to refer all things to what the Senses present us with. *Cicero*, St. *Austin*, *Albertus Magnus*, *Guliel, Parisiensis*, and, above all, Experience have taught, us the same, we may see a Proof of it in the *Sadduces* and *Epicureans*, who admitting nothing but what is Corporeal, find themselves among those Sensless Persons, of whom *Solomon* speaks in *Ecclesiasties*, and the Book of *Wisdom*, who have push'd their

Part I. p. 61.

Folly so far, that they cannot own they have a Soul, and effects that cannot be produc'd but by Spirits. I would there were no more Persons of that Mind; but we shall always find some, who will tell us in cold Blood, that they cannot believe *Prodigies*, nor *Miracles*, because they have seen nothing of extraordinary. Dispute not with such Persons; when a Man will be incredulous, he will be so in the midst of *Prodigies* and *Miracles*; there are always found People tempered like *Celsus* and *Lucian*, who will have all things to be Fable, Illusion, and Imposture. Many Persons measure all things by what they ordinarily see, and hold all for false, that surpass the bounds of Nature. They believe Facts while they appear Natural; convince them that they cannot so be, and you shall see them presently conclude them Impostors.

It's manifest, that we conceive but two sorts of Beings, *Spirits* and *Bodies*, and that since we can reason but according to our Ideas, we ought to ascribe to Spirits what cannot be produc'd by Bodies. So far the Abstract from Father *Le Brun*.

The Author of the *Republick of Learning*, in the Month of *August*, *An.* 1686, has given us a rough Draught for writing a good Tract of *Witchcraft*, which he looks upon as a *Desideratum*; where, among other things, he writes thus: Since this Age is the true time of *Systems*, one should be contrived concerning the Commerce, that may be betwixt *Dæmons* and Men.

Ib. part 3. c. 14.

On this Passage Father *Le Brun* writes thus: Doubtless here the Author complies with the Language of a great many Persons, who, for want of Attention and Light, would have us put all Religion in *Systems*. Whatever regard I ought to have for many of these Persons, I must not be afraid to say, that there is no *System* to be made of those Truths, which we ought to learn distinctly by Faith; because we must advance nothing here, but what we receive from the *Oracle*. We must make Systems to explain the effects of the *Load-stone*, the ebbing and flowing of the *Sea*, the motion of the *Planets*; for that the Cause of these Effects is not evidently signified to us, and many may be conceiv'd by us; and to determine us, we have need of a great number of Observations, which, by an exact Induction, may lead us to a Cause that may satisfie all the *Phænomena*. It's not the same in the Truths of Religion, we come not at them by groaping; and it were to be wish'd Men spake not of them but after a decisive and infallible Authority. It's thus we should speak of the Power of *Dæmons*, and of the Commerce they have with Men. It's of Faith that they have Power, and that they attack Men, and try to seduce them divers ways: We find it in *Job*, in *Tobit*, and in a thousand other places of Scripture and Tradition. It's certain also, that the Power they have depends not of us, that they have it over the Just, since they may tempt them as they did *Christ*: Tho' they have it not ordinarily, but over those that want Faith, or fear not to partake of their Works; and that to these last particularly the disorder'd *Intelligences* try to make exactly succeed, what they wish; Inspiring them to have recourse to certain Practises, by which those seducing Spirits enter in Commerce with Men. All this is discover'd without *System*. So far, *Le Brun*.

Dialog. 4.

    Gregory setting forth the Orthodox Opinion Concerning Spirits, says, That all things in this visible World are govern'd by an invisible Being; but *Aristotle*, tho' he assign'd spiritual Substances to the Celestial Bodies, whose number he conceiv'd according to the number of the Spheres mov'd; yet he tells us of none that preside over Inferior Bodies, unless, haply, Human Souls: And this because he thought of no Operations, in reference to inferior things, but natural, for which the Motion of the Celestial Bodies suffic'd.

    But the Assertors of Christian Truth, who affirm many things to be done here which exceed the Power of Nature, have thought it necessary that *Angels* should preside immediately over us. *Avicenna* was of Opinion, that only one Immaterial Substance presided over all Inferior Bodies, which he call'd the *Intellectus Agens*: But the Holy Doctors not disagreeing with the *Platonicks*, have taught, that distinct Spiritual Substances presided over differing Corporeal Things. So far *Greg*.

Having set forth the Opinion of Christians, concerning Spirits, establish'd, as well by Reason, as by Authority, both Divine and Humane, I shall now consider the Opinions of the *Perapateticks*, *Epicureans*, and *Sadduces*, denying the existence of Spirits; and shall here set down the notorious Principles they generally go upon, leaving those that please to follow them, and to partake of the Consequents of them.

First, *Aristotle* held, That God is not the Creator of the World, but that it was from Eternity, and will so continue, *Phys.* 8. *& Met.* 12. where *Aquinas, lect.* 2. says. That he held this Opinion firmly, and not problematically, tho' in his *Topicks* he says, it was a Problem among the ancient Philosophers.

2. That God does not take care of Inferior Things; nay, That he would become Vile if he minded them. *Met.* 12. *Text.* 3.

3. That God is a necessary, and no free Agent, as being the Soul of the first Sphere, which he cannot but move; and, that he cannot move a Stone with us. *Phys.* 8. *& Met.* 12.

4. That Heaven and Hell are the Fables of Legislators. *Met.* 2. *& in* 12.

5. That the particular Souls of Men die with the Body; and, That there is only one Immortal Soul, which is not the Form of the Body, but assisting to all Bodies.

6. That there are no *Dæmons* nor *Angels*, but the Movers of the Spheres, who are in Bliss by that motion, and cannot but move them. *Met.* 12. *& l. de Mundo.*

7. That God does not send *Dreams*, because he would send them to the Wise, and not to Idiots, as it commonly happens. *L. de Insomm.*

8. That Prophets are not Inspir'd by a Divine *Afflatus*, but grow Mad through Melancholy, and Prophecy in their Madness. *In Problem, Sect.* 30.

These *Dogma*'s, with others of his, were censur'd by the Councils and Fathers; and if admitted, all Religion and Government must fail: And *Aristotle*, for holding them, was forc'd to fly from *Athens*, otherwise he had been question'd by the Court of the *Areopagites*.

Secondly, The *Epicurean Philosophy* contains these *Errata* in *Physicks*.

1. It takes away the two chief Causes of Nature, *viz*. the eternal efficient, and final Cause.

2. It feigns all things to arise from a casual concourse of Atoms.

3. It feigns the Sun and Stars to be Vapours kindled and burning.

4. It affirms the Souls of Men to die with the Body.

Thirdly, The *Sadduces*, 1. Deny the *Resurrection*.

2. They reject all Tradition of the Fathers; and some of them, all the Prophets, but *Moses*.

3. They believe the Souls of Men to be Mortal, and to die with the Body. The *Arabian* Heresy, which was trump'd up, about 231 Years after *Christ*, (as it's observ'd by the Learned *Wigandus*, in his *Tract de Homine*) having some Alliance with this Opinion of the *Sadduces*, it asserting the Souls of Men to die with the Body, tho' it allows it to be restor'd with the Body at the Redurrection. Which *Dogma* has been new vampt of late by some of our Authors. Whereas *Christ* plainly says, *Matth*. 10. 28. *They cannot kill the Soul*.

4. They deny God's Providence, and ascribe all things to Man's Free-Will.

5. They deny Angels and Spirits.

Now, the *Sadduces* being a Sect among the *Jews*, and owning, at least, the Books of *Moses*, and finding mention there made of *Angels* and *Spirits*, they say that by the word *Spirit* in the Scriptures we are not to understand any substantial Being, but either certain Qualities, Motions, or Inspirations in Men, or else certain Divine Phantasms, or Appearances created by God to serve some present occasions, which cease to be as soon as they disappear.

And indeed, as Mr. *Lawrence* observes, in his *Discourse of Angels*, c. 1. sect. 2. the word *Spirit* is sometimes us'd in these Senses in the Scriptures; because Spirits being very active Natures, working, tho' powerfully, yet insensibly, therefore such Impressions, Qualities and Affections in Men, as powerfully and secretly move them, are call'd Spirits. Again, Because *Spirits* are such pure Substances as cannot be perceiv'd by our Senses, therefore meer Phantasms and Appearances are sometimes call'd *Spirits*. But when it's said, *John* 4. 24. that *God is a Spirit*, &c. Is God only a Quality or meer Phantasm? Is He not a proper Spirit, or a spiritual Substance?

The *Sadduces* Notion of *Spirits*, seems to resemble that which *Monsieur Charas* has of the Venom of *Vipers*: He thinks no Man can assign any part in a *Viper* where there is real Venom; and says, the Venom has nothing material in it, that it's a pure effect of the Imagination of the *Viper*, which forms to it self an Idea of Vengeance, which he produces but in the Instant of his Anger; and that its annihilated as soon as he ceases to be irritated: For confirming which he gives us this Experiment, that upon swallowing the Blood of a *Viper*, or pouring it on a Wound, no ill accident follows, which a Man would think it would, if Venom were really included in it.

Having laid down the general Principles of these Philosophers, I shall now particularly consider their Ground for rejecting Spirits, and their Operations.

These Philosophers, especially the two later, who have many adherents even to this Day, chiefly reject Spirits, because they say, they can have no Notion of such a thing as a Spiritual Substance. Now, as to this, I think our late Mr. *Lock*, in his Elaborate *Essay on Humane Understanding*, has fairly made out, that Men have as clear a Notion of a Spiritual Substance, as they have of any Corporeal Substance, Matter, or Body; and that there is as much Reason for admitting the Existence of the one, as of the other; so that if they admit the latter, it is but Humour in them to deny the former. He reasons thus: If a Man will examine himself, concerning his Notion of pure Substance, in general, he will find he has no

L. 2. c. 29.

other Idea of it, but only a supposition of he knows not what support of such Qualities, which are capable of producing simple Ideas in us, which Qualities are commonly called Accidents; thus, if we talk, or think of any particular sort of Corporeal Substance, as Horse, Stone, &c. though the Idea we have of either of them, be but the Complication, or Collection of those several simple Ideas, or sensible Qualities, which we use to find united in the thing call'd Horse, or Stone; yet because we cannot conceive how they should subsist alone, nor one in another, we suppose them to Exist in, and supported by some common subject; which support we denote by the name of Substance, though it be certain we have no clear, or distinct Idea of that thing we suppose a support.

The same happens concerning the Operations of our Mind, *viz.* thinking, reasoning, fearing, &c. which we concluding not to subsist of themselves, and not apprehending how they can belong to Body, we are apt to think these the Actions of some Substance, which we call spirit: Whereby its evident, that having no other Notion or Matter, but something wherein those many sensible Qualities, which affect our Senses do subsist; by supposing a Substance wherein thinking, knowing, doubting, and a Power of moving, &c. do subsist, we have as clear a Notion of the Nature, or Substance of Spirit, as we have of Body; the one being suppos'd to be (without knowing what is the *Substratum* to those simple Ideas, which we have from without; and the other suppos'd (with a like ignorance of what it is) to be the *Substratum*, of those Operations which we Experiment in our selves within; 'tis plain then, that the Idea of Corporeal Substance in Matter, is as remote from our Conceptions and Apprehensions as that of Spiritual Substance; and therefore from our not having any Notion of the Substance of Spirit, we can no more conclude its *Nonexistence*, than we can for the same reason deny the Existence of Body; it being as Rational to affirm, there is no Body, because we cannot know its Essence, as its called, or have the Idea of the Substance of Matter, as to say, there is no Spirit, because we know not its Essence, or have no Idea of a Spiritual Substance.

Mr. *Lock* also comparing our Idea of Spirit with our Idea of Body, thinks there may seem rather less Obscurity in the former, than in the latter. Our Idea of Body he takes to be an extended solid Substance, capable of communicating Motion by Impulse; and our Idea of Soul is a Substance that thinks, and has a Power of exciting Motion in Body, by Will, or Thought. Now some, perhaps will say, they cannot comprehend a thinking thing. Which perhaps is true; but he says, if they consider it well, they can no more comprehend an extended thing; and if they say, they know not what 'tis thinks in them, they mean, they know not what the Substance is of that thinking thing; no more, says he, do they know what the Substance is of that solid thing; and if they say, they know not how they think, he says, neither do they know how they are extended, how the solid Parts of Body are United, or Cohere to make Extension, *&c.*

The Learned Monsieur *Le Clerc*, who generally considers how far Humane Reason can bear, in judging of Points laid before it, argues consonantly to what is before deliver'd by Mr. Lock, in his *Coronis*, added at the end of the Fourth Volume of his Philosophical Works, in the Third Edition of them. Where he writes as follows.

When we contemplate the Corporeal Nature, we can see nothing in it but Extension, Divisibility, Solidity, Mobility, and various determinations of Quantity, or Figures; which being so, it were a rash thing, and contrary to the Laws of right reasoning, to affirm other things of Bodies; and consequently from meer Body, nothing can be deduc'd by us, which is not joyn'd in a necessary connection with the said Properties: Therefore those who have thought the Properties of perceiving by Sense, of Understanding, Willing, Imagining, Remembring, and others the like, which have no Affinity with Corporeal things, to have risen from the Body, have greatly transgress'd in the Method of right Reasoning, and Philosophizing, which has been done by *Epicurus*, and those who have thought as he did, having affirm'd our Minds to be compos'd of Corporeal *Atoms*; but whence shall we say, they have had their rise? Truly, they do not owe their rise to Matter, which is wholly destitute of Sense and Thought; nor are they spontaneously sprung up of nothing, it being an *Ontological Maxim* of most evident Truth, that *nothing springs from nothing*.

Therefore the most Ancient *Physiologers*, as the very Learned Dr. *Cudworth* has shewn in his *Intellectual System of the World*, when they saw nothing in Matter, beside what we have said, and had consider'd the *Maxim* alleged; they pass'd from the Consideration of Bodies, to the Contemplation of a much more excellent Nature, by which they gathered Humane Minds were created, and all other Intelligent Natures, therefore the Consideration or the Corporeal Nature, joyned with the knowledge of the Properties of our Mind, lead Men the strait way to two *Tenents* of the greatest Moment, *viz.* the Existence of a Supream Deity, and the Creation of Man's Soul, by God, whence also is deduced its Immortality, to which we may add, that though the Authority of Divine Revelation be worthy of Credit by it self, yet it is not a little confirm'd in our Minds, when we see the Lights of Revelation and right Reason friendly conspire betwixt themselves, for they are two Sisters fall'n from Heav'n together, wherefore their Agreement must necessarily be very great, as being Sprung from one Father, but we do not apprehend their Agreement, at first sight, nor can understand it without an intent Meditation. If right Reason deny'd what right Revelation affirms, and we thought they disagreed we should stand doubtful betwixt them, nor should we well satisfie our selves which we ought to believe; but they agreeing, who can with-hold his Faith from them, but he that would be accounted not only to have little Religion, but likewise wholly destitute of Reason? Wherefore there is no cause for those that give not Credit to Revelation to flatter themselves, as though they were Wiser than the vulgar, when

Chap. I.

at the same time they naturally exclude themselves from the Number of Men that use Reason. *See there also what he further smartly argues for the Immortality of the Soul.*

The same Monsieur *le Clerc*, in his *Pneumatologia*, has delivered several things concerning Spirits and their Operations, of which I have extracted the few following Heads, as thinking them of use for directing our Judgments in Considerations of that Nature.

1. Those who affirm, or deny that Spirits can be without any Corporeal property, go farther than they ought; for we cannot gather from the Nature of Spirits, which is unknown to us, whether they are without all Corporeal proprety, or have a subtle Body. *Sect.* 2. *c.* 1.

2. As for Apparitions of Spirits, he says, we cannot by any Reason, shew from the Nature of the thing it self, that it is not possible for Spirits to be joyn'd with a subtle Body; nor is it likely that so many Nations, and so remote in Places and Opinions agreed in a Lye, as to all they have said concerning Apparitions of Spirits. Its much more likely, that the ground of the Lyes invented about this Matter, was some true Apparition, to which, as it's usual, a World of other Relations of the like kind have been feign'd. *Ibid.*

3. We are so far from determining what is the Nature of an Angels Intellection, that we do not comprehend ev'n the Nature of our own Intellection. *Sect.* 2. *c.* 2.

4. In what the *Gentiles* say of *Dæmons*, and the *Hebrews* of *Angels*, there is nothing contrary to any certain Knowledge we have; therefore it may be they say true, if the thing be consider'd in it self. *Sect.* 2. *c.* 3.

5. As it cannot be doubted, but there are many Lyes in what is related concerning strange Performances by Witches, upon a contract with *Dæmons*, so it would be rashness to Charge them all of Falshood, especially, since the Scriptures relate some things like them; and truly the thing it self is not so known to us, that we may gather from the Nature of *Dæmons*, which may not consist at least with many things that are related of them; if any Man, because both good and evil *Angels* are believed to be thinking Substances, should

contend that they have no Power on Bodies, because naked thought has no Power on Bodies, before this were granted him, he ought to shew, and that evidently, *First*, That there is nothing in Angels beside Thought; *Secondly*, That there is no tye instituted by God betwixt their Wills, and some Changes of Bodies; for if either of these may be admitted without absurdity, they may also be thought able to Act on Bodies without absurdity. *Sect.* 2. *c.* 4.

6. Some say no true Miracles, but Cheats are perform'd by *Dæmons*; but to Understand what this means, we must define the Words that are here us'd; a Portent, a Miracle, or a Prodigy are here the same things, and they denote an Effect. *First*, Above Humane Power. *Secondly*, Beside the constant Course of Nature. *Thirdly*, That it's done at Mans Pleasure, or at the Moment he will. Now, who can make but by certain Arguments, that nothing can be done by evil *Dæmons* above Humane Power, beside the usual Course of Nature, at the Moment the Magician, pleases, since the bounds of Angelical Power are unknown, we can here assert nothing but from Experience. *Ibid.*

7. Those that deny some wonderful Facts, for the most part contend they are *Præstigia*; but beside that, they affirm what they know not; this word may be taken in a twofold Sense; *Præstigia* by some are so understood, as tho *Dæmons* present to the Senses, a thing that is not, as if it were; as that an House, for Instance, may seem to be there where there is none; but to do this, either they move the Brain of Spectators, as its wont to be moved when an House is before them; or they present a certain sort of an Appearance of an House in the Air, which strikes the Eyes of Spectators; but choose either of these, it must be shewn how this is no Miracle, for both are done above Humane Power, and beside the Order of Nature, and at the time the Magician pleases. *Ibid.*

8. Those Opinions, or Diseases of the Brain which Witches have, who think they go to Feasts and Dancings, upon their talking of it to others that are of a timorous Disposition, and weak Brains, bring others into the same Fits of Fury, and like a contagion spread far and near, infecting many Heads.

Though it's observable that those Diseases are more frequent among Inhabitants of Mountains and Solitary places, than among those that live in Cities, or among a Concourse of People. Whence also it appears, that the Terror of vast Solitudes, which is apt to move the Brain, contributes much to this Madness; we must add to this, that Persons abounding with Melancholy, are more capable of this Madness; and on the contrary, those are freest from it, who are of a merry Disposition; which raises my Suspicion, that all these Visions are nought but the Sports of a timerous and melancholy Brain.

If it shall seem strange, that so many Men should be impos'd on by their fear and temper of Body, all Admiration may be taken away by Instances of a greater fury; many Diseases so trouble the Brain, that those that labour under them, seem to themselves to see things that are no where; that kind of Disease if it be join'd with a vehement Motion of the Blood, and lasts long, it at length consumes the Diseas'd; and if the Motion of the Blood abates, the Disease is lessen'd, and the Diseas'd returns to a sound Mind; but if the Disease does not so vehemently affect the Blood, but that it may continue a long time, without destroying the Diseas'd, or a lessening of his strength, strange things are presented to his Mind for many Years, as it's manifest in many Instances. Nor are there only those who think they see without themselves things that are nowhere; but also such as obstinately assert themselves to be Wolves, or I know not what Wild Beasts. Whoever weighs these things will not wonder if Opinions of Witches are accounted melancholy Diseases.

Yet tho' these things may be so, I will not affirm that those things which Witches relate, have never happen'd; but for one thing that has truly happen'd, I believe there have been a thousand Dreams of a deluded Mind. So far Monsieur *le Clerc. Sect.* 2. *c.* 5.

But, to return a little to the *Epicureans* and *Sadduces*, perhaps they may desire of me a clear Definition of a Spirit, or such an one as they would like. Now, I think, Monsieur *le Clerc*, has well answered this, in his Preface to his *Pneumatologia*, writing thus: We call all things endow'd with an Understanding and a Will, Spirits; but as we consider them as Spiritual Substances, he says, he has shewn in his Logick, that the inward Nature of any Substances, whatsoever, as well as that of Spirits is unknown to us, wherefore Men ought not to expect from us an absolutely compleat Description of Spirits.

Part I. *c.* 3.

But since these Gentlemen are for having all things made out very plainly to them, let us examine their Physical Principles, *Democritus* and *Epicurus* would have all Natural Effects whatsoever, to proceed from a Conflux of Attoms variously Figur'd, so that in every Body there are Particles that are round, acuminated, square, cylindrical, striated, and of other Configurations, and that according to the various locking together of them, a subject is of this, or another Figure, Operation, or Efficacy.

Now, as our Learned Dr. *Willis* has observed, this *Epicurean* Opinion, rather supposes than demonstrates their Principles, and teaches of what sort of Figure those Elements of Bodies are, not what they are, and also induces Motions very subtle, and remote from our Senses, and which do not satisfie the *Phænomena* of Nature, when we descend to Particulars; and thinks it concerns them to shew that those Conceptions of theirs are Real; he being too short sighted to discern them so.

L. de Parmi c. I.

Again, As for *Aristotle*'s reasoning against the Existence of Spirits, in his Book *De Mundo* (if it be his) *viz.* that since God can do all things of himself, he does not stand in need of Ministring *Angels* and *Dæmons*, a multitude of Servants shewing the weakness of a Prince. But if this Argument would hold good, *Aristotle* should not suppose Intelligences moving the Celestial Spheres, for God suffices to move all without ministring Spirits, nor would there be need of a Sun in the World, for God can enlighten all things by himself, and so all Second Causes were to be taken away. Therefore there are Angels in the World for the Majesty of God, not for that he wants them; and for Order, not for his Omnipotency: and who told *Aristotle* there were Intelligences that moved the

Celestial Spheres? Is not this Hypothesis as precarious, as any Man may pretend that of Spirits to be? And I believe there are few Philosophers at present, who agree with *Aristotle* in that Opinion. And indeed, I think *Kircher* in the right, where he tells us, it's certain, *Aristotle* took his Intelligences from the *Hebrews*, who beholding the Multiform face of the World, and the discording concord of things, believed it to be govern'd by certain presiding Angels; and hence also the Fiction of the Nine Muses took its rise.

Obel. Pamph. Pag. 292.

Moreover, when *Aristotle* lays down his Principles of Natural Things, he tells us, they are Matter, Form, and Privation, unintelligible Terms; and when he comes to define his Matter, he tells us, it is what is neither *quid*, nor *quantum*, nor *quale*, nor *aliquid eorum quibus ens determinate*, a notable clear Notion of Matter, *obscurum per obscurius*, and I think no Man will pretend the notion we have of Spirits, to be more obscure than this.

In short, those that will take upon them to rectify our notions of things, ought to bring us notions of things more clear than what we have, especially where Religion is concern'd; as in this case it is, and Young Wits, who are well opinioned of their Parts, may do well to try here, what they can suggest to us beyond what is here argued, and I am apt to think whatever conceit they may have of themselves, they will not be found so overdoing in Argument, but they will find a valid reply ready for them.

CHAP. XI.

Considerations on Dr. Bekker's *Books against* Spirits, *with a Conclusion to this Book.*

F*Rommannus* in his Tract of *Fascination*, tells us, that *Voetius*, above all others, has made out by firm Reasons, that there is such a thing as Diabolical and Magical *Fascination*, and this he undertook, as he says, because upon reading Mr. *Scot*'s Book (in which he has openly deny'd, and professedly oppugn'd the Crime of Magick, and ascribes all its wonderful effects, either to Melancholy, or other natural Diseases, or to Art, Industry and Agility of Men, imposing on us by their *Præstigia*, or to the foolish Imaginations of the said Magicians, or to (their vain Fables and Fictions) after it was Translated into *Low Dutch*, not a few, from that time, both Learned and unlearned began to Scepticize and turn Libertines concerning *Magick*.

L. 3. *part* 1. *c.* 2.

From this Source, I conceive, among other Works, the Four Volumes of the late Dr. *Bekker*, Entituled, *Le monde enchantè*, that is, *the World Bewitched* (of which the First Volume is Translated into *English*) have flown: he generally therein agreeing with Mr. *Scot*, and rejecting all Magical Incantations.

Indeed the great Principle Dr. *Bekker* goes upon, is, That there were Devils once in the World, who corrupted Humane Nature, but since that time, God Almighty put them in Chains, so that they have never made any Figure in the World since, by acting any way against Mankind, or otherwise.

As I perused Dr. *Bekker*'s said Volumes in *French*, I found some Persons had writ against him, and thereupon I sent to *Holland* for all that was Writ against him, and any Reply's he had made; but could get only one small Volume writ by *Monsieur Binet*, in *French*, Entitled, *A general Idea of the Pagan Divinity, Serving for a refutation of Monsieur* Bekker's *System, concerning the Existence and Operations of Dæmons.*

Printed at *Amsterdam*, *An*. 1698. This Book is composed of Six letters, writ by Mr. *Binet* to a Friend, and I shall here give you an Abstract, of what I find most material in them, in reference to Dr. *Bekker*'s System. In his first Letter he tells us, He finds in Mr. *Bekker*'s Works, much Zeal and Confidence in advancing Novelties, but no proofs to Maintain them, and unless you suffer your self to be surprized with a certain Air of Triumph, wherewith he animates his Expressions, you will run a risque of remaining still Inchanted, especially if you deny certain Principles, which he has laid down without proof, all the Work will fall of it self.

He observes, that where Mr. *Bekker* speaks of Spirits, all things seem to him perplext with difficulties, you shall scarce find a passage in the Scripture that speaks of them, all is Mysterious, Allegorical. The proper Names of Angels, Devils, Dæmons, *&c*. are but Men sent, Calumniators, Evil Thoughts, or, at most mere Symbols to give us some Metaphorical *Idea* of the Majesty of God.

He next cites the Passage following from Mr. *Bekker*'s Preface to his first Vollume.

It's now look'd on as a piece of Piety for a Man truly to Fear God, and also the Devil: if we do not this, a Man passes for an Atheist, that is, for a Man who believes no God; because he cannot believe there are two, one Good, and another Evil; but I believe, says he, we may with reason call those Men *Ditheists*, or such as believe two Gods. On this Passage Mr. *Binet* writes as follows.

This Passage extreamly reflecting on our Belief, I have rendered it word for word from the Text, because the Translator has corrupted it, by his usual softnings. This Accusation which Mr. *Bekker* charges us with, of making the Devil a God Almighty, strikes an Horror; mean while it's the foundation on which he builds his whole Work, it's the Idol he will pull down, it's in which the force of his Proofs consists, and you shall scarce read a Chapter in him, but you will find this Imputation. But whoever believ'd amongst us, that the Devil, properly speaking, is the absolute Author of all the Works, they say, we ascribe to him? What Divine has ever consider'd him as a First and Independent Cause? If we ascribe much Power to the Devil, it's manifest we speak with the Scriptures, and if there be any thing which does not agree with the Authors Conceptions, we use but the Expressions which the *Holy Ghost* has Consecrated; and thus all Mr. *Bekker*'s Objections Address themselves to God himself, who has prescribed us a way of expressing our selves in this respect.

Again, he writes beneath. You pretend to be well grounded in maintaining that we unjustly ascribe to the Devil, the Works that are ascribed to him, because he is but an Instrument, who borrows from God all his Actions, and I think we have as much reason to say that we deceive our selves, in ascribing to Man all his operations, since of himself he can do nothing; therefore it will no longer be Man that Moves himself, Speaks, Eats, Drinks, but God himself, for the Devil and Man are in this Case, in reference to God, one and the same thing, in an equal Impotence, and an entire Dependency.

You may object that this comparison of the Devil with Man is not Just: the business is to know, if the one be the Author of those high and sublime Operations that are ascribed to him; whereas, we consider in the other but actions proper and natural to him; but this difference tho' real betwixt the two Creatures, is but a meer Illusion, in reference to God, in which properly consists the state of the Question. We consider the Devil always as an Instrument in the hand of God, as a Rod of Fury, which strikes but when God lets it fall on those he will Visit. To explain this farther, I ask what vertue had *Moses* or *Aaron* and his Rod to do so many Miracles? to Inflict so many Plagues on *Pharaoh* and his People? the simple Rod in the hand of a Man could not produce so many Miracles of it self, but one was the Minister, the other the Visible Sign which God accompanied with a Divine Efficacy. And what would you say of a Man that would impute it to us to believe, that *Moses*, *Aaron* and his Rod were the sole cause of all these Miracles; if he inlarged himself in writing great Volumes, and making large Reflections, for giving colour to this Absurdity? and in the mean time the Scripture says, *Ex.* 8. 5. That *Aaron*, having stretcht forth his Hand with his Rod, on the Rivers, Brooks, and Ponds, caused Frogs to Issue from them to cover the Land of *Ægypt.* Therefore when we conceive the Devil as a Rod of Fury, without any Vertue of his own, it is but by relation to God, the first cause who precedes, determines, accompanies, bends the Creature, how excellent soever it may be. But it's manifest if you compare the Devil with Man, you will find more excellency in his Nature, light in his Knowledge, penetration in his Sight, facility and power in his Operations, his natural Knowledge is more extended, not only because he beholds things with a more Ample view, but also by reason of the experience of all Ages, which discovers to him the connexions, which makes him penetrate the bottom of Nature; whose Springs, Causes and Effects he knows after a more perfect manner than the greatest Philosopher: and it's this great Knowledge the Devil has of Nature, which teaches him how to move the various parts; whence it is that we, who know not these Springs, and the manner to make them act, are strangely struck at the sight of his operations, and that we look on as a Miracle, what is often but the operation of a *Dæmon,* produced by Causes otherwise apply'd and moved, than according to the ordinary course of Nature; and thus as the Devil has much more Light, Penetration and Activity than Man, we must not doubt but his Power is much superiour to his. You see therefore that the Author's odious Imputations vanish of themselves, and that our Doctrine is neither repugnant to Reason, nor Revelation, nor to the Idea of the Divine Perfections.

And I cannot comprehend how these Persons will find opposition betwixt the Almighty Power of God, and the Ministry of the Devil, for by this Objection the Author so often makes, he wholly overthrows his own Hypothesis: He will have it, that the clear and distinct Idea of the Divine Perfections exclude the operations of *Dæmons,* that there is a contradiction in believing, that those Spirits oppose themselves to the Will of God: Now this *Devil,* this *Satan,* these *Dæmons,* according to you are some Calumniating

Men, some Adversary, Humane Passions, Irregular Motions of the Spirits, what you please; but you cannot deny at least but these Men thus Characterized, are as many Enemies of God, and of his Gospel, Seducers, Persecutors; give me leave to ask you then, whether it be not a thing much more Inconsistent with the Idea of God's Perfections, to oppose to himself weak Creatures, these Mortal Men, rather than the Devil, who is a Spirit disengaged from Matter, of a consummate experience.

And beneath. It's in vain Mr. *Bekker* imputes to us the fear of the Devil, no he is an Enemy overcome, the Seed of the Woman has bruised his head; if he has any Power remaining, he derives it from God alone, he is in his Hand as a Rod of Fury to Chastise Men, and I fear him but as the Chastisements that God displays by his Ministry are to be fear'd. You see then that the Author Condemns himself, while having established for Principle that according to us, this abominable and Curs'd Creature does things more Miraculous than God himself has ever done. He adds, That supposing what is usually ascrib'd every where to the Devil and his Angels, there cannot be convincing Proofs that *Jesus* is the *Christ*, or that there is but one God: And I confess, says he, that if I do not possess the Reader with a clear Conception of this, in what I have Writ, it's in vain that I have Composed it. Now supposing that the Devil acts but Ministerially, and dependently of God, supposing that we attribute nothing to the Devil, properly speaking, of Miraculous, that can be put in opposition to, or parallel with the Works of God, our Proof that *Jesus* is the *Christ*, and that there is but one God, are exclusive to all other, in regard that it being very far from there being any prerogative in this Curs'd Spirit, that can be confounded with those which God possesses in the highest degree of Eminency; he has deprived himself, by his revolt, of his most pure advantages, and has precipitated himself into an Abyss of Miseries, where the Idea of a severe God makes him tremble.

In his Fifth Letter he writes thus.

Because a truth has been corrupted by divers Fictions, must it presently be rejected? there is no Principle, no natural Notion that can undergoe this examen, without being condemned: there is none but has been ill conceived and abused, then there will be none that can lawfully be admitted. Let us conclude therefore in general, that tho Men have err'd infinite ways, concerning the Doctrine of *Dæmons*, that they have been conceived as Substances either Material, or Spiritual, or mixt, tho' some have placed them in the Stars, others on the Earth, others in Hell; tho' there have been as many Sentiments, as Heads concerning their Offices; tho' they have been call'd *Sylphes, Gnomes, Salamanders*, all this will but prove at most that Men have ill conceived the nature and operations of *Dæmons*, but no way that we must entirely reject the ground of this Doctrine, by reason of the Fables Superstition has mixt with it.

And beneath. Were it true, as it's gathered from the expositions of Mr. *Bekker*, always opposite to himself, that there were in the *Old Testament* no Term which signified properly, or that could according to the *Genius* of the *Hebrew Language* and the use then, signifie those Spirits which we call *Satan, Devils*, &c. the *Jews* would have taken these Terms in their proper signification; so that by this name *Satanin*, they had not understood *Satans*, Angels of Destruction, or of Death, but only Adversaries, Men Enemies to God and his Truth; the *Sadduces*, for example, had had grounds to accuse. St. *Paul* of Ignorance, for following the sentiments of the *Pharisees*, who took the affirmative, since the *Pharisees* would have ill understood all the Terms of the *Old Testament*, which had signified Originally, and according to the then use, not Angels and *Satans*, but only Men either Good or Evil. If then the *Jews* were Imbibed in Substance with the common Doctrine of Devils; it's because they took these Expressions either for these pure and favourable Intelligences, or for these impure and adversary Spirits; and if they understood them in this Sense, being the same which the *Holy Ghost* has us'd in the Books of the *Old Testament*, they will have the same Signification, and if they have the same Signification; they will consequently be these same Spirits which operate here below; for there is not one Passage where these Terms are found, but formally teaches us their Operations; so that it's an uncontestable Principle, Which Mr. *Bekker* did not foresee, that if the *Old Testament* teaches us the Existence of Devils, we ought necessarily to infer their Operations, because they there appear every where operating.

Again, If those Terms of the Old Testament, which some pretend we abuse, to establish the Operations of *Dæmons*, signifie properly but Men, Adversaries, and if the Holy Tongue had never employ'd them to express these wicked Spirits, it's not to be doubted but the *Jews*, would have thrown it in our Dish; you should have seen them exagerate the easiness of the Christians to admit this fable of the Operations of *Dæmons*, as being purely pagan, and reproach them their gross Ignorance in Understanding the *Hebrew Tongue*. If they forbear it, and concur with us in defending the Opinion of the Operations of *Dæmons*, tho' they have added to them some Fables, it's because, that beside they know the true Signification of these Terms, and that we do not make use of them to contend against them, there would be too much absurdity to contest the Sense of them.

We find, according to Mr. *Bekker*, that what we believe of *Dæmons*, is in substance, but what the *Babylonians* taught the *Jews*. It's what this Gradation from the *Babylonians* to the *Jews*, from the *Jews* to the first *Christians*, from the first *Christians* to the *Papists*, from the *Papists* to the *Protestants*, evidently makes out; but I wonder God has suffer'd his Church always to be infected with this Error, and that neither the Prophets that were at *Babylon*, nor those that Instructed the *Isrælites*, after their re-establishment, who thundred with so much vehemency against Errors, did not oppose themselves to a Superstition so gross and Impious.

Christ came into the World to Destroy the Works of the Devil; his Prophetick Office oblig'd him to instruct the Ignorant, and oppose Superstition; you see him every where reprehending Vices, and thundering against Errors without any bearing of them: But as for the Operations of Angels and Devils, we find not the least Censure, nor the least Correction; would he have suffer'd these wanderings of Mans Mind, without recalling it to its Duty when these Errors, says Mr. *Bekker*, have undermined the Foundation of the Christian Religion, and would *Jesus Christ* have left them in their full vigour; in using the same Terms the *Jews* had corrupted, the *Pagans* had abus'd, and giving then the same Ideas?

If the Jews had corrupted the Terms of Angels and *Dæmons*, in giving them a false Signification, would *Jesus Christ* instead of dissipating these Prejudices of the *Jews*, have confirm'd them in their Error, in expressing himself in the same Terms, without having restor'd them to their true Sense, and in fomenting Superstition, by fabulous Examples of Men, obsess'd and deliver'd from *Dæmons*? Would the *Apostles* have Authoriz'd Error, in ascribing every where Operations to Devils; which neither the *Jews*, nor *Pagans* could have took in another Sense, than that which was then in use; compare this Objection with the 28th Chapter of the Author's Second Book; for I pretend, that the way Mr. *Bekker* there Answers, renders my Objection wholly unanswerable.

In his Sixth Letter, he writes thus: Mr. *Bekker* owns, that all the *Pagans* Ancient and Modern, *Europeans*, *Asians*, *Africans*, *Americans*, both North and South, agree in these three chief Points, which are of an incontestable Truth, 1. That there is only one first Being, or one supream Deity. 2. That there are Spirits that have had a Beginning, and that are distinct from Humane Souls. 3. That those Spirits are either Good or Evil; and that some of them are Friends to Men, and others Enemies.

See here then all the World imbib'd with an Opinion of *Dæmons*; whence I infer, that what they know, how erroneous soever it may be, must be known to them by the way of Operation; and to set this Truth in a clear Light, observe: It's impossible, that one self same Belief universally disperst, and constantly receiv'd, can be entirely false in the Bottom; I say in the Bottom, not to confound with the Substance of this

Doctrine, the erroneous Ideas under which it has been conceiv'd, and which have been divers, according to the diversity of the Imagination.

And beneath. We cannot find by any certain History, that the *Americans* had any Communication with the rest of the World till of late Years, yet this Imagination of *Dæmons* has been preserv'd among them for a great number of Ages, notwithstanding their Ignorance, Brutishness and Extravagances.

You may say, you cannot maintain that the knowledge of *Dæmons* carries the Characters proper to natural Truths. God has not imprinted them in the Imagination; and Reason, how clear soever it may be, cannot raise it self so far without the aid of Revelation; but I say, if *Dæmons* have been universally and constantly receiv'd by all the People of the World, this Knowledge must, flow from some solid Cause. It comes neither from the Scripture, nor from Reason, nor from the Imagination, it's deriv'd therefore only from the Operations of *Dæmons*.

Again, As for the surprizing Operations of *Dæmons* on the Idolaters. Mr. *Bekker* says, Those who know not God as Christians, know not also the Devil; but a Clown would have reason to Laugh at Mr. *Bekker*, if he would perswade him, that because he knows not the Nature of the Soul, and of the Body, and the Laws of Motion, he should not pretend to feel a sound Box on the Ear given him; and it's ridiculous to deny the Operations of *Dæmons* on People, because they are not so good Divines, as to raise themselves to the Knowledge of God, and the Mysteries which his Word has revealed to us, or because they are Ignorant of the true Doctrine of *Dæmons*. So far Mr. *Binet*.

This Author having made the foregoing Reflexions on Dr *Bekker*' Four Volumes, I shall have the less to say to them. However, as I think it proper for me to add some Considerations of my own, I shall first set down, as briefly as I may, what I find most Material in Dr. *Bekker*'s Volumes, deserving an Answer, and then offer what I have to reply.

In his First Volume, he sets forth the various Opinions of People in the World, concerning evil Spirits and their Operations; and having there giv'n an account of many Christian Authors, as well as others, who have countenanc'd their Operations in several respects, in his 22d Chapter, he writes thus: But I find no Author, who in time pass'd, has ascrib'd so little Understanding, and Vertue to the Devil, as for what relates, to all those Knowledges and Effects set forth by me, as *Reginald Scot*. We have at present *Antony Van Dale*, who ascribes no more to him in his Book of *Oracles*. These two Authors hold, that there is no other efficient Cause of all those things that are practis'd or wrought, but the Impostures of Men, the Devil having nothing to do in them. I hear also every Day while I am employ'd in this Work, that the Men of the best Sense among us, ascribe but very little Power and Knowledge to the Devil, and that there are many more than I thought, who, as to Persons possess'd and bewitch'd, are of the same Opinion with Monsieur *Daillon*, who, in what he has writ in *French* concerning *Dæmons*, maintains, that all that is contained in the Scriptures concerning evil and impure Spirits, ought not to be understood otherwise, than of certain Diseases, to which the *Jews* were wont to give such Names; he believing, nevertheless, that it might be that evil Spirits came at the same time to concern themselves in it. And beneath, he adds, My scope here is to relate what is said of the Devil and his Power, and to examine whether it be true or not, and I hold the Negative; because it's much contrary to me to maintain an Opinion which ascribes so much Power and Vertue to Spirits, especially evil Spirits; wherefore I must rank myself with *Scot, Van Dale*, and many others, who are opposite to the belief Men have of this Power.

In his 24th Chapter, §. 10. 11. he tells us, We have all the Reason of the World to hold for *Pagan Legends*, all the *Pagans* have published concerning Miracles, Oracles of their Gods, æreal Spectres, Dreams, and so many other Prodigies, as well as all the Papists obtrude upon us in that kind. And he thinks it's clearly enough prov'd by all the Citations he has made in this Book, that there are no Miracles, Oracles,

Purgatories, Apparitions of Spirits or Souls, of Diabolical Arts and Illusions, or Sorceries, by Letters and Characters, or of Choice of Days, neither in *Judaism*, nor *Papism*, but draws its Origine from *Paganism*. We must reject all at once, or leave all to subsist together, of what kind soever it be; we ought to discharge our selves of all these Prejudices, and joyn Reason with the Scriptures to ground our selves on them, and look upon those alone as pure Sources.

In his Second Volume, C. 7. §. 7. he writes thus: All the Learned agree, that *Affirmanti incumbit probatio* but he that denies a thing, or doubts only of it, does enough when he alledges Reasons of his doubts; and much more yet when he sifts and curiously examines those Reasons he might expect from the Persons concerned. It's what he has resolved to do in this place: first as to what has never been alledg'd by Reason, and afterwards as to what has never been taught by the Scriptures.

C. 19. §. 19. He says, That the Devil by the first Sin that was committed in Paradice, is the Cause of all evil, and consequently all the evil that is done, ought with just Reason to be imputed to him. And beneath, You can find nothing that can prove, that the Devil after having seduc'd Man at the beginning of the Creation, has had since, in Person, the least Power on him, or his Actions; but indeed that all the evil that ever happen'd, or is still committed in the World is consider'd by Reason of this, as if the Devil himself did it.

C. 20. §.19. He says, As for the Fall of Man, it's certain it was caused by the Devil, but to know the way how, it's altogether uncertain.

C. 27. §. 1.5. He argues thus: As it's manifest, that that which has no Existence can produce nothing, whence comes it that the Devils, or unclean Spirits did those things, which the Gospel mentions, and by those that were possess'd by them? I answer, The pretended unclean Spirits are always named in case of Maladies, and that so it was understood by those that were attaqued, or infected with Diseases and Scourges of God, that reign'd at that time. And he says, If you say, the Apostles since Christ have not freed us from that

Error, that the *Dæmons* are really such Spirits, and that they have such a Power, he answers, This is not so easily granted, because *Eidola*, false Gods or Idols, and the *Dæmonia* are one and the same thing. Now St. Paul tells us, that the Idols, or false Gods are nothing at all.

C. 32. §.10. He says, As for *Angels* he does not deny but they have appear'd sometimes, but he believes not so many Apparitions of the Devil, §. 12. He owns, there are Men that naturally see Spectres and Phantomes more often than others, but he says it's the natural Disposition of the Body of the Man, of his Blood and Spirits, which makes him believe he really sees, what he sees no farther than he believes.

C. 33. §. 10. He says, He concludes, that the Devil has not the least Knowledge of the World, nor of the things that concern Religion, nor of the Affairs of Faith.

C. 34. §. 16. He says, He has shewn that the Devil can do nothing in reality, nor in appearance. §. 25. He says, The Angels are the Ministers of God in all Places, both to Punish Men, and to Protect and Defend them; but as for the Devil, he is God's Prisoner. After which he has no more to say on this Matter.

In his Third Volume, C. 1. §. 6. He says, The Question is not, whether there are Enchantments, or the like; but what we ought to understand by Enchantments, and in what it consists; whether it be Deceit, Subtlety, Covert wickedness, *&c.* or whether those they call Magicians really work by the Devil.

C. 5. §. 5. He says, He is of Opinion, That what the *Ægyptians* did was only in Appearance, and nothing real.

C. 4. §. 13. He says. If we think to fright People with *Spectres*, to teach them so much more to fear God, it's a miserable thing in Christianity, that People must be brought to God by a servile Fear, which naturally makes us fly God, or that we serve him without love. If it be with this Fear, with which we ought to serve God, has not *Christ* rendred us a poor Service for having delivered us?

C. 22. §. 18. As for those they call possess'd Persons; he says, He confesses he has no Knowledge of the least Operation of the Devil, on the Body, in the Body, and by means of the Body, no more than of those some will have him do on the Soul of Man; for none of all these evil Spirits ever were, or are in any place of all the Bible, Devils so called, but the evil Spirits were troublesome Torments, and incurable Ills, of which *Christ* cured many Persons by his sole Word, and assisted the Apostles when they undertook to do it.

In his Fourth Volume, *C*. 2. §. 1. He says, He has shewn that the Ancient *Magick* was nothing but surprize, or imposture according to all the Scripture says of it. §. 3. He says, That all which Men think to be an Action of Spirits, by Reason of the subtlety with which it's done, is an effect of subtle and indivisible Substances. The knowledge of the most subtle Matters, and of the extent of their Motion may shew us, that all that is commonly ascribed to Magick, or the Operations of the Devil may be natural. The most subtle Parts of Bodies, entring in, issuing forth, and passing through Bodies, are the Cause of all the Changes which happen. §. 10. He says, All he has said, is to shew that there are sometimes very surprising things done, whereof we cannot outwardly know the Causes, and which nevertheless ought to be ascribed to the Motion, assembling, or reparation of these little Bodies, oneway, or other.

C. 2. §. 11. He says, We shall now examine, whether there has ever happened in the World, that any thing of the Nature of those we call Apparitions, Phantoms, or Magick, that ought not to be ascribed to those Atoms, which often, in moving themselves, in separating, or joyning themselves to one another, can cause the same Aspects, the same Sounds, the same Motions in Men, and about them, that are ascribed to Spirits, or the Devil in particular.

C. 34. §. 10. He says, Men take the word Devil, Satan, Witch and Magick, in quite another Sense than it's found in the Scripture, searching with all the exactness Imaginable. So much from Dr. *Bekker*.

On what I have set forth from this Author, a Man has room to write a large Volume; but I shall contract my self in a little compass.

As for this Persons undertaking from Scripture and Reason to introduce a new Doctrine amongst us, concerning Evil Spirits, contrary to what the whole stream of those Learned Teachers, who have convey'd Religion to us, have constantly taught us hitherto, I think it may be look'd upon as a very bold and surprising attempt. And I believe the Learned part of Christians will consider the Matter very maturely, before they part with a Doctrine so long taught them.

It seems to me a strange Confidence in a Dr. *Bekker*, and indeed, no less than that of *Socinus*, and other Innovators, that through a self-presuming Conceit of his out-doing insight in the Scriptures, he should now pretend to tell us, That tho' he allows good Angels have appear'd sometimes, yet there has been no Devil in the World since he tempted our first Parents to sin; whereas the Scriptures every where speak as plainly of Evil Spirits, and their Operations since the Fall, as of Good Spirits. Neither do I believe, that any Person adhering to Dr. *Bekker*'s Doctrine, will ever be able to assign the least Reason, why God Almighty should have permitted the Devil to tempt Man before the Fall, and not since. And tho' Dr. *Bekker*, and Dr. *Van Dale* have shewn themselves Men of Learning; yet we know there have been many *Protestant* Divines, since the Reformation, who have given the World much greater *Specimens* of their Insight in the Oriental Languages, which the others so much pretend to, for inabling them to a right understanding of the Scriptures; who, notwithstanding, never took the words, *Devil*, *Satyr*, *Witch*, and *Magick* in that sense they have done.

But as for the Origin of Idolatry, and the Doctrine of *Dæmons* among the *Gentiles*, I think no Man has better set it forth than *Kircher*, in his *Oedipus Ægyptiacus*, whom those Authors have not pleas'd to take notice of, as I think it might have been proper for them; he having given an account of it quite contrary to what they have writ. This Man had all the Advantages that a great Writer could have: He had great

Natural Parts, us'd great Industry, had a great Correspondence with the Learned in most Parts of the World, had the Command of near twenty Languages, and the Favour of many great Princes, who assisted him with all sorts of Books, and other Necessaries, for carrying on so great a Work; in which he acquaints the World, he spent Twenty Years Labour, with a very intent Study. In his first Tome of his said Work he writes thus: *Pag.* 171.

St. *Ambrose* wisely and truly says, that Humane Error was the cause of Idolatry: And with him *Hermes Trismegistus*, that the Origin of the detestable Idolatry of the *Ægyptians* was the Error and Incredulity of their Ancestors, in which *Ægypt* always wallowed: For as they did not apply their Minds with a due Reverence and Consideration to the Worship of the true God, and the Divine Religion; and nevertheless were possest with a desire of some Religion, they found out the Art of making Idols; but as they knew not how to animate them, using wicked Arts, and a Diabolical Conjurations, and calling forth *Dæmons*, they forc'd them into them; and to give them more Vertue and Strength, they consecrated to them Animals of divers kinds, which they called Sacred, adoring in them the Souls of those Persons, who have been Famous for Vertues, and Facts, they had perform'd, calling by their Names those Cities, that had been either built, or instructed with wholsome Laws and Ordinances by them. To their Honour also they instituted various Sacrifices, which sort of Rites and Ceremonies, *Mor. Isaack*, a *Maronite*, most elegantly describes in his *Syrian Philosophy*, as follows, *Ad. Asclep.c.* 13.

Then arose Men of the Seed of *Cham*, having corrupt Manners, whose Minds were corrupted through Ignorance, and *Dæmons* that seduc'd them, and they taught one thing for another, and thought the Stars were endowed with a Spirit of Intelligence, that they had a free Liberty and Power, and by degrees the Devil made them Err, till they thought the Stars to be Creators and Makers; and they gave to each Star the Name of a God, and they Worship'd them with various Ceremonies, falling down before them, and adoring them; and they set up various Idols in their Names, and plac'd them on the tops of High Pillars, and Walls of Houses, exhibiting their Figures after various Manners; and to these they offer'd Victims, and Sacrifices, burning Incense before them; and the Devil at certain times, speaking from each of them, gave Answers to those that ask'd them, predicting future things, and revealing things hidden, and presently told of things that, were done in Places very remote; and put Thoughts into their Minds, which he revealed to others; and he has seduc'd very many of those Men even to this Day. Now these Rites were proper to the *Ægyptians,* which afterwards, passing to others, infected by degrees the whole World.

Now, from what is here deliver'd by *Kircher* we find we may allow what Dr. *Bekker* says, *viz.* That the *Eidola,* false Gods, or Idols, and the *Daimonia* of the *Gentiles,* are in a manner one and the same thing; and say with St. *Paul* that the Idols, or false Gods are nothing at all; for as the *Pagans* adored in their Idols the Souls of Persons, that had been Famous for Vertues, or great Actions done for the Benefit of Mankind, or their suppos'd Spirits of the Stars, these indeed were nothing there; but as they apply'd themselves to these, for receiving Answers, they desired, or for being otherwise gratifyed by them in other desires, it was the Devil who deluded them, in giving them Answers, and doing other things as they desired; so that their Conversation was with him, who kept them in continual Idolatry, though they did not direct their Worship directly to him.

So again, *Kircher* in his *Second Tome,* of his said *Oedipus, Part* 2. treating of *Hieroglyphical Magick,* in his Third Chapter, which treats concerning the Divinations and Oracles of the *Ægyptians,* sets forth, that the Mind of Man being still agitated with a desire of the goods both of Body and Soul, and eagerly wishing to secure them perpetually to himself, applies its Study to the Knowledge of future things; whence the Devil, as being Enemy of Mankind, laying as many Snares, as there are Appetites of Humane Machinations, at length sets upon him with an Hope of the Knowledge of those future things. Now there are two chief Nets he lays, *Astrology* and *Polymancy*; by the first he teaches the Lot,

P. 441. *& seq.*

which each Man has gotten from the first Minute of his Nativity, as to a good or bad Fortune; by the latter he presents, as under the Veil of natural Causes, various kinds of Divinations, with which the uncautious, while they unadvisedly go about to pursue Good, and shun Evil, are justly depriv'd of the eternal Good. These Arts *Cham*, the Son of *Noah*, first introduc'd into the World, by the Instigation of the Devil; which the *Ægyptians*, instructed by *Cham*, have transfus'd into the whole World, as it were by a certain Hereditary Tradition. As for their *Astrology*, he has treated amply of it before, and here he takes upon him to give an Account of their Divinations, and their Origine, and concerning the Nature of their Oracles.

Before I give you an Account of what he says, concerning the latter, I shall give you two or three Particulars of what he says concerning their *Astrology*.

In his forementioned *Tome, p.* 141. he writes thus: I dare solemnly affirm, that all our present *Judicial Astrology*, relating to Nativities and horary Questions, retains even to this Day, that occult pact with Devils, which the Ancient *Ægyptian Astrology* did.

P. 176. He says, The *Ægyptians* did not so much ascribe to the Stars, as to the *Genii* presiding in them, the Events of things; hence there was an earnest desire, care, and solicitude to render them Propitious, by previous Ceremonies and Sacrifices, otherwise then the *Astrologers* of our Times deal, who rashly ascribe the Fortune of Men to a certain fatal necessity of the Stars.

P. 200. He says, The *Ægyptians* held, that Gods or *Genii*, inhabited the Stars; for they thought the Inferior World depended on their Vertue and Efficacy, not by the proper influsive force of the Stars, but by the disposing Power of the Deities, who being seated in the Stars as an Instrument for the Disposition of Inferiors, *&c.* As for what is said more concerning their *Astrology*, I refer the Reader to the Author.

As for the *Ægyptians* Divinations, and their Origine, and the Nature of their Oracles, they thought, that beside the Celestial Gods, there were certain middle Natures, which they call'd *Angels*, *Dæmons*, *Genii*, or *Terrestrial Gods*, to which they ascribed the rise and fall of their Oracles, and so, that the Oracles lasted so long, as the said *Genii* continued in the *Statues*, which deliver'd Oracles, and that they ceas'd, When the *Statues* were deserted by the *Genii* or *Dæmons*. Now they affirmed these *Genii* to Inhabit the Region betwixt the Heavens and the Earth, and to consist of Herbs, Stones, Spices, and other Terrestrial Matters, containing a natural Power of a Divinity in them; and that as living near us, they were joyned to us by a friendly Alliance; and they thought them to be affected with a singular Love towards Mankind, according as their Nature bears; predicting future things by Oracles, and taking care of other things belonging to us. Wherefore they entred *Statues* rightly prepared by Men, and gave Answers from them to those that consulted them; and stayed in them many Years, by so much the more willingly, by how much the *Statues* were made of Matters more agreeing to them; and by how much the more skilful they were to detain them by Sacrifices, Hymns, Prayers, and Harmonies, with which only Allurements of them, they are delighted. And *Trismegistus* in his *Pymander* says, their Ancestors had not a perfect Knowledge of the celestial Deity, for God being known, they had not cared for terrestrial Gods, but as being uncertain of him, greatly straying from the Divine Religion, they excogitated an Art whereby they might make Gods, erecting *Statues*; and as they could not create Souls for them, they called the Souls of *Angels* or *Dæmons* into them, which came upon calling, both because the Power of these Men was great, and because *Angels* and *Dæmons* have so great an Alliance with Men, that they are drawn by a natural Obsequiousness to them.

But to return to the Oracles, they were the Root and Foundation of all Divinations and Superstition; nor did the Devil always give Answers with a sensible Voice, but discovered what he pleased by certain Signs. Hence first arose the various kinds of Rites and Ceremonies, with which, as it were with previous Dispositions, they were wont to purge the Mind, that it might become conscious of future things;

then turning themselves to vain observances, they took all the Ludibria of obvious things for Auguries. But let us explain them in particular. I find that, in a manner, in all the Prefectures of *Ægypt*, there was an Oracle, from which Consulters received Answers concerning various Events; not that every particular Oracle answered concerning every thing proposed to them, but only concerning things agreeing to their Nature: Thus the Oracle of *Serapis*, about things that concerned Agriculture; of *Anubis*, of things relating to Sciences; of *Horus*, about things concerning the good of the Body and Soul; of *Isis*, about things concerning *Nilus*, or Fertility; but the Oracle of *Ammon*, as being the most Famous of all, gave Answers concerning all things proposed. So in Innumerable other Places Oracles were set up, all which gave Answers in obscure Places, obsess'd by evil Spirits, by a Voice, Dreams, a Gesture, and a Nod of the *Statues*, by a sound, a ringing, or other Signs; and they were given either by the *Dæmon* himself, or by *Pythonists*, or by Priests inspir'd with a Fate-telling Spirit, which from Caves, and obscure deep Vaults, with an horrible sound and noise, rush'd out on the Enthusiasts, in the likeness of Fire, with which being wholly surrounded, and driven into a fury, they uttered those things which the *Dæmon* suggested to them, with a Palpitation of all their limbs, their Eyes turn'd upwards, and their Mouths distorted. After this manner *Satan* the Architect of Superstitions, insinuating himself by stealth into the Minds of Men by Idolatry, made it his Business to inculcate to them, devoted Services of Rites and Ceremonies, by which they should Worship his Commentitious Gods under a pretext of Piety and Vertue, that under these Colours he might involve and pollute them in all kinds of Impiety and Wickedness, and derive to himself the Honour due to God.

And as there was nothing so obvious to our Senses, which the *Dæmon* did not assume, as certain Signs, to shew his Will, and nilling to those that consulted him; hence manifold kinds of Divinatory Magick arose, hence issued the Spawn of all kinds of portentous Sorceries, and Divinations, *&c.* So far *Kircher*.

Now, laying this before us, I must say, That notwithstanding all Dr. *Van Dale* has writ concerning *Oracles*, as being wholly contrived by the Impostures of Men, I must wholly assent to what *Kircher* has here set forth concerning them; and this, not only because *Kircher*, and others, have so deliver'd it to us, but chiefly, because, even at this Day, there are Persons, who upon calling themselves into a Trance, and otherwise, can, and do predict future things, reveal things hidden, and tell of things done in Places very remote, like to what was done by the Oracles, as I have set forth in this Work, which must be ascribed to the Agency of evil Spirit, as I shall shew beneath.

Indeed that many things in the *Ægyptian Oracles*, were done by the Impostures of their Priests; it's what *Kircher* freely owns in the Third *Tome* of his said *Oedipus*, *p*. 46. where he writes as follows.

We have shewn in several Parts of this Work, that *Dæmons* did not only speak from various *Statues*, as from certain Oracles, but that ev'n Priests themselves, to keep the People in a greater cult and veneration towards the Gods, impos'd on their Simplicity by their Craft; and the use of these *speaking Statues* was so frequent in *Ægypt*, that there was scarce a Prefecture without them; and so that the chief end of the Priests seems to have consisted in this, to draw *Dæmons* by Magical Adjurations, and various Incantations into *Statues*, first consecrated by due Rights, in the *Adyta*, and being drawn to consult them concerning various Demands. And because the *Dæmons* did not always give Answers agreeing to Truth, but wholly fool'd those that consulted them many ways, hence the Priests performing the Office of a *Dæmon*, and applying themselves to Fraud, made *Statues* with such an Artifice, that by occult Pipes convey'd to the Head of the *Statues*, they mutter'd Voice's, as it were of the Gods, and what Answers they pleas'd, to interpose on the Superstitous People; who being deluded by this impious Cheat of the Priests, were more and more animated to make Oblations, and offer Gifts, due, as they thought, to the Gods, but, in Truth, to those deceitful Priests, who thought they had done some great thing, if what was done by the Craft of a fraudulent Wit, obtain'd in the Minds of the simple People, the Opinion of a Divine Work of the Gods, and of a Miracle. So far *Kircher*.

But to conclude from this with Dr. *Van Dale*, that all that pass'd in the Oracles of the Ancients, was done by Humane Contrivance, without any Agency of evil Spirits, is what I can no way assent to, for the Reason above giv'n.

To return to Dr. *Bekker*. As to what he says, That the Knowledge of the most subtle particles of Matter, and of the Extent of their Motion may shew us, that all that is commonly ascrib'd to Magick, and the Operations of the Devil, may be Natural, and that all Apparitions and Phantomes, Sounds, *&c.* commonly ascribed to the Operations of *Dæmons*, may be caus'd by the Action of those Atoms. I should ask'd him here, whether the Action of those subtle Particles of Matter can exert it self to an intellectual and voluntary Agency, (for this is the true State of the Question) and not to tell us, that seemingly occult Sympathies and Antipathies, and the like, may be solv'd that way, which we own may be true; and I think I have sufficiently shewn in this Book, in the foregoing several Heads of Mens preception of Spirits, that the Actions I there ascribe to Spirits have resulted from intellectual and voluntary Agents. If he should say, the Actions of such subtle Particles could arise to such Agency; I think I have fairly shewn before from Mr. *Lock*, and Monsieur *le Clerc*, that the Notions of Matter, and of an intellectual and voluntary Agent, are clearly distinct, and incommunicable to each other.

Again, As for his raising the Action of the Particles of Matter to this pitch, this would equally take away the Operations of good Spirits, as well as evil, whereas he allows the former; So that I think he had been more consonant to his Principles, in setting up for Sadducism or Epicurism, denying both good and evil Spirits, than to take up with this half-spirited Opinion, which I know not whether any Man has ever held but himself.

Chap. 6.
Sect. 5.

Indeed we may allow what Dr. *Bekker* says, That good Angels may sometimes Punish Men by God's Appointment, as well as protect and defend them; but we say there have been frequent manifestations of wicked Facts, done by Spirits, and such as could no way consist with the Nature of good Angels, therefore there must be allowed of both Kinds; unless the *Doctor*'s subtle Particles shall solve all. And whereas in his *Second Volume*, he says, The Facts ascribed to Spirits, are perhaps such as a Man's Spirit can do, as when a Man possess'd with a pretended evil Spirit, speaks strange Languages, which he had never Learned before: this he says may be solv'd, if we embrace the Opinion of *Justin*, viz. that the Souls of the Dead can enter into the Bodies of the Living; for then he says, Why may it not be, that the Soul of a Man, skill'd in many Languages, is that which after, the Death of its Body, speaks by the means of that which is yet alive, those same Languages he had learned Living? But, he says, He is not of this Opinion, though this may suffice to convince those by what they say themselves, that confound one thing with another, in believing this of the Soul, and that there are Angels for the same Reason, which Experience proves not that there are, or that they exist.

Now, as to this, since the *Doctor* did not hold the Opinion of *Justin*, nor deny that strange Languages had been spoken by Ignorant Persons; he might have done well to have explain'd how that could be done without the Agency of Spirits; and as for his charging those with an inconsistency that hold this Opinion, and with all the Agency of Spirits, is it that because some particular Person has set up such an Hypothesis for solving that Fact, there must be no Spirits? So we know that *Marcus Marci* (who generally takes upon him to solve all *Phænomena* without God, Angel, or Devil) has set up another Hypothesis for solving the said Fact, he supposes, that Ideas are convey'd into all Persons, with the seminal Principles, derived from Parents and Ancestors; and that when these Ideas, upon certain critical Junctures, come to an Evolution, a Man may come to speak any of those Languages, which any of his Ancestors were skilled in: But what if Men set up such Hypothesis, the Question will still be whether these Hypothesis are more cogent upon our understanding for their Admittance, than that of Spirits, or whether our Reason acquiesces more easily in them?

And I think, I may here justly charge these Men, as *Justin Martyr* does others, in a like Case, saying, Some oppose to us *Marcion*, who even now teaches Men to deny God, the Maker of all things in Heaven and Earth, and Christ his Son predicted by the Prophets, and introduces another God beside the Maker of all things, and also another Son; by whose Authority many being sway'd, they deride us, as though he were the only Man that knew Truth: and as they have no Demonstration of those things they say, without all Reason, being seized as Lambs by a Wolf, they become the foul prey of Mens *Dogma*'s, and of Devils.

Apol. 2.

Tandlerus, in his Answer to a Question propos'd concerning the Divination, and other wonderful Effects of Melancholick Persons, first tells us, that those Melancholick Facts or Energies may be reduc'd to two kinds; one is, of those who are said to have spoken Languages of which, while they were themselves, they were wholly Ignorant, or to have shewn an understanding of those Arts, which they never acquired to themselves by Learning; the other is, of those who are said to have had a certain Power and Faculty of discovering occult things, of commemorating past things that were unknown to them, and of predicting future Events, whose Truth experience it self, at length, has shewn to be so. To the first kind belongs that rustick mentioned by *Guainerius*, who always, the Moon being combust, made Verses, and the combustion being pass'd about two Days, till she came to another combustion, could not speak a word of *Latin*; and this Man had never Learned Letters. And here that Saylers Boy has place, who, as *Forestus* tells, having received a Blow on his Head, as he pass'd a Bridge, in his *Delirium*, always made *Syllogisms* in the *German Tongue*, and that excellently; and that afterwards being cur'd he knew not how to do it.

Of the latter kind we have *Rhasis* a Witness, among the *Arabians*; and *Alexander*, who was in no mean rank among the Ancient Physicians, and among these Persons, he thinks we may not unfitly place, *Exstaticks*.

Now, he says, There is a very great Dissention among Authors, in assigning the Causes of these stupendious Actions of Persons seized with a Melancholy Distemper, some laboriously inquire into the natural Causes of them, others ascend to Supernatural; as for those who acquiesce in natural Causes, he finds two Sets of them. The first is of *Astrologers*, ascribing all the Works of Melancholick Persons to the Influences of the Stars, as *Guainerius* does, building on certain *Platonick* and *Astrological Principles*, he says, That the Soul before it's infus'd into the Body, contains the Knowledge of all things in it self, but that it's in a manner abolish'd, by the Union with the Body, with whose Fetters it's held ensnared, after it's infused; nor can it be otherwise recovered, but by teaching, or by an influx, or impression of the Planet, which presided over his Nativity at the very time the Soul was infused into the Body. He will have the force of this impression to be so great, that it may endow the Soul with a Faculty of producing such Actions, as the Star is wont to produce elsewhere; so that it may make a well Man sick, and a sick Man well; also cause Snow and Rain; but that the Body and corporeal Senses resist this Impression, especially as to Knowledges, it being otherwise of efficacy enough in it self; these Senses therefore being bound, as it happens in Melancholick Persons, and the Star working on the Soul without resistency, it comes to pass that the Soul understands all things without Discourse, foresees future things, answers concerning Arts, to which it inclines by the force of the influencing Planet. The second Sect is of natural Philosophers, who seeing that the Minds of Men are variously affected with the Melancholick Humour, and that most that have excelled others in Understanding, or in Learning Arts, or in Administration of government, or in performing other things, were naturally Melancholick, they stuck not to ascribe so great force to it; for as there are many found, who are naturally enclined to divers Arts, so Melancholy, they say, is naturally inclined to Work wonderful things; and as high fermented Wine, immoderately taken, changes Mens Manners, and Causes them to differ from themselves; so they contend, that if the Melancholick Juice exceeds its convenient Measure in a Person, or be rendred more hot, or cold than is fitting, gets a certain singular force wholly to change the Mind, and to stir up wonderful Motion in it.

Now, *Tandlerus*, after having stated these Opinions, rejects them; for though he does not deny the Power of the Stars, for changing the temperament of the whole Body, and of each of its Parts in particular, and for giving an Inclination either for the Knowledge of Tongues, or for divers Disciplines; yet this he stifly denies, that the very Knowledge of Tongues is any way conferr'd by the Stars, without teaching, or their use without any precedent Knowledge, for certain Reasons he gives; nor can he acquiesce in their Opinion, who think these kinds of Prodigies ought to be ascribed to the property of the Melancholick Humour; for though there be a certain occult force of the Melancholick Juice, that it may produce Operations causing Admiration, yet it cannot be so great as to beget a Knowledge of Languages, and of occult and future things; these certainly are owing to a superior Cause, not that while he denies these things to have place in the Melancholick Humour, he therefore denies what *Aristotle* says, *viz.* that Melancholick Persons are, that is have direct Dreams, by which they may have a fore-perception of certain future things; for there are two kinds of Divination, one natural, common to Men with Brutes, whereby without Discourse, by the sole guidance of Nature, some Animals have a foresense of things, as well for avoiding hurtful things themselves, as for admonishing Men of certain iminent Events; so Ants have a natural fore-sense of the approaching Winter; from the going away of Sparrows, many Physicians believe we are admonish'd of an approaching Pestilence; such a presaging faculty is often found in some Fools, who by Nature have a vitiated Reason, in whom doubtless Nature makes a recompence one way for what it takes away in another. So *Marcus Maci* says,

<small>Phil. vet. Rest. par. 2. Sect. 4.</small>

Those whose Minds are employed in Speculations, which take up the Soul, do not easily perceive sympathetical Impressions, whence presaging and predictions are wont to be sent to simple Persons, rather than to Wise Men; and that happens much more to brute Animals, than no Men, those being presently filled with the celestial Image, being void of any of their own.

The same things haply sometimes occur in Melancholick Persons, especially in those whom Nature has particularly brought forth such. The other kind is Artificial, which is grounded on an observation of Events, or on certain Signs; and because it consists, for the greatest part, in a comparing together of natural Causes, as well betwixt themselves, as of the Effect, it is also called Natural; though this depends on certain Rules, yet the Inclination of Nature which proceeds partly from the temperament and Humours, and partly from a fortunate, and meet position of certain Stars, hold the chief place in it; for we see some by a peculiar guidance of Nature, being cultivated with an indifferent knowledge of the Stars, far more truly and readily to hit out future things from obvious, or little previous Marks, than those who excel only in Art, being destitute of the Aids of Nature. Nay, some by this very force of Spirit arrive at a full insight in many things, which Art with Labour would not Come to the Knowledge of, or attain with Difficulty. Such a Facility of conjecturing, since it happens for the most part in Persons inclin'd to Melancholy, which happily may be increas'd by a fortunate Concourse of the Stars, I easily grant that Melancholick Persons are not only, but likewise that they excel others in the Prediction of future Things. But here we speak of another kind of Divination, when Ignorant Persons, without Conjectures and Observation of Events, bring secret Things to light, Prophesie of those future Things which are neither known to themselves, nor others; nay, when they come to themselves, they know not that any such thing was done by them. These things, he says, he judges could no way arise from an Humour, especially exceeding the Bounds Of Nature.

He concludes therefore, That the Devil is the Author of all these things, tho' not alone, but join'd with the Melancholick Humour, which he exagitates at his pleasure, and causes certain Operations, which that Humour had not been able to produce by its own force.

Since we are upon this Point of Ignorant Peoples speaking unknown Languages, I shall give you one particular Instance of it, taken from a Letter sent by the late Lord *Lauderdale* to Mr. *Baxter*; which Letter was printed *Anno* 1691. in Mr. *Baxter's Historical Discourse of Apparitions and Witches*. He there writes, among other things, as follows:

"I shall here tell you of a real Possession near the place where I was born. About thirty Years ago, when I was a Boy at School, there was a poor Woman generally believ'd to be really possess'd: She liv'd near the Town of *Duns* in the *Mers*; and Mr. *John Weems*, then Minister of *Duns*, (a Man known, by his Works to be a Learned Man, and I know him to be a Godly Honest Man) was perswaded she was possess'd: I have heard him many times speak with my Father about it, and both of them concluded it a real Possession. Mr. *Weems* visited her often; and being convinc'd of the truth of the thing, he, with some neighbour Ministers, apply'd themselves to the King's Privy-Council for a Warrant to keep Days of Humiliation for her; but the Bishops being then in Power, would not allow any Fasts to be kept. I will not trouble you with many Circumstances; one I shall only tell you, which, I think, will evince a real Possession. The report being spread in the Country, a *Knight* by the Name of *Forbes*, who liv'd in the *North* of *Scotland*, being come *Edenborough*, meeting there with a Minister of the *North*, and both of them desirous to see the Woman, the Northern Minister invited the *Knight* to my Father's House (which was within ten or twelve Miles of the Woman) whither they came, and next Morning went to see the Woman. They found her a poor Ignorant Creature, and seeing nothing extraordinary, the Minister says in *Latin* to the *Knight, Nondum audivimus Spiritum loquentem*; presently a Voice comes out of the Womans Mouth, *Audis loaquentem, audis loquentum*. This put the Minister into some amazement (which I think made him not mind his own *Latin*) he took off his Hat, and said, *Misèreatur Deus peccatoris*: The Voice presently, out of the Woman's Mouth, said, *Dic peccatricis, Dic peccatricis*; whereupon both of them came out of the House fully satisfied, took Horse immediately, and return'd to my Father's House, at *Thirlestane Castle* in *Lauderdale*, where they related this Passage. This I do exactly remember. Many more Particulars might be got in that Country, but this *Latin Criticism*, in a most Illiterate Ignorant Woman, where there was no pretence to dispossessing, is Evidence enough, I think."

So far the Lord *Lauderdale*.

This leads us to consider another Assertion of Dr. *Bekker's*, where he says, that all the Possessions mention'd in the Scriptures, were but incurable Diseases that tormented Men, the Devil having nothing to do in them, and of which Christ cur'd many Persons by his sole Word.

As to this *Gulielmus Adera*, Physician of *Tolouse*, Printed a Book there, *Ann.* 1623. concerning the Diseases and Diseas'd cur'd by Christ. In the third Part of this Book, he enquires, how the Devil becomes the external Cause of many Diseases.

He there tells us, that those Persons whom Christ Cur'd, were such as the Interpreters of the Scriptures call *Energumens*, or such as were possest with an Evil Spirit, concerning whom it's a Crime to doubt: Nay, he says, those strive and contend against all Truth, Faith, Experience, and the Authority of most Wise and Pious Men, who obstinately deny those *Energumens*, and Persons obsest and possest with the Devil; and set nought by of the vexatious Power the Devil has in moving natural Causes, and if the obsest do any thing excessively violent or stupendious, believe it to be, and ascribe it to Melancholy, preternaturally mov'd in the Brain, or the whole Body. These Men bring it so to pass, that by understanding they understand nothing, who exploding the Power of *Dæmons*, accuse all ancient Writers, and all the Fathers of the Christian Church, whose Negligence he should rather choose to imitate, than the unaccountable Diligence of those Men.

To distinguish Persons possest, from those infested with a melancholick Enthusiasm, he says, the learned Physician *Massaria* gives two Signs, which are most certain Marks of a demoniacal seizure. First, if a Rustick or Ideot speaks Greek or Latin: Secondly, if he predicts future Things. Now it is not to be doubted, but these things have been often observ'd in melancholick Persons by *Levinus Lemnius* and others. *Riolanus* brings Reasons for it, and an Instance in *Philaretus* of *Spoletto*, who being infested with Worms, fell into a new kind of Madness; so that in his Disease, he spake very well the *German Tongue*. *Huartus* in his *Scrutinium Ingeniorum*, tells us of a Woman seiz'd with a Frenzy in a great Fever, who spake *Latin*, and predicted many things as a Prophet. She predicted to a *Chirurgion* who let her Blood, that he would die within a Month, and that his Wife would after Marry a Neighbour Smith, which fell out accordingly. *Psellus* also tells us of a Woman who being ill after Child-bearing, spake in the *Armenian Tongue* with a certain *Armenian Physician*, tho' she had never seen an *Armenian* before, and knew nothing but her Chamber and Distaffe.

In Lib. fern de abd. rer. caus.

He thinks every Man knows it to be a great and difficult Task to distinguish melancholick Persons from such as are possest: No Man as far as he knows, having as yet, given us true Marks of it. He says, therefore, that a Man must inspect the Nature, Manners, Humours, and Disposition of the Diseas'd. What he does betide the usual Nature of the Disease, and of the Nature of its Symptoms; as to cry out violently, to be vehemently agitated and tortur'd, to contract, wrest, or extend his Limbs without a manifest Convulsion, to be

Delirious without a Frenzy, to speak prodigious Things and use an unusual Tongue. In short, to do or suffer those things which are very unusual in Diseases.

These things being discover'd, as far as a Physician may, he must explain how the Devil becomes the cause of Diseases, how he acts with natural Causes, entangles the Body in Distempers, stirs up Symptoms with such Enormity, that it may be justly doubted whether it be a monstrous Disease, or a severe *Dæmon*. And he concludes with the unanimous Assertion of Divines and Physicians, that it's done by the Devil's managing of the Humours at his Pleasure in those that are left to him, whereby he can cause an Epilepsie, Palsie, and the like Diseases, as also Blindness, Deafness, *&c.*

If any one wonders why he awakens and stirs up Fits of Diseases according to the Motion and Quarters of the Moon, he says, it's because at that time the Humours being encreas'd by the Motion and Influence of the Moon, are more conveniently agitated.

And in his 8*th Ch.* of his said *Third Part*, treating, concerning the Difference of an *Epilepsie*, from a divine *Exstasie*, and that which proceeds from the Devil, he says, a divine *Exstasie* is a sacred rapt of the Mind, in which God, by a Condescent presents himself to any humane Creature, not by the means of any Disease, or other preternatural morbisick Cause; the Doctrine of Divines being, that God insinuates himself into our Minds by a Rapt, and then shews us by a divine Representation those Things he pleases we shall see. Therefore it is really God who forcibly draws Man to him by an *Exstasie*, no natural Cause, nor the Mind spontaneously mov'd; for as the Sun is not seen without the Sun, so neither can God be known without God.

If you had seen the Prophets, or others rapt in *Exstacies*, you would have been apt to say they were fallen into an Apoplectick or Epileptick Seisure, for they remain'd immovable; their Eyes open, and fixt towards Heav'n; their Faces pale, either standing upright, or being on their Knees; till being fill'd with the light of Celestial Visions, and saturated with a feast of holy Thoughts, they return'd to themselves.

But it's easie to distinguish these from Epileptical Persons, and we shall shew that extatical Persons, and such as are rapt by a *Dæmon*, are not Epileptical.

Christian Divines and Physicians, agree that *Dæmons* stir up Raptures and Exstasies in Men, binding or loosing the exterior Senses, and that, either stopping the Pores of the Brain, that the Spirits do not pass forth, as it's done naturally by Sleep, or by recalling the sensitive Spirits from the outward Senses to the inward Organs, which he there retains; so the Devil renders Women Witches exstatical and Magicians, who while they lie fast asleep in one place, being deceiv'd, they think they have been in various places, and done many things.

That these Exstasies are not Epileptick Seisures, it appears from *Bodin* in his *Theatre of universal Nature*, where he says, That those that are rapt by the Devil, feel neither Stripes, nor Cuttings, nor no wresting of their Limbs, nor burning Torches, nor the burning of a red hot Iron. Nay, nor is the beat of the Pulse, nor the Motion of the Heart perceiv'd in them, but afterwards returning to themselves, they feel most bitter Pains of the Wounds receiv'd, and tell of things that were done at 600 Miles distance, and affirm themselves to have seen them done. So far *Bodin*.

An *Exstasie* therefore is an Abolishment of Sense and Motion, and not a Depravation of it, as in an Epileptick Seisure; for Persons in an *Exstasie* lie wholly immoveable, in an Epileptick Fit they are most violently agitated. And, as *Bodin* says, Demoniacal Exstaticks breath forth an horrid stink: Epilepticks foam at the Mouth, and their Seed and Excrements pass from them thro' a violent Agitation of the Muscles; and infinite Evils which Demoniacks Commit in their Raptures, shew that they were not agitated with a Convulsion, but gave themselves too much to the Devil's Covenants. Nor need I say much concerning the difference betwixt a *Madness*, a *Syncope*, and a *Stupor* caus'd by narcotick Medicines, and an *Exstasie*. For as *Bodin* rightly argues, a Mad Man is always agitated without ceasing, and a Man rapt in an *Exstasie* lies immoveable, destitute of all Sense and Motion of all his Parts, and rather like a Man seiz'd with an

Apoplexy. A *Syncope* is a Hidden failing of all the Strength, and soon ends in Death, or a Recovery; an *Exstasie* lasts a long time without the loss of a Man's Strength. A *Stupor* caus'd by narcotick Medicines, takes away Sense, not Motion, for otherwise Motion being abolish'd together with Sense, Death would be at Hand, therefore a *Stupor* is not *Exstasie*. So far Dr. *Ader*.

<small>*Inst. med. l. 2. p. 3. Sec. 2. c. 4.*</small>

To this I may add, what *Sennertus* writes of the *Demoniacal Sopor* of Witches, who think they are carried through the Air, Dance, Feast, have Copulation with the Devil, and do other things in their sleep, and afterwards believe the same things waking. Now, he says, whether they are really so carried in the Air, *&c.* or being in a profound sleep, only dream they are so carried, and persist in that Opinion after they are awake, these Facts or Dreams cannot be natural, for it cannot be that there should be so great an Agreement in Dreams of Persons, differing in Place, Temperament, Age, Sex, and Studies; that in one Night, and at the same Hour they should Dream of one such Meeting, and should clearly agree of the Place, Number and Quality of the Persons, and the like Circumstances. But such Dreams are suggested from a supernatural Cause, *viz.* from the Devil to his Confederates, God permitting it. Whence also to those Witches seriously converted, and refusing to be longer present at those Meetings, such Dreams no longer happen; which is a Mark that they proceeded not before from a natural Cause.

Schottus, in his Book *De Mirabilibus Energumenorum*, gives us some signs for knowing *Dæmoniacks*, and first he says, A revealing of occult things, which surpass the natural Knowledge of the Revealers, is a probable sign of a Possession, unless we may rationally presume it to be from God, or a good Angel; And this, because, since that revealing must necessarily be suggested from some Mind or Spirit, and it is not from the private Spirit of the Man, since it surpasses his natural Knowledge, nor from God, or a good Sprit, as it's prudently suppos'd; of necessity it must proceed from an Evil Spirit. He says, it's a probable sign, not certain, since that revealing may be caus'd by *Dæmons* not possessing a Person, as it appears by many Histories. But if there are other signs it's a Presumption that the revealing in the said Circumstances, is from a Dæmoniacal Possession.

Secondly, He says, a Skill in, and speaking of unknown Tongues which the Speaker never learnt, is also a probable Sign of a Possession, if it may not otherwise be rationally presum'd that it is from God or a good Angel, because it cannot naturally be, that a Person ignorant of a Tongue, should speak it, since we learn not foreign Tongues but with great Labour. The same is to be understood of the Knowledge of Reading, Writing, Singing, and of the Knowledge of other Sciences, if a Person had never learnt them. *Levinus Lemnius* therefore lies under a Mistake, where he tells us, that melancholick Persons, and such as are in a frenzie, thro' a fervent ebullition of the Humours, and a vehement agitation of the Spirits, may speak various Languages, tho' before they knew nothing of them. *Schottus* there sets forth many other Signs of *Dæmoniacks* tho' not so certain as the former: and he sets forth also the Signs giv'n by *Voetius* and others of them, for which I refer you to his Book.

This, I think, is enough in answer to Dr. *Bekker*'s Assertion, that the Devil has nothing to do in Diseases.

As for the Cavils of many Writers against the possibility of a covenanting Witch, I am throughly convinc'd, that if an Apparition presents itself to any Person, as many have to my self; if that Person be fallen from God, and sunk into despair, thro' the Miseries of human Life, having not that Christian Armour on which St. Paul speaks of, he may make a Covenant with him, as well as with at Man, and if they say there can be no Covenant with a Spirit, how comes it that there has has been a Covenant betwixt God and Man?

There is one Point of Dr. *Bekker*'s Doctrine, which remains to be answer'd, where he says, if we think to fright People with *Spectres*, to teach them so much the more to love God, it's a miserable thing in Christianity, that People must be brought to God by a servile Fear, instead of Love.

Now this seems not to me so extraordinary a Lesson in Divinity, for, as we know the Love of God to be the consummation of Wisdom, so the Fear of God is the beginning of it; and I think a servile Fear still necessary to the generality of Mankind; for Parents have Rods for their Children, Masters for their Scholars, Princes for their Subjects and tho' all three would persuade those under them to do what they are enjoyn'd for Love, yet such generally is the reluctancy of humane Nature, from doing what is enjoyn'd it, thro' an exorbitancy of our Passions, that till these are broken by a Christian or Philosophical Training, or we are come to a clearness of Judgment, by a long Practice and Experience in the Affairs of humane Life, Love alone will not do; and the servile Fear of those Rods must be upheld; and the Scriptures teach us that we must be content with the Bond Woman for a while, till we may deserve to Marry the Free Woman.

Thus, I think, I have sufficiently answer'd what has been stated from Dr. *Bekker*. But there is one thing remains for me to take notice of in him. In his fourth *Volume* he has taken upon him to examine the Proofs that are brought from Experience for the Existence and Operations of *Dæmons*, and to refute them. I have intimated before how groundlessly he has there rejected the *Dæmons* of *Tedworth* and *Mascon*; and here I shall observe how he rejects what is said of the *Piper* at *Hamelin*: He tells us, that his Master *Schookius*, has refuted that Story in his little Book in Latin, Entituled; *Fabula Hamelensis*, of whose Reasons he leaves the Reader to judge, and adds many Suggestions of his own against it.

Part. 4. Sec. 1. c. 7. De præser. Dæm. c. 16.

Now, *Frommannus*, in his third Book of *Magical Fascination*, after having given us the Relation of this *Piper*, as it's set down by *Kircher*, and *Schottius*; and after having told us, that *Wierus* says, This Story is entred in the publick Records of the Town, and Painted in the Church Windows, of which himself was an Eye Witness, and that the Magistrate there was wont to date the publick Acts from the Year of the going forth of their Children, together with the Year of Christ; and that its observed, even to this Day in Mark of the

Fact, that the Sound of a *Timbrel* is never admitted in that Street, by which the Boys went forth, if any Bride hap'ly be led forth that way, till she be gone forth; nor is dancing permitted there. I say, after having set forth this, he says, That *Martin Schookius* strongly endeavoured in a peculiar little Book, to rank this story among fabulous Relations, but *Theo. Kirchmeierus* egregiously shammed all his effort, in a peculiar Deputation at *Witteberg, Anno* 1671.

Now, Dr. *Bekker*, has not been so Candid as to take notice of this in *Frommannus*, as he ought to have done; he having read *Frommannus*, as it appears by his quoting him, in his 4th Volume, *c.* 2.

I could add much more against Dr. *Bekker*, but this shall suffice at present.

And now, before I make an end, in regard that in the front of my Book, I have promis'd some Account of my particular Experience as to a sensible Perception of Spirits, perhaps it may be expected from me, that I should set forth some more particulars, than I have yet done concerning it. As to this, I shall only say, that in regard I do not urge my own Experience, as Argumentative, for proving the existence, of Spirits, and their Operations, I think it may be looked upon as a thing of more Curiosity than Use to enlarge upon it; though I shall add the following particulars relating to it.

I declare then, with all the Sincerity of a Christian, that it never so much as entred into my Thoughts to use any practice for raising, or calling Spirits, as some Men have done; and that when they came, it was altogether a surprize to me. At their first coming they did not appear to me, nor come into my Chamber, but kept at my Chamber Windows, and in a Court adjoyning to one of my Chamber Windows, and in a Garden adjoyning to another Window. They called to me, sung, play'd on Musick, rung Bells, sometime crowed like Cocks, *&c.* and I have great Reason to believe these to be all good Spirits, for I found nothing in them tending to ill; their drift in coming, as far as I could perceive, being only to compose my Mind, and to bring it to its highest Purity; they used no Threats to me, but the surprize kept always a Terror upon me, and they continued with me about two Months.

Their second coming to me was some Years after, when at first there came Five, as I have set forth in my Fourth Chapter; and presently after there came Hundreds, and I saw some of them Dance in a Ring in my Garden, and Sing, holding Hands round, not facing each other, but their Backs turned to the inner part of the Circle. I found these of a promiscuous Nature, some good, and some bad, as among Men; for some of them would now and then Curse and Swear, and talk loosely, and others would reprehend them for it. Yet none of these ever perswaded me to any ill thing; but all would diswade me from drinking too freely, and any other irregularity; and if at any time I was upon going to any Neighbouring Town, they would tell me they would go with me, which I found they did, for they would there call at my Curtain, by my Beds side, as they usually did at my House, and talk to me.

Beside these two great Visitations, they have come to me now and then for some Years, and sometimes have stay'd with me a Week, sometimes two or three Days; and all along from their first coming, they have very often suggested things to me in my Dreams, as now and then they do still. At their first coming I heard no name of any of them mentioned, as I did at their second coming. I had a perception of them by four of my Senses, for I saw them, heard them, and three of them had a dark smoak coming out of their Mouths, which seemed somewhat offfensive to the Smell, it being like the smoak of a Lamp; and three of them bid me take them by the Hand, which I did, but it yielded to my touch, so that I could not find any sensible resistency in it; neither could I perceive any coldness in them, as it's said some Apparitions have had. I did not ask them many curious Questions, as I find many Men think I should, and, as they say, they would have done; but I always kept me on my guard, and still requir'd them to be gone, and would not enter into such Familiarity with them. Indeed I ask'd them once, what Creatures they were, and they told me, they were an Order of Creatures superior to Mankind, and could Influence our Thoughts, and that their Habitation was in the Air; I ask'd them also several things relating to my own concerns in this World, and I found sometimes both in their Answers, and in what they suggested in my Dreams, things very surprizing to me. One of them lay down upon my Bed by me, every Night, for a considerable time, and pretended great kindness to me, and if some others at any time would threaten me, that Spirit told me, they should do me no hurt.

If you ask me, whether I really think these Apparitions to be Spirits, or only an effect of Melancholy, I can only say, what St. *Paul* said of the Nature of His Rapture, God knows, I know not, but they appear'd to me Real.

Tandlerus, in his *Dissertation concerning Melancholy*, tells us, That the affect of Melancholy chiefly happens to Persons from the Fortieth to the Sixtieth Year of their Age, and that it's contracted chiefly in the Summer and Autumn, and comes to an Head in the Spring; and I must own that I was above Forty Years of Age, before any thing in this kind happen'd to me, but it was about *Christmas*, that the Apparitions came to me, both times.

As for Melancholy, I know not whether my Temperament may have some allay of it, but I think, I carry more of a Sanguine. Indeed, there was this, that might help to exalt the other. When they first came to me, I was just upon a recovery from an intermittent Fever, which had held me above twelve Months; and I confess at that time I was unfortunately involv'd, in an unnatural Suit in Law, with a too near Relation, which might somewhat discompose my Mind; and at the Spirits second coming, that suit in Law was continued, and I cannot say, but at that time I might have been somewhat affected by that saying of the Wise Man, *Prov.* 25. *Si Dedas te vino, oculi tui videbunt extraneas, nempe, visiones, & mirabiles Apparitiones,* as *Lavaterus* explains it; but it's much if such an occasion should cause them to continue then with me above three Months.

De Spect. l.
I. *c.* 4.

    I could add many more particulars of what pass'd betwixt the Spirits and my self, for indeed I kept a Journal of it for some Years, as well for what pass'd in my Dreams, as other wise; but I shall forbear to trouble the Reader farther, only adding, that as these Visitations of Spirits, gave me an occasion to consider how far Humane Reason could bear, as to a making out of the Exigence of Spirits, and their Operations, so I must declare, I firmly believe, that as the whole visible World has proceeded from the invisible World (which will hold good even according to the *Epicurean* Doctrine) so, that Spirits both good and bad are concern'd in the Administration of it, as Agents subordinate to the first Cause; and this I adhere to as well by a *Medium* of Reason, as that of Faith, in which, I think, we are all bound to acquiesce. And it appears plain enough to me, that those that will not so do, will but lose themselves in a vertiginous *Doxomania*, and never center, in any solid Truth.

A POSTSCRIPT.

Having lately had the Honour to hear a Relation of an Apparition, from the Lord Bishop of *Gloucester*, and it being too late for me to insert it in its proper place, in this Book; I give it you here, by way of Postscript, as follows.

"Sir *Charles Lee*, by his first Lady, had only one Daughter, of which she died in Child-Birth; and when she was Dead, her Sister, the lady *Everard*, desir'd to have the Education of the Child; and she was by her very well Educated, till she was Marriageable; and a Match was concluded for her, with Sir *William Perkins*, but was then prevented in an extraordinary manner. Upon a *Thursday* Night, she, thinking she saw a Light in her Chamber, after she was in Bed, knock'd for her Maid, who presently came to her; and she ask'd, why she left a Candle burning in her Chamber? The Maid said she left none, and there was none, but what she brought with her at that time. Then she said it was the Fire; but that her Maid told her was quite out; and said, she believ'd it was only a Dream, whereupon she said it might be so, and compos'd her self again to sleep; but about two of the Clock she was awaken'd again, and saw the Apparition of a little Woman, between her Curtain and her Pillow, who told her she was her Mother, that she was Happy, and that by Twelve of the Clock, that Day, she should be with her, whereupon she knok'd again for her Maid, called for her Clothes, and when she was dress'd, went into her Closet, and came not out again till Nine; and then brought out with her a Letter sealed to her Father, brought it to her Aunt, the Lady *Everard*, told her what had happen'd, and desir'd, that assoon as she was Dead, it might be sent to him; but the *Lady* thought she was suddenly fall'n Mad; and thereupon sent presently away to *Chelmsford*, for a Physician and Surgeon, who both came immediately, but the Physician could discern no Indication of what the Lady imagin'd, or of any Indisposition of her Body, notwithstanding the *Lady* would needs have her let Blood, which was done accordingly; and when the Young Woman had patiently let them do what they would with her she desir'd that the Chaplain might be called to read Prayers; and when Prayers were ended, she took her *Gittar* and *Psalm Book*, and sate down upon a Chair without Arms, and play'd and sung so melodiously and admirably, that her Musick-Master, who was then there, admired at it; and near the stroke of Twelve, she rose, and sate her self down in a great Chair with Arms, and presently fetching a strong Breathing or two, immediately Expired, and was so suddenly cold, as was much wondred at by the Physician and Surgeon. She dyed at *Waltham*, in *Essex*, three Miles from *Chelmsford*; and the Letter was sent to Sir *Charles*, at his House in *Warwickshire*; but he was so afflicted with the Death of his Daughter, that he came not till she was Buried; but when he came, caus'd her to be taken up, and to be buryed by her Mother at *Edminton*, as she desir'd in her Letter, This was about the Year 1662 or 63.

And this Relation the Lord Bishop of *Gloucester*, had from Sir *Charles Lee* himself.

FINIS.

NOTES
CONCERNING
GENII,
OR
FAMILIAR SPIRITS.

HAVING some Years since published a Book of *Genii*, or *Familiar Spirits*, I shall here give you a few short Notes relating to them.

Lomeierus, in his Book, *De Veterum Gentilum Lustrationibus*, c. 11. where he writes of visible Appearances of the Gods of the *Gentiles*, sets down a Passage we have in *Heliodorus, Æth.* 1. 3. where *Calasiris* tells *Cnemon*, that he had seen *Apollo* and *Diana* not in a Dream, but really; and adds, The Gods and Deities, *Cnemon*, as they come to us, and go from us, transform themselves, for the most part, into a human Shape; but very rarely into that of other Animals. And tho' they are not seen by the Prophane, they cannot escape being known by the Wise: for they may be discerned by their Eyes, they having always a sted-fast Look, and never closing their Eye-lids. And they are much more known by their Motion, which is, not by setting one Foot before the other, but by a certain ærial *Impetus*, readily cleaving the Air, rather than by a walking through it. Wherefore the *Egyptians* make the Statues of their Gods with their Feet join'd together, and as it were united. Which things also *Homer* knowing, as being an *Egyptian*, and instructed in their secret Learning, has intimated after an occult and intricate manner, leaving them to be understood by those that can understand them. So he says of *Pallas*,

Atque truces oculi fulsere tuenti:

And of *Neptune*,

Namque pedum crurumque simul vestigia pone
Perfacile agnovi, remeante aurasque secante.

The Words *perfacile remeante* importing a flowing Passage: from this sort of passing, the Gods are said by the *Greeks* to slide along. *Theocritus*, Idyll. 27. writes,

Immortales vero vocantur Dii sine pedum usu facti.

From such a Passage *Æneas* knew his Mother going from him, *Virg.* 1. *Æneid. v.* 400. & 5 *Æneid* 647, 648, 649.

Et vera incessu patuit Dea.

viz. As carried on by a light Wind, as a small Vessel, or as Hiding away by a slippery Motion, as on Ice. Nor have such Appearances of the Gods been accounted vain, but efficacious, and carrying with them some salutiferous Aid, as being wont to portend, either Health to the Sick, or Comfort to the Afflicted, or Aid to those that labour under any Difficulties. So far *Lomeierus*.

I have noted this Passage of *Heliodorus*, with the Additions of *Lomeierus*, because I think the Tradition of this Fact well deserves to be transmitted to Posterity, it being a faithful Account of the manner after which *Genii*, or Familiar Spirits, appear to those who see them, when other Persons present see no such thing. And as I have averr'd my own Experience in this kind, I must declare, that as often as those *Genii* have appear'd to me, it has always been with that swimming Motion through the Air, and not setting one Foot before the other, as usual with Men, when they pass from one place to another. I know many Persons laugh at all Apparitions; and it's not for those I record these things, but for those to whom such *Genii* may appear; who, as they will be much surprized at the first Sight of them, I know will be glad to find that others have had the like Experiences, and to be instructed in the manner of their Appearance, and in what they may portend.

I shall farther here observe to you, that whenever such *Genii* have appeared to me, I have always look'd on my self to have been, for that time, in an extatick State of Mind; and conclude, that most Persons, who see Apparitions, unseen by others, present with them, are in such a state, tho' many times unobserv'd by themselves; the various Dispositions of Mens Minds not being to be understood without a good share of philosophical Learning, and much Application used. In this extatick state of Mind, Men are said to dream waking; and the antient Poets call'd this a dreaming on *Parnassus*, in which Dream their Minds were opened, and they were led into Knowledges incommunicable to others in a common state. And as common Dreams, according to what many Persons may observe in themselves, often carry in them a prophetick Energy, so that what they dream comes to pass; so it's no wonder, if in this extatick State of Dreaming (during which the Astral Impulses are incomparably stronger than in common Dreams, or in the ordinary Course of Life) that prophetick Energy more efficaciously exerts itself, so that Persons then, both sleeping and waking, surprizingly see, foresee, and predict what the Mind of Man in a common state cannot bear to. And I doubt not but the true Prophets were in these extatick Dreams when they prophesied: But as their Minds were purified by a due prophetick training, their divining Impulses always directed them to deliver wholesome Truths. Whereas others, who either by some severe Circumstances of human Life, or by being magically wrought on by some villanous Abusers of that Art, are brought into this extatick State without a due training, so that they have not pass'd a purgative Life, but have their Minds strongly possest with Passions and vicious Habits: These Persons, I say, tho' their strong Impulses may now and then direct them to deliver useful Truths, yet they more often deliver vain Falshoods, and many times are led away by deplorable Delusions; as we may see in those Wretches who are accused of Witchcraft, and who commonly confess things as really transacted, which only pass in them in these extatick Dreams, and who for want of Judges knowing in this mysterious State of Mind, have been barbarously prosecuted and murthered, even to the Ridicule of Mankind; since Men may be as well executed for falling into a Fit of an Epilepsy, the other being as involuntary, and as much out of the Person's power to avoid.

I may here also acquaint you, that this Extatical Disposition of Mind is many times contagious, according to the Dispositions of Persons who may be with such as are in it. This is manifest in the Visitation which happen'd some Years since in *New England*, where one Person happening to have the Specter Sight, it became in a short time so general, that two hundred were accused of Witchcraft, and about twenty executed; the like having happen'd in many other Countries. Indeed all Persons are not infected with this extatick Contagion, tho' much using with those that are in those waking Extasies, but only such as are disposed for it, as it happens in contagious Diseases. The late Mr. *Emes*, famous for his Assurance of his Resurrection, when he went among the Prophets first, little thought of his becoming one; but had not been long with them, when he found himself seiz'd with the same Spirit: and I have been present when, upon a young Woman's falling into a Convulsion Fit, to which she was much subject, presently another young Woman, who chanced to be present, and who never had a Fit, nor seen any one in a Fit, fell into the like Fit, after a more severe manner than the other.

I shall farther give you here my Thoughts concerning those People in *Scotland*, who are said to have the Gift of the *Second-Sight* by Inheritance from Father to Son; and it is my Opinion, that those who first had this Gift by Descent, were begotten when one of their Parents were in an extatick State: and I recommend this Notion to a farther Consideration. I know some of the Ancients tell us what Methods have been used to bring Men to a Converse with *Genii*; but I shall not enlarge upon this here: and I hope and believe the Explication I have given of these Matters, may, and will prove of good use to some Persons, who may not easily find the like in their common Reading.

As for those who laugh at all Apparitions, as only imaginary, I shall give them two or three Instances, and leave them to their Consideration.

The learned *Nicholaus Seneccerus*, in *Analect. l. 4. b.* writes thus: It's true that many Spirits walk about, and are often seen; and we do not only read of Instances, but I my self have known Instances, and have both seen and heard Specters; concerning which the *Gentiles* said,

Sunt aliquid Manes, Lethum non omnia finit.

Melancthon, L. de Animâ, tells us, he had seen Specters, and knew many Men worthy of Credit, who affirm'd they had both seen, and discoursed with them.

Campanella, L. 4. de Sensu Rerum, writes thus: *Plotinus* and *Porphyrius* say there are Angels both good and bad, as daily Experience teaches, and my self also have found by manifest Experience, not when I earnestly endeavour'd it, but when I was minding another thing; and therefore it's no wonder if they did not appear to curious *Nero*. The same Author in the same Work, *L. 2. c. 25.* tells us, he knew many other Persons, who from Disbelievers, became afterwards convinc'd of the Reality of such Apparitions by their Sight, and a Converse with them. The same Author again, *Met.p. 2. c. 6. Art.* 3 writes thus: We know there are both good and evil Spirits, from Persons being tormented by the latter, and visited by the former; and my self, when I was upon a long Enquiry after them, found nothing of them, but only when I thought not of them. Therefore let *Pliny, Aristotle,* and their Followers be silent; for, it's most certain there are *Dæmons* in the World, and it's a foolish thing, not to say impious, to deny it: for there are many of the best of Men, and of the most learned, who certify this from their own Experience, Men not Deceived nor Deceivers: And I know this now my self, and am not led by the Credulity of others. So far *Campanella*; and here you may read much more for confirming this Truth. See also the same Author, *Met. p.* 3.

l. 12. *c.* 2. where he proves the Existence of Angels and *Dæmons*, by Reason, Experiences, Witnesses, Authorities, and the Consent of all Nations.

Now if any Man shall confidently tell me that these are all Illusions, as many are apt to do, and laugh at such Experiences; when I am convinc'd that these Laughers are Men of more Learning and Candor than the foregoing Testimonies, I may consider farther of it: Mean while, I hope they will give me leave to have such Regard for their negative against three good positive Evidences, as a Court of Judicature is commonly wont to have.

I know it's made a Question by some, whether Specters are ærial Images having a real Existence, or only imaginary Appearances and the Fancies of melancholick and weak Persons, who fancy they see Specters, when there is nothing real. But to grant there are sometimes such Fancies, must all Apparitions be so? In my Book of *Genii*, or *Familiar Spirits*, C. 4. I have given a Relation of some Women condemned for Witchcraft, at *Chelmsford*, in *Essex, Anno* 1645. one of whom, whose Name was *Elizabeth Clark*, said more than once to the Company present with her in the Night-Time, that she would call her *Imps* for them to see them; and she did call for seven or eight *Imps* by their several Names; and all the Persons present, to the number of Eight, saw them appear in the shapes of Dogs and Cats, *&c.* and this they deposed on Oath before a Magistrate.

Now I would ask any Man, whether he looks on these *Imps* only as the melancholy Fancies of this Woman: Indeed some who maintain that all Apparitions are only imaginary, tell us that the imaginative Species in the Mind can form the Air into the same Likeness; wherefore they think it in the power of melancholick Persons to form Specters in the Air; and *Helmont de Ortu Med. Tit. de injectis Mater.* says, The Power of the Imagination is so great, that it's able to produce some real external Things; which being produced by the imaginative Power as it's join'd with the *Archæus*, constitutes a sort of shadowing Apparition, which walks about, and has a proper Substance.

Now if this Doctrine could hold, it might account for the aforementioned things; but others are of opinion this Doctrine cannot hold according to sound Philosophy, *viz.* That the imaginative Faculty in Man has so great a Power, that of it self, it can produce some real Effect, either within or out of the Body of the Person who imagines. I say of itself, because the imaginative Faculty of itself produces no Effect, but by Accident and indirectly, as it changes the Body of the Person, or that of the Embryo within it, by stirring up the Appetite, and this the removing Faculty, which moves the Spirits and Humours; but it produces no Effect on an external Body, there being no assignable Vehicle, Way, or Medium for it to perform it by. If therefore there are Apparitions which have a real Subsistence, they must be explained some other way, which will be hard to do but by the Hypothesis of Spirits. There is this to be said for a real Subsistence of some Specters, *viz.* That they are seen by all Persons present, as the Imps before-mentioned, and not only by some particular Person, who may say, he sees them, when others do not. Secondly, that they are perceived not only by the Sight, but likewise by the Touch; as some have been struck by them, when others have been present. Thirdly, they have sometimes carried away, or removed things from one place to another, and given other Marks of some real and understanding Agents. If we find it difficult to account for what Experience evinces of the Beings and Operations of Spirits, you may consider what *Campanella* writes concerning it. *Met.p.* 3. *L.* 12. *C.* 3. *Art.* 3. the Head of which Article is thus: That the way is unknown to us by which an Angel adapts a Body to himself; yet it is most true, that he appears and operates in a Body, and Experience must not be deny'd for an Opinion. In the Article itself he freely owns, that these things cannot be understood, nor does he find them well explained by any Divines; yet he says they ought to be believed, tho' the Way is unknown to us: for the Art of the Superior Intelligences is not perceived by the Inferiors; as the *Americans* thought it impossible that a Paper should convey Thoughts, and that Clocks should tell the Hours of the Day, by a spontaneous Sound, which things are obvious to us.

Mr. *Saurin*, in his Defence of the Doctrine of the Reformed Church, concerning the Principle of Faith, has a material Passage relating to the foregoing Subject, *c.* 27. *p.* 329. where he writes thus: Mr. *Witsius* proves by many Examples, that the inward Instructions of God's Spirit go in some Subjects to a Revelation of particular Events; which is contradicted by some Divines: and tho' I make not myself a Party for Mr. *Witsius*, or those Divines, I think Mr. *Witsius*'s Opinion the more probable; and it's certain, that those who are for the Negative, cannot maintain it but two Ways: First, in shewing the Characters of Falshood, in some of the particular Relations, on which the Affirmative is established. Secondly, in saying that if a Man be not sure, that these Relations are false, he is no more sure that they are true. It is not necessary, he says, to advertise, that he does not speak here of the Examples given in the Old and New Testaments: The same Restrictions are made in the famous Controversy betwixt the *Esprits Forts* and *Foibles* concerning Apparitions, the Operations of the Devil, and the Enterprizes of Witches and Magicians. Wise and pious Men, who are neither of the *Esprits Forts* nor *Foibles*, in that evil Sense which is commonly given to this Title, believe, by a divine Faith, the Truth of the Histories contain'd in the Word of God; but they judge after a differing manner concerning common Relations, which are the Subject of the People's Wonder, and of the Raillery of those who look on themselves as above the People: Some of these Relations are possible, the greater part are false; and there are very few of them certain; or perhaps none of them at all are so.

Here we find Mr. *Saurin* seems inclined to think (as many do) that there is nothing real in what is said of Apparitions, or the Operations of evil Spirits, Witches, and Magicians; but I see not how he should be so inclined, if he kept to what he has laid down before concerning God's Revelation of particular Events; where he says, that those who are for the

Negative, cannot maintain it, but either by shewing the Characters of Falshood in the particular Histories on which the Affirmative is established, or by saying, that if a Man is not sure those Relations are false, he is no more sure they are true. And here I must ask Mr. *Saurin*, or any Man else, whether they can shew Characters of Falshood in the foregoing Relations I have given of Apparitions, or say the Truth of the Facts I have instanced, is not fairly insured.

Aventinus, in his *Annals* of *Bavaria*, *l*. 4. gives us the following remarkable Relation concerning an Apparition:

In *Germany*, not far from the Town *Bing*, where the River *Navas* mixes itself with the *Rhine*, there is a Village, commonly call'd *Camont* (*quasi Caput Montium*) a Name given it by the *Romans*, when they possessed that Country, because there begin the Mountains which run along with the *Rhine* towards the North: There, in these our Days, a revolted and roving Spirit has done many strange things, playing prestigiating Tricks, and infesting the Inhabitants. First, this cursed Spirit, seen by no Man, began to throw Stones at Persons, and to knock at Doors. Soon after, this pestilent and wicked Genius, taking a Human Shape, gave Answers, discover'd Thefts, accused many of Crimes, and set a Mark of Infamy on them, stirr'd up Discords and Ill-Will among Persons: By degrees, he set fire to, and burnt down Barns and Cottages, but was more trouble-some to one Man than the rest, always keeping with him wherever he went, and burnt his House; and, to stir up the whole Neighbourhood to destroy this innocent Man, the wicked Impostor openly declared, that for this Man's Crimes the Place lay under a Curse, and would be unfortunate; so that the Man was forced to lie without doors, all Persons denying him entrance into their Houses, they looking on him as one follow'd by evil Spirits: He, to satisfy his Neighbours, carry'd a burning-hot Iron in his Hand, with which not being hurt, he prov'd his Innocence: nevertheless the wicked Spirit burned his Stacks of Corn in the Fields; and as he was daily more and more troublesome, the Country People were forced to acquaint the Archbishop of *Mentz* with it, who sent Priests to expiate and lustrate the Fields and Villages; which they did with solemn Prayers and consecrated Water and Salt. The wicked and disturbed Spirit at first strove against them, and wounded some with Stones: but being overpowered by divine *Exorcisms*, and adjured by efficacious Prayers, he at length ceased, nor did he any where appear. When the Priests were gone, this pestilent Spirit return'd again, and said, while those bald-pated Priests mutter'd I know not what, I lay hid under the *Amiculum* of one of them (whom he named) who, by my persuasion, lay the last Night with his Host's Daughter. And having said this, the wicked Ghost went off with a mighty roaring Noise, and left the Country quiet.

An Occasion being here given, it will not be besides our Purpose to take things a little higher, concerning the burning-hot Iron, the scalding Water, and single Combat, and the expiatory and pretorial Ceremonies used on their account: Our Ancestors being most religious Persons, confided more in God than themselves, rely'd more on the Divine Justice and God's Promises, than on their own Wit, or Wisdom; and rather stood to the Divine Decrees, than their own Opinions: They look'd on God as present in all Acts and Things done and thought; things were then ratify'd, when the Divine Pleasure had adjudged them: they concluded that all things were done in the Theatre of Heaven, God looking on them: and therefore in doubtful Causes, especially in Crimes which could not be proved by any Human Testimony, they fled to the Divine Pleasure, to the Supreme Majesty, who could not be deceiv'd, as to an honorary Umpire, and Judge of all things. The Senate, People, and Priests, who came in Crowds to see a single Combat, as I find in the *Salick-Law*, implored the Divine Aid, they commemorated the Benefits which, on a like Occasion, our Saviour, through his Benignity and Clemency had conferr'd on them; they minded him of his Promises, recited Examples, prayed that his mighty Power would show itself on the present Occasion, according to his Promise, as it had always done hitherto; and that, according to his Justice, he would be present to the Innocent, and grant him Victory. Free leave was granted the Accused of making choice of, and hireing whom he pleased to fight for him, the Accuser was forced to fight himself. I find in the antient Books of Sacrifices, the burning-hot Iron, and the scalding-hot Water were consecrated by the Priests with the following Prayers:

God, just Judge, strong and patient, who are Author and Lover of Justice, who judge equitably; judge, O Lord, that which is just, because your Judgments are right; who look on the Earth, and make it tremble. You Almighty Lord, who have saved the World by the coming of your Son our Lord Jesus Christ, and redeemed Mankind by his Passion, do you sanctify this scalding-hot Water, as you preserv'd the three Children *Sidrach, Misach*, and *Abdenago*, who were cast into a burning Furnace by the Command of the King of *Babylon*; do you most clemently bring it to pass, that if any Innocent puts his Hand into this Water, it may be drawn out safe and unhurt, as you preserved the three fore-mention'd Children from the Fiery-Furnace, and freed *Susanna* from the Crimes falsely laid to her charge. But if any culpable Person, having his Heart harden'd by the Devil, shall presume to put his Hand into it, let your most just Piety vouchsafe to declare it, that your Power may be manifested on his Body, and his Soul may be saved through Repentance.

God, just Judge, who are Author of Peace, and judge equitably, we humbly pray you, that you will vouchsafe to bless and sanctify this *Iron*, appointed for making a just Tryal of some Doubts; so that if an Innocent (in the fore-mentioned Cause where a Purgation is fought) shall take it Fire-hot in his Hand, he may appear unhurt: and if the Person be culpable and guilty, let your Power be most just in this, by declaring it in him; so that Iniquity may not prevail over Justice, and Falshood may yield to Truth, through our Lord, *&c.*

And these things were so far from being judged impious, that I find those Ceremonies for Purgation were used by the most holy Pontiffs, the most Christian Princes, and by Men and Women consecrated to the Service of God. That was then to be Wise, to trust in God, to place all our Hope in him. In our Age nothing less is practised, for it's now look'd upon only as a Folly and a provoking the immortal God to Anger by irritating him: Thus we see, the same Fact, in divers Ages, is accounted in one place Piety, and in another Error. So far *Aventinus*.

Now there are many things to be noted in this Relation: First, as to the evil Spirit's throwing Stones, knocking at Doors, and burning Stacks of Corn, we have had the like Instances in *England* and *Scotland*; and there is now a House in *London*, in which, for the three Years last past, there have been heard, and are still, almost continual knockings against the Wainscot, and Over-head; and sometimes a Noise like telling of Money, and of Mens sawing, to the great disturbance of the Inhabitants; and often Lights have been seen there like to flashes of Lightning; and the Person who rents the House has told me, that when she has removed eight Miles from *London*, the knockings have followed her.

Secondly, It's remarkable, that the Person chiefly concerned in the Disturbance at *Camont*, put himself upon the fiery Tryal for his Purgation, which I do not remember to have met with else-where, on the like Occasion. Those who are unacquainted in the Tryals of *Ordeal*, may have recourse to several Authors concerning them. *Bangertus* in his Notes on the *Chronicon Slavorum*, writ by *Helmoldus* and *Arnoldus*, has drawn together many Instances of them: In his Notes on the First, he writes, That there occur many Examples of those Tryals from the fifth to the thirteenth Age, and some later: And if what *Aventinus* relates, past in his own time, it must be so late as about the Year 1500. for he was born *An.* 1466. and died in the 68th Year of his Age. If there were Truth in those Tryals, and to be relied on, we might justly lament our Times.

Heu! tam præsentes nobis cognoscere Divos
Non licet. ———

But *Trithemius* in his *Chron. Hirsang.* tells us, that about the Year 1215. when many Persons of both Sexes had incurred a Suspicion of Heresy, *Conradus de Marpurg*, an Apostolical Inquisitor, put them all, without distinction, on the fiery Tryal; but *Trithemius* owns he burnt many Innocents, and says, that after he had exercised this cruel Butchery till the Year 1233, he was kill'd.

Bangertus examines also whence these sorts of Tryals came among the Christians; whether they used them in imitation of the *Gentiles*, or of the Divine Rites of the *Jews*, and says, they seem in the Tryal by Water, to have had a mind to imitate the divine Law of the *Jews*, in their *Cup of Jealousy*: but the Fiery-Tryal may seem to have been derived to them from the *Gentiles*; for the Messenger who told *Creon*, King of *Thebes*, that the Body of *Polynices*, which he had order'd, on pain of Death, to be thrown out in the Fields, and lie unburied, was privately buried, (which was done by his Sister *Antigone*) when he found the King was much incensed at it, and would excuse himself and his Companions, who were set to guard the Body, said, as we find in the *Antigone* of *Sophocles*,

> No Man is found who did it, and it is hid to us.
> But we are ready both to take a red-hot Iron in our
> Hands, And to walk on burning Coals, and to swear
> by the Gods, That we neither did it, nor had any
> Knowledge Of him that either advised it, or did it.

And here I may note what *Strabo* writes, *l.* 5. as follows, concerning these Tryals: Under the Mountain *Soracte*, stands the City *Feronia*, by which Name also a certain Goddess is call'd, to whom the People of that Country pay a wonderful Veneration, and she has a Temple there with a wonderful sort of sacred Mysteries, for those that are inspired by that Goddess, walk with their bare Feet on burning Coals, without being hurt; and a world of People flock there every Year, at a certain time, to see this perform'd. Others think the antient Christians introduced the Fiery-Tryal from the Bible ill-understood by them; for in the Prayers with which they consecrated the red-hot Iron, they often referred to the Examples of *Sidrach*, *Misach*, and *Abednago*, and God has often manifested his Presence by the Fire, as a thing agreeable to the Deity.

Bangertus concludes thus: Who may not have cause to wonder that, tho' the Cælestial Deity has given no Command for Mens making use of these Tryals; yet often by them he has given a Testimony of Guilt and Innocency. *Grotius* in his *Prolegomena* to his History of the *Goths*, answers, That because God was better pleased with plain Honesty, than with nice studied ways of Address, he accommodated his wonder-working Power to the Laws of those innocent People, who fought to find out the Innocence of particular Persons by the Touch of fire-hot *Ploughshares*.

But notwithstanding God was sometimes pleased to give Testimony of Guilt and Innocency by those Tryals, yet all Men were convinced, at long run, that many unjust Judgments had pass'd in them. All the famous Civilians in *Germany* unanimously concluded, that in criminal Causes those obscure, divinatory, superstitious, and indeed, *null* Proofs, did not suffice; but Proofs more clear than the Noon-Day, were required, and all the most learned Divines, Politicians, Physicians, and Philosophers exploded this mad way of Tryal, calling it a superstitious Invention, introduced by Satan and credulous hearkeners to him, the Devil's May-game, the ground of dangerous and scandalous Tragedies: so that, at length, they were totally abolish'd.

Thus we see; that after Christianity had egregiously plaid the fool about a thousand Years, they began to grow wiser, and Men have had fairer Play in criminal Causes; and as Man's Condition is somewhat mended in this respect, it may be wish'd, and I am sorry I cannot say hoped, that all those who administer Justice, as to *Meum* and *Tuum*, in Christian Governments, would seriously consider they are incomparably out-done in that respect by the *Turks*, and the more rational *Pagans*, and would think of some Amendment. I cannot now enlarge on this Subject, but must say, I think Men cannot enough resent those villanous and execrable Abuses daily put on them by the delays of Justice and the Corruptions used in the Administration of it in the generality of Christian Governments:

> ―― *Non hic Arcana revelo,*
> *Non ignota loquor, liceat vulgata referre.*

And as *Aventinus* observes, that what at one time is accounted Piety, at another time is accounted Error, we may consider what Christians, partly by their Policy, and partly by their Zeal without Knowledge, have brought Religion to.

> *Nunc gerit hanc, aliam Speciem nunc induit anno*
> *Relligio, ad procerum Sensa parata loqui.*

> *This, or that Mask Religion every Year*
> *Puts on, as Rulers whisper in her Ear.*

I shall only add one Observation here, *viz.* That as all Men must allow there was a Reality in the fore-mentioned Tryals, both among Christians and Pagans; so that some carried burning-hot Irons in their Hands, some dip'd their Arms up to their Elbows in scalding-hot Water, some walk'd on burning Coals, *&c.* without hurt; I say, as these Facts must be allow'd, unless we take all History for a Ballad, this seems to me a strong Proof for the Existence of Spirits, or invisible Intelligent Beings; and if any Man will be Refractory, and admit those Facts, but deny the Existence of the other, I desire him to shew me wherein the Admittance of those Facts, fits more easy on his Understanding, than the Admittance of the other. And so I conclude this Work.

FINIS.

www.ingramcontent.com/pod-product-compliance
Lightning Source LLC
Chambersburg PA
CBHW021116300426
44113CB00006B/173